MW01242669

Shenandoah County Virginia

A STUDY OF THE
1860 CENSUS
WITH SUPPLEMENTAL DATA

Volume 1

Marvin J. Vann

HERITAGE BOOKS
2010

HERITAGE BOOKS

AN IMPRINT OF HERITAGE BOOKS, INC.

Books, CDs, and more—Worldwide

For our listing of thousands of titles see our website
at
www.HeritageBooks.com

Published 2010 by
HERITAGE BOOKS, INC.
Publishing Division
100 Railroad Ave. #104
Westminster, Maryland 21157

Other books by the author:

CD: *Virginia, Volume 7: Shenandoah Valley*

*Shenandoah County, Virginia: A Study of the 1860 Census
with Supplemental Data, Volume 1*

*Shenandoah County, Virginia: A Study of the 1860 Census
Volumes 2–5*

Shenandoah County, Virginia: The 1870 Census

International Standard Book Numbers
Paperbound: 978-1-55613-852-2
Clothbound: 978-0-7884-8333-2

CONTENTS

FOREWORD

Within many of us there is a strong desire to know who we are through an understanding of the events and individuals that have shaped our development. This task leads the researcher to spend countless hours in the courthouses, libraries and archives that may provide insight necessary to clarify our evolution.

Looking back, the current project had a simple beginning. The mission was merely to locate the author's relatives in the 1860 census of Shenandoah County. There was obvious merit in such an undertaking as the author is a direct descendent of many of the families residing in the county in 1860.

What should have been an easy task, was compounded in difficulty by the printed quality of this census. Portions of the document are extremely difficult to decipher. It was necessary to spend hours examining many of these households to find some clue that might assist in the identification of the residents. Often one distinguishable letter, or a series of first names were the only clues available in this process. As the identification process continued, data regarding hundreds of these households was accumulated. However, much of the data had no relationship to the original mission of the author. Yet, the task needed to go forward because there was the possibility that the next household would unearth the discovery of a relative long forgotten.

At some point, an awareness began to develop that a great deal had been learned about the residents of Shenandoah County in 1860. The next step was to share this data with others to facilitate the quest for information regarding their ancestors.

As you read this document please keep these thoughts in mind. It is not possible for one individual to know everything about the citizens of Shenandoah County in 1860. Would that we could! It would certainly simplify our genealogical research. While I have attempted to employ high standards of scholarship I am certain there must be errors. The process of transcribing thousands of dates and numbers, in itself, presents the possibility of numerous pitfalls for a researcher. I encourage you to use this as a starting point in your own research. Accept no portion of this as the final word! Check information related to your family against data you have accumulated or the data readily available in documents listed in the bibliography of this document.

Nothing in this document has been carved in granite. It has become a constantly growing and changing document. Every time the work is touched it changes as new data is accumulated. Much has been learned, but so much remains unknown. The search could, and should go on for an indefinite period. However, it is also time for this research to see the light of day.

At least five additional volumes will be necessary to complete this project. Even as final preparations are being made to send this work to press, research has begun in earnest on the second volume. There is much that remains to be done. However, the ultimate goal would be the publication of a second, more accurate and detailed, edition of this work. To this end, I request your input. Please let me know your reaction. I would like you to share information regarding errors you have discovered. I would appreciate information on individuals we have not identified or information that is incomplete. In a second edition, I would like to include more pictures of the individuals and the dwellings of the individuals represented in this census. If you can provide assistance in any of these areas it would be greatly appreciated. Please address any correspondence to:

Marvin J. Vann
200 Sun Valley Drive
Waldorf, Maryland 20603

ACKNOWLEDGEMENTS

Shenandoah County, Virginia is blessed by the scholarship of large numbers of individuals who have and are continuing to preserve the history of the county. Without the efforts of those who have provided us with information on such varied topics as cemeteries, deaths, marriages, and the military record of county citizens, a work of this type would have been impossible. Equally important are the genealogical studies which continue to be developed. They run the range from those that are but a few pages to the more detailed works such as the **History of the Hottel Family**. Yet each in it's own way plays a vital role in preserving the past and contributes to a work of this type.

Mary Ann Williamson, President of the Edinburg Heritage Foundation, offered assistance and encouragement throughout this project. In particular, her assistance in securing information on the Grandstaff family was appreciated. The town of Edinburg is fortunate to have an individual of her talent to promote the historic preservation of that community.

A vital, and probably an undervalued resource in the preservation of the history of Shenandoah County, Virginia is Jeannette Connor Ritenour. Jeanette has not been accorded due recognition for her role in collecting and preserving cemetery and marriage records in the county. She was an invaluable resource in providing information on the Powells Fort section of this document. In addition, she was responsible for securing many of the pictures included in this work. Her encouragement and excitement about this project were an important source of motivation. Jeanette's husband, George Ritenour, also shared her enthusiasm for the project and assisted with some of the proof reading.

This project would not have been possible without my parents. Marvin H. Vann and Ruth Catherine McNaney Vann, residents of Shenandoah County, were the primary motivators in this undertaking. My appreciation for the study of history is directly related to my father's interest in the past. An avid reader of history, he often planned early family trips to include visits to historic sites. Ironically, many of these sites were the scenes of battles that were the arenas where individuals described in this work participated. My mother was the guiding light in this project. She is the individual who introduced me to the value of genealogical study. She assisted me in organizing, proofing and typing this work. It would not be inappropriate to list her as co-author of this study. If this work is judged by readers as having merit, my parents, at their hill-top home in the Fort Valley, may justifiably derive great satisfaction for their role in this project.

Lastly, I salute a wonderful wife, Sally Ann Layman Vann. No one could undertake a project of this magnitude without the support and understanding of a devoted spouse. The time on task and the expense in such a project is not insignificant. I am grateful for her understanding and encouragement. My children, Kimberly, Dorian and Melissa, a continuing source of pride to me have also encouraged my effort.

TO MY PARENTS RUTH C. McNANEY VANN AND MARVIN H. VANN
With love, I dedicate this work.

Dwelling 1   Family 1

Henry Jennings	47	Clerk	500	500	Virginia	
Mary Jennings	31				"	
Mary L. Jennings	20				"	School
Jewett M. Jennings	15				"	School
Theodore Jennings	6				"	
Frank DeWitt Jennings	4				"	
Fannie B. Jennings	1				"	

Henry Jennings, was listed as a minister in the 1850 census.   In that capacity he performed a number of marriages in Shenandoah County during this period. He was married twice. On 28 Jul 1838 he was married in Rockingham County, Virginia to Lucinda ----son. The marriage record is faded and Lucinda's surname is illegible. The record for his second marriage to **Mary M. Jennings** has not been located.

Mary L. Jennings, daughter of Henry and Lucinda, was married on 12 Jul 1866 to Charles Neff. Charles was born and resided in Rockingham County, Virginia. The son of Peter Neff, Charles was a farmer.

Jewett M. Jennings, son of Henry and Lucinda, enlisted as a private in Company M of the 62nd Virginia Infantry. He enlisted on 3 May 1864 at Paris, Virginia. He was present on 31 Oct 1864 through 31 Dec 1864.

Theodore C. Jennings, son of Henry and Mary, was married on 30 Sep 1880 to Catherine "Kate" Belle Windle. Kate was the daughter of Jack and Matilda. Andrew Jackson Windle married Matilda Valentine on 8 Aug 1854. Andrew and his family resided in **dwelling 4** in this census. Theodore died 29 Dec 1917 at the age of 64. Kate Windle Jennings died at Columbia, Virginia in Oct 1935. She was 75 at the time of her death.

Frank DeWitt Jennings, son of Henry and Mary, was born in 1855 and died 3 Jan 1922. He was a student at the time of his marriage on 29 Aug 1880 to Adesta Fidelas "Addie" Miller. Addie was the daughter of Richard and Artemisia. Richard Miller married Artemisia Grandstaff on 18 Jun 1842. Richard Miller and his family may be found in **dwelling 291**. Frank DeWitt Jennings eventually became a teacher in Shenandoah County. Addie F. Miller Jennings

was born in 1857 and died 12 Nov 1926. Frank and Addie
were buried in the Cedarwood Cemetery in Edinburg.

1850 CENSUS: Henry Jennings and family resided in dwelling
            721 on page 51.

PAGE 1 EDINBURG   (Microfilm Page 579)

Dwelling 2   Family 2

Samuel Rinker	46	Court Receiver 800	500		Va.
Rachel C. Rinker	34		Va.		
Mary C. Rinker	23		"	School	
Jacob Z. Rinker	19		"	School	
Elizabeth M. Rinker	11		"		
John V. Rinker	9		"	School	
Margaret V. Rinker	7		"	School	
Emma J. C. Rinker	2		"		
Samuel P. Rinker	8m		"		
William H. Cone	28	Luth. Clergyman 0	240		Penn.

        Samuel Rinker was born 14 Mar 1814 and died 15 Jan
1883. He was the son of Jacob and Mary. His father, a
captain in the militia, married Mary Fravel on 20 Mar 1808.
Samuel also served in the Shenandoah County militia and
attained the rank of major. He was a trustee and founding
member of the Woodstock Female Seminary on 13 Mar 1847.
Samuel was married three times. His first marriage was to
Margaret Ann (Anna Margaretha) Hottel on 23 Sep 1835.
Margaret Ann was born 16 Feb 1817 and died 23 May 1847.
Margaret Ann Hottel Rinker was buried in the St. Paul's
Reformed Lutheran Church Cemetery in Woodstock, Virginia.
She was the daughter of John George and Maria Catherine.
John George Hottel married Maria Catherine Ocks on 5 Nov
1799. Rachel C. Vance, of Bath County, Virginia, was the
second wife of Samuel Rinker. Rachel died 1 Mar 1874. On
24 Nov 1874, Elizabeth "Lizzie" Catherine Cooper Farra
became Samuel's third wife. Elizabeth was the daughter of
Joseph and Harriet. Joseph P. Cooper and Harriet Artz were
married on 3 Feb 1834. Joseph Cooper and his family
resided in dwelling 17 in this census. Elizabeth was
initally married to William H. Farra on 6 Nov 1854.
William and Elizabeth have not been located in this census.
William was the son of John and Mary. John W. Farra
married Mary Hockman on 29 May 1828. Mary Hockman Farra
resided in dwelling 98. William H. Farra enlisted in the
service at the outset of the war and was reported to have

died at Richmond as a result of wounds received in battle. The service record of William has not been located. However, John Wayland indicates in his history of Shenandoah County that an individual named Will Farrar was killed while a member of Company C of the 7th Virginia Cavalry. Lizzie Cooper Farra Rinker was born 21 Jun 1838 and died 1 Mar 1908 at Milford Center, Ohio. She had moved to Ohio to reside with her daughters Mae and Clara. These girls were born to Samuel and Lizzie when Samuel was over sixty years of age.

Mary Catherine Rinker, daughter of Samuel and Margaret, married a gentleman with the surname of Houl and moved to Pataskala, Ohio.

Jacob Zwinglius Rinker, was also the son of Samuel and Margaret. He was born 12 May 1841 and died in Lovettsville, Virginia 15 Aug 1916. He is buried in the Mt. Olivet Cemetery in that Loudoun County community. At the outbreak of the war Jacob became a member of Company C of the 10th Virginia Infantry. In June of 1862 Company C ceased to function as a unit. Many members of the unit transferred to Company F. This unit, given the large number of Shenandoah County men in its membership, was called the Muhlenberg Rifles. Later in the war Jacob also appears on the roster of Company K of the 12th Virginia Cavalry. Hottel family records indicate that Jacob participated in 23 battles and received no injuries other than the rheumatism he contracted from the unpleasant living conditions. He was taken prisoner at Bull Run on 12 May 1864 and sent to Ft. Delaware until his parole on 13 Jun 1865. On 26 Nov 1868 he was married to Sophia Jefferson. Sophia died in 1885. On 12 Oct 1886 Jacob married Greta D. Kalb, the daughter of Silas D. and Mary Wire Kalb. Greta was born 12 Aug 1864. After the war Jacob had returned to Edinburg and served as postmaster. Upon his marriage to Greta, he opened a store in Lovettsville in partnership with his father-in-law Silas D. Kalb.

Elizabeth Marshall Rinker, daughter of Samuel and Rachel, was born 22 Mar 1849 and died 15 Oct 1917. She married George W. Dinges on 28 Oct 1874. George was a student at the time of their marriage. He was the son of William J. Dinges and Mary Frances Grandstaff. William and Mary were married on 25 Mar 1847 and resided in **dwelling 58**. George William Dinges was born 8 Feb 1847 and died 8

Mar 1920. Elizabeth and George were buried in the Cedarwood Cemetery in Edinburg.

John Vance Rinker, son of Samuel and Rachel, was born 28 Feb 1851 and died 6 May 1860 as a result of an injury inflicted by a horse.

Margaret Virginia Rinker, daughter of Samuel and Rachel, was born 4 Feb 1853 and died in 1932. Margaret was married on 10 Apr 1878 to Samuel James Hoffman. Samuel was born 17 Sep 1852 and died 1 Nov 1914. He was the son of N. Milton and Mary. Nimrod Milton Hoffman had married Mary C. McCord on 5 Feb 1845. Nimrod Hoffman and family resided in **dwelling 278.** Samuel James Hoffman was a very prominent man in Shenandoah County. He was a medical doctor and served two terms as a Representative in the Virginia State Legislature. Margaret and Samuel are buried in the Massanutten Cemetery in Woodstock, Virginia.

Emma Jane Rinker, also the daughter of Samuel and Rachel, was born 5 Aug 1857 and died 20 Mar 1924. She died at the Memorial Hospital in Winchester, Virginia. Emma married late in life. She had served as the matron of the Massanutten Academy in Woodstock prior to her marriage. She married William A. McGinnis on 23 Dec 1903. William was a 60 year old widowed real estate broker at the time of their marriage. He was the son of William and Susan and had been born in Preston County, West Virginia. After their marriage William and Emma resided in Terra Alta, West Virginia. Emma was buried in the Dinges plot in the Cedarwood Cemetery in Edinburg.

Samuel Prescott Rinker, son of Samuel and Rachel, was born 24 Sep 1859. He was a railroad clerk at the time of his marriage to Elizabeth Watt Rinker on 30 Mar 1892. Elizabeth was the daughter of Samuel W and Sallie. Samuel Watt Rinker married Sallie C. Miller on 27 Sep 1866. After Elizabeth died, Samuel Prescott Rinker married Virginia Cosgrove.

William H. Cone was a minister in the Lutheran Church. He was born in Union City, Pennsylvania on 11 Dec 1831 and died in Shenandoah County on 23 Dec 1902. William was the son of Jacob and Elizabeth. He was assigned to a church in Shenandoah County but was relocated for a period of time to Rowan County, North Carolina. At some point he had married. Upon the death of his first wife he married Barbarba Ann Shirley in December of 1876. Barbara was the daughter of Zachariah and Barbara. Zachariah Shirley married Barbara Kagey on 15 Aug 1825. Zachariah Shirley and family resided in **dwelling 840** at the time of this census. Barbara Ann Shirley Cone was born 18 Feb 1839 and died 3 Apr 1926. The Reverend and Mrs. Cone were buried in the Reformation Lutheran Church Cemetery in New Market, Virginia.

RELATED FAMILY:

        Sarah Ellen Rinker, daughter of Samuel and Margaret, married John Henry Rau on 11 Aug 1857 and resided in **dwelling 64.**

        Mary Rinker, sister of Samuel Rinker, married Daniel Henry Fravel and resided in **dwelling 1441.**

1850 CENSUS: **Samuel Rinker** and family were residents of dwelling 1553 on page 110.

PAGE 1 EDINBURG   **(Microfilm Page 579)**

Dwelling 3   Family 3

Phillip Miller	43	Master Plaster	0	75	Virginia
Elizabeth Miller	36			Va.	Can'tRead
Jane Miller	11			"	School
Joseph Miller	8			"	School
John Miller	4			"	
Edward Miller	3			"	

      There was a marriage on 7 Oct 1849 for **Phillip Miller** to **Elizabeth Long.** Elizabeth was the daughter of Mary Ann Long. Conclusive evidence that this was the same couple has not been established.

      John E. Miller was born in November of 1855 according to birth records in the Shenandoah County Courthouse.

      The same document indicates that **Edward Miller** was born 22 May 1857.

1850 CENSUS: No record of this family.

6

PAGE 1 EDINBURG   (Microfilm Page 579)

Dwelling 4   Family 4

Andrew J. Windle	42	Potter	100	50	Virginia
Matilda Windle	22				"
Ellen Windle	3				"
George Windle	5m				"

Andrew Jackson Windle was the son of William and Margaret. William Windle married Margaret Gaines on 19 Apr 1824 in Frederick County, Virginia. William Windle resided in **dwelling 28** at the time of the 1860 census. Andrew, or Jack as he was called, married **Matilda Valentine** on 8 Aug 1854. Matilda was born in Powells Fort, Virginia. She was the daughter of Rachel Valentine. Rachel Valentine resided in **dwelling 27**.

Mary Ellen Windle was married on 18 Dec 1884 to James E. Jones. James was a painter. He was the son of Joseph W. and Mary. Joseph W. Jones married Mary Malvina Windle on 28 Aug 1856.

RELATED FAMILY:
George Windle, brother of Andrew, married Mary Krenb on 1 May 1848 and resided in **dwelling 32**.
Margaret Malvinia Windle, sister of Andrew, married Henry Bowman on 3 Jan 1856 and resided in **dwelling 28**.
Cyrena Windle, sister of Andrew, resided in **dwelling 28** with her father and sister.

1850 CENSUS: **Andrew Jackson Windle** was a resident in dwelling 715 on page 50.

PAGE 1 EDINBURG   (Microfilm Page 579)

Dwelling 5   Family 5

Robert Newman	26	(Black)	Barber	230	0	Virginia

Robert Newman, was a tanner at the time of his August 1868 marriage to Caroline Price. Caroline was from Alexandria, Virginia. The parents of the couple were not reported. In the 12 Jan 1866 issue of the **Shenandoah Herald**, "Robert Newman would inform the public that he is prepared to disinter soldiers and others, whose friends desire to have them removed. His charges will be reasonable. Address him at Woodstock, Virginia." Descendants of Robert and Caroline were buried in the Mt. Zion United Methodist Church Cemetery in Strasburg. A daughter, Caroline Newman, was born 12 Oct 1880 and died 29 Oct 1929. She married John Curry of Hampshire County, West Virginia on 22 Apr 1901. John and Caroline were buried in the Mt. Zion Cemetery.

1850 CENSUS: No record of this individual in the census.

PAGE 1 EDINBURG (Microfilm Page 579)

Dwelling 6   Family 6

| Catherine Kidwalder | 48 | Weaver | 0 | 100 | Virginia |
| Henry H. Evans | 19 | Plasters | Apprentice | " | School |

Catherine Ann Loyd was married to John Evans on 12 Oct 1829. The bondsman for that marriage was Jacob Fisher. After the death of John, Catherine Ann Loyd Evans was married to Ezra Cadwalder on 29 Mar 1849. Her marriage to Ezra took place in Frederick County, Virginia.

Henry H. Evans was born 22 Nov 1840 and died 7 Feb 1914. He was the son of John and Catherine Ann Loyd Evans. At the outbreak of the Civil War Henry enlisted in Company C of the 10th Virginia Infantry. He had a notation on his record which stated that he was assigned to heavy artillery. When Company C disbanded Henry joined Company F of the 10th Virginia Infantry. Like many young men in the Confederate service, Henry moved to other units. When he left the Muhlenberg Rifles he served for a period of time as a member of the Confederate States Navy. Records indicate that he was also a member of Company E of the 28th Virginia Infantry. On 9 Dec 1866, Henry H. Evans, a plasterer, married Rebecca J. Downey, the daughter of Thornton and Amelia. Thornton Downey married Amelia Ann Miley on 12 Dec 1838. Thornton Downey and family resided in **dwelling 76.**

RELATED FAMILY:
Marilla Evans, daughter of Catherine Loyd Evans Cadwalder, married Josephus Willard on 29 Jun 1856 and resided in **dwelling 608.**

1850 CENSUS: **Catherine Kidwalder** was a resident of dwelling 981 on page 68.

Henry H. Evans was a resident of dwelling 1040 on page 72. He was listed with his sister Matilda in the household of Samuel Bowman.

PAGE 1 EDINBURG   **(Microfilm Page 579)**

Dwelling 7   Family 7

Israel Orndorff	44	Wagoner	1000	180	Virginia
Rebecca Orndorff	45				"
Jefferson Orndorff	18	Stage Driver			"
Isabella Atta Orndorff	13				" School

Israel Orndorff was married on 16 Jan 1837 to **Rebecca Hisey**. The bondsman for this marriage was William Allison. This marriage was recorded in both Frederick and Shenandoah County records.

Jefferson Orndorff was listed in the 1850 census as Israel J. Orndorff. During the war he enlisted in Company C of the 10th Virginia Infantry. This unit was known as the "Southern Grays". The unit ceased to exist in June of 1862. Most men went into other units, but no further record of service has been located for Jefferson.

Isabella Orndorff was listed in the 1850 census as Billetta. Isabella was married on 12 Jun 1866 to David H. Lamen. David was a merchant from Maryland. He was the son of David and Mary.

1850 CENSUS: **Israel Orndorff** and family were residents of dwelling 741 on page 52.

PAGE 1 EDINBURG (Microfilm Page 579)

Dwelling 8 Family 8

William Shea	40	Day Labor	0	100	Ireland	Can't Read
Sarah A. Shea	41				Virginia	Can't Read
Mary A. Shea	14				"	School
Nancy Shea	2m				"	

William Shay (Shea) was born in Ireland 8 May 1808 and died 10 Apr 1898. He was the son of John and Ann. William married **Alla Ann Martin** on 7 Oct 1854. Alla was born in Warren County, Virginia and lists her parents as Thomas and Catherine. Alla was listed as Sarah in this census, Ellie on the marriage record of her daughter and as Allie on her tombstone. Allie Martin Shay was born in 1827 and died 31 May 1893. William and Allie are buried in the Cedarwood Cemetery in Edinburg.

Mary Ann Martin, daughter of Allie Martin and the stepdaughter of William Shay, married George Copenhaver on 9 Mar 1871. George was the son of William and Mary. William Copenhaver married Mary Ann Burner on 8 Oct 1839. William Copenhaver and family resided in **dwelling 1866.** Mary Ann Martin Copenhaver was born 9 Feb 1845 and died 28 Feb 1921. George S. Copenhaver was born 9 Feb 1850 and died 6 Mar 1931. Mary and George were buried in the Cedarwood Cemetery in Edinburg.

Nancy "Nannie" Shea was born 9 Mar 1860 and died 18 Mar 1915 in Taylortown, Virginia. She was married on 15 Sep 1885 to William C. Dunnavan. William was a carpenter. He was born 18 Aug 1860 and died 3 Jul 1923 in Taylortown. William was the son of Lawrence and Elizabeth. Lawrence Dunivan married Elizabeth Bussey on 25 Aug 1853. Lawrence and his family were located in **dwelling 245** at the time of this census. Nannie Shea Dunnavan (Donovan) and her husband were buried in the Cedarwood Cemetery in Edinburg. Please note that Shenandoah County records reveal many different spellings for the surname Donovan.

1850 CENSUS: No record of this family in the census.

NOTE REGARDING MILITARY RECORD:
There is a military record for William Shay. The name Shay was not common in the Shenandoah Valley area, however, precise evidence has not been developed to prove that the individual who served in the Confederate Army was the head of this household. The record indicates that William Shay enlisted on 1 Feb 1863 in Company K of the 2nd Virginia Infantry as a Private. He entered the unit as a substitute for Isaac Marshall. In November of 1863 he was wounded in the middle third of his thigh in a battle at Payne's Farm. He was subsequently hospitalized and retired to the Invalid Corp. The primary argument against declaring these two the same man is the age of the head of this household. Men forty years of age and older were generally exempt from military service.

PAGE 2 EDINBURG   (**Microfilm Page 580**)

Dwelling 9   **Family 9**

Payton Southard   59   Day Labor 0 0 Virginia
Rhoda Southard   76   "
Sarah C. Southard 30   "

Despite the recorded age difference, Payton and Rhoda were husband and wife. They originally resided in Frederick County, Virginia and were married there in 1821. **Payton Southard** married **Rhoda Rhodes** on 27 Jun 1821. The bondsman for the marriage was John Rhodes.

RELATED FAMILY:
    Mary C. Southard, daughter of Payton and Rhoda, married Benjamin D. Holden on 6 Sep 1855 and resided in **dwelling 42**.

1850 CENSUS: No record of this family in the census.

PAGE 2 EDINBURG   (**Microfilm Page 580**)

Dwelling 10   **Family 10**

Henry M. Hockman   29 Master Mason 400 100 Virginia
Isabella F. Hockman 24   "
Francis Hockman   7   "
Robert M. Hockman 4   Mosouri
Samuel Hockman   1   Virginia
Catherine Ruby   26 Seamstress   "

Henry M. Hockman was a member of the 12th Virginia Cavalry. He enlisted at New Market on 2 Apr 1862 in Company E as a private. He was wounded on 9 Jun 1863 at Brandy Station, the largest cavalry battle of the war. He returned to his unit and was present through April of 1864.

There is no confirmation, but it is possible that **Isabella F. Hockman** and **Catherine Ruby** were sisters. They may have been the daughters of Isaac and Elizabeth Kibler Ruby. Isaac and Elizabeth were wed on 21 Jul 1832. Isaac Kibler and his family resided in **dwelling 55**. In the 1850 census Isaac and Elizabeth had a 17 year old daughter named Mary Catherine and a 15 year old daughter named Isabella.

Francis "Frank" M. Hockman was born 24 Nov 1853 and died 14 Mar 1913. Frank was buried in the Cedarwood Cemetery in Edinburg. He was a bricklayer at the time of his 29 Mar 1883 marriage to Lorena Belle Evans. Lorena was the daughter of Joseph W. and Hannah Via Evans. Joseph and his family resided in **dwelling 38**. Lorena was born 24 Jan 1864 and died in New York on 30 Jun 1947. She was buried with Frank at the Cedarwood Cemetery. Her second marriage was to William R. Hite. The marriage took place after 1926. William was the son of Isaac R and Rhoda Frances. Isaac R. Hite married Rhoda Frances Miley on 26 Aug 1857. William was a widower at the time of their marriage. He had originally been married on 22 Sep 1887 to Nannie Reilly. Nannie was the daughter of Patrick and Mary. Patrick Reilly and his family resided in **dwelling 284**. Nannie Reilly Hite died 29 Aug 1926. William died on 12 Apr 1939 in Harrisonburg, Virginia. He and Nannie were buried in the Massanutten Cemetery in Woodstock, Virginia.

The birth place of **Robert M. Hockman** was listed as "Mosouri" instead of Missouri.

Samuel M. Hockman was married on 19 Jan 1888 to Maggie L. Jennings. She was the daughter of Henry and Mary M. Jennings. Henry Jennings and family resided in **dwelling 1**.

RELATED FAMILY:

Caroline Susan Ruby, sister of Catherine, married William Hockman on 19 Dec 1854 and resided in **dwelling 12**.

1850 CENSUS: No record of this family in the census.

PAGE 2   EDINBURG   (Microfilm Page 580)

Dwelling 11   Family 11

Isaac R. Bowman	47	Master Carpenter	0 200	Virginia
Rebecca P. Bowman	49			"
Joseph C. Bowman	22	Baggage Master R.R.		"
Mary E. Bowman	21			"
Ann E. Bowman	18			"
John H. Bowman	14			" School

Isaac R. Bowman was the son of Jacob and Rebecca. Jacob Bowman married Rebecca Fravel on 23 Feb 1807. Isaac was married to **Rebecca Cooper** on 7 Jan 1833. The bondsman

for the marriage was George Cooper. George Cooper's will,
dated Jan of 1821, refers to Rebecca as his daughter.
Isaac R. Bowman was a master carpenter and was responsible
for building railroad depots in Woodstock, Mt. Jackson and
Edinburg.   In addition he worked on the flour mill in
Edinburg that was constructed in 1848. The Hottel family
history indicates that Rebecca Cooper Bowman died in 1859.

Joseph C. Bowman, enlisted in Company C of the 10th
Virginia Infantry on 1 Apr 1862. It was reported that he
deserted in the winter of 1864 with the intended purpose
of joining the cavalry. No record of his enlistment in a
cavalry unit has been located.

All of the children of Isaac and Rebecca in the
household at the time of this census would eventually
remove to the west.   This period of westward movement
occurred during 1862 and 1863.

RELATED FAMILY:
            Joseph Bowman, brother of Isaac R. Bowman,
married Sarah A.Johnson on 20 Oct 1847 and resided in
dwelling 258.

1850 CENSUS: No record of this family in the census.

PAGE 2 EDINBURG   (Microfilm Page 580)

Dwelling 12   Family 12

William Hockman	32	Collier 1000	200	Virginia
Caroline Hockman	23			"
Mary E. Hockman	4			"
Sarah E. Hockman	1			"
Ann S. Ruby	13			"

William Hockman was born 8 Dec 1827 and died 14 Mar
1865. He was the son of Abraham and Elizabeth. Abraham
Hockman married Elizabeth Pennywitt on 7 Feb 1827. Abraham
and his family resided in **dwelling 625.** William lived most
of his life in the vicinity of Strasburg, Virginia. He was
a farmer at the time of his marriage on 19 Dec 1854 to
Caroline Susan Ruby. Caroline was the daughter of Isaac
and Elizabeth. Isaac Ruby married Elizabeth Kibler on 21
Jul 1832. Isaac Ruby and his family resided in **dwelling
55** when this census was taken. At some point Caroline

Susan Ruby Hockman was married to John H. Downs. Caroline
was born in 1838 and died 9 Jun 1913. According to
obituary records, John H. Downs had died 25 years earlier.
She was buried in the Riverview Cemetery in Strasburg.

Mary E. Hockman was born in 1856 and died in 1908.
She did not marry. Mary was buried next to her mother in
the Fletcher family plot in the Riverview Cemetery in
Strasburg.

Sarah "Sallie" Ellen Hockman was born in 1859 and died
in 1931. She married Charles Leslie Fletcher on 10 Feb
1880. Charles was the son of Thomas and Elizabeth. He was
a bridge builder at the time of his marriage to Sallie.
Charles was born in 1850 and died in 1889. He was
originally from Fauquier County, Virginia. Sarah and
Charles were buried in the Riverview Cemetery in Strasburg.

Caroline Susan Ruby's sister **Ann S. Ruby** resided in
this household. She was born in 1844 and died in February
of 1912. Ann was married on 31 Dec 1868 to James W. Ash.
James was a widower. He was a 40 year old carpenter who
was born and was residing in Fauquier County, Virginia.
He was the son of Francis T. and Serepta. Francis T. Ash
married Serepta Bowie on 11 Feb 1825 in Fauquier County.
Ann S. Ruby Ash was buried in the Fletcher plot at the
Riverview Cemetery.

RELATED FAMILY:
> **Jacob H. Hockman,** brother of William,
married Sarah Ellen Haun on 20 Feb 1855 and resided in
dwelling 621.
> **Isaac Hockman,** brother of William, married
Rebecca M. Walton on 14 Jul 1857 and resided in **dwelling
1416.**
> **Martha Ruby,** sister of Caroline, married
William Shutters on 12 Nov 1857 and resided in **dwelling
1062.**
> **Catherine Ruby,** sister of Caroline, resided
in **dwelling 10.**
> **Samuel Hockman,** brother of William, resided
in **dwelling 121.**

1850 CENSUS: **William Hockman** was a resident of dwelling
1347 on page 96.
Caroline Ruby was a resident of dwelling 726
on page 51.

14

PAGE 2 EDINBURG   (Microfilm Page 580)

Dwelling 13 Family 13

George W. Grandstaff	26	Day Labor	1000	100	Virginia
Eliza B. Grandstaff	23				"
Samuel M. Grandstaff	3				"
Jacob Grandstaff	58	Day Labor			"

George W. Grandstaff was the son of **Jacob Grandstaff** and Miss Lambert. George was married to **Elizabeth Ann Artz** on 18 Jun 1856. Elizabeth was the daughter of Mary Artz. Elizabeth was the twin sister of Samuel A. Artz. Samuel resided in **dwelling 264** at the time of this census. He was listed as the son of Mary in his 30 Jul 1862 marriage to Mary L. Miley. In 1850 Mary Artz and her twins resided in the household of her parents John and Mary. John Artz married Mary "Polly" Hoffman on 25 Mar 1805. All of this goes by way of saying that there is reason to doubt that Mary Artz was married when the twins were born.

Samuel M. Grandstaff is not listed in records contained in the Grandstaff family history. He may have died young.

Jacob Grandstaff was the father of George W. Grandstaff. He was the son of George and Barbara. George Grandstaff Jr. married Barbara Halderman on 21 Jan 1792. Jacob was born in Aug 1802. He married Mary Koontz on 3 Oct 1827. His second wife was Elizabeth Lambert. His marriage to Elizabeth took place on 1 Apr 1830.

RELATED FAMILY:
          Catherine Ann Grandstaff, sister of George, married Abraham Miley on 24 Mar 1859 and resided in **dwelling 30.**

1850 CENSUS: **George W. Grandstaff** was a resident in dwelling 168 on page 12. This was the residence of Nimrod Milton Hoffman.
          Jacob Grandstaff was a resident of dwelling 2123 on page 152. This was the residence of George Thompson, a cooper.
          Elizabeth Ann Artz was a resident of dwelling 172 on page 13. She resided with her grandfather.

15

NOTE REGARDING MILITARY RECORD:

In all probability George W. Grandstaff served in the Confederate Army. However, at this moment the unit or units he served with have not been identified. There was a George W. Grandstaff with the 35th Battalion Cavalry and the 5th Virginia Infantry.

PAGE 2 EDINBURG (Microfilm Page 580)

Dwelling 14 Family 14

Isaac Ritter	40	Farmer 1000 696	Virginia		
Amanda Ritter	31		"		
Phillip Ritter	11		"	School	
Joseph Ritter	9		"	School	
Mary E. Ritter	9		"		
William Ritter	6		"	School	
Prescott D. Ritter	1		"		

Isaac H. Ritter died 3 Sep 1882. He was 63 years, 8 months and 25 days old. Isaac had married **Amanda Grandstaff** on 7 Mar 1848. The bondsman for the marriage was Phillip Grandstaff. Phillip Grandstaff is believed to have been Amanda's father. Phillip had married Mary Cooper on 6 Aug 1816 and resided in **dwelling 267**. Amanda F. Grandstaff Ritter was born 29 Nov 1822 and died 19 Jan 1904. Isaac and Amanda were buried in the Old Edinburg Cemetery.

Mary Elizabeth Ritter was born 1 Dec 1850 and died 2 Oct 1859. She may have been the twin sister of Joseph. Mary had died prior to this census and it is difficult to know if Mary and Joseph were the same age or that her age reflects age at the time of death. It was customary to list individuals who had died within the preceding year. Amanda Ritter was pregnant at the time this census was taken with a set of twins. August 1860 death records for the county indicate that one day old male and female twins died. Their parents were Isaac and Amanda Ritter.

William G. Ritter was a merchant at the time of his marriage to Emma Lee Gochenour. Emma was the daugfter of Levi and Mary. Levi Gochenour married Mary Wiseman on 29 Jan 1839. Levi and family resided in **dwelling 1608**. Emma was born 16 Aug 1861 and died 15 Apr 1928. William G. Ritter was born 19 Dec 1854 and died 17 Jul 1910. Emma and William were buried in the Levi Gochenour Cemetery. After William died, Emma married Adolph Brill on 7 Nov 1915.

Adolph was a widower and a farmer. He was the son of
Purnell B. and Mary. Purnell B. Brill married Mary
Elizabeth Orndorff on 6 Nov 1850. Adolph was born 29 Dec
1851 and died 10 Aug 1925. He was buried in the St. John's
United Church of Christ at Toms Brook. Adolph was initally
married to Virginia Ellen Shillingburg on 6 Feb 1873. She
was the daughter of John and Rebecca. His second marriage
took place on 2 Aug 1898. He was a carpenter at the time
he married Martha M. Orndorff, the daughter of Benjamin and
Maria. It was the second marriage for Martha. She was an
Orndorff prior to her marriage to Lewis Orndorff Jr. on 15
Oct 1874. He was the son of Samuel and Comfort.

RELATED FAMILY:
        Joseph Grandstaff, brother of Amanda,
married Louise C Riddleberger on 25 Oct 1851 and resided
in **dwelling 54.**
        Jane Grandstaff, sister of Amanda, married
William H. Hisey on 7 Feb 1842 and resided in **dwelling 69.**
        Branson Grandstaff, brother of Amanda,
married Elizabeth Eveline Liggett on 9 Jun 1842 and resided
in **dwelling 313.**

1850 CENSUS: No record of this family in census.

PAGE 2 EDINBURG (Microfilm Page 580)

Dwelling 15 Family 15

Samuel Hisey	38	Carpenter	1200	175	Virginia	
Rebecca Hisey	33				"	
Alice Hisey	11				"	School
Sarah C. Hisey	10				"	School
Joseph H. Hisey	8				"	School
John F. Hisey	6				"	School
------- Hisey	10days (Female)				"	

        Samuel Hisey was married to **Rebecca Rhodes** on 7 Feb
1848. The bondsman for this marriage was Joseph Rhodes.
While not proven, it is probable that Samuel was the son
of Frederick Hisey in **dwelling 18.** Frederick Hisey was
married to Mary Artz on 7 Nov 1812.

        Sarah C. Hisey did not marry. She is buried in the
Old Edinburg Cemetery near the family of her brother
Joseph. She was listed on the tombstone as Aunt Sallie C.
Hisey. Sallie was born 22 Jan 1853 and died 27 Jun 1928.

Joseph Homer Hisey was born 27 Nov 1851 and died 22 Feb 1919. He was a plasterer at the time of his marriage on 29 Dec 1881 to Phoebe Scothern. Phoebe was the daughter of David Scothern. David Scothern married Sarah Walker on 13 May 1845. David and his family resided in **dwelling 660.** Phoebe Scothern Hisey was born in 1852 and died in 1886. Joseph and Phoebe were buried in the Old Edinburg Cemetery.

1850 CENSUS: Samuel Hisey and family resided in dwelling 704 on page 50.

PAGE 3 EDINBURG (**Microfilm Page 581**)

Dwelling 16 Family 16

Andrew Shank	49	Tailor	0 50	Virginia
Emily Shank	44			"
Catherine Shank	16			"
James W. Shank	13			"

1850 CENSUS: No record of this family in the census.

PAGE 3 EDINBURG (**Microfilm Page 581**)

Dwelling 17 Family 17

Joseph P. Cooper	59	Lawyer	0 100	Virginia	
Harriet Cooper	46			"	Can't Read
John E. L. Cooper	18			"	School
Mary E. Cooper	14			"	School
Alberta J. Cooper	11			"	School
Phillip Ann Cooper	8			"	School
William M. Cooper	6			"	School
Joseph H. Cooper	1			"	

Joseph Pollard Cooper was married to **Harriet Artz** on 3 Feb 1834. Harriet was listed as the daughter of John Artz. In 1850 she was listed as Henrietta in the census. Joseph is believed to have been the son of George Cooper.

John E. L. Cooper was born in 1840 and died in 1927. He entered Company C of the 10th Virginia Infantry at the outbreak of the Civil War. He was wounded early in the conflict. After a period of recovery he re-enlisted in Company F of the 10th Virginia Infantry. John surrendered at Fort Steadman on 25 Mar 1865 and was discharged at Point Lookout, Maryland on 24 Jun 1865. He was employed as a shoemaker when he returned to Shenandoah County. On 7 Nov

1867 he was married to Catherine Ann Comer. Catherine was the daughter of Christian and Maria. Christian Comer married Maria Bigby on 1 Jan 1828. Christian and his family resided in **dwelling 74**. Catherine Ann Comer Cooper was born in 1843 and died in 1915. This couple was buried in the Cedarwood Cemetery in Edinburg.

Mary Ellen "Ella" Cooper was born 5 Mar 1846 and died 18 Jan 1916. She was married to Raphael P. Proctor on 9 Dec 1869. Raphael, a carpenter, was the son of Harrison and Edith. Harrison Proctor married Edith Funk on 12 May 1836. Raphael and his family resided in **dwelling 573**. Raphael died prior to 1884 and Ella was married to the widower John W. B. Woods on 11 Sep 1884. John was a bridge builder who was born in Rockingham County, Virginia. He was the son of Ephramin and Dorothy. At the time of this census he resided with his first wife in **dwelling 645**. John W. B. Woods had married Frances Ellen Ruby on 31 Oct 1854. She was the daughter of Jacob and Diana. Jacob Ruby married Diana Brinker on 9 Jun 1831. Frances was born 3 Feb 1835 and died 29 Jun 1882. She was buried in the Old Union Cemetery near Mt. Jackson. John W. B. Woods died 5 Apr 1904 at the age of 84. Ella was buried in the Cedarwood Cemetery in Edinburg.

Phillipann (Phillip Ann) Cooper was born in 1851 and died in 1910. This burial took place at the Old Edinburg Cemetery.

William Milton Cooper was born 14 Jan 1854 and died 27 Oct 1937. He was a painter at the time of his marriage to Mary E. Newland on 30 Dec 1880. Mary was the daughter of Isaac and Susan. Isaac Newland married Susan Rinker on 30 Dec 1852. Isaac and his family resided in **dwelling 1620**. Mary E. Newland Cooper was born 7 Dec 1857 and died 7 Jun 1913. They were buried at the Cedarwood Cemetery.

RELATED FAMILY:

        Elizabeth Catherine Cooper, daughter of Joseph and Harriet, married William H. Farra on 6 Nov 1856. They do not appear in this census. When William was killed in the war, Lizzie married Samuel Rinker on 24 Nov 1874. Samuel Rinker resided in **dwelling 2**.

        Josephine M. Cooper, daughter of Joseph and Harriet, married William A. Mohler on 1 Jan 1857 and resided in **dwelling 1065**.

George Jacob Cooper, son of Joseph and Harriet, married Drucilla C. Downey on 15 Mar 1860 and resided in **dwelling 77.**

Mary Cooper, believed to have been the sister of Joseph, married Phillip Grandstaff on 6 Aug 1816 and resided in **dwelling 267.**

1850 CENSUS: Joseph P. Cooper and family resided in dwelling 162 on page 12.

PAGE 3   EDINBURG   (Microfilm Page 581)

Dwelling 18   Family 18

Frederick Hisey	68	Farmer	3730	250	Va.	Just Md.
Harriet Hisey	54				"	Just Married
John Hisey	45	Farmhand			"	
Isaac Hisey	29				"	
Elizabeth Hisey	25				"	
Elizabeth Hisey	64				"	

Frederick Hisey was the son of Christian and Rosena Foltz Hisey. He was originally married to Mary Artz on 7 Nov 1811. Mary Artz Hisey died 4 Oct 1841. His second wife was **Elizabeth Balthis Higgins.** Elizabeth was a widow at the time of this marriage. Her first marriage was to Henry Higgins on 21 May 1822. The bondsman for that marriage was Leonard Balthis. Elizabeth died 11 Apr 1859, yet continues to be listed in this household in 1860. It should be noted that individuals who had died within the preceding year were often listed with their family. On 29 Mar 1860 Frederick Hisey married **Harriet Beckwith Boehm.** Harriet had been born in Hardy County and was the daughter of Samuel and Susan. She was a widow at the time of her marriage to Frederick. On 3 Jan 1827 Harriet Beckwith married Isaac Boehm. Frederick Hisey departed this life on 26 Jan 1862. On 1 Jun 1875 Harriet Beckwith Boehm Hisey entered into marriage with Jacob Pence. Jacob was an 80 year old widower. The former blacksmith was the son of Jacob and Catherine. Harriet was born 16 Jan 1804 and died 27 Jun 1892. Frederick Hisey and all three of his wives were buried in the Old Edinburg Cemetery. Frederick was a most unusual man. He was an ordained minister in the United Brethren Church at a time when most preachers were not educated. He never accepted pay for his pastoral duties. He chose instead to work as a farmer and blacksmith. Frederick Hisey gave the town the land needed as the site of the church and then paid to have the church built.

John Hisey, son of Frederick and Mary Artz Hisey, died 13 Dec 1864.

Elizabeth C. Hisey, daughter of Frederick and Mary, died 15 Jan 1889. She was buried next to her brother in the Old Edinburg Cemetery.

RELATED FAMILY:
                    Robert F. Hisey, son of Frederick and Mary, married Amelia Riddleberger on 9 May 1852 and resided in **dwelling 21.**

1850 CENSUS: Frederick Hisey and family resided in dwelling 706 on page 50.
              Harriet Beckwith Boehm resided in dwelling 447 on page 32.

PAGE 3 EDINBURG   **(Microfilm Page 581)**

DWELLING 19 FAMILY 19

Abraham Saum	49	Col. of Claims 0	200	Va.
Ellen A. Saum	43			Va.
Louisa C. Saum	12		"	School
Martha D. Saum	9		"	School
Mary E. Saum	6		"	School
Catherine Sonnestine	75		"	C't Rd
Ann Robinson	21	(Mulatto) Housegirl	"	

Abraham Saum was born 8 Apr 1811 and died 1 Apr 1883. He was the son of John and Anna. John Saum married Anna Brubaker on 13 Aug 1808. Abraham was married to **Ellen A. Sonnestine** on 26 Jul 1836. Ellen was the daughter of Joseph and Catherine. Dr. Joseph F. Sonnestine and Catherine Bozeman were married on 23 Jul 1802. Ellen A. Sonnestine Saum was born 28 Mar 1818 and died 1 Jun 1893. Her mother **Catherine Bozeman Sonnestine** was a resident of this household. It is believed that she was the daughter of Frederick Bozeman.

Louisa Catherine Saum was born 8 Nov 1847. She died on 13 Apr, but the year is illegible on her tombstone. Louisa, or Lou as she was called, was married to John D. Milligan on 17 Nov 1868. John D. Milligan was living in the hotel of James N. Swann **(dwelling 51)** at the time of this census. John was a merchant from Cumberland, Pennsylvania. He was the son of William B. and Mary. John D. Milligan died 5 Aug 1909. John and Lou were buried in the Cedarwood Cemetery. This couple did not have children.

Martha D. "Mattie" Saum was born 16 Sep 1850 and died in 1924. She married Arthur P. Belew on 28 Oct 1873. Arthur was a physician. He was the son of Peter and Elizabeth. Peter Belew and family resided in **dwelling 36**. Dr. A.P. Belew was born 27 Oct 1848 and died 4 Dec 1909. Mattie and Arthur were buried in the Cedarwood Cemetery.

Mary Ellen Saum was born 19 Aug 1853 and died 22 Aug 1877. She was married to Edward B. Tapley on 9 May 1872. Edward was a tin plate worker and preacher from Newbury Port, Massachusetts. He was the son of William S. and Caroline. Edward was born 30 Jul 1848 and died 21 Jan 1885. Mary Ellen and Edward are also buried in the Cedarwood Cemetery. Edward Tapley married again after Mary Ellen died. He married Lucy May Saum on 21 Jan 1878. Lucy was the daughter of Samuel and Catherine Hisey Saum. Samuel and his family resided in **dwelling 1888**.

RELATED FAMILY:

John Addison Saum, son of Abraham and Ellen, resided in **dwelling 1092**. This was the home of Levi Rinker.

John Saum, brother of Abraham, married Elizabeth Wilkin on 11 Jul 1854 and resided in **dwelling 1876**.

Catherine Saum, sister of Abraham, married Christian Miller on 1 Apr 1844 and resided in **dwelling 1615**.

Sarah Saum, sister of Abraham, married Noah Bauserman on 8 Jul 1846 and resided in **dwelling 1978**.

Lorenzo Saum, brother of Abraham, married Mary Ellen Lutz on 25 Dec 1856 and resided in **dwelling 2171**.

1850 CENSUS: **Abraham Saum** and family resided in dwelling 714 on page 50.

Catherine Bozeman Sonnestine was a resident of dwelling 847 on page 59. This was the home of her daughter Catherine, the wife of Isaac F. Allen. She had married Isaac on 12 Nov 1833.

Ann Robinson resided in dwelling 223 on page 21. She is listed as a 14 year old in the household of Clara Miller, an ordinary keeper.

PAGE 3 EDINBURG   (Microfilm Page 581)

Dwelling 20   Family 20

John W. Miley	36	Tailor	1000	200	Virginia	
Frances Miley	35				"	
Arabella Miley	11				"	School
Bertha V. Miley	9				"	School
Alfaretta Miley	5				"	
Philippa Miley	4				"	
Clarence L. Miley	1				"	

John W. Miley was born 13 Feb 1824 and died 28 Jul 1901. He was married to **Frances Artz** on 16 Feb 1848. The bondsman for the marriage was Christian Comer. Frances Artz Miley was born 24 Jun 1824 and died 17 Oct 1902. They were buried in the Old Edinburg Cemetery.

Arabella R. Miley was born 20 Nov 1848 and died 31 Jul 1921. She was married to William Ira Riddleberger on 14 Oct 1869. William was the son of Madison and Susan. Madison Riddleberger married Susan Shyrock on 15 Dec 1830. Madison and family resided in **dwelling 40** at the time of this census. William, a tailor at the time of his marriage, was born 7 Dec 1847 and died 30 May 1920. Arabella and William were buried in the Cedarwood Cemetery in Edinburg.

Bertha V. Miley was born 29 Sep 1851 and died 5 Dec 1934. She was married on 26 Dec 1878 to Francis M. Evans, a young shoemaker. Francis was the son of David and Mary. David D. Evans married Mary M. Walters on 4 Jul 1843. They were residents of **dwelling 1873**. Francis M. Evans was born 17 Mar 1849 and died 19 Sep 1927. Bertha and Francis are buried in the Cedarwood Cemetery.

Alpharetta (Alfaretta) Miley was born in 1854 and died in 1923. She is buried with her sister **Philippy** in the Old Edinburg Cemetery near their parents. Philippy Miley was born in 1856 and died in 1941.

Clarence L. Miley was born 3 Jul 1858 and died 12 Mar 1862. He is also buried in the Old Edinburg Cemetery.

1850 CENSUS: John W. **Miley** and family resided in dwelling 699 on page 49.

PAGE 3   EDINBURG   (Microfilm Page 581)

Dwelling 21   Family 21

Robert Hisey	34	Master Blacksmith	1600	1400	Va.
Amelia S. Hisey	25				"
Frederick M. Hisey	5				"
Charles P. Hisey	6m				"
Samuel Evans	23	Blacksmith Apprentice			"
Artemisia Newman	16	(Mulatto) Housegirl			"

Robert Ferguson Hisey was born 17 May 1824 and died 22 Feb 1907.   He was the son of Frederick and Mary. Frederick Hisey married Mary Artz on 7 Nov 1812. Frederick and his second wife Elizabeth Balthis Higgins Hisey resided in **dwelling 18.**   Robert was married to **Amelia Riddleberger** on 9 May 1852.   Amelia was the daughter of Madison and Susan. Madison Riddleberger married Susan Shyrock on 15 Dec 1830.   Madison and his family resided in **dwelling 40.** Amelia was born 8 Apr 1835 and died 27 Apr 1915.   Robert and Amelia were buried in the Cedarwood Cemetery in Edinburg.   On 23 Mar 1862 Robert enlisted at Rudes Hill in Company K of the 5th Virginia Infantry.   He was a private and he was hospitalized on 10 Jun 1862.   He was carried on the rolls until February 1864 when he was dropped. According to the Hisey family history he had been wounded and was brought home to convalesce. When U. S. troops heard he was at home they came for him.   He pretended deafness and was not taken.   Robert is said to have been a great reader all of his life and was particularly interested in ancient history.

Frederick M. Hisey, named for his paternal grandfather, was born 30 May 1855 and died 22 Dec 1926. He was a medical doctor. Dr. Hisey married Mary "Mollie" E. Wightman on 6 Dec 1883. She was the daughter of William and Julie.   William Wightman married Julie A. Grandstaff on 20 Jul 1852.   William Wightman and family resided in **dwelling 290.** Mollie Wightman Hisey was born 5 Apr 1857 and died 9 Apr 1924.   Frederick and Mollie were buried in the Cedarwood Cemetery.

Charles Phillip Hisey was born 2 Dec 1849 and died 30 Dec 1899.   He was a druggist.   Charles was married on 16 Dec 1885 to Emma Jane Evans, the daughter of Joseph and

24

Hannah Via Evans. Joseph Evans and family resided in
dwelling 38. Emma was born in 1866 and died in 1954.
After Charles died, Emma was married to Dr Rutherford
Benton Mitchell on 20 May 1909. Dr. Mitchell was a
minister from St. Albans, West Virginia. Rutherford was
the son of Archibald H. and Mary. He had served with the
1st West Virginia Volunteers during the Civil War.
Rutherford Benton Mitchell died 29 Aug 1938. Emma Jane
Evans Hisey Mitchell and both of her husbands were buried
in the Cedarwood Cemetery.

Samuel Evans was married to Amanda Trook on 15 Mar
1870. Amanda was the daughter of Phillip and Ann Rebecca.
Phillip Trook married Rebecca Painter on 30 May 1826.
Phillip and his family may be located in **dwelling 344.**
Amanda was born 1 Jan 1848 and died 24 Mar 1872. Samuel
married for a second time on 30 Dec 1870. His second wife
was Mary C. Cook of Rockingham County. She was the
daughter of John and Mary. Mary C. Cook Evans resided in
dwelling 737. Rockingham County records report that a John
Cook married Mary Ward on 23 Nov 1848. It is not certain
that these were her parents. There is also some question
regarding Samuel's parents. His mother was Susan. The
identity of his father is less clear. On his 1870 marriage
certificate his father was listed as C. Artz Evans. On his
1873 marriage certificate his father was listed as William.
Samuel C. Evans was a member of Company C of the 7th
Virginia Cavalry.

RELATED FAMILY:
Louisa C. Riddleberger, sister of Amelia,
was married to Joseph F. Grandstaff on 25 Oct 1851 and
resided in **dwelling 54.**
Sarah E. Riddleberger, sister of Amelia, was
married to Benjamin Holtzman and resided in **dwelling 56.**
John Evans, brother of Samuel, resided in
dwelling 277.

1850 CENSUS: Robert Hisey resided in dwelling 708 on page
50. This was his fathers household.
Amelia Riddleberger resided in dwelling 721
on page 51. She also resided with her
parents.
Samuel Evans lived in dwelling 2125 on page
152. This was the household of his
brother. Samuel's mother Susan was in the
household at that time.

25

PAGE 4   EDINBURG   (Microfilm   Page 582)

Dwelling 22   Family 22

Edward H. Berry	60	Clerk	300 100	Va.
Lucy A. Berry	30	Teacher in Common School		"
Jane Whissen	15			"

Edward H. Berry was born 25 Nov 1799 and died 28 Aug 1870.   He was married to Mary W. Hunston on 8 Aug 1825. The bondsman for the marriage was Thomas Hunston.   It is probable that Thomas was her father.   Mary W. Hunston Berry was born 2 Jan 1802.   Mary's grandfather Edward Hunston Sr. owned a number of slaves.   In his Will dated 13 Dec 1820 he designated that his granddaughter Mary W. Hunston should receive "one negro boy named Thomas (son of Hannah)."   At least eight slaves were given to members of his family at the time of his death.   Edward H. Berry was listed in Samuel Kercheval's 1833 history of the valley   as one of the prominent men in Shenandoah County.   Edward H. Berry and Mary W. Hunston Berry were buried in the Cedarwood Cemetery in Edinburg.

Lucy A. Berry, a school teacher, never married.   She was 60 years, 9 months and 3 days old when   she died on 27 Nov 1890.   She was buried next to her parents.   Lucy had a brother Milton A. Berry who was a dentist.   It is known that he returned to practice in the county.   Milton may have been away at school.

Jane Whissen was listed twice in this census.   She appears in this household and the household of her parents Edward and Mary.   She is listed in **dwelling 80** as 17 year old Elizabeth J. Whissen.   Her father was Edward B. Whissen and her mother was Mary G. Miller Whissen.   Elizabeth Jane "Bettie" was married to Joseph Comer on 28 Jan 1861. Joseph was the son of Christian and Maria.   Christian Comer married Maria Bigby on 1 Jan 1828.   The family of Christian Comer was located in **dwelling 73**.   Joseph Comer was born 25 Apr 1837 and died 1 Apr 1899 in Washington, D. C. Bettie was born 2 Jul 1842 and died 22 Apr 1915.   They were buried in the Cedarwood Cemetery.

1850 CENSUS: Edward H. Berry resided with his family in dwelling 1067 on page 74.
   Elizabeth Jane Whissen resided with her parents in dwelling 734 on page 52.

PAGE 4   EDINBURG   (Microfilm Page 582)

Dwelling 23   Family 23

Jacob Bovey	36	Clergyman 0 0	Maryland	
Rebecca Bovey	32		"	
Augustus Bovey	11		"	School
Albert Bovey	9		"	School
William T. Bovey	8		Va.	School
George A. Bovey	5		"	
Arabella Bovey	2		"	

The **Reverend Jacob A. Bovey** died 7 Nov 1859 in the 36th year of his life. This suggests that the Reverend Bovey was dead at the time this census was taken. This is another illustration of the tendency of census takers to report individuals who had died during the preceding year. He was a Minister in the United Brethren Church of Christ. Reverend Bovey was buried in the Old Edinburg Cemetery.

1850 CENSUS: No record of this household in the census.

PAGE 4   EDINBURG   (Microfilm Page 582)

Dwelling 24   Family 24

Robert Riddleberger	55	Stage Driver	50	75	Va.
Elizabeth Riddleberger	41				"

1850 CENSUS: No record of this household in the census.

PAGE 4 EDINBURG   (Microfilm Page 582)

Dwelling 25   Family 25

Samuel Jack	49	Wagon Maker	500	250	Virginia
Catherine Jack	39				"
Robert F. Jack	16				" School
Mary S. Jack	9				"
Marcus P. Jack	5				"

Samuel Jack was married to **Catherine Liggett** on 21 Mar 1837. Catherine was born 12 Oct 1820 and died 11 Jun 1871. She was buried in the Old Edinburg Cemetery. Catherine was the daughter of Peter Liggett. Peter Liggett married Catherine Gibler on 8 Nov 1802. Peter was a resident in **dwelling 26.**

Robert W. Jack was born ca. 1843. He was a laborer at the time of his enlistment in Company C of the 10th Virginia Infantry. He enlisted as a Private at Harpers Ferry on 29 May 1861. He was detached to the Brigade Commissary on 28 Jun 1861. There is no record of his activities in Company C after 6 Feb 1862. Robert enlisted at New Market as a Private in Company K of the 12th Virginia Cavalry on 9 Aug 1862. He was taken prisoner on 11 Aug 1862. The location of the prison he was assigned to is not reported. He was exchanged on 21 Sep 1862. He was absent in Oct 1862. He was reported as present for muster in Sep and Oct 1863. His record demonstrates that he was periodically present and absent during 1863 and 1864. Robert was paroled at Edinburg at the conclusion of the war. Robert W. Jack had blue eyes, brown hair and a fair complexion. He was 5'5".

Marcus Perry Jack was a wagon maker at the time of his marriage to Jennie R. Clem on 18 Nov 1879. Jennie was the daughter of Ammon and Regina. Ammon W. Clem married Regina Lutz on 30 Mar 1854. Ammon Clem and his family resided in **dwelling 1474**.

RELATED FAMILY:

   William Liggett, brother of Catherine Liggett Jack, resides in **dwelling 26**.
   Elizabeth Liggett, sister of Catherine Liggett Jack, married John Grandstaff on 27 Feb 1826 and resides in **dwelling 46**.

1850 CENSUS: **Samuel Jack** and family resided in dwelling 737 on page 52.

PAGE 4   EDINBURG   (Microfilm Page 582)

Dwelling 26   Family 26

William Liggett	40	Gunsmith	1500	650	Va.
Mary Liggett	40				Va. Can't Read
Catherine E. Liggett	13			"	School
Clay Liggett	9			"	School
Peter Liggett	83				Pennsylvania

   William Liggett was the son of **Peter Liggett**. The elder Liggett resided in this household. **Peter Liggett** had married Catherine Gibler on 8 Nov 1802. Catherine was the daughter of Phillip and Margaret. The surname of William's wife **Mary** is not known.

Elizabeth Catherine Liggett was married on 25 Nov 1869 to George W. Snider Jr. George, a shoemaker, was born and resided in Hardy County, West Virginia. He was the son of George W. and Elizabeth.

RELATED FAMILY:
Catherine Liggett, daughter of Peter Liggett, was married to Samuel Jack on 21 Mar 1837 and resided in **dwelling 25**.
Elizabeth Liggett, daughter of Peter Liggett, was married to John Grandstaff on 27 Feb 1826 and resided in **dwelling 46**.

1850 CENSUS: William Liggett resided with his family in dwelling 707 on page 50.

PAGE 4   EDINBURG   (Microfilm Page 582)

Dwelling 27   Family 27

Rachel Valentine   64   Weaver   0   40   Virginia   Can't Read

It is not known whether **Rachel Valentine** was ever married. In 1850 she resided in a household with her 13 year old daughter. Her marriage has not been located in Shenandoah County records.

RELATED FAMILY:
Matilda Valentine, the daughter of Rachel, was married to Andrew Jackson Windle on 8 Aug 1854 and was located in **dwelling 4**.

1850 CENSUS: Rachel Valentine resided in dwelling 688 on page 49. Her 13 year old daughter Regina was also in the household. It is possible Regina and Matilda Valentine Windle are one and the same.

29

Dwelling 28   Family 28

Stephen Bowman	72	Farmer	8000	100	Va. Cn't Rd
Henry Bowman	38		0	128	"
Malvinia Bowman	27				"
Virginia Bowman	2				"
Henrietta Bowman	3m				"
William Windle	70	White Smithe			"
Cyrena Windle	21	Seamstress			"

        Stephen Bowman died 24 May 1868 of "old age". He
was the son of Henry and Elizabeth. Henry Bowman was
married to Elizabeth Hockman Stover on 9 Apr 1823. The
bondsman for this marriage was Thomas McCord. Elizabeth
was the widow of Joseph Stover.   She had married Joseph
on 6 Mar 1811.   Elizabeth was the daughter of Henry
Hockman.

        Henry Bowman was the son of Stephen and Elizabeth
Hockman Bowman. Henry was a farmer at the time of his
marriage to **Margaret Malvinia Windle**. They were married
on 3 Jan 1858. Malvinia was the daughter of William and
Margaret.

        Virginia C. Bowman was the daughter of Henry and
Malvinia. She was born in 1858 and died in 1940. Virginia
married James E. Beazley on 9 Dec 1879. James was a clerk
and was born and resided in Page County, Virginia. He was
the son of Isaac and Rebecca. James was born in 1846 and
died 18 Jan 1914. James enlisted on 2 Jun 1861 at Luray,
Virginia in Company K of the 10th Virginia Infantry.   On
9 Aug 1862 he was wounded at Cedar Run. He lost his leg
as a result of the wound and was discharged to the invalid
corp. Virginia and James were buried in the Cedarwood
Cemetery in Edinburg.

        William Windle was the father of Malvinia. He had
married Margaret Gaines on 19 Apr 1824. Their marriage
took place in Frederick County, Virginia.

        Cyrena Windle, the daughter of William and
Margaret, was married to Joseph T. Crickenberger on 25 Feb
1868. Cyrena was born in Augusta County, Virginia. Joseph
T. Crickenberger was a minister and was the son of James
and Elizabeth.

30

RELATED FAMILY:
     Andrew Jackson Windle, son of William Windle, was married to Matilda Valentine on 8 Aug 1854 and resided in **dwelling 4.**
     George Windle, son of William Windle, was married to Mary Krebs on 1 May 1848 and resided in **dwelling 32.**
     Isaac Bowman, was probably the son of Stephen Bowman. He resided in **dwelling 280.**

1850 CENSUS: **Stephen Bowman** and family resided in dwelling 711 on page 50.

PAGE 4   EDINBURG   (Microfilm Page 582)

Dwelling 29 Family 29

John W. Smoot	29	Cabinet Maker	0	400	Virginia
Mary E. Smoot	29			Va.	
Clarisa C. Smoot	7		"		School
Benjamin P. Smoot	6		"		
Franklin P. Smoot	4		"		
Theodore Smoot	1		"		
Ellenora Miller	16	Housegirl	"		

    John W. Smoot was married to **Mary E. Pirkey** on 4 Dec 1851. In their marriage record they are listed as John Smutz and Mary E. Parkey. Mary E. Pirkey Smoot was born 7 Jul 1829 and died 21 Jan 1900. She is buried in the Mt. Zion United Methodist Church Cemetery in Strasburg, Virginia. John W. Smoot was drafted on 16 Apr 1862. He enlisted at Rude's Hill as a member of the 2nd Virginia Infantry in Company K. On 27 Nov 1863 he was wounded in the left leg at Payne's Farm. John was hospitalized at Chimborazo #3 on 29 Nov 1863. He was recorded as back with his unit in March of 1864.

    Benjamin P. Smoot was born 16 Mar 1854 and died in Mt. Jackson on 18 Aug 1941. He was married on 30 Jul 1876 to Barbara C. Rush. Barbara was the daughter of Samuel and Catherine. Samuel Rush married Catherine Hupp on 28 Jan 1845. Samuel Rush and family resided in **dwelling 985.** Barbara Rush Smoot was born 19 Jun 1854 and died 19 Mar 1918. Benjamin and Barbara were buried in the New Mount Jackson Cemetery.

    Theodore Smoot was born 3 May 1859 and died 4 Feb 1890. He was buried next to his mother in the Mt. Zion

United Methodist Church Cemetery. They were buried next to the Reverend John Pirkey, a prominent minister in Shenandoah County. Reverend Pirkey was born in Washington County, Maryland and was the son of Abraham and Catherine. He was located in **dwelling 1645** at the time of this census. He may have been the brother of Mary E. Pirkey Smoot.

1850 CENSUS: **John W. Smoot** was a resident in dwelling 746 on page 52. This was the residence of Henry and Catherine Kern.

Mary E. Pirkey was a resident in dwelling 468 on page 34. This was the household of Samuel and Clarissa Kern.

PAGE 5 EDINBURG   (Microfilm Page 583)

Dwelling 30 Family 30

Abraham Miley	48	Collector of Claims	0	700	Virginia
Catherine Miley	29				"
Louisa Miley	18				"
Annie B. Miley	2m				"

Abraham Miley was the son of David and Magdalena. He was married originally to Sarah Roads on 17 Feb 1834. The bondsman for that marriage was David Rhodes. Upon the death of Sarah Roads Miley, Abraham, a constable at the time, was married on 24 Mar 1859 to **Catherine Ann Grandstaff.** Catherine was the daughter of Jacob and Elizabeth. Jacob Grandstaff was married to Elizabeth Lambert on 1 Apr 1830.

Mary Louise Miley was born 26 Feb 1842 and died 15 Feb 1912. She was married to Samuel J. Artz, the son of Mary Artz. Samuel J. Artz was born 6 Mar 1837 and died 18 Feb 1918. Samuel was a farmer from Maurertown at the time of the wedding. Samuel and Mary Louise were buried at the Zion Christian Church Cemetery in Maurertown. Samuel was the twin brother of Elizabeth Ann Artz Grandstaff. Elizabeth resided in **dwelling 13** at the time of this census.

Annie B. Miley, or Fannie as she appears in marriage records, married Hamilton J. Mathias on 25 Mar 1883. He was a 24 year old farmer from Hardy County, West Virginia. Hamilton was the son of Joseph and Susan.

32

RELATED FAMILY:

Joseph R. Miley , son of Abraham and Sarah, was a resident in **dwelling 35**. This was the household of Hiram Carver.

Jacob **Grandstaff**, father of Catherine, resided with his son **George W. Grandstaff** in **dwelling 13**.

1850 CENSUS: **Abraham Miley** and family resided in dwelling 710 on page 50.

PAGE 5 EDINBURG (Microfilm Page 583)

Dwelling 31 Family 31

James M. Hisey	44	Clerk 0 100	Virginia	
Elizabeth Hisey	34		"	
Mary M. Hisey	11		"	School
Florence A. Hisey	9		"	
William A. Hisey	6		"	School
Edgar Hisey	2		"	

James M. Hisey died 2 Jun 1870 at the age of 54. He married **Sarah E. Windle** on 28 Jun 1849. The bondsman for the marriage was William Herman. Sarah E. Windle Hisey died 6 Apr 1894 at the age of 68 years, 7 months and 25 days old. James and Sarah were buried in the Old Edinburg Cemetery.

Florence Ann Hisey was born 19 Oct 1852 and died 11 Feb 1924. She is buried near her parents. Information published regarding her death indicates that she had been the wife of James T. Goodall.

William Arthur Hisey was born in 1854 and died in 1939. He was a farmer when he married Mollie F. Lowery on 1 Oct 1885. Mollie was the daughter of Alexander and Catherine. Mollie was born in 1854 and died in 1937. They were buried in the Cedarwood Cemetery in Edinburg.

Edgar L. Hisey was born 22 Jun 1857 and died 18 Oct 1918. He was married to Minnie H. Murray on 7 Jun 1886. Minnie was the daughter of Ben and Sallie. Ben Murray married Sallie F. Allen on 26 Jan 1864. Minnie was born 31 Mar 1860 and died 18 Jul 1923. This couple was buried in the Old Edinburg Cemetery. Edgar was a printer.

1850 CENSUS: James M. Hisey and his family resided in dwelling 710 on page 50. This was the household of Abraham Miley.

PAGE 5 EDINBURG   (Microfilm Page 583)

Dwelling 32 Family 32

George Windle	32	Trade	400 300	Virginia
Mary Windle	35			"
Robert Windle	11			"

*****A Note on a possible discrepancy:
There are at least two, and possibly a third George W. Windle listed in the 1860 Census. Two of these men were located in Edinburg and the third was in the New Market area. This is important because data regarding birth, death and possibly military records of the two individuals living in Edinburg may have been interpreted incorrectly.

The **George W. Windle** located in this household is known to have married **Mary Krenb (Krebs)** on 1 May 1848. The bondsman for that marriage was Joseph Roads. He was a potter at the time of the 1850 Census. Andrew Jackson Windle, believed to have been his brother, was in the same residence. This leads to the deduction that George's parents were William and Margaret. William Windle married Margaret Gaines on 19 Apr 1824. William resided in **dwelling 28.** The other George W. Windle resided in dwelling 317. His parents were George and Sarah. His wife was also named Mary (Barton). Military records for the Danville Artillery indicate that George Washington Windle, husband of Mary C. Barton died 25 Feb 1904 at the age of 76 years, 5 months and 13 days old. His wife Mary died 10 Nov 1900. She was 76 years, 2 months and 2 days old. Military records contend that George W Windle and Mary Barton Windle were buried in the Cedarwood Cemetery in Edinburg. Here is the dilemma. The ages on the tombstone more closely match those attributed in the census to George and Mary Krebs Windle. In addition they are buried next to Robert W. Windle, known to have been the son of George W. Windle and Mary Krebs Windle.

THERE IS THE POSSIBILITY THAT THE COUPLE BURIED IN THE CEDARWOOD CEMETERY IS THE COUPLE IN THIS HOUSEHOLD. INDIVIDUALS INTERESTED IN THE HISTORY OF THE WINDLE FAMILY NEED TO CAREFULLY STUDY THIS MATTER.

Robert W. Windle was born 8 Mar 1849 and died 1 Nov 1915. His wife Sarah C. was born 5 Dec 1853 and died 12 Jan 1914. Her surname may have been Burke. Robert and Sarah were buried in the Cedarwood Cemetery. Historian John Wayland recounted one of the more memorable events of Shenandoah County's involvement in the Civil War in his history of the county. The event involved Captain George J. Grandstaff and his efforts to free Confederate pickets who had been captured by Major Young and his Yankee troops. Grandstaff was alerted to the Union raid by Martin Luther Grove (dwelling 52) who at the time was too young to serve in the army. Grandstaff, Lt. Joseph R. Miley (dwelling 35) who happened to be home on leave at the time and M. L. Grove gathered other Shenandoah County men and pursued the raiders down the Valley Pike striking them aggressively from the rear. By the time they had reached Maurerstown, Grandstaff and his forces had captured five of the Yankee troops. These troops were sent back to Edinburg under the guard of Martin Luther Grove and another local youth identified as "Bob Windle". Eventually Grandstaff and his men freed all of the Confederate pickets and captured 15 of the Union forces.

RELATED FAMILY:

Andrew Jackson Windle, brother of George, married Matilda Valentine on 8 Aug 1854 and resided in dwelling 4.

1850 CENSUS: George W. Windle resided in dwelling 715 on page 50. His wife, son Robert and brother Andrew resided with him.

PAGE 5 EDINBURG (Microfilm Page 583)

Dwelling 33   Family 33

Samuel Boehm	37	N.R.	300	700	Virginia
Frances Boehm	32				"
William H. Boehm	13				" School
Joseph J. Boehm	11				" School
Victoria C. Boehm	7				" School
John E. Boehm	4				"
Letcher Boehm	2				"
Ann Rudy	25				"

Samuel Boehm was born 17 Aug 1817 and died 1 Jul 1886. He was married to Frances Miller on 14 Oct 1844. Frances was born 7 Aug 1826 and died 23 Aug 1900. Samuel and Frances are buried in the Old Edinburg Cemetery. Frances was listed as the daughter of Susan Miller. Susan Miller was residing as a mid-wife in the home of Edward B. Whissen (dwelling 80) at the time of this census. Susan Miller died 2 May 1871 and was buried next to Samuel and Frances. She is believed to have been the Susan Kibler who married Joseph Miller on 19 Nov 1818.

William H. Boehm was a teacher. He died 8 Sep 1864 at Elmira, New York of Typhoid Fever. This suggests that he was a soldier and died at the prison camp in Elmira. According to Shenandoah County death records he was 17 years, 10 months and 23 days old at the time of his death.

Victoria C. Boehm died in Edinburg on 30 Mar 1937. She was 83 years old and had never married.

John E. Boehm was a miller. Samuel Boehm, his father, was also reported to have been a miller at the time of the 1850 census. John E. Boehm was married to Lucy M. Belew on 28 Oct 1881. Lucy was the daughter of Dr. Peter Belew and his wife Elizabeth. Lucy and her parents resided in dwelling 36 at the time of this census.

Letcher Boehm was born 1 Mar 1858 and died 19 Aug 1861. He is buried with his parents in the Old Edinburg Cemetery.

1850 CENSUS: Samuel Boehm and family resided in dwelling 736 on page 52.

PAGE 5   EDINBURG   (Microfilm Page 538)

Dwelling 34   Family 34

Joseph W. Hoffman	32	N.R.	100	150		Va.	
Eveline V. Hoffman	29					"	
Emma F. Hoffman	6					"	School
Lydia C. Hoffman	1					"	
Levi D. Wanzer	39	(Mulatto)	Shoemaker			"	

Joseph W. Hoffman was born 10 Nov 1827 and died 12 Mar 1898. Joseph may have been the son of Andrew and Fanny. Andrew J. Hoffman married Fanny Stover on 1 Apr

1820. He married **Eveline V. McCord** on 24 Nov 1849. The bondsman for the marriage was John Gaw. Eveline may have been the daughter of Thomas and Catherine. Thomas McCord married Catherine Hunt on 13 Oct 1818. Eveline was born 9 May 1830 and died 17 Aug 1890. They are buried in the Cedarwood Cemetery in Edinburg.

      Emma Hoffman was married on 29 Jan 1885 to R. H. Lacey. Mr. Lacey was a widowed merchant who had been born in Loudoun County, Virginia. He was the son of Joseph and Frances. Emma was 29 years old and R. H. was 34.

      Lydia Catherine Hoffman was born 27 Jul 1858 and died 7 Nov 1932. Lydia never married and was buried in the Riverview Cemetery in Strasburg.

RELATED FAMILY:
      Nimrod Hoffman, believed to have been the brother of Joseph W. Hoffman, married **Mary C. McCord,** believed to have been the sister of Eveline on 5 Feb 1845. They resided in **dwelling 278** at the time of this census.

1850 CENSUS: Joseph Hoffman and his family lived in dwelling 169 on page 12.

NOTE: Evidence has not been discovered to positively identify the parents of Joseph and Eveline, nor the relationship of this couple to Nimrod and Mary. Members of related families will need to research this in greater detail.

PAGE 5 EDINBURG (Microfilm Page 583)

Dwelling 35 Family 35

Hiram Carver	32	Machinist	1100	200	Pennsylvania
Mary Carver	36				Virginia
Joseph R. Miley	22				"

      Hiram Carver was listed as a cabinetmaker in the 1850 census.

      Joseph R. Miley was the son of Abraham and Sarah. Abraham Miley married Sarah Roads on 17 Feb 1834. Abraham and his family resided in **dwelling 30.** On 30 Nov 1865 Joseph R. Miley was married to Mary F. Bowman. Mary F. Bowman was a housegirl in **dwelling 267.** She was reported to have been the daughter of Samuel Bowman. In the 1850 census, 7 year old Mary was a resident in the household of Samuel and Elizabeth. There is a discrepancy in the site of Joseph R. Miley's burial site. Records at the Strasburg Museum indicate that Joseph was buried in the Riverview Cemetery at Strasburg. Terrance V. Murphy in his book **10th Virginia Infantry** indicates that Joseph R. Miley was buried in the Old Edinburg Cemetery. Murphy indicates that Joseph was born ca. 1832 and was a clerk at the time of his enlistment in Company C. He enlisted on 29 May 1861 at Harpers Ferry, West Virginia. He was promoted to 3rd Corporal. On 25 Dec 1861 he was promoted to 4th Sergant. Joseph transferred to Company F of the 10th Virginia Infantry when Company C was disbanded. He later transferred to Company K of the 12th Virginia Cavalry. He was eventually elected to the position of Lt. Col. with that unit. Evidence of a tombstone for Joseph R. Miley in either the Riverview Cemetery or the Old Edinburg Cemetery has not been reported. Joseph was home on leave when he became involved in one of the more memorable incidents in Shenandoah County during the Civil War. Union forces under the command of Major Young captured a group of Confederate troops who were assigned picket duty near Edinburg. When Lt. Joseph Miley learned of this, he and an area youth named Martin Luther Grove (**dwelling 52**) rode out to advise Captain George J. Grandstaff. Grandstaff and Miley rounded up a group of area men and rode off in pursuit of the Union forces and their captives. The local men fought an aggressive action against the rear guard of Major Young's forces. They eventually were able to free all of the hostages and capture 15 of the Union forces in the process. This incident is recounted in John Wayland's **A History of Shenandoah County, Va.**

1850 CENSUS: **Hiram Carver** resided in dwelling 709 on page 50.

Joseph R. Miley resided in dwelling 710 on page 50.

38

PAGE 5 EDINBURG   **(Microfilm 583)**

Dwelling 36 Family 36

Peter Belew	40	Physician	16,700 4775	Va.
Elizabeth M.Belew	35			Va.
Emma V. Belew	13			" School
Arthur P. Belew	11			" School
George H. Belew	8			" School
Albert L. Belew	7			"
Lucy M. Belew	2			"
Laura C. Belew	8m			"
Solomon F. Belew	83			"
Barbara J. Rau	35			"

Dr. Peter Belew was born 4 Dec 1819 and died 9 Jul 1904. His wife **Elizabeth M.** was born 17 Apr 1825 and died 23 Sep 1890. They were buried with several of their children at the Cedarwood Cemetery in Edinburg. Dr. Belew was one of the five trustees responsible for the incorporation of Edinburg, Virginia on 24 May 1852. Belew, John J. Grandstaff and Richard Miller were authorized to hold elections for trustees.

Emma V. Belew was born 16 Nov 1846 and died 4 Oct 1916. She was married to Captain Harrison H. Riddleberger on 29 Nov 1866. Harrison was a clerk at the time of their marriage. He was the son of Madison and Susan. Madison Riddleberger married Susan Shryock on 15 Dec 1830. Madison and family resided in **dwelling 40**. Harrison attained the rank of Captain in the Confederate Army. He was born 4 Oct 1843 and died 24 Jan 1890. Emma and Harrison were buried at Cedarwood Cemetery

Arthur Page Belew became a physician like his father. He was born 27 Oct 1848 and died 4 Dec 1909. He was married to Martha "Mattie" D. Saum on 28 Oct 1873. Mattie was the daughter of Abraham and Ellen. Abraham Saum married Ellen Sonnestine on 26 Jul 1836. Abraham and his family resided in **dwelling 19**. Mattie D. Saum Belew was born 16 Sep 1850 and died in 1924. They were buried in the Cedarwood Cemetery.

George Hupp Belew was born 24 Jun 1851 and died 27 Oct 1884. He was buried in the family plot at Cedarwood.

Laura C. Belew was born 8 Sep 1859 according to Shenandoah County birth records. Her tombstone at Cedarwood indicates that she was born 21 Sep 1859. Laura died 1 Sep 1939. In 1890 Laura was engaged to marry Page L. Eaton a 35 year old potter from Washington County, Virginia. It is not known if the marriage actually took place.

Barbara Jane Rau was the daughter of Henry and Amelia. She was 53 years old when she married Peter E. Zeiler of Morgan County, West Virginia on 14 Mar 1876.

RELATED FAMILY:

John Henry Rau, brother of Barbara Jane Rau, married Sarah Ellen Rinker on 11 Apr 1857 and resided in **dwelling 64.**

David S. Rau, brother of Barbara Jane Rau, married Lydia S. Boehm on 7 Dec 1858 and resided in **dwelling 65.**

1850 CENSUS: Peter Belew resided in dwelling 1685 on page 121.

PAGE 6   EDINBURG   (Microfilm Page 584)

Dwelling 37   Family 37

George Funk	43	Boot & Shoemaker	1500	252
Ann Funk	43			H. C. Germany
William Funk	9			Virginia
Mary M. Funk	5			" School
Ellen Funk	1			"
Sarah Funk	9m			"
Elizabeth Rinker	23			"

George Funk was born in Germany. He was married to **Anna Painter** on 21 Apr 1846. The bondsman for the marriage was David Craig.

The **Reverend Joseph W. Funk,** son of George and Ann, was married to Annie E. Clapper on 6 Feb 1873. She was born in Grant County, West Virginia. Annie was the daughter of Gideon and Ann Marie. Remarks at the ceremony were given by Jacob E. Ridings who was listed as her step-father. Joseph W. appears to have been listed as William in this household.

40

Sarah Elizabeth Funk resided in Mt. Jackson. She was 78 when she died on 4 Feb 1938.

Elizabeth Rinker is not known. However, there is a possibility that she was listed twice in the census. She may have been the 24 year old listed in the household of her parents William and Sallie. William Rinker married Sallie Painter on 29 May 1833. They resided in dwelling 932 at the time of the census. Elizabeth "Lizzie" Rinker was born 9 Sep 1835 and died 23 Jun 1888. She was married to Harrison Lindamood on 20 Feb 1868. Harrison Lindamood resided in dwelling 563. Harrison, a blacksmith at the time of their marriage, was the son of Michael and Elizabeth. Michael Lindamood married Elizabeth Rinker on 10 Mar 1834. Harrison Lindamood married again after Elizabeth died. He was married to Mary M. Funk. Information regarding the marriage of these two individuals was found in the notice of his death. A marriage record has not been found. It is possible that she was the five year old in this household. Mary M. Funk Lindamood was born 26 May 1855 and died 4 Oct 1912.

1850 CENSUS: George Funk and family resided in dwelling 716 on page 50.

PAGE 6   EDINBURG   (Microfilm Page 584)

Dwelling 38   Family 38

Joseph W. Evans   42   Master Boot & Shoemaker 600   202
Virginia

Hannah T. Evans   28   Va.
William H. Evans   9   "   School
Lucy E. Evans   7   "
Mary C. Evans   5   "
Julann Evans   4   "
Albert A. Evans   1   "
Mary Evans   70   "   Can't Read

Joseph W. Evans was born 28 Jan 1818 and died 3 Oct 1892. His wife was Hannah T. Via. She was born 15 May 1832 and died 21 Jan 1906. Joseph and Hannah were buried in the Old Edinburg Cemetery.

William Henry Evans was born 22 Mar 1845 and died 19 Jul 1914. He was buried in the Cedarwood Cemetery at Edinburg. William was a shoemaker at the time of his 23

Dec 1869 marriage to Virginia T. Downey. Virginia was the daughter of Thornton and Amelia. Thornton Downey married Amelia Ann Miley on 12 Dec 1838. Thornton and his family were residents of **dwelling 76**.

Lucy Ellen Evans was born 31 Oct 1852 and died 9 Apr 1928. She was married to Joseph W. Downey, a blacksmith, on 24 Dec 1874. Joseph was the brother of Virginia T. Downey, the wife of William Henry Evans. Joseph W. Downey was born 4 Jun 1849 and died 17 Jul 1892. Lucy and Joseph were buried in the Cedarwood Cemetery. Lucy Ellen Evans Downey, married Thomas A. Hoffman on 23 Jul 1896. He resided in **dwelling 278**. He was a widower. His first wife was Kate A. Balthis. She died in 1890. Thomas was the son of Nimrod and Mary. Nimrod Hoffman married Mary C. McCord on 5 Feb 1845. Thomas A. Hoffman was born in 1846 and died 25 Jun 1924. He was also buried in the Cedarwood Cemetery.

Mary C. Evans was born in 1854 and died in 1936. She was married to Absolom Coffman on 17 Sep 1876. Absolom was the son of Ezra and Mary. Ezra Coffman reportedly married Mary Haun. Absolom Coffman was born 1852 and died in 1936. He and his parents were residents of **dwelling 273**. Mary and Absolom were buried in the Cedarwood Cemetery.

Albert A. Evans was a shoemaker. He was born in 1858 and died in 1912. He was married to Julia A. Baker on 15 Mar 1881. She was the daughter of Jacob and Elizabeth. Jacob Baker was married to Elizabeth Funk on 15 May 1851. They are located in **dwelling 575**. Julia Ann Baker was born in 1856 and died in 1929. They are buried in the New Mount Jackson Cemetery.

1850 CENSUS: **Joseph W. Evans** and family resided in dwelling 718 on page 51.

Mary Evans, believed to have been the mother of Joseph, resided in dwelling 160 on page 12. She was located in the residence Phillip Stover. Aaron Evans, apparently her son, was also in the residence.

PAGE 6   EDINBURG   (Microfilm Page 584)

Dwelling 39   Family 39

Joseph H. Spengler   26 Merchant   O 510   Virginia

Joseph H. Spengler was born 21 Nov 1833 and died 19 May 1894. At times he is referred to in historical records as "Spangler". Joseph was the son of John and Margaret. John Spengler married Margaret Russell on 29 Jan 1833 in Frederick County, Virginia. At the outbreak of the Civil War he was a merchant. When the conflict began he enlisted on 18 Apr 1861 as a 2nd Lt. in Company C of the 10th Virginia Infantry. He was elected 1st Lt. on 26 Dec 1861. Company C disbanded on 22 Apr 1864 and Joseph joined the 35th Battalion of the Virginia Cavalry. He rose to the rank of 2nd Lt. but was force to resign his position on 9 Jan 1864 because of physical disabilities. The military roll of the 12th Virginia Cavalry reports that Joseph H. Spengler was a member of that unit and was paroled on 21 Apr 1865 as a private in K Company. He was 5'9 1/2" and had a fair complexion.

During the war Joseph H. Spengler was married to Mary C. Allen on 31 Mar 1863. Mary was the daughter of Israel and Amanda. Mary and her parents were residents of **dwelling 564**. Mary C. Allen Spengler was born 1 Aug 1843 and died 22 Jan 1870. After a five year period of mourning, Joseph H. Spengler was married to Mary Caroline Bryant on 6 Jun 1876. Mary Caroline Bryant was the daughter of Enoch and Catherine. She resided in **dwelling 620** with her parents at the time of this census. Mary Caroline was born 17 Apr 1842 and died 6 Aug 1879. Joseph Spengler, Mary C. Allen Spengler and Mary Caroline Bryant Spengler were all buried in the Old Union Church Cemetery in Mt. Jackson, Virginia.

1850 CENSUS: **Joseph H. Spengler** was a resident in dwelling 240 on page 17. The head of that household was Reuben Walton, a merchant.

PAGE 6 EDINBURG   (Microfilm Page 584)

Dwelling 40 Family 40

Madison Riddleberger	54	Stage Driver	800 75	
		Virginia	Can't Read	
Susan H. Riddleberger	44		Va.	
Harrison H. Riddleberger	16		"	School
William I. Riddleberger	12		"	
Amanda E. Riddleberger	16	Housegirl	"	

43

Madison Riddleberger was the son of Samuel and Sarah Compton Riddleberger. His parents were married in Botecourt County, Virginia in 1794. He was born 22 Apr 1809 and died 23 Nov 1880. Madison earned his living as a stage driver and gunsmith. He married **Susan Shryock** on 15 Dec 1830. Susan was the daughter of Jacob and Amelia. Jacob Shryock married Amelia Heiskell on 1 Jun 1793. Historian John Wayland recounted that the Shryock family owned " a considerable part of land on which Edinburg stands". In fact when a gentleman named Shryock applied for a license to open a tavern in 1802 the town that eventually became Edinburg was known as Shryock. For a period of time it had also been called "Stony Creek". Madison and Susan were buried at the Cedarwood Cemetery in Edinburg.

U.S. SENATOR HARRISON HOLT RIDDLEBERGER
John Walter Wayland Collection, Winchester-Frederick County Hist. Society Archives, Winchester, Virginia

Harrison Holt Riddleberger was born 4 Oct 1843 and died 24 Jan 1890. Shortly after this census he began working at Harrisonburg, Virginia as a clerk. When the Civil War broke out he organized a company of cavalry in the Harrisonburg area. He was commissioned a Lt. in the 10th Virginia Infantry on 10 Apr 1862. He was shot by accident on 22 Oct 1862. On 1 Jan 1863 he was commissioned as the Enrolling Officer for Shenandoah County. At some point he was promoted to Captain with a cavalry unit. It is believed that this was Imboden's troop with the 18th Virginia Cavalry. He was captured and sent to Camp Chase, Ohio. While in prison he began to take an interest in the study of law. After the war he was the publisher of the **TENTH LEGION BANNER.** He would also serve as a commonwealth attorney and in the Virginia House of Delegates. Harrison Holt Riddleberger was elected to serve in the United States Senate from 1883 to 1889. Harrison was married to Emma V. Belew on 29 Nov 1866. She was the daughter of Dr. Peter and Elizabeth Belew of **dwelling 36.** Their home was one of the buildings that now house the Massanutten Academy. Harrison and Emma were buried at Cedarwood Cemetery.

William Ira Riddleberger, a tailor, was born 7 Dec 1847 and died 30 May 1920. He was married to Arabelle R. Miley on 14 Oct 1869. Arabelle was the daughter of John and Frances. John W. Miley was married to Frances Artz on 16 Feb 1848. Arabelle and her parents resided in **dwelling 20.** Arabelle R. Miley Riddleberger was born 20 Nov 1848 and died 31 Jul 1921. He was reported to have been a veteran of the war. No record has been found to substantiate this. William and Arabelle were buried in Cedarwood Cemetery.

RELATED FAMILY:

Amelia Riddleberger, daughter of Madison and Susan, was married to Robert Hisey on 9 May 1852 and resided in **dwelling 21.**

Louisa C. Riddleberger, daughter of Madison and Susan, was married to Joseph F. Grandstaff on 25 Oct 1851 and resided in **dwelling 54.**

Sarah E. Riddleberger, daughter of Madison and Susan, was married to Benjamin B. Holtzman and resided in **dwelling 56.**

1850 CENSUS: Madison Riddleberger and family resided in dwelling 719 on page 51.

45

PAGE 6 EDINBURG   (Microfilm Page 584)

Dwelling 41 Family 41

John R. Wierman	38	Clerk 800	150	Virginia
Isabella B. Wierman	34			"
Mary C. Wierman	1			"
John W. Wierman	9m			"

    John R. Wierman was born in 1822 and died in 1891. He was a millwright at the time of the 1850 census. He was the son of John and Elizabeth. John's father was born in Adams County, Pennyslvania and his mother was born in Frederick County, Maryland. On 11 Jun 1856 John R. Wierman married Isabella B. Leeper. Isabella was born in 1825 and died in 1886. She was the daughter of William P. and Jane E. William P. Leeper married Jane E. Blackford on 25 Jan 1817. Isabella was born in Page County, Virginia. John and Isabella were buried in the Old Edinburg Cemetery. John R. Wierman enlisted in the Eighth Star New Market Artillery on 4 Mar 1862. He was present on all rolls. In September of 1862 he was reassigned to the Danville Artillery. He is reported as being present through 3 Aug 1863. He appears under the name of John R. Wireman. There was also a John Wireman who was listed on the role of Company H of the 11th Virginia Infantry. Robert C. Ruby a resident of **dwelling 55** was hired as a substitute for John R. Wierman.

    John W. Wierman died on 18 Jul 1860 of the "summer complaint" according to county death records. He was 1 year old.

RELATED FAMILY:
    Benjamin B. Wierman, brother of John, was married to Catherine A. Moore on 12 Mar 1857 and resided in **dwelling 1024.**

1850 CENSUS: John R. Wierman appears in dwelling 30 on page 3. This was household of his parents.

        Isabella B. Leeper resided in dwelling 305 on page 22. This was household of William A. Crawford, a teacher in Shenandoah County. Mary C. Leeper, sister of Isabella, was also a teacher and a resident in the household.

PAGE 6 EDINBURG   (Microfilm Page 584)

Dwelling 42   Family 42

Benjamin D. Holden	47	Confectioner	0	150	Virginia
Mary C. Holden	34				"
George D. Holden	10				" School
William L. Holden	3				"
Sarah V. Holden	1				"

Benjamin D. Holden is reported to have been born in Harrison County, Virginia. He was the son of Alexander and Nancy. Benjamin was a widower at the time of his marriage to **Mary C. Southard**, the daughter of Peyton and Rhoda. Payton Southard married Rhoda Rhodes on 27 Jun 1821 in Frederick County, Virginia. Mary was born in Frederick County. Peyton Southard and family were residents of **dwelling 9**. Benjamin D. Holden was a prominent merchant in the community. On 13 May 1862, Mr. Holden applied for a license to sell "wine and ardent spirits". He was granted the license to sell these items for one year.

1850 CENSUS: No record of this family in census of 1850.

PAGE 6 EDINBURG (Microfilm Page 584)

Dwelling 43   Family 43

Martin M. Wetzel	31	Cabinet Maker	0	0	Virginia
Mary A. Wetzel	25				"
Sarah M. Wetzel	3				"
Elizabeth C. Wetzel	1				"
Nancy Viands	60			0 50	"
Mary L.Hollar	8				"

The marriage of **Martin M. Wetzel** to **Mary A. Viands** took place on 16 Oct 1855 in Page County, Virginia. **Nancy Viands** was her mother. Thomas Viands was listed in marriage records as the husband of Nancy. Martin's parents were Jacob and Delila and he was born in Rockingham County. Jacob Wetzel and family resided in **dwelling 268**. Mary A. Viands Wetzel died prior to 1874 as Martin was married to Mary Olinger on 14 Jun 1874. Mary Olinger was the daughter of Phillip and Catherine. Phillip Olinger married Catherine Hollar on 21 Jun 1831. Phillip Olinger and family resided in **dwelling 889**. Mary Olinger Wetzel was born 14 Jul 1833 and died 9 Nov 1910. She is buried in the Zirkle Family Cemetery near New Market, Virginia.

Sarah M. "Maggie" Wetzel was married on 14 May 1885 to Charles C. Kibler. He was a blacksmith who was born in Augusta County, Virginia. His parents were Isaac and Margaret. Charles was born 23 Jun 1854 and died 29 Nov 1919. Maggie had been born on 8 Oct 1854 and died 24 Jun 1936. They were buried in the Union Forge Cemetery.

Elizabeth Catherine Wetzel died 5 Jul 1938 at the age of 79. She married Robert L. Hockman on 11 Jan 1887. He was a shoemaker and was the son of William and R. F. Robert was born in 1864 and died in 1953. They were buried in the Cedarwood Cemetery.

RELATED FAMILY:

It is interesting to speculate if there was a relationship between **Nancy Viands** of this household and Hannah T. Via Evans of **dwelling 38**. The names Vine, Viands or Via were not commonly found in Shenandoah County.

1850 CENSUS: **Martin Wetzel** resided with his parents in dwelling 545 on page 306 in Page County.

PAGE 7 EDINBURG   (Microfilm Page 585)

Dwelling 44   Family 44

Jacob B. Snapp	53	Farmer	2000	1000	Virginia
Barbara Snapp	40				"
George H. Snapp	23	Carpenter			"
William H. Snapp	20				"
Sarah E. Snapp	18				" School
Mary F. Snapp	13				" School
Sarah Keiran	79				New Jersey
John Sprigs	9	(Black)			Virginia

Jacob B. Snapp was born 24 Jul 1806 and died 1 Jan 1873. He was the son of Abraham and Sarah. Abraham Snapp Jr. married Sarah Miller on 20 Aug 1800. Sarah Miller Snapp Keiran was a member of this household. Jacob B. Snapp married Rebecca Grandstaff on 4 Apr 1831. The bondsman for the marriage was John Fry. Rebecca was the daughter of Phillip and Elizabeth. Phillip Grandstaff married Elizabeth Haas on 21 Dec 1784. Rebecca Grandstaff Snapp died 1 Nov 1855 in her 49th year. Jacob and Rebecca were buried in the Old Edinburg Cemetery. Upon the death of Rebecca, Jacob B. Snapp married **Barbara Pitman** on 1 Jan 1857. Barbara was the daughter of Abraham and Catherine. Abraham Pitman was married to Catherine Eschelman on 8 Jun

1816.   Barbara Pitman Snapp was born 4 Jul 1823 and died
12 Jan 1907.   She was buried in the Saumsville Cemetery.

George H. Snapp was born 10 May 1834 and died 6 Apr
1901.   He was buried next to his parents in the Old
Edinburg Cemetery.

William Harrison Snapp was born 13 Jul 1839 and
died 4 Oct 1919.   On 18 Apr 1861 William joined Company C
of the 10th Virginia Infantry as a 4th Corporal.   He was
elected to the position of 2nd Lt. on 25 Dec 1861.   On 3
Oct 1862 he entered Company F of the 2nd Virginia Infantry
at Bunker Hill.   He was listed as a private and was AWOL
on 13 Dec 1862.   On 11 Sep 1863 he was listed as a member
of Company K of the 12th Virginia Cavalry.   He was a
private.   He was taken prisoner at Edinburg 16 Feb 1865 and
was in the POW camp at Fort McHenry on 22 Feb 1865.   He
took the oath of allegiance on 1 May 1865.   *Note: a
William Snapp was also a member of the 35th Battalion of
the Virginia Cavalry.   William H. Snapp worked in the post
office at New Market after the war.   He was married to
Maria Louise Rice on 14 Dec 1869.   Maria was the daughter
of Charles and Mary.   Charles Edward Rice married Mary
Beaver on 2 Dec 1844 in Page County, Virginia.   Maria and
her parents resided in **dwelling 763**.   Maria Louise Rice was
born 9 Feb 1846 and died 11 Mar 1918.   William and Maria
were buried in the Lutheran Reformation Church Cemetery in
New Market, Virginia.

Sarah Elizabeth Snapp was born in 1841 and died in
1915.   She was married to Casper Funkhouser on 11 Mar 1861.
Casper was the son of Andrew and Elizabeth.   Andrew
Funkhouser married Elizabeth Rinker on 11 Feb 1833.   Andrew
and family resided in **dwelling 1425**.   Casper was born 27
Jan 1836 and died 9 Jan 1918.   They were buried in the
Otterbein Cemetery (a.k.a. Funkhouser Cemetery) in Mt.
Jackson, Virginia.

Fannie Mary Snapp was born in 1846 and died in
1913.   She married James W. Funkhouser on 28 Nov 1867.
James was the son of Henry and Hannah.   Henry Funkhouser
married Hannah Maphis on 23 May 1830.   Hannah Funkhouser
and her family resided in **dwelling 2285**.   James Funkhouser
died 22 Dec 1878 at the age of 41 years, 6 months and 10
days old.   He is buried in the John Funkhouser Cemetery in
Mt. Olive.   Upon the death of James, Fanny Mary Snapp
Funkhouser was married to Daniel Spiker on 15 Feb 1881.
Daniel was the son of Ezra and Rebecca.   Ezra Spiker

married Rebecca Naugle on 4 Nov 1852. Fannie Mary Snapp Funkhouser Spiker was buried in the Mt. Hebron Cemetery in Toms Brook.

Sarah Miller Snapp Keiran was the daughter of Jacob Miller. She married Abraham Snapp Jr. on 20 Aug 1800. Abraham was the son of Phillip and Sallie.
In his will dated 18 Jun 1812, Phillip Snapp makes reference to his sons John, Jacob and Joseph. Sarah Miller Snapp , a widow, was married to Samuel Keiran on 31 Oct 1808. Her deceased husband's father Phillip was the bondsman for the marriage.

RELATED FAMILY:
Martha Ellen Snapp, daughter of Jacob and Rebecca, was married to John H. Hoffman on 17 Mar 1856 and resided in dwelling 928.
Elizabeth Liggett, sister in law of Jacob B. Snapp, had married John I. Grandstaff on 27 Feb 1827. John I Grandstaff, the brother of Rebecca Snapp Grandstaff, had died in 1852. Elizabeth resided in dwelling 46.
George P. Grandstaff, brother in law of Jacob B. Snapp, had married Mary Reedy on 3 Oct 1810 and resided in dwelling 63.
Phillip Grandstaff Jr., brother in law of Jacob B. Snapp, had married Mary Cooper on 6 Aug 1816 and resided in dwelling 267.
Benjamin Grandstaff, brother in law of Jacob B. Snapp, had married Elizabeth "Betsy" Clinedinst on 14 Oct 1820 and resided in dwelling 324.
Catherine A. Grandstaff, sister in law of Jacob B. Snapp, had married John A. Fry on 10 Jun 1815 and resided in dwelling 353.

1850 CENSUS: Jacob B. Snapp and family resided in dwelling 729 on page 51.
Barbara Pitman and her parents were located in dwelling 534 on page 38.

PAGE 7   EDINBURG   (Microfilm Page 585)

Dwelling 45   Family 45

Robert H. Grandstaff	25 Farmhand	0	100	Virginia
Elizabeth V. Grandstaff	27			"
Ida E. Grandstaff	3			"
John M. Grandstaff	1			"

Robert Henry Grandstaff was born 18 Feb 1835 and died 13 Aug 1913. He was the son of John and Elizabeth. John I. Grandstaff was married to Elizabeth Liggett on 27 Feb 1826. Elizabeth Liggett Grandstaff, a widow, and other family members resided in dwelling 46. Robert married Elizabeth "Bettie" V Johnson on 15 Sep 1856. She was born 15 Aug 1834. Judy Coffman Stickley's book indicates that Elizabeth Grandstaff (nee Johnson) died 25 Jun 1922. She was reported to have been the wife of Robert. There is no record of their marriage in Shenandoah County. Robert and Elizabeth were buried in the Old Edinburg Cemetery. Robert Henry Grandstaff enlisted as a private in Company C of the 10th Virginia Infantry at Edinburg, Virginia on 18 Apr 1861. He was ill with Typhoid Fever on 20 Sep 1861. Robert then enlisted as a private in Company K of the 12th Virginia Cavalry on 8 Aug 1862. He was AWOL in Sep and Oct of 1862. He was detailed as a Provost Guard at Brigade Headquarters in Sep and Oct of 1863. His record indicates a pattern of alternating attendance and absence through 1864.

Ida E. Grandstaff was born 30 Jul 1857 and died 17 Dec 1924. She was married on 20 Jul 1876 to James M. Rudasill, a widower from Rappahannock County, Virginia. Some accounts indicate he was born in Rockingham County, Virginia. James was the son of John and Susan. James was born 7 Jun 1844 and died 12 Nov 1923. Ida and James are buried in the Old Edinburg Cemetery.

John M. Grandstaff was born 3 May 1859 and died 13 Nov 1882. He was buried near his parents.

RELATED FAMILY:
John Henry Rau, brother in law of Robert, resided in dwelling 64. John Henry had married Eveline B. Grandstaff on 11 Jan 1854. Eveline, the sister of Robert died in 1856. John married Sarah Ellen Rinker on 11 Apr 1852.
Susan Elizabeth Grandstaff, sister of Robert, married Dorilas J. Martz on 8 May 1848 and resided in dwelling 257.

1850 CENSUS: Robert Henry Grandstaff resided with his parents in dwelling 730 on page 52.

PAGE 7 EDINBURG (Microfilm Page 585)

Dwelling 46 Family 46

Elizabeth Grandstaff	52	0 200	Virginia	
Presley H. Grandstaff	21		"	
Mary F. Grandstaff	17		"	

Elizabeth Grandstaff was born in 1807 and died in 1875. Her maiden name was Liggett. She was married to John I. Grandstaff on 27 Feb 1826. The bondsman for the marriage was Peter Liggett. John I. Grandstaff was the son of Phillip and Elizabeth. Phillip Grandstaff married Elizabeth Haas on 21 Dec 1784. John Grandstaff was born in 1789 and died in 16 Jul 1852. Elizabeth and John are buried in the Old Edinburg Cemetery.

Presley Hues Grandstaff was born in 1838 and died in 1914. He was 5'5" tall, was dark complexed with black eyes and hair. He was a farmer at the time he enlisted on 18 Apr 1861 in the 10th Virginia Infantry Company C. He was wounded at the battle of 1st Manassas on 21 Jul 1861. Presley spent the months of August, September, October and November recuperating from his wounds. He returned to duty on 20 Dec 1861 and was transferred to Company F of the 10th Virginia Infantry on 18 Apr 1862. On the 2nd of June 1862 he joined Company K of the 12th Virginia Cavalry. On 13 Aug 1862 he was detailed to the Provost Guard at Brigade Headquarters. Presley was paroled at Edinburg on 4 May 1865. He was buried in the Old Edinburg Cemetery.

Mary F. Grandstaff was born in 2 Jan 1842 and died in 8 Feb 1925. She was buried near her brother Presley.

RELATED FAMILY:

Robert Henry Grandstaff, son of John and Elizabeth, was a resident in **dwelling 45.**

Evaline B. Grandstaff, daughter of John and Elizabeth, married John Henry Rau on 11 Jan 1851. Evaline died in 1856 and her husband John Henry was married on 11 Aug 1857 to Sarah Ellen Rinker. John Henry and his second wife resided in **dwelling 64.**

Susan Elizabeth Grandstaff, daughter of John and Elizabeth, married Dorilas J. Martz on 8 May 1848 and resided in **dwelling 257.**

George P. Grandstaff, brother in law of Elizabeth, married Mary Reedy on 3 Oct 1810 and resided in **dwelling 63.**

Phillip Grandstaff Jr. brother in law of Elizabeth, married Mary Cooper on 6 Aug 1816 and resided in **dwelling 267**.

Benjamin Grandstaff, brother in law of Elizabeth, married Elizabeth "Betsy" Clinedinst on 14 Oct 1820 and resided in **dwelling 324**.

Catherine A. Grandstaff, sister in law of Elizabeth, married John A. Fry on 10 Jun 1815 and resided in **dwelling 353**.

Jacob B. Snapp, brother in law of Elizabeth, married Rebecca Grandstaff on 4 Apr 1831 and resided in **dwelling 44**.

1850 CENSUS: **Elizabeth Liggett Grandstaff** and family resided in dwelling 731 on page 52.

PAGE 7 EDINBURG   **(Microfilm Page 585)**

Dwelling 47 Family 47

John Hamman	27	Miller	600	100	Virginia
Lydia Hamman	28				"
Mary M. Hamman	4				"
Jane C. Hamman	2				"

John George Hamman was the son of George and Catherine. George Hamman married Catherine Schmucker on 25 Mar 1827. Catherine Schmucker Hamman was the daughter of Jacob Schmucker Sr. Upon the death of her husband, Catherine Schmucker Hamman was married to George Kibler. John George Hamman was born 27 Nov 1832 and died 28 May 1869. He was married to **Lydia Maphis** on 13 Apr 1854. Lydia was the daughter of George and Magdalene. George Maphis married Magdalene Gochenour on 13 Dec 1817. John George Hamman was a member of the 33rd Virginia Infantry during the Civil War. He enlisted in Company B on 10 Aug 1862. He was wounded in action at Second Manassas on 28 Aug 1862. He never returned to his unit after the wound. John died 28 May 1869 and was buried in the Maphis-Hamman Cemetery in Alonzoville, Virginia. It may be that his war wounds were a contributing factor to his early death. Upon the death of John, Lydia Maphis Hamman was married to William Gouhl on 8 Jan 1871. William was born in Germany and was the son of George and Catherine. Lydia Maphis Hamman Gouhl was born 12 Feb 1831 and died 7 Dec 1909. She was buried in the Mt. Zion Lutheran Church Cemetery near Woodstock.

Mary Magdalene Hamman was born 28 May 1855. She was married to John G. Clower on 4 Dec 1873. John was the son of John and Leah. John G. Clower married Leah Schmitt on 14 Apr 1845.

Virginia Catherine Hamman was born 6 Jun 1857 and died 6 May 1907. She was married to Jonathan Luther Wisman on 26 May 1881. Jonathan was a banker in Woodstock. He was born 27 Apr 1856 and was the son of Martin and Catherine. Virginia Catherine Hamman Wisman was buried in the Emmanuel Lutheran Church Cemetery near Woodstock.

RELATED FAMILY:

George Christopher Hamman, brother of John George Hamman, was a clerk in the residence of Samuel Williams. They were located in **dwelling 174.**

NOTE: Two of his brothers removed from Shenandoah County shortly before this census. Jacob Schmucker Hamman left in 1855 with his wife Dorothy Hottel. They moved to Corydon, Harrison County, Indiana. Another brother, William Harrison Hamman went to Texas. It is reported that he was Brigadier General during the Civil War. He later was an independent candidate for Governor of Texas and practiced law before the Supreme Court.

1850 CENSUS: John George Hamman resided in the household of his mother and step-father, George Kibler. They resided in dwelling 773 on page 54.
Lydia Maphis Hamman resided in dwelling 785 on page 55.

PAGE 7 EDINBURG (Microfilm Page 585)

Dwelling 48 Family 48

John G. Zimmerman	41	Tailor	800	200	Maryland
Caroline Zimmerman	42				New York
Maria C. Zimmerman	17				Virginia
Mary C. R. Zimmerman	15				" School
Ann E. Zimmerman	11				"

John G. Zimmerman is listed as George J. Zimmerman in the marriage records of his daughter and in the 1850 census. His wife **Caroline** was born in New York. A Miss Lydia Rebecca Zimmerman, the daughter of John Zimmerman and his wife Rebecca of Emmitsburg County, Maryland is buried

54

in the Zion Lutheran Church Cemetery in Edinburg. She died
8 Jul 1842 at the age of 17 years, 11 months and 24 days
old. She may have been the sister of John G. Zimmerman.
Emmittsburg, the site of Mt. Saint Mary's College, is a
town and is not a county in the state of Maryland.

Maria Catherine Zimmerman was married to James N.
Swann on 11 Mar 1868. James M. Swann was a widower and was
the keeper of a hotel in Edinburg. He and his wife
Isabella Blackford Swann resided in that hotel at the time
of this census (dwelling 51). James N. Swann was born 15
Sep 1815 in Georgetown, Washington, D. C. He died 7 Apr
1878. It appears that the marriage of James N. Swann and
Maria Catherine Zimmerman was of short duration as James
N. Swann was reported to have wed for a third time on 6 Sep
1871. Their marriage must have been annuled or ended in
divorce because Maria Catherine Zimmerman did not die
until 16 Aug 1922 at the age of 79. James N. Swann married
Sarah Riddleberger Holtzman on 6 Sep 1871. Sarah was the
daughter of Madison and Susan. Madison Riddleberger and
Susan Shryock were married on 15 Dec 1830. Sarah
Riddleberger was originally married to Benjamin B.
Holtzman. James N. Swann, his first wife Isabella and
Sarah Riddleberger Holtzman Swann were buried in the
Cedarwood Cemetery in Edinburg.

Mary C. Rebecca Zimmerman died 12 Aug 1933.

Anne Elizabeth Zimmerman was born 30 Jun 1847 and
died 12 Aug 1912. She was married to Lewis Chrisman in Sep
1872. Lewis was a blacksmith from Hesse Darmstadt,
Germany. He was a recent widower at the time of this
marriage. Lewis had married Sarah Catherine Clem on 1 Sep
1868. Sarah was the daughter of Jonathan and Sarah.
Jonathan Clem married Sarah Black on 2 May 1842. She was
buried in the John Funkhouser Cemetery. Lewis Chrisman was
born 30 Jun 1841 and died 15 Nov 1927. Anne and Lewis were
buried in the Cedarwood Cemetery in Edinburg. In the
marriage record for Anne and Lewis, he was reported to have
been the son of Joshua Chrisman. When he married Sarah
Clem he was listed as the son of Lewis and Elizabeth.

1850 CENSUS: John G. Zimmerman and family resided in
                dwelling 725 on page 51.

PAGE 7   EDINBURG   (Microfilm Page 585)

Dwelling 49 Family 49

Daniel W. Prescott	36	Physician 2500	750	Maine
Ann V. Prescott	35			Maryland
Ida R. Prescott	5			Virginia
William F. Prescott	2			"
Mary H. Rhorback	36			Maryland
Walter Grayson	15	(Mulatto)		Virginia

Dr. Daniel W. Prescott was born in Kennebeck County, Maine on 22 Jun 1823. He died 27 Sep 1881. When the Civil War broke out he served as a 2nd Lt. in the 10th Virginia Infantry Company C. He was promoted to 1st Lt. on 21 Aug 1861. He was Assistant Surgeon for the unit. He was promoted to Captain but was dropped from the company roster on 22 Apr 1862. His wife **Ann V.** was born in Maryland on 2 Dec 1824 and died 12 May 1891. Daniel and Ann were buried in the Old Edinburg Cemetery. It is possible that **Mary H. Rhorback** was a relative of Ann. They were close in age and share a birth place in Maryland. Several Prescott children were buried near their parents in Old Edinburg Cemetery.

Walter Grayson was the son of Washington Grayson and his wife Winney. Walter appears in the household of his parents in 1850. His father, Washington, was born in Maryland. Walter is reported to have had at least two brothers. Henry was born ca. 1845 and Silas F. was born ca. 1848. Both appear with Walter in the 1850 census.

1850 CENSUS: Daniel W. Prescott was located with his family in dwelling 701 on page 49. Walter Grayson was located in dwelling 2118 on page 152.

PAGE 7 EDINBURG   (Microfilm Page 585)

Dwelling 50 Family 50

John J. Stoneburner	42	Merchant	3000 15,000	Virginia
Ann E. Stoneburner	32			"
Lewis T. Stoneburner	3			"
John J. Stoneburner	4m			"
Martha Kibler	18			"
Charles H. Bolen	19			"

56

John J. **Stoneburner** was born 20 Jan 1817 and died
6 Nov 1898. His wife **Ann E.** was born 5 Jun 1827 and died
15 Dec 1907. During the Civil War John J. Stoneburner was
located in Powells Fort. He and George W. Windle operated
the Caroline Furnace from the beginning of the war until
it was burned by Union forces in 1865. The iron that was
manufactured at the furnace was shipped to the Tredegar
Iron Works in Richmond. John and Ann were buried in the
Cedarwood Cemetery in Edinburg, Virginia.

Lewis T. Stoneburner was born 13 May 1857 and died
7 Feb 1933. Lewis was married to Mary Moore Wierman on 20
Jun 1878. Lewis was a merchant at the time of this
marriage. Mary was the daughter of Benjamin and Kate.
Benjamin Wierman married Catherine A. Moore on 12 Mar 1857.
Mary and her parents were located in **Dwelling 1024.** Mary
Moore Wierman Stoneburner was born 21 Dec 1857 and died 14
May 1948. They were buried in the Cedarwood Cemetery.

Martha Kibler was the daughter of John and Mary.
John Kibler married Mary Wolverton on 1 Jun 1840. They
resided in **dwelling 360** at the time of this
census. Martha Kibler was born 2 Apr 1840 and died 25 Apr
1876. Martha Kibler was married to Perry Jefferson Allison
on 27 Dec 1860. Perry was a house carpenter at the time
of the marriage. He was the son of William and Ann.
William Allison married Rosanna Hisey on 23 Nov 1836.
Perry and his parents were located in **dwelling 85.** Perry
Jefferson Allison was born in 1838 and died in 1912. He
was wed at least three times. Upon the death of Martha,
Perry married Sarah M. Coffman, the daughter of Levi and
Elizabeth. Levi Coffman married Elizabeth S. Nichols on
12 Apr 1842. Levi Coffman and his family resided in
dwelling 1238. Sarah M. Coffman Allison died 29 Aug 1895.
Perry's third wife was Ann E Coffelt. Ann was the daughter
of William and Katherine. William Coffelt married
Katherine Fultz and resided in **dwelling 1217.** Ann was born
in 1852 and died in 1932. Perry, Sarah and Ann are all
buried in the Old Edinburg Cemetery. Martha Kibler Allison
is also thought to have been buried there.

1850 CENSUS: John J. **Stoneburner** and family resided in
dwelling 658 on page 46. This was the
household of Israel P. Rinker.
Martha Kibler was a resident with her parents
in dwelling 684 on page 48.

PAGE 8   EDINBURG   (Microfilm Page   586)

Dwelling 51 Family 51

James N. Swann	44	Hotel Keeper	2000	1250	D.C.
Isabella B. Swann	50				Virginia
Willis G. Swann	14				" School
Emma E. Swann	12				" "
John C. Swann	10				" "
Elenora Dellinger	37				"
Mary L. Visery	18	(Mulatto)			"
John D. Milligan	17				Penn.

NOTE: December 19, 1860 the Swann Hotel was destroyed by fire.

  James N. Swann was born in the Georgetown section of Washington, D. C. He was the son of Nathaniel and Mary E. Swann. James was born 15 Sep 1815 and died 7 Apr 1878. He was married to **Isabella Blackford**. Isabella died 16 Dec 1866 at the age of 57 years and 1 day old. James N. Swann enlisted in Company C of the 10th Virginia Infantry. He was appointed a Captain in the unit. He resigned from the army on 12 Dec 1861. Upon the death of Isabella, James was married on 11 Mar 1868 to Maria Catherine Zimmerman, the daughter of John G. and Caroline. The Zimmerman family resided in **dwelling 48** at the time of this census. The marriage of James Swann to Maria Catherine may have ended in a divorce as Maria did not die until 1922. Speculation regarding the status of this marriage is created because James N. Swann was married on 6 Sep 1871 to Sallie Riddleberger Holtzman. Sarah E. Riddleberger was the daughter of Madison and Susan. Madison Riddleberger had married Susan Shryock on 15 Dec 1830. Sarah married Benjamin B. Holtzman and resided in **dwelling 56**. Sarah E. Riddleberger Holtzman Swann died 25 Jul 1890. James, Isabella and Sarah were all buried in the Cedarwood Cemetery.

  Willis G. Swann was born in 1840 and died in 1926. He was married on 14 Nov 1869 to Isabel V. Miley, the daughter of Isaac W. and Elizabeth. Isaac W. Miley married Elizabeth C Cooper on 21 Oct 1844. Isaac Miley and family resided in **dwelling 75**. Isabel V. Miley Swann was born in 1852 and died in 1933. Willis and Isabel are buried in the Cedarwood Cemetery.

58

John C. Swann was born 24 Jan 1850 and died 3 May 1915.

Eleanora Dellinger may have been the Elenora Eppley who married Jacob Dellinger on 28 May 1845. The bondsman for that marriage was John Stoneburner.

John D. Milligan was a merchant from Cumberland County, Pennsylvania. He was the son of William B. and his wife Mary. John and his parents were residents of Shenandoah County as early as 1850. William B. Milligan, the father of John, was reported to have been born in New York. His mother Mary was a native of Virginia according to census data. John D. Milligan died 5 Aug 1909. He was married to Louisa Catherine Saum on 17 Nov 1868. Lou was the daughter of Abraham and Ellen. Abraham Saum married Ellen A. Sonnestine Saum on 26 Jul 1836. Abraham Saum and family resided in **dwelling 19**. Lou was born 8 Nov 1847 and died 13 Apr---(date does not appear on tombstone). John and Louisa were buried in the Cedarwood Cemetery.

1850 CENSUS: **James N. Swann** and family resided in dwelling 723 on page 51.
Elenora Dellinger resided in dwelling 55 on page 5.
John D. Milligan resided in dwelling 21 on page 2.

PAGE 8   EDINBURG   (Microfilm Page 586)

Dwelling 52   Family 52

Lewis W. Grove	36	Saddle and Harness Maker	0	600
				Virginia
Ann E. Grove	36		Virginia	
Francis Grove	13	"	School	
Martin L. Grove	11	"	School	
Henrietta J.Grove	6	"	School	
William B. Grove	2	"		
Mary J. Lewis	31	"		

Lewis William Grove died 23 Feb 1905. He was 81 years, 4 months and 23 days old. His wife **Ann Elizabeth** died 1 May 1887. She was 64 years, 1 month and 9 days old. They were buried in the Cedarwood Cemetery.

Martin Luther Grove was born 11 Sep 1848 and died 24 Apr 1944. He was a merchant at the time of his marriage

on 7 Aug 1872 to Julia Allen Miller Rosenberger. Julia was
a widow.   She was reported to have been the daughter of
John R and Ellen M.   John R. Miller, father of Julia, and
his family resided in **dwelling 53.**   Julia A. Miller
Rosenberger Grove was born 19 Feb 1852 and died 19 Aug
1910.   Martin and Julia were buried in the Cedarwood
Cemetery in Edinburg.   Martin Luther Grove was involved in
one of the most memorable Civil War incidents.   He was too
young to serve in the army.   However he was present when
a group of Union troops under the command of Major Young
captured Confederate pickets as they guarded the town of
Edinburg.   When he observed this, Martin and another
resident of Edinburg, Lt. Joseph R. Miley **(dwelling 35)** who
happened to be home of leave at the time, set off in search
of Captain George J. Grandstaff to advise him of the
incident.   Grandstaff and Miley began a pursuit of the
Union troops, gathering additional men as they rode.   They
delivered aggressive attacks to the rear of the Union
forces.   By the time they had reached Mauerstown they had
captured five of the troops of Major Young.   These five
troops were sent back to Edinburg under the guard of Martin
Luther Grove and another area youth Bob Windle **(dwelling
32)**.   Eventually all of the pickets were freed and 15 of
the enemy was captured. This event was recounted in the
history of Shenandoah County that was written by John
Wayland.

        Henrietta J. Grove died 1 May 1934.   She was 80
years, 11 months and 19 days old.   Henrietta was married
on 3 Nov 1875 to William Marion Boyd of Warren County,
Virginia. He was the son of John F. and Sommerville. John
F. Boyd married Sommerville A. King on 9 Dec 1841 in Warren
County, Virginia.   William Marion Boyd died 1 May 1888.
He was 36 years, 9 months and 12 days old.   Henrietta and
William were buried in the Cedarwood Cemetery.

1850 CENSUS: No record of this family has been found in
               the 1850 census.

PAGE 8 EDINBURG   **(Microfilm Page 586)**

Dwelling 53 Family 53

```
John R. Miller   35  Merchant 150  150 Virginia
Ellen M. Miller  28                  "
Julia A. Miller   8                  "      School
Dollie Miller     2                  "
Caroline Holler  23                  "
```

John R. Miller was born 5 Feb 1825 and died 10 Aug 1887. His wife Ellen M. Grandstaff was born 9 Jun 1830 and died 23 Feb 1899. She was the daughter of George and Mary. George P. Grandstaff married Mary Reedy on 17 Mar 1810. They were buried in the Old Edinburg Cemetery.

Julia Allen Miller was married initially to a man named Rosenberger. However, Mr. Rosenberger died and Julia was married on 7 Aug 1871 to Martin L. Grove. Martin was the son of Lewis and Ann. Martin and his parents resided nearby in **dwelling 52**. Julia A. Miller Rosenberger was born 19 Feb 1852 and died 19 Aug 1910. Martin L. Grove was born 11 Sep 1848 and died 24 Apr 1944. Martin and Julia were buried in the Cedarwood Cemetery in Edinburg.

Dollie Miller died 25 Oct 1861 at the age of 3 years, 7 months and 1 day old. She was buried at the Old Edinburg Cemetery.

Caroline Holler died 26 Feb 1904 at 64 years of age. She was the daughter of Isaac and Elizabeth. Isaac Holler was married to Elizabeth Marshall on 24 Dec 1828. Caroline was buried next to her older sister Amelia "Milly" Holler in the Cedarwood Cemetery.

RELATED FAMILY:

Mary Frances Grandstaff, sister of Ellen, married William J. Dinges on 25 May 1847 and resided in **dwelling 58**.

Elizabeth Ann Grandstaff, sister of Ellen, married William J. Koontz on 12 Aug 1837 and resided in **dwelling 60**.

Milton M. Grandstaff, brother of Ellen, married Emily J. A. Frye on 19 Nov 1846 and resided in **dwelling 61**.

Phillip Marcus Grandstaff, brother of Ellen, married Sarah Miller and resided in **dwelling 62**.

Artimissia Grandstaff, sister of Ellen, married Richard Miller on 18 Jan 1842 and resided in **dwelling 291**.

John Jackson Grandstaff, brother of Ellen, married Isabella Murray on 5 Mar 1835 and resided in **dwelling 328**.

1850 CENSUS: John R. Miller and family appear in dwelling 115 on page 9.

Caroline Holler was in the household of her parents in dwelling 732 on page 52.

PAGE 8 EDINBURG   (Microfilm Page 586)

Dwelling 54   Family 54

Joseph F. Grandstaff	32	Master Plaster	550	150	Va.
Louisa G. Grandstaff	25				Va.
Mary A. Grandstaff	5				" School
Madison R. Grandstaff	11m				"
------- Grandstaff	1m	(Male)			"

Joseph F. Grandstaff was born 31 Jan 1827 and died 15 Jul 1913. He was married to **Louisa C. Riddleberger** on 25 Oct 1851. Louisa was the daughter of Madison and Susan. Madison Riddleberger married Susan Shryock on 15 Dec 1830. Madison Riddleberger and family resided in **dwelling 40**. Louisa was born 21 Aug 18?? and died 16 Oct 1908. Joseph and Louisa were buried in the Old Edinburg Cemetery. Joseph F. Grandstaff was the son of Phillip Grandstaff and his wife Mary. Phillip Grandstaff Jr. married Mary Cooper on 6 Aug 1816. Phillip and Mary resided in **dwelling 267**.

NOTE: Joseph F. Grandstaff may have provided a substitute for service in the Civil War. The records of the Danville Artillery record that a Joseph Grandstaff hired Phillip Ready, a resident of **dwelling 67** in this census as a substitute.

Mary "Mollie" Amelia Grandstaff was born 5 Feb 1855 and died in Washington, D.C. on 5 Feb 1924. Mollie was married to John Robert Hutchinson on 25 Nov 1880. John was born 28 Dec 1853 and died 21 Jan 1926. He was the son of Joseph and Mary Ann. Joseph Hutchinson married Mary Ann Long on 4 Sep 1853. Joseph and his family resided in **dwelling 1187**. Mollie and John Robert were buried in the Old Edinburg Cemetery.

Madison R. Grandstaff was named in honor of his maternal grandfather. He was born 21 Aug 1858 and died 3 Jun 1859. He was buried in the Old Edinburg Cemetery. Several other infant children of Joseph and Louisa were buried in the same cemetery.

Joseph H. Grandstaff was the new born male baby. He was born in 1860 and died in 1862.

62

RELATED FAMILY:

Amelia Riddleberger, sister of Louisa, married Robert Hisey on 9 May 1852 and resided in **dwelling 21.**

Sarah E. Riddleberger, sister of Louisa, married Benjamin Holtzman and resided in **dwelling 56.**

Amanda Grandstaff, sister of Joseph, married Isaac H. Ritter on 7 Mar 1848 and resided in **dwelling 14.**

Jane Grandstaff, sister of Joseph, married William A. Hisey on 7 Feb 1842 and resided in **dwelling 69.**

Branson Grandstaff, brother of Joseph, married Elizabeth Eveline Liggett on 9 Jun 1842 and resided in **dwelling 313.**

1850 CENSUS: **Joseph F. Grandstaff** and his parents resided in dwelling 695 on page 49.

Louisa Riddleberger was living with her parents in dwelling 719 on page 51.

PAGE 8 EDINBURG (Microfilm Page 585)

Dwelling 55 Family 55

Isaac Ruby	50	Workman on R.R.	1500	150	Virginia
Susan Ruby	39				Virginia
Sarah R. Ruby	17			"	
Robert C. Ruby	14			"	School
Louisa E. Ruby	12			"	
Josephine Ruby	6			"	
Lucy M. Ruby	4			"	
Alice Ruby	3			"	
Ellenore Ruby	1			"	

Isaac Ruby was the son of Henry F. and Catherine. Henry Ruby married Catherine Rodeheffer on 9 Jan 1802. Isaac Ruby was married to Elizabeth Kibler on 21 Jul 1832. Elizabeth was the daughter of John Kibler. Upon the death of Elizabeth, Isaac married **Susan Artz** on 6 Oct 1853. Susan was the daughter of John and Mary. On 25 Mar 1805, there was a marriage record for John Ortz to Mary "Polly" Hoffman.

Robert C. Ruby was born ca. 1846. He enlisted in the Eighth Star Artillery of New Market, Virginia as a substitute for John R. Wierman of **dwelling 41.** Robert was later reassigned to the Danville Artillery in Sep of 1862. He was paroled at Appomattox on 9 Apr 1865.

Josephine Ruby was born in 1854 and died in 1912. She was married on 6 Mar 1879 to Albert M. Funk, the son of Obed and Mary S. Obed Funk married Mary S. Hoffman on 12 Nov 1847. Albert M. Funk was born 3 Aug 1854 and died 12 Nov 1933. Josephine and Albert were buried in the Riverview Cemetery in Strasburg.

Lucy M. Ruby was born in 1856 and died in 1912. She was married to William L. Ray, a carpenter, on 20 Jan 1876. William was from Frederick County, Virginia. He was the son of Harvey J. and Catherine. William L. Ray was born in 1849 and died in 1908. They are buried in the New Mount Jackson Cemetery in Mount Jackson, Virginia.

Alice Ruby was married to Levi Steadman, a bridge builder, on 22 Jul 1875. Levi, the son of Levi and Catherine, was from Harpers Ferry, West Virginia.

Ellenora Ruby was born in 1859 and died in 1925. She did not marry and was buried in the New Mount Jackson Cemetery near her sister Lucy.

RELATED FAMILY:

Mary C. Ruby, daughter of Isaac and Elizabeth, is believed to have been the Catherine Ruby in **dwelling 10.**

Isabella Ruby, daughter of Isaac and Elizabeth, is believed to have been the Isabella Hockman in **dwelling 10.**

Caroline Ruby, daughter of Isaac and Elizabeth, married William Hockman on 19 Dec 1854 and resided in **dwelling 12.**

Ann S. Ruby, daughter of Isaac and Elizabeth, resided with her sister in **dwelling 12.**

Martha Ruby, daughter of Isaac and Elizabeth, married William Shutters on 12 Nov 1857 and resided in **dwelling 1062.**

1850 CENSUS: Isaac Ruby and his family resided in dwelling 726 on page 51.
Susan Artz resided with her parents in dwelling 172 on page 13.

PAGE 9 EDINBURG   (Microfilm Page 587)

Dwelling 56   Family 56

Benjamin B. Holtzman	35	Laborer on R.R.	O	60	Va.
Sarah E. Holtzman	23				Virginia
Joseph F. Holtzman	5				"
Susan E. Holtzman	4				"

Benjamin B. Holtzman was born 17 Feb 1827 and died 22 May 1861. At the time of this census, Benjamin was a laborer on the railroad. In 1850 he was reported to have been a miller. His early death may have been in some way job related. There is no record of his marriage having been recorded in Shenandoah County. It is known that he married **Sarah Elizabeth Riddleberger.** Sarah was the daughter of Madison and Susan. Madison Riddleberger married Susan Shryock on 15 Dec 1830. Madison and his family resided in **dwelling 40.** After Benjamin's death, Sarah was married to James N. Swann, the hotel proprietor, on 6 Sep 1871. James was a neighbor in **dwelling 51** at the time of this census. He resided with his first wife Isabella Blackford. Isabella died 16 Dec 1866. James was then married for a short period of time to Maria Catherine Zimmerman. They were married on 11 Mar 1868. Maria was the daughter of John G. and Caroline. She resided with her parents in **dwelling 48.** Maria's marriage to James may have ended in divorce as she is reported to have lived until 1922. James N. Swann was born 15 Sep 1815 in Washington, D.C. The son of Nathaniel and Mary did not die until 7 Apr 1878. Sarah E. Holtzman Swann died 25 Jul 1890. Benjamin, Sarah and James N. Swann are all buried in the Cedarwood Cemetery.

Joseph Frederick Holtzman was born 27 Jul 1854. He died 3 Mar 1935. Joseph was married to Ella A. Dinges on 5 Mar 1878. Ella was the daughter of William J. and Mary Frances. William J. Dinges married Mary Frances Grandstaff on 25 May 1847. Ella and her parents resided in **dwelling 58.** Ella A. Dinges Holtzman died 5 Oct 1886. Joseph was married for a second time on 26 Sep 1898. He married Bettie Belle Lantz, the daughter of George and Mary. Bettie was born 28 Jul 1867 and died 2 Jun 1934. Joseph, Ella and Bettie were all buried in the Cedarwood Cemetery. At the time of his second marriage Joseph is reported to have become a hotel proprietor. This may have resulted from his association with his step father James N. Swann.

Susan E. Holtzman was named after her maternal grandmother Susan Shryock Riddleberger. She was born 17 May 1856 and died 6 Nov 1872. She is also buried in the Cedarwood Cemetery.

RELATED FAMILY:
Louisa C. Riddleberger, sister of Sarah E. Holtzman, was married to Joseph F. Grandstaff on 25 Oct 1851 and resided in dwelling 54.
Amelia Riddleberger, sister of Sarah E. Holtzman, was married to Robert Hisey on 9 May 1852 and resided in dwelling 21.

1850 CENSUS: Benjamin B. Holtzman, a miller, resided in the residence of Charles Hutcheson. They resided in dwelling 728 on page 51.
Sarah E. Riddleberger, was located with her parents in dwelling 719 on page 51.

PAGE 9 EDINBURG (Microfilm Page 587)

Dwelling 57 Family 57

Jerimiah S. Evans 38 Boot & Shoemaker 800 150 Virginia
Mary A. Evans 85 Penn.

Jerimiah S. Evans was born 18 Oct 1822 and died 7 Jun 1890. He was the son of Jerimiah Evans Jr. and Mary Ann Biedlman. Mary Ann Biedlman, the daughter of Stephen, was married to Jerimiah Evans Jr. on 20 Jun 1801. Jerimiah S. Evans was 5'2", fair complexed with blue eyes and black hair. He enlisted in the 10th Virginia Infantry on 18 Apr 1862 as a private in Company C. He transferred to Company F on 18 Apr 1862. He was discharged from the army on 18 Jul 1862 as overaged. On 21 Dec 1865 Jerimiah was married to Sarah Jane Gochenour Copp. Sarah was the daughter of Levi and Mary. Levi Gochenour married Mary Wisman on 23 Jan 1839. Levi and Mary were residing in dwelling 1608. Sarah Jane was married to George W. Copp on 23 Mar 1863. George was born in Ohio. He was the son of Jacob and Barbara. George was a resident in dwelling 1911. George W. Copp was born 7 Jul 1832 and enlisted in the 33rd Virginia Infantry. He was wounded in action at First and Second Manassas. On 7 May 1864 George W. Copp was killed in action at the Wilderness. George was buried in the Brumback Cemetery. Sarah Jane Gochenour Copp Evans was born 9 Nov 1839 and died 11 Oct 1890. Jerimiah and Sarah were buried in the Levi Gochenour Cemetery.

66

RELATED FAMILY:
            Aaron B. Evans, brother of Jerimiah S. Evans, was married to Evaline Rau on 12 Feb 1856 and resided in **dwelling 71.**

1850 CENSUS: Jerimiah S. Evans was a resident in dwelling 176 on page 13.

PAGE 9 EDINBURG   (Microfilm Page 587)

Dwelling 58   Family 58

William J. Dinges	41	Lumber Dealer	1000	500	Virginia
Mary F. Dinges	37				"
George W. Dinges	12				" School
Ella A. Dinges	4				"

        William J. Dinges was born 27 May 1819 and died 18 Jul 1884. He was married to **Mary Frances Grandstaff** on 25 May 1847. The bondsman for the marriage was George Grandstaff. Mary was the daughter of George and Mary. On 17 Mar 1810 George Grandstaff was married to Polly Reedy. George Grandstaff resided in **dwelling 63.** Mary Frances Grandstaff Dinges was born 12 Mar 1828 and died 22 Sep 1875. William and Mary were buried in the Old Edinburg Cemetery.

        George William Dinges was born in 1848 and died in 1920. He was married to Elizabeth Rinker on 28 Oct 1874. Elizabeth was the daughter of Samuel and Rachel. Samuel Rinker was married to Rachel C. Vance. Elizabeth and her parents were residing in **dwelling 2.** When the marriage took place George was a student. Elizabeth Marshall Rinker Dinges was born 22 Mar 1849 and died 15 Oct 1917. They were buried in the Cedarwood Cemetery in Edinburg.

        Ella A. Dinges was 31 years, 2 months and 29 days old when she died on 5 Oct 1886. Ella was married to Joseph Frederick Holtzman on 5 Mar 1878. Joseph was the son of Benjamin B. and Sarah Riddleberger Holtzman. Joseph and his parents were residents of **dwelling 56.** Joseph Frederick Holtzman was born 27 Jul 1854 and died 3 Mar 1935. Upon the death of Ella, Joseph was married to Bettie Belle Lantz on 26 Sep 1898.   Bettie was the daughter of George and Mary. She was born 28 Jul 1867 and died 2 Jun 1934. Ella, Joseph and Bettie were buried in the Cedarwood Cemetery.

RELATED FAMILY:

Milton M. Grandstaff, brother of Mary, married Emily J. A. Frye on 19 Nov 1846 and resided in **dwelling 61**.

Phillip Marcus Grandstaff, brother of Mary, resided with his wife Sarah in **dwelling 62**.

Elizabeth Ann Grandstaff, sister of Mary, married William J. Koontz on 12 Aug 1837 and resided in **dwelling 60**.

Artimissia Grandstaff, sister of Mary, married Richard Miller on 18 Jan 1842 and resided in **dwelling 291**.

John Jackson Grandstaff, brother of Mary, married Isabella Murray on 5 Mar 1835 and resided in **dwelling 328**.

Ellen Grandstaff, sister of Mary, married John R. Miller and resided in **dwelling 53**.

1850 CENSUS: No record of this family in 1850.

PAGE 9 EDINBURG (Microfilm Page 587)

Dwelling 59 Family 59

Calvin Wilcher	23	Wood Sawyer	Virginia
Mary Frances Wilcher	17		"
Adline Wilcher	1		"

George Calvin Wilcher was reported to have been born in Rockingham County, Virginia. He was the son of Joseph and Isabella. George Calvin Wilcher married **Mary Frances Webb** on 8 Apr 1858. Mary Frances was the daughter of David and Elizabeth. Shenandoah County marriage records indicate that a David Webb married Elizabeth Foltz on 4 Oct 1841. They are believed to have been living in **dwelling 1535**. There is no evidence that this couple were the parents of Mary Frances. In the 1850 census Mary Frances, who would have been seven or eight, was not in their household. George Calvin Wilcher joined Company G of the 33rd Virginia Infantry on 1 Jul 1861. He was wounded on 21 Jul 1861 at the Battle of First Manassas. He was admitted to Chimborazo on 5 Mar 1863 and was transferred to Lynchburg on 7 May 1863. Calvin was absent wounded until Oct 1863. He was reported to have deserted on 20 Nov 1863.

1850 CENSUS: No record of this family in 1850 census.

68

PAGE 9 EDINBURG (Microfilm Page 587)

Dwelling 60 Family 60

Elizabeth A. Koontz	40	0 100 Virginia		
Ellen F. Koontz	16		Virginia	School

Elizabeth Ann Grandstaff was born 30 Sep 1818 and died 7 May 1898. Elizabeth was the daughter of George and Mary. George Grandstaff, a resident of **dwelling 63**, married Mary "Polly" Reedy on 10 Mar 1810. Elizabeth Ann Grandstaff was married to William J. Koontz on 12 Aug 1837. William was born 7 Mar 1816 and died 2 Apr 1844. Elizabeth and William are buried in the Old Edinburg Cemetery.

Ellen "Nelly" F. Grandstaff was born 13 Jan 1845 and died 19 Sep 1927. She was married to Newton F. McCann on 24 Jun 1869. Newton French McCann was a printer residing in Norfolk, Virginia at the time of their marriage. He was the son of James and Sarah. Newton French McCann was born 31 Mar 1837 and died 10 Feb 1884. They were buried in the Old Edinburg Cemetery. Nelly Grandstaff is one of the more colorful characters in the history of Edinburg during this period. There are many interesting escapades recounted. However, the most memorable one involved Nelly and her cousin Mary Melvinia Grandstaff who resided in **dwelling 61**. When Sheridan and his troops rode into Edinburg they commenced to burn many of the buildings in the area. When Sheridan's men had torched the Edinburg Mill, Nelly and Mary went to Sheridan and pleaded with him to spare the mill because so many of the women and children in the area depended on the mill for survival. Sheridan ordered his men to put out the fire. They were assisted by a bucket brigade formed by the women of Edinburg.

RELATED FAMILY:
       Mary Frances Grandstaff, sister of Elizabeth, married William J. Dinges on 25 Mar 1847 and resided in **dwelling 58**.
       Milton M. Grandstaff, brother of Elizabeth, married Emily J. A. Frye on 19 Nov 1846 and resided in **dwelling 61**.
       Phillip Marcus Grandstaff, brother of Elizabeth, and his wife Sarah Miller resided in **dwelling 62**.

Artimissia Grandstaff, sister of Elizabeth, married Richard Miller on 18 Jan 1842 and resided in **dwelling 291**.

John Jackson Grandstaff, brother of Elizabeth, married Isabella Murray on 5 Mar 1835 and resided in **dwelling 328**.

Ellen Grandstaff, sister of Elizabeth, married John R. Miller and resided in **dwelling 53**.

Milton Koontz, son of Elizabeth and William, resided in **dwelling 785**. He was a painter apprentice in residence with William Wickes.

NOTE: George William Koontz, son of Elizabeth and William has not been located. Perhaps he was away at school. He enlisted in the Eighth Star Artillery in June of 1861. This was Rice's Battery in the New Market area. He served with great distinction and rose through the ranks to the position of captain. He was transferred with the rest of the unit in September of 1862 to the Danville Artillery. He was wounded in action during the seige at Petersburg. He was paroled on 9 Apr 1865 at Appomattox. He moved to Hightown in Highland County after the war and operated Heaveners Store. George William Koontz married Mollie C. Newman on 4 Dec 1871. George returned to Shenandoah County and became very active in business and in politics. He served for 30 years as Shenandoah County Treasurer. He was also Commander of the Shenandoah Camp of Confederate Veterans. He was a Democrat with independent tendencies. He opposed prohibition and according to sources had no sympathy for the League of Nations. George was born 12 Feb 1839 and died 16 Mar 1925. In addition, **Mary Elizabeth Koontz**, the sister of George does not appear in this census. She had married the Reverend Henry Tallhelm on 16 Dec 1858. He was a very prominent minister.

1850 CENSUS: **Elizabeth Ann Grandstaff Koontz** and family resided in dwelling 692 on Page 49.

PAGE 9 EDINBURG (Microfilm Page 587)

Dwelling 61 Family 61

Milton M. Grandstaff	31	Sawyer	0	171	Virginia
Emma E. Grandstaff	32				" Can't Read
Margaret M. Grandstaff	12				" School
Samuel G. Grandstaff	10				" School
John P. Grandstaff	7				" School
George M. Grandstaff	2				"

Milton M. Grandstaff was the son of George and Mary. His father George Grandstaff married Mary "Polly" Reedy on 3 Oct 1810. George Grandstaff resided in **dwelling 63.** Milton was married in Frederick County, Virginia and appears as Wilton M. on the marriage record. He married **Emily J. A. Frye** on 19 Nov 1846. Doris Brown in her history of the Grandstaff family acknowledge this marriage. However, Milton's wife is referred to as Emily E (Emma) Roundtree. In reading that information it was not clear if Emily Frye and Emily Roundtree are one and the same individual. This information needs clarification.

Melvinia Mary Grandstaff, Margaret in this census, was married to George W. Calohan, a lumber merchant who was born in Pennsylvania. Their marriage took place on 4 Dec 1871. George was the son of William and M. W. Calohan. Mary and her cousin Nellie Koontz **(Dwelling 60)** are remembered for their efforts to save the Edinburg Mill during the Civil War. When Phil Sheridan's forces were in the process of burning the mill, Mary and Nellie pleaded with him to spare the building because so many of the women and children of the town depended on what was produced at the mill for survival. Sheridan was move by their pleas and instructed his men to cease their burning. Union forces, assisted by a bucket brigade formed by the women of Edinburg, put out the fire.

Samuel G. Grandstaff and his brother **George M. Grandstaff** removed to the west. Samuel may have married Fannie L. Fry. She was the daughter of Jonathan and Elizabeth. She was born in 1856 and died in 1933. This information was reported in the Grandstaff family history.

John Osceola Grandstaff was born 4 Apr 1852 and died 13 Dec 1925. He was 74 years old. John married Martha F. Heaton on 23 Oct 1877. Mattie was born in 1857 and died in 1927. John and Mattie are buried in the Cedarwood Cemetery. Martha was the daughter of John M. and Julia A. Jonathan W. Heaton married Ann Julia Barton on 19 Jul 1853. Jonathan Heaton and his family were residents in **dwelling 316.** The name Heaton also appears as Eaton in Shenandoah County records.

RELATED FAMILY:
          Mary Frances Grandstaff, sister of Milton, married William J. Dinges on 25 Mar 1847 and resided in **dwelling 58.**

71

Phillip Marcus Grandstaff, brother of Milton, married Sarah Miller and resided in dwelling 62.

Elizabeth Ann Grandstaff, sister of Milton, married William J. Koontz on 12 Aug 1837 and resided in dwelling 60.

Artimissia Grandstaff, sister of Milton, married Richard Miller on 18 Jan 1842 and resided in dwelling 291.

John Jackson Grandstaff, brother of Milton, married Isabella Murray on 5 Mar 1835 and resided in dwelling 328.

Ellen Miller, sister of Milton, married John R. Miller and resided in dwelling 53.

1850 CENSUS: Milton M. Grandstaff and family resided in dwelling 692 on page 49.

PAGE 9 EDINBURG (Microfilm Page 587)

Dwelling 62 Family 62

Marcus Grandstaff	34	Farmhand	2700	491	Virginia
Sarah M. Grandstaff	30				"
George H. Grandstaff	9				" School
Lucy A. Grandstaff	7				" School
Catherine L. Grandstaff	4m				"
Julia A. Myers	30	Housegirl			"

Phillip Marcus Grandstaff, was the son of George and Mary. George Grandstaff married Mary "Polly" Reedy on 17 Mar 1810. George was a resident in dwelling 63 at the time of this census. Marcus was born 9 Dec 1825 and died 7 Mar 1905. His wife Sarah Miller died 27 Sep 1890 at the age of 61 years and 8 days old. Marcus and Sarah were buried in the Old Edinburg Cemetery.

George Homer Grandstaff was born in 1850 and died in 1916. He was married to Ellen McElroy. Ellen was born in 1857 and died in 1907. She was the daughter of Samuel and Kate. George and Ellen were buried in the Old Edinburg Cemetery. There is a report in the Grandstaff family history that George was married to Ida Proctor after the death of Ellen.

Lucy A. Grandstaff died 16 Jun 1883 at the age of 30 years and 7 months old. Lucy was married to Joseph S. Allison on 11 Aug 1875. He was the son of William and Anna. William Allison married Rosana Hisey on 23 Nov 1836.

Joseph and his parents resided in **dwelling 85**. Lucy's brother George Homer Grandstaff was a witness to this ceremony. Joseph was a plasterer. Lucy was buried in the Old Edinburg Cemetery.

Catherine "Kate" L. Grandstaff died 29 Sep 1863 at the age of 4 years, 5 months and 21 days old.

RELATED FAMILY:

Mary Frances Grandstaff, sister of Marcus, married William J. Dinges on 25 May 1847 and resided in **dwelling 58**.

Elizabeth Ann Grandstaff, sister of Marcus, married William J. Koontz on 12 Aug 1837 and resided in **dwelling 60**.

Milton M. Grandstaff, brother of Marcus, married Emily A. J. Frye on 19 Nov 1846 and resided in **dwelling 61**.

Artimissia Grandstaff, sister of Marcus, married Richard Miller on 18 Jan 1842 and resided in **dwelling 291**.

John Jackson Grandstaff, brother of Marcus, married Isabella Murray on 5 Mar 1835 and resided in **dwelling 328**.

Ellen Grandstaff, sister of Marcus, married John R. Miller and resided in **dwelling 53**.

1850 CENSUS: Marcus Grandstaff resided with his father in dwelling 692 on page 49.

PAGE 9 EDINBURG (Microfilm Page 587)

Dwelling 63 Family 63

George Grandstaff   73   Farmer   17,125 12,835 Virginia

George P. Grandstaff, was the son of Phillip. There are many interesting stories widely reported in Shenandoah County about the origin of the Grandstaff family name. However, recent genealogical studies dismiss most of these accounts as inaccurate. Mindful that the following accounts are of questioned validity, they are nonetheless included because they have been widely circulated. According to one of these disputed accounts, the patriarch of this family was John Jacob Bischoff. He arrived in this country from Palatinate, Germany on the ship "Two Brethren". John Jacob's son George was responsible for changing the name from Bischoff to Grandstaff. There are

GEORGE GRANDSTAFF HOUSE

drawing by Mardi Fadely

two versions of the story related to the change. One
story is told that George Bischoff, the grandfather of the
individual in this household, was captured by Indians and
escaped. However he feared to retain his name and called
himself Grandstaff. The other story and perhaps the more
credible is that the same individual was helping his
neighbor John Stone bring in the hay. They were set upon
by a tribe of Shawnee Indians led by "Kill Buck". Stone
and others in the party were killed. George Bischoff and
one of the Stone children were taken prisoner and more or
less adopted by the tribe. Bischoff in particular was
known for his hunting prowess. He lived with the tribe for
three years. During that time the Indians were impressed
with his fine physique as he stood tall and erect. As he
presented such a fine image they said he stood like a
"grand staff". Bischoff liked the image and the name and
when he left the Indians he became George Grandstaff.
Grandstaff family genealogists reject this story. While
willing to concede that George was captured by the Indians
they absolutely reject the notion that the name was

changed. He was George Grandstaff when he was captured and George Grandstaff when he obtained his freedom. This gentleman's son Phillip was the father of the head of this household. George Grandstaff was born 22 Apr 1787 and died 26 Apr 1878. He was married to Mary "Polly" Reedy, the daughter of Augustine Reedy on 3 Oct 1810. Mary died 19 Sep 1847 at the age of 51 years and 15 days old. George and Mary were buried in the Old Edinburg Cemetery. George was a Major during the War of 1812. Wayland's history of the county reports that George had a rifle factory and made guns for the War of 1812. Some of the guns he created were carried by Shenandoah County men into conflict during the Civil War. George Grandstaff was also responsible for building and operating the Edinburg Mill in 1848.

RELATED FAMILY:

    Mary Frances Grandstaff, daughter of George, married William J. Dinges on 25 May 1847 and resided in **dwelling 58.**

    Elizabeth Ann Grandstaff, daughter of George, married William J. Koontz on 12 Aug 1837 and resided in **dwelling 60.**

    Milton M. Grandstaff, son of George, married Emily A. J. Frye on 19 Nov 1846 and resided in **dwelling 61.**

    Phillip Marcus Grandstaff, son of George, married Sarah Miller and resided in **dwelling 62.**

    Artimissia Grandstaff, daughter of George, married Richard Miller on 18 Jan 1842 and resided in **dwelling 291.**

    John Jackson Grandstaff, son of George, married Isabella Murray on 5 Mar 1835 and resided in **dwelling 328.**

1850 CENSUS: George P. Grandstaff resided in dwelling 692 on page 49.

PAGE 9 EDINBURG (Microfilm Page 587)

Dwelling 64 Family 64

John H. Rau	34	Master Carpenter	1200 300	Va.
Sarah E. Rau	20			"
Horace B. Rau	5			"
William S. Rau	1			"
James W. Rau	23	Carpenter		"
Elias Sheetz	21	Carpenters Apprentice		"

John Henry Rau a resident of Greenbriar, West Virginia, was born in Augusta County, Virginia. He was the son of Henry and Amelia. John was born 8 Nov 1825 and died 18 Sep 1879. He was married on 11 Jan 1854 to Evaline B. Grandstaff, the daughter of John and Elizabeth. John Grandstaff married Elizabeth Liggett on 27 Feb 1826. John Grandstaff resided in **dwelling 46**. Evaline B. Grandstaff Rau was born in 1832 and died in 1856. She was buried in the Old Edinburg Cemetery. John Henry Rau then married **Sarah Ellen Rinker** on 11 Apr 1857. Sarah was the daughter of Samuel and Margaret. Samuel Rinker married Margaret Ann Hottel on 23 Sep 1835. Samuel Rinker resided in **dwelling 2**. Sarah Ellen Rinker Rau was born 6 Apr 1839 and died 30 Apr 1886. According to data in John Wayland's history of Shenandoah County John Henry Rau was a member of Company C of the 7th Virginia Cavalry.

William Samuel Rau was born 19 Aug 1858. He was a minister in the United Brethren Church. William was married to Sarah McDermott on 9 Mar 1887. Sarah died 8 Jun 1892. William then married Laura Bruce of Boonesville, Virginia on 28 Nov 1895.

James W. Rau was born 15 Jan 1837 and died 17 Jan 1912. He was born in Pochanatas, Virginia. He was the brother of John Henry Rau. James was married to Amanda Hisey on 27 Feb 1867. Amanda was the daughter of William and Jane. William Hisey married Jane Grandstaff on 7 Feb 1842. William and his family resided in **dwelling 69**. **Amanda Hisey Rau** was born 10 Jan 1846 and died 22 Jul 1909. James W. Rau served in Company C of the 7th Virginia Cavalry with his brother. James and Amanda were buried in the Old Edinburg Cemetery.

Elias W. Sheetz was the son of George of Jacob and Elizabeth. George Sheetz married Elizabeth Bowman on 14 Feb 1826. Elias was married to Artimisia Fry on 26 Nov 1862. Artimisia died 4 Dec 1912 at the age of 74 years. She was the daughter of John A. and Catherine. John A. Fry married Catherine Grandstaff on 10 Jun 1815. John A. Fry and family resided in **dwelling 353**. Elias W. Sheetz enlisted in Company C of the 10th Virginia Infantry on 18 Apr 1861. There is no record of his service with that unit after 1 Mar 1862. He is known to have been a member of Company C of the 7th Virginia Cavalry. There was a report that he had been wounded in combat. There is a marker for him in the Cedarwood Cemetery in Edinburg.

RELATED FAMILY:

      David S. Rau, brother of John Henry Rau, married Lydia S. Boehm on 7 Dec 1858 and resided in **dwelling 65.**

      Evaline Rau, sister of John Henry, married Aaron Evans on 12 Feb 1856 and resided in **dwelling 71.**

      Barbara J. Rau, sister of John Henry, appears in the residence of Peter Belew. They were located in **dwelling 36.**

      Robert H. Grandstaff, brother of Eveline Grandstaff Rau, married Elizabeth V. "Bettie" Johnson on 15 Sep 1856 and resided in **dwelling 45.**

1850 CENSUS: **Elias W. Sheetz** was a resident in the household of his father. They were located in dwelling 154 on page 11.

                      John Henry Rau was listed twice in the 1850 census. He was listed with his father in dwelling 81 on page 6. He also appears in household of John C. Clower. He was an apprentice joiner. They resided in dwelling 276 on page 20. In both households John Henry was listed with the surname "Rowe".

PAGE 9 EDINBURG   (Microfilm Page 587)

Dwelling 65   Family 65

David S. Rau	27	Carpenter	700	753	Virginia
Lydia S. Rau	19				"
Carrol W. Rau	1m				"

      David S. Rau was the son of Henry and Amelia. Amelia Rau may have been Amelia Brooke. This information was provided in the marriage record of David's sister Evaline. David was born in Pocahontas, Virginia. He was married to **Lydia S. Boehm** on 7 Dec 1858. Lydia was the daughter of David and Regina. David Boehm married Regina Swanyie on 29 Aug 1828.

RELATED FAMILY:

      John Henry Rau, brother of David, married Sarah Ellen Rinker on 11 Apr 1857 and resided in **dwelling 64.**

      Evaline Rau, sister of David, married Aaron Evans on 12 Feb 1856 and resided in **dwelling 71.**

Barbara J. Rau, sister of David, resided with the family of Peter Belew in **dwelling 36.**

Lucinda Boehm, sister of Lydia, married William H. Few on 13 Sep 1852 and resided in **dwelling 100.**

1850 CENSUS: David S. Rau was a resident in the household of his father Henry and his second wife Esther. Henry Rau married Esther Haun on 8 Oct 1842. They resided in dwelling 81 on page 6.

Lydia S. Boehm was a resident with her parents in dwelling 2025 on page 146.

PAGE 10 EDINBURG (Microfilm Page 588)

Dwelling 66 Family 66

Timothy Coffer	30	Day Labor on R.R.	Can't Read	Ireland
Johanna Coffer	35		Ireland Can't Read	
John Coffer	13		" School	
Johanna Coffer	5		Virginia	
Michael Coffer	2		"	

1850 CENSUS: No record of this family in Shenandoah County.

PAGE 10 EDINBURG (Microfilm Page 588)

Dwelling 67 Family 67

Anne M. Reedy	50	Washerwoman 0	100	Can't Read Virginia
Catherine Reedy	23	Housegirl		Virginia
Sarah A. Reedy	21	Seamstress		"
Eliza A. Reedy	17	Seamstress		"
Phillip L. Reedy	14			"

Anne M. Reedy was the wife of Phillip Reedy. She was born 25 Sep 1807 and died 21 Oct 1873. She was buried in the Old Edinburg Cemetery. There was a marriage reported for Phillip Reedy to Ann Getz on 5 Aug 1839 but it has not been confirmed. The bondsman for that marriage was Christian Miller. If it were the correct marriage, the presence of older children in this household suggest that it may have been the second marriage for Phillip.

Phillip L. **Reedy** is reported to have been a member of the New Market Eighth Star Artillery. The record lists him as Phillip Ready and indicates that he was born ca. 1846. He enlisted on 4 Mar 1862 as a substitute for Joseph Grandstaff. It is probable that this was the Joseph F. Grandstaff who resided in **dwelling 54.** Phillip was reassigned to the Danville Artillery in Sep 1862. He was paroled at Appomattox on 9 Apr 1865. Phillip died at the Lee Camp Soldiers Home on 10 Aug 1908. He was buried in the Hollywood Cemetery in Richomond, Virginia.

1850 CENSUS: Anne M. Reedy, her husband Phillip and family resided in dwelling 171 on page 13.

PAGE 10 EDINBURG (Microfilm Page 588)

Dwelling 68 Family 68

Charles Hutchinson	60	Miller	600	100	Virginia
Eliza B. Hutchinson	55				Virginia
John S. Hutchinson	18	Clerk	"		
Sarah E. Hutchinson	15		"		School
Charles W. Hutchinson	13		"		School
Francis M. Whissen	10		"		School

Charles Hutcheson was born in Loudoun County, Virginia on 11 Apr 1799. He died of consumption 29 Jun 1864. Charles was the son of George and Mary. George Hutcheson married Mary Hottle on 27 Nov 1793. Charles was married on 15 Mar 1827 to **Eliza B. Whissen.** Eliza was born 24 Jul 1804 and died 10 Mar 1868. She died of pneumonia. She was the daughter of Joseph and Salome. Joseph Whissen married Salome Snapp on 8 Nov 1802 in **Frederick** County, Virginia. Salome Snapp Whissen was a resident of **dwelling 79** at the time of this census. Charles and Eliza were buried in the Old Edinburg Cemetery.

John Samuel Hutcheson was born 29 May 1842 and died 20 Mar 1911. He was married to Alice Adele Miller on 17 Mar 1869. Alice Adele Miller Hutcheson was born 31 Aug 1846 and died 31 Aug 1926. Alice was the daughter of Richard and Artimisia. Richard Miller married Artimisia Grandstaff on 18 Jun 1842. John was fair complexed, with light hair and gray eyes. He was 6' tall. John enlisted at Edinburg as a private in Company C of the 10th Virginia Infantry on 18 Apr 1861. He transferred to Company F on 18 Apr 1862. An interesting story is told regarding the exploits of Private "Jackie" Hutcheson. He was captured by Yankees during one of the battles fought around Edinburg. As he was being marched out of town he waved and shouted to towns people, "see you in the morning boys". When the prisoners were being marched across the bridge at Opequon Creek, young Jackie hid under the bridge and successfully escaped. To the delight of his friends he made good on his promise to be back in Edinburg by morning. He was wounded 25 May 1862 at Winchester. On 16 Feb 1864 he was promoted to 4th Corporal. He was taken prisoner at Spotsylvania Courthouse on 12 May 1864. He was imprisoned at Point Lookout on 23 May 1864. John was transferred to Elmira, New York on 6 Jul 1864. He was exchanged in Feb 1865 at James River and was paroled on 4 May 1865 at Edinburg. He was a resident of Baltimore in 1900. John served as editor of the **CHRISTIAN ALLIANCE** and was awarded the Cross of Honor at Fredericksburg, Virginia in 1904. He also edited a book **BLUE AND GRAY** that was published after the war in 1869. He entered the ministry of the Methodist Episcopal Church and was the Presiding Elder for Roanoke, Lewisburg, Baltimore and Washington Districts. He also served for 30 years as a trustee at Randolph Macon College.

Sarah Elizabeth Hutcheson was born 1 Sep 1844 and died of typhoid fever on 1 Oct 1864.

Charles William Hutcheson was born 22 Nov 1847. He was married twice. He held office in the State Prison System at Jefferson City, Missouri and died around 1900.

RELATED FAMILY:

Eliza B. Whissen Hutcheson's brother Edward B. Whissen and his wife Mary Miller Whissen resided in **dwelling 80.**

NOTE: Most of the children in this family eventually removed to the west. However, one of the children of Charles and Eliza, **Calvin Amos Hutcheson** married Sarah Bailey. Sarah Bailey was from Edinburg. She was the sister of the Bailey of Barnum and Bailey Circus. Calvin Amos Hutcheson and his son Charles toured with the circus for years.

1850 CENSUS: **Charles Hutcheson** and his family resided in dwelling 728 on page 51.

PAGE 10 EDINBURG (Microfilm Page 588)

Dwelling 69   Family 69

William H. Hisey	40	Blacksmith	200	100 Virginia
Jane E. Hisey	39			"
Lemuel M. Hisey	16			" School
Amanda M. Hisey	14			" School
Artimesia L. Hisey	11			" School

William H. Hisey was 63 years, 2 months and 19 days old when he died on 10 Jun 1883. William was married to **Jane E. Grandstaff** on 7 Feb 1842. The bondsman for the marriage was Phillip Grandstaff. Jane was the daughter of Phillip and Mary. Phillip Grandstaff Jr. married Mary Cooper on 6 Aug 1816. Phillip Grandstaff resided in **dwelling 267.** Jane was 66 years, 7 months and 12 days old when she died on 9 May 1880. William and Jane were buried in the Old Edinburg Cemetery.

Lemuel M. Hisey was born in 1844 and died in 1900. He is buried near his parents.

Amanda M. Hisey was born 10 Jan 1846 and died 22 Jul 1909. She was married on 27 Feb 1867 to James W. Rau, a farmer, who was born in Pocahontas, Virginia. He was the son of Henry and Amelia Brooke Rau. James was born 15 Jan 1837 and died 17 Jan 1912. James was residing in **dwelling 64** with his brother John Henry. Amanda and James were buried in the Old Edinburg Cemetery.

Artimesia L. "Artie" Hisey was born 17 Jan 1849. She was married to Stephen P. Hollingsworth, a cabinet maker from Frederick County, Virginia. They were married on 28 Oct 1875. Stephen was born 20 Nov 1850 and died 24 Sep 1933. He was the son of Isaac and Mary. Isaac Milton Hollingsworth married Mary C. Pritchard in Frederick County, Virginia on 20 Feb 1843. Artie and Stephen were buried in the Old Edinburg Cemetery.

RELATED FAMILY:
Branson Grandstaff, brother of Jane, married Elizabeth Evaline Liggett on 9 Jun 1842 and resided in **dwelling 313.**
Joseph F. Grandstaff, brother of Jane, married Louisa C. Riddleberger on 25 Oct 1851 and resided in **dwelling 54.**

Amanda Grandstaff, sister of Jane, married Isaac Ritter on 7 Mar 1848 and resided in **dwelling 14**.

1850 CENSUS: **William H. Hisey** and his family resided in dwelling 717 on page 50.

PAGE 10 EDINBURG   (Microfilm Page 588)

Dwelling 70   Family 70

John W. Branin	26	Cabinet Maker	500	100	Virginia
Virginia F. Branin	20				"
Lucy L. Branin	3				"
John Thomas Branin	10m				"

John W. Branan was married to **Virginia Danavan** in Jul 1854.

John W. Thomas Branin is reported in Shenandoah County birth records to have been born in Sep 1859.

1850 CENSUS: No record of this family has been located in 1850.

PAGE 10 EDINBURG (Microfilm Page 588)

Dwelling 71   Family 71

Aaron B. Evans	56	Wool Carder	0	50	Virginia
Evaline Evans	31				"
Dillard O. Evans	2				"
Joseph H. Evans	2m				"

Aaron B. Evans was born 1 Jan 1802 and died 19 Dec 1872. He was married to **Evaline Rau** on 12 Feb 1856. Evaline was born 21 Jan 1828 and died 2 Feb 1892. Evaline was the daughter of Henry and Amelia. There is no record for the marriage of Henry and Amelia in Shenandoah County. However, Evaline's marriage record reports that she was the daughter of Amelia Brooke. Aaron was the son of Jeremiah and Mary. Jeremiah S. Evans Jr. and Mary A. Biedleman were married on 20 Jun 1801. Mary Biedleman Evans was living with her son Jeremiah in **dwelling 57**. The muster roll of 1835 indicates that Aaron B. Evans was a private in the militia. He was a member of the 13th Regiment 2nd Battalion.

Joseph Henry Evans was buried at the Union Forge Cemetery in Edinburg. He was born 19 Jan 1860 and died 11 Dec 1928. Joseph was married three times. His first marriage was to Arabela C. Windle on 20 Nov 1884. Arabela was born 10 Jul 1861 and died 14 Nov 1892. She was the daughter of George W. and Mary C. Joseph was working as a stone mason when he married Annie Lee Bradford. Annie was the daughter of William and Amanda. She was born in Delaware on 30 Dec 1869 and died 30 Sep 1900. The final marriage of Joseph was to Lovina Myers on 10 Oct 1901. She was the daughter of Jacob and Elizabeth. Jacob Myers married Elizabeth Bowers on 11 Oct 1855. All three of these women were buried near Joseph in the Union Forge Cemetery.

Dillard O. Evans died 11 Dec 1911 at the age of 54. He married Josephine Lydia Racey on 22 Jul 1894. She was the daughter of James and Mary. James Madison Racey married Mary Fadely on 12 Oct 1858. Dillard was a bricklayer at the time of his marriage.

RELATED FAMILY:

John Henry Rau, brother of Evaline, married Sarah Ellen Rinker on 11 Apr 1857 and resided in **dwelling 64.**

Barbara J. Rau, sister of Evaline, resided with the family of Peter Belew in **dwelling 36.**

James W. Rau, brother of Evaline, resided with his brother John Henry in **dwelling 64.**

David S. Rau, brother of Evaline, married Lydia S. Boehm on 7 Dec 1858 and resided in **dwelling 65.**

Jeremiah S. Evans, brother of Aaron, resided with his mother in **dwelling 57.**

1850 CENSUS: **Aaron B. Evans** was located in the residence of Phillip and Susan Ann Ruddell Stover. They were found in dwelling 160 on page 12.

Evaline Rau resided in the household of her father Henry and his second wife Esther Haun Rau. This household was located in dwelling 81 on page 6.

PAGE 10 EDINBURG (Microfilm Page 588)

Dwelling 72 Family 72

William H. Marshall   38   Saddle and Harness Maker   Virginia

William H. Marshall was the son of John and Amelia. John Marshall married Amelia Carrier on 21 Dec 1818. He was married to Sarah Miller on 3 Oct 1871. She was the daughter of Isaac and Catherine. There was a marriage on 7 Jan 1828 of Isaac Miller to Catherine Stickley. There was evidence that a William H. Marshall was a member of the Second Virginia Infantry during the Civil War. He was reported to have been born in 1818. He was a member of Company G. He was discharged on 14 Oct 1862. The reason was not stated but he was older than most soldiers in this conflict. He is reported to have died in Augusta County on 15 Apr 1893.

1850 CENSUS: No record of this individual in 1850.

PAGE 10   EDINBURG   (Microfilm Page 588)

Dwelling 73   Family 73

Christian Comer	53	Farmer and Tanner 7170 7498	Virginia
Maria Comer	53		"
Joseph Comer	23	Farmhand	"
Mary E. Comer	20	Teacher Common School	"
Catherine A. Comer	16		" Sch.
Maria J. Comer	12		" "
Thomas J. Hanson	23	Farmer	"C'tRd
Elizabeth Wetzel	20	Housegirl	"
Granville Grayson	14	(Mulatto)	"
Sarah Grayson	6	(Mulatto)	"

Christian Comer was born 20 Aug 1806 and died 11 Aug 1880. He was the son of Barbara Comer Buracker. Barbara had married Michael Buracker on 2 Dec 1811. George Garner was the bondsman for the wedding. It is not known if Barbara was married at the time of Christian's birth. Christian was married to **Maria Bigby** on 1 Jan 1828. Maria Bigby Comer was born 7 Nov 1806 and died 2 Jun 1881. Christian and Maria were buried in the Cedarwood Cemetery.

Joseph Comer was born 25 Apr 1837 and died 1 Apr 1899 in Washington, D.C. He was a farmer at the time of his marriage on 28 Mar 1861 to Elizabeth Jane Whissen. Elizabeth was the daughter of Edward and Mary C. Miller Whissen. Edward Whissen and his family resided in **dwelling 80**. Bettie was listed twice in this census as she also appears in **dwelling 22**. Elizabeth "Bettie" Jane Whissen was born 2 Jul 1842 and died 22 Apr 1915. Joseph and Bettie were buried in the Cedarwood Cemetery. Joseph Comer was 6'1" with dark complexion, black eyes and dark hair. He enlisted on 18 Apr 1861 as a Color Sergeant in Company C of the 10th Virginia Infantry. He was promoted to 1st Sergeant on 21 Aug 1861. Later in the war, Joseph was enlisted in Company K of the 12th Virginia Cavalry with the rank of 1st Sergeant. He was paroled at Edinburg on 4 May 1865.

Mary E. Comer, a school teacher, was married to Franklin J. Kibler on 22 Apr 1869. Franklin was a farmer. He was a widower. He had married Emily Amiss on 10 Jun 1852. Franklin was the son of David and Rebecca.

Catherine Ann Comer was born in 1843 and died in 1915. She was married to John E. L. Cooper on 7 Nov 1867. He was employed as a shoemaker. John was born in 1840 and died in 1927. Catherine and John were buried in the Cedarwood Cemetery in Edinburg. John was the son of Joseph and Harriet. Joseph Pollard Cooper married Harriet Artz on 3 Feb 1834. Joseph and his family resided in **dwelling 17**.

Maria J. Comer was married on 25 Nov 1869 to John W. Kibler. John was from Page County, Virginia. He was the son of David and Mary Ann. David Kibler married Mary Ann Level on 19 Aug 1837 in Page County, Virginia.

Thomas J. Hanson was a tanner. He was born ca. 1838. Thomas enlisted in Company C of the 10th Virginia Infantry as a private on 18 Apr 1861. He later re-enlisted on 13 Aug 1862 at New Market as a private in Company K of the 12th Virginia Cavalry. He is reported to have died soon after the war. Thomas was the son of Thomas and Rachel. He was married to Catherine Brown on 9 Aug 1864. Catherine was the daughter of John and Catherine. His name is sometimes listed as Henson in Shenandoah County records.

Very little is known for certain about **Elizabeth Wetzel**. There was a marriage on 30 Dec 1862 for an Elizabeth Wetzel to Joseph Fox. He was the son of Samuel and Elizabeth. Her parents were not recorded. However she did indicate in marriage records that she was born in Page County, Virginia.

Granville Grayson and **Sarah Grayson** are believed to have had some relationship to Washington Grayson and his wife Winney. In the 1850 census this couple had a son

named Henry G. Grayson (perhaps Granville) who was the
correct age.

1850 CENSUS: **Christian Comer** and family resided in
dwelling 739 on page 52.
    Thomas J. Hanson appears in dwelling 694 on
page 49. The family of Washington Grayson
were residents of dwelling 2118 on page
152.

PAGE 11 EDINBURG   (Microfilm Page 589)

Dwelling 74   Family 74

Joseph H. Marston	25	Carpenter	Virginia
Eve R. Marston	32		"
Catherine Grove	64		"

    Joseph H. Marston was the son of Lewis and
Margaret. Lewis Marston and his family resided in **dwelling
373.** Lewis was one of three or, according to some sources,
four Marston brothers. The patriarch of the family is
reputed by Marston family historian Eunice Boyer Marston
to have been Thomas Marston. The family originally was
located in Spotsylvania County and later moved to
Rappahannock County, Virginia. For a period of time some
members of the family may have settled near Culpepper.
Joseph, Powell and Lewis have definitely been identified
as Marston brothers and all appear in Shenandoah County.
Another possible brother was the Fountain Marston who
settled in the Mt. Jackson area. Joseph Marston, uncle of
the head of this household was instrumental in
establishing furnaces in the Powells Fort area. Lewis
Marston, father of Joseph H. Marston settled in the
Edinburg area. Joseph H. Marston was married to **Eve R.
Grove** , the daughter of Catherine on 19 Dec 1858. William
Marshall provided the affidavit for the marriage. Joseph
H. Marston was a carpenter. He was born 15 Sep 1841.
Joseph enlisted as a private in Company C of the 10th
Virginia Infantry. In September of 1861 he attained the
rank of 4th Corporal. He transferred to Company F of the
10th Virginia Infantry on 18 Apr 1862. Joseph was captured
at Gettysburg on 3 Jul 1863. He was sent to Fort McHenry
on 6 Jul 1863 and was transferred to Fort Delaware on 8 Jul
1863. Joseph was sent to Point Lookout on 27 Oct 1863 and
was exchanged on 30 Oct 1864. 10th Infantry records report
that he died 1 Jun 1916 at the Robert E. Lee Confederate
Soldiers Home in Richmond, Virginia.

1850 CENSUS: **Joseph H. Marston** was a resident in the household of his father dwelling 740 on page 52.

Eve R. Grove and her mother are believed to have been located in dwelling 385 on page 28. The young lady listed with Catherine was called Rebecca. The age is correct and Eve's middle initial was R.

PAGE 11 EDINBURG **(Microfilm Page 589)**

Dwelling 75   Family 75

Isaac W. Miley	35	Farmer 800 935	Virginia	
Elizabeth C. Miley	36		"	
Mary Susan Miley	14		"	School
Joseph W. Miley	12		"	School
Isabella V. Miley	8		"	School
Ann E. Miley	8		"	School

Isaac Miley was married to **Elizabeth C. Cooper** on 21 Oct 1844. The bondsman for the marriage was Isaac Bowman. She was the daughter of George and Mary Magdalene. George Cooper married the widow Mary Magdalene Saum Bowman on 12 Feb 1822. Mary Magdalene Saum, the daughter of Nicholas, had married Benjamin Bowman on 13 Nov 1800. Benjamin had died 6 Nov 1820.

Mary Susan Miley was married to Richard S. Richardson on 2 Jul 1867. Richard was a widower. He was born in Bristol, Tennessee and was residing in Baltimore, Maryland at the time of this marriage. He was employed as a house joiner. Richard was the son of Lewis D. and Catherine A.

Joseph W. Miley was born 26 Mar 1848 and died 23 Oct 1864. County death records indicate that he was killed "accidentally". He is buried in the Old Edinburg Cemetery.

Isabel V. Miley was born in 1852 and died in 1933. She was married on 14 Nov 1869 to Willis Green Swann, the son of James N. and Isabella Blackford Swann. Willis resided with his parents at the hotel (**dwelling 51**) at the time of this census. He was born in 1840 and died in 1926. Isabel and Willis were buried in the Cedarwood Cemetery in Edinburg.

Annie E. Miley was born 16 Feb 1852 and died 29 Aug 1904. She was married to James Littleton Coates of Louisa County, Virginia. James was the son of James R and Elizabeth B. Annie and James were married 15 Nov 1881. James was a farmer. He was born 18 Jul 1851 and died 25 Oct 1917. They were buried in the Old Edinburg Cemetery.

1850 CENSUS: **Isaac W. Miley** and his family resided in dwelling 2057 on page 148.

PAGE 11 EDINBURG (Microfilm Page 589)

Dwelling 76 Family 76

Amelia A. Downey	39	Seamstress	1000	140	Virginia
Angelo Downey	17				" School
Rebecca Z. Downey	15				" School
Joseph W. Downey	11				" School
Virginia Downey	8				" School

Amelia Ann Miley was married to **Thornton Downey** 12 Dec 1838. The bondsman for the marriage was Andrew Hoffman. Thornton Downey died 24 Mar 1853 at the age of 39 years, 8 months and 21 days old. Thornton Downey was the son of Eleazer and Fanny. Eleazer Downey married Fanny Hoffman on 30 Aug 1811. Thornton was buried in the Downey Cemetery. In 1835 Thornton was listed as a private in the militia. He was a member of the 13th Regiment, 2nd Battalion.

Angelo Downey was born ca. 1843. He was of light complexion, dark hair with gray eyes. Angelo was a 5'10" carpenter. He enlisted as a private in Company C of the 10th Virginia Infantry. He transferred to Company F of the 10th Virginia Infantry on 18 Apr 1862. Angleo was taken prisoner of war at Spotsylvania Courthouse on 12 May 1864. He was sent to Fort Delaware on 21 May 1864. Angelo was released under the Oath of Allegiance on 15 Jun 1865. He was a resident of Springfield, Ohio after the war.

Rebecca Z. Downey was married to Henry H. Evans on 9 Dec 1866. He was the son of John Evans and Catherine Lloyd Evans. Henry and his mother resided in **dwelling 6**. Henry H. Evans was born 22 Nov 1840 and died 7 Feb 1914. He was buried in the Cedarwood Cemetery.

Joseph W. Downey was born 4 Jun 1849 and died 17 Jul 1892. He was a blacksmith at the time of his marriage to Lucy Ellen Evans. Lucy and Joseph were married on 24 Dec 1874. Lucy Ellen was born 31 Oct 1852 and died 9 Apr 1928. Joseph and Lucy were buried in the Cedarwood Cemetery. Lucy Ellen Evans was the daughter of Joseph W. and Hannah Via Evans. Joseph Evans and family resided in **dwelling 38.**

Virginia T. Downey was married to William Henry Evans on 23 Dec 1869. William was the brother of Lucy Ellen Evans and appears with his family in **dwelling 38.** William Henry Evans was born 22 Mar 1845 and died 19 Jul 1914. He was buried in the Cedarwood Cemetery.

RELATED FAMILY:

Eleazer Downey Jr., brother of Thornton Downey, married Lydia Haun on 4 Dec 1848 and resided in **dwelling 274.**

Andrew Jackson Downey, brother of Thornton Downey, married Mary Ann Bowman on 25 Jan 1839 and resided in **dwelling 1779.**

Sarah Jane Downey, sister of Thornton Downey, married Daniel Keller on 15 Jan 1845 and resided in **dwelling 270.**

Drucilla C. Downey, daughter of Thornton and Amelia, married George Jacob Cooper on 15 Mar 1860 and resided in **dwelling 77.**

Andrew Jackson Downey, son of Thornton and Amelia, resided with his uncle Andrew Jackson Downey in **dwelling 1779.**

1850 CENSUS: **Amelia Miley Downey** and her family resided in dwelling 976 on page 68.

PAGE 11 EDINBURG (Microfilm Page 589)

Dwelling 77 Family 77

| Jacob Cooper | 24 | Farmer | Va. | Just Married |
| Drucilla Cooper | 22 | Seamstress | " | Just Married |

George Jacob Cooper was born 1835 and died 1907. He was the son of Joseph and Harriet. Joseph P. Cooper married Harriet Artz on 3 Feb 1834. Joseph and Harriet were located in **dwelling 17** at the time of this census. George had married **Drucilla A. Downey** on 15 Mar 1860. Drucilla was the daughter of Thornton and Amelia. Thornton

Downey married Amelia Ann Miley on 12 Dec 1838. At the time of this census Thornton was deceased but Amelia Ann Miley Downey and other members of the family were located in **dwelling 76**. Drucilla C. Downey Cooper was born in 1838 and died in 1907. They are buried at the Cedarwood Cemetery. George Jacob Cooper was a tanner at the time he enlisted at Edinburg as a private in Company C of the 10th Virginia Infantry. He enlisted on 18 Jun 1861 and was listed as a 5th Sergeant in October of 1861. George was transferred to Company F of the 10th Virginia Infantry on 18 Apr 1862. George was 6'2" and had a dark complexion with gray eyes and black hair. He enlisted as a private in Company K of the 12th Virginia Cavalry on 10 Aug 1862. He was absent in September of 1862. George was taken prisoner of war on 9 Jun 1863 at Beverly Ford. He was kept at the Old Capitol Prison. It is reported that he had a bay horse appraised at $500 that was killed when he was captured. He was eventually released from the Old Capitol Prison. He was on the company sick roll on 2 Sep 1863 and was paroled at Edinburg on 4 May 1865.

RELATED FAMILY:

      Josephine M. Cooper, sister of George, was married to William A. Mohler on 1 Jan 1857 and resided in **dwelling 1065**.

      Andrew Jackson Downey, brother of Drucilla, resided with his uncle Andrew in **dwelling 1779**.

1850 CENSUS: **George Jacob Cooper** was located in the household of his father in dwelling 162 on page 12.

           Drucilla A. Downey was located in the household of her father in dwelling 976 on page 68.

PAGE 11 EDINBURG   (Microfilm Page 589)

Dwelling 78   Family 78

Charles W. Hutcheson	32	Cooper	400	45	Virginia
Caroline Hutcheson	28				"
Susan S. Hutcheson	8				"
Franklin P. Hutcheson	7				"
Emma C. Hutcheson	3				"

    Charles W. Hutcheson was born 25 Jan 1825 and died in 1908. He was the son of Jacob and Margaret. Jacob Hutcheson married Margaret Mauck on 10 Jun 1822. Jacob and

Margaret were located in **dwelling 319**. Charles was married on 6 Apr 1850 to **Caroline Clinedinst**. Caroline was born 13 Jan 1831 and died 20 Oct 1925. Caroline was the daughter of Isaac and Lydia. Isaac Clinedinst was married to Lydia Holler on 7 Mar 1825. Lydia Holler Clinedinst and her family resided in **dwelling 322**. Charles and Caroline were the parents of eight children. Charles is reported to have been a member of the Confederate army during the Civil War. No information has been located to determine his unit. He may not have participated in battle as he was detailed to make saltpeter used in the manufacture of munitions. Caroline Clinedinst Hutcheson was known in the Edinburg area as the "Grand Old Woman" and "Granny Reb". She earned these accolades when she successfully challenged the Yankees when they tried to burn a barn at the old Clinedinst place.

Susan S. Hutcheson was born 5 Jun 1851 and died 21 May 1893. She was reported to have wed Newton W. Branham on 3 Nov 1880. He was the son of William and Catherine. William Branham and his family were located in **dwelling 691**. Newton was born 12 Dec 1857 and died 4 Nov 1924. The Hottel Family history indicates that Newton "dropped dead on top of a carload of coal." Susan was buried in the Old Union Cemetery in Mt. Jackson. The burial site of Newton has not been located.

Franklin P. Hutcheson was born 11 Apr 1853 and died 25 Jun 1934. He married Jennie D. Craig in May 1877. Jennie was born 11 Apr 1858 and died 27 Nov 1920. They were buried in the Cedarwood Cemetery. Frank lived for a period of time in Canton, Ohio and served as a gardner in Morgantown, West Virginia.

Emma C. Hutcheson was born 24 Apr 1857. She was married to Joseph S. Bowman on 20 Jan 1885. Joseph was the son of Isaac and Eve. Isaac Bowman married Eve Sheetz on 15 Sep 1852. Isaac and Eve resided in **dwelling 280**. Joseph was born 31 Aug 1855 and died 23 Feb 1912.

RELATED FAMILY:

William H. Hutcheson, brother of Charles, married Mary E. Hockman on 14 Feb 1854 and is located in **dwelling 359**.

Jacob Amos Hutcheson, brother of Charles, is located in **dwelling 81**.

91

Joseph Franklin Hutcheson, brother of
Charles, married Mary Ann Long on 4 Sep 1852 and resided
in **dwelling 1187**.

John T. Hutcheson, brother of Charles,
married Mary Margaret Dirting on 20 Oct 1849 and resided
in **dwelling 357**.

John C. Clinedinst, brother of Caroline,
married Sarah Catherine Bowman on 30 Sep 1858 and resided
in **dwelling 261**.

1850 CENSUS: Caroline Clinedintst resided in dwelling 698
on page 48.

Charles Hutcheson and his wife Caroline
Clinedinst Hutcheson resided in dwelling
995 on page 69. Caroline was listed twice
in the 1850 census.

PAGE 11 EDINBURG (Microfilm Page 589)

Dwelling 79 Family 79

Salome Whissen   76   2166 100   Virginia

Salome Snapp was married to Joseph Whissen on 8 Nov
1803. They were married in Frederick County, Virginia.
The bondsman for the marriage was Joseph Snapp. Salome
Snapp Whissen was born in 1784 and died in 1862. Her
husband, Joseph, was born in 1776 and died in 1846. They
were buried in the Old Edinburg Cemetery.

RELATED FAMILY:

Edward B. Whissen, son of Salome, was a
resident in **dwelling 80**.

Eliza B. Whissen, daughter of Salome,
married Charles Hutchinson on 15 Mar 1827 and resided in
dwelling 68.

1850 CENSUS: Salome Whissen was a resident in dwelling 735
on page 52.

Dwelling 80 Family 80

Edward B. Whissen	43	Farmer	9854	2088	Virginia
Mary G. Whissen	38				"
Elizabeth J. Whissen	17				"
Susan S. Whissen	14				" School
Frances C. Whissen	11				" School
Ellen C. Whissen	9				" School
Josephine M. Whissen	7				"
Henry A. Whissen	4				"
William E. Whissen	1				"
Phillip S. Whissen	12				Ohio/Sch
George W. Sibert	23	Miller			Va.
Albert Winter	35	Millwright			Ohio
Susan Miller	60	Mid-Wife			Va.

Edward B. Whissen was the son of Joseph Whissen and Salome Snapp Whissen. Joseph and Salome were married in Frederick County, Virginia on 18 Nov 1803. Salome Whissen was a resident in **dwelling 79**. Edward was born in 1816 and died in 1899. His wife **Mary G** is listed as Mary Miller Whissen in the death records of her children. Mary was born in 1821 and died in 1905. Edward and Mary were buried in the Old Edinburg Cemetery.

Elizabeth Jane Whissen was born 2 Jul 1842 and died 22 Apr 1915. Elizabeth was listed twice in this census. She also appears in **dwelling 22**. She was married to Joseph Comer on 28 Mar 1861. Joseph was a farmer and was the son of Christian and Maria. Christian Comer married Maria Bigby on 1 Jan 1828. Christian and his family resided in **dwelling 73**. Joseph Comer was born 25 Apr 1837 and died 1 Apr 1899. Elizabeth and Joseph were buried in the Cedarwood Cemetery.

Susan Salome Whissen was born in 1845 and died in 1938. She was married to Joseph Arthur Osborn on 1 Dec 1870. Joseph was a farmer and was the son of Joseph and Rosanna. Joseph Osborn married Rosanna Bender on 29 Sep 1828. Joseph and his family resided in **dwelling 1409**. Joseph was born in 1836 and died in 1891. They were buried in the Old Edinburg Cemetery.

Frances "Fannie" C. Whissen was married to William H. Dinges on 10 Nov 1874. He was a farmer and a widower from Frederick County, Virginia. In the Dinges Cemetery a woman named Pauline E Smith was buried. She died on 17 Jul 1870. She was listed as the wife of William H. Dinges and the daughter of William and Lucy Smith. Williams parents were David and Catherine. David Dinges married Catherine Miller on 26 Feb 1822.

Ellen C. Whissen was born 15 Aug 1851 and died 9 Dec 1922. She was married to Andrew J. Hopewell on 19 Jan 1876. Andrew was a watch maker and jeweller. He was the son of Samuel and Amelia. Samuel Hopewell married Amelia McInturff on 25 Jul 1836. Samuel and his family resided in **dwelling 576**. Andrew J. Hopewell was born 7 Apr 1842 and died 18 Dec 1923. They were buried in the Cedarwood Cemetery.

Henry Amos Whissen was born in 1856 and died in 1938. His obituary reports that he died in D.C. He was buried in the Cedarwood Cemetery.

George W. Sibert enlisted on 18 Apr 1861 in the 10th Virginia Infantry Company C. He was a private and he was reported missing in action with a wound on 21 Jul 1861. On 2 Aug 1861 he died of his wound at Culpepper, Virginia.

Susan Kibler was married to Joseph Miller on 19 Nov 1818. She died on 2 May 1871 at the age of 72 years, 1 month and 16 days old.

RELATED FAMILY:
Elizabeth Whissen, sister of Edward, married Charles Hutchinson on 15 Mar 1827 and resided in **dwelling 68**.
Frances Miller, daughter of Susan Kibler Miller, married Samuel Boehm on 14 Oct 1833 and resided in **dwelling 33**.

1850 CENSUS: Edward B. Whissen and his family were located in dwelling 734 on page 52.
Susan Kibler Miller was a resident in dwelling 722 on page 51.

NOTE: Wilson's book on Edinburg during the Civil War relates the story of 8 year old Lucy Whissen. (A review of household members in the census would suggest that the Lucy in this story may have been Josephine M. Whissen.) She had been ill and died during the shelling of Edinburg. The situation was so dangerous that the family was unable

94

to bury her in a cemetery. As a result she was buried in
the garden of the Whissen home. After the war her body was
exhumed and buried in a local cemetery.

PAGE 11 EDINBURG   **(Microfilm Page 589)**

Dwelling 81   Family 81

Amos Hutcheson   26   Wagoner   300   0 Virginia

     Jacob Amos Hutcheson was the son of Jacob and
Margaret. Jacob Hutcheson married Margaret Mauck on 10 Jun
1822. Jacob and Margaret were residents of **dwelling 319.**
Jacob Amos was born 4 Jul 1830 and died 22 Nov 1905. He
was 5'2" with dark complexion, black hair and blue eyes.
He enlisted in the 10th Virginia Infantry Company C as a
private on 26 Apr 1861. He transferred to Company F of the
10th Virginia Infantry on 18 Apr 1862. He was detailed as
a teamster in Feb 1863. He was paroled at Mt. Jackson on
20 Apr 1865. He initally served as a substitute for his
brother William and then enlisted on his own. Jacob Amos
Hutcheson is reported to have served during the Mexican
War. On 17 Jul 1865 he married Martha Ann Bowers, the
daughter of Reuben and Mary. Reuben Bowers married Mary
Holler on 8 Aug 1832. Martha and her parents resided in
dwelling 1207. Martha Ann Bowers Hutcheson was born 20 Apr
1839 and died 29 May 1902. Jacob and Martha were buried
in the Union Forge Cemetery in Edinburg.

RELATED FAMILY:
          William H. Hutcheson, brother of Amos, was
married to Mary E. Hockman on 14 Feb 1854 and resided in
dwelling 359.
          Charles W. Hutcheson, brother of Amos, was
married to Caroline Clinedinst on 6 Apr 1850 and resided
in **dwelling 78.**
          Joseph Franklin Hutcheson, brother of Amos,
married Mary Ann Long on 4 Sep 1852 and resided in **dwelling
1187.**
          John T. Hutcheson, brother of Amos, married
Mary Margaret Dirting on 20 Oct 1849 and resided in
dwelling 357.

1850 CENSUS: Jacob Amos Hutcheson and his parents resided
              in dwelling 679 on 48.

95

PAGE 11   EDINBURG   (Microfilm Page   589)

Dwelling 82   Family 82

Clarence L. Broadus	27	Teacher Common School 10 100 Virginia
Sarah J. Broadus	26	"
Thomas M. Broadus	4	"
Ellen B. Broadus	1	"

Clarence L. Broadus enlisted in the 10th Virginia Infantry Company C on 18 Apr 1861. He was a private. He later transferred to Beckham Battery of the Laurel Brigade. On 16 Sep 1861 company records indicate that he suffered the loss of his arm as a result of a wound.

1850 CENSUS: No record of this family in 1850.

PAGE 12 EDINBURG   (Microfilm Page 590)

Dwelling 83   Family 83

Lewis Pence	34	Master Blacksmith	3000	671 Virginia
Rebecca Pence	33			"
William A. Pence	9			"
Samuel E. Pence	7			"
Virginia J. Pence	5			"
Amanda E. Pence	2			"
David L. Pence	2m			"
Israel Dellinger	28	Blacksmith	300	0 "
Mollie	20	(Black)		"

Lewis Pence was married on 21 May 1849 **Rebecca Fry**. The bondsman for this marriage was John A. Fry. Rebecca was the daughter of John A. and Catherine. John A. Fry married Catherine Grandstaff on 10 Jun 1815. John A. Fry and his family resided in **dwelling 353**. Lewis Pence was born 21 Jun 1825 and died 14 Jan 1904. Ann Rebecca Fry Pence was born 25 Nov 1826 and died 2 Sep 1908. They were buried in the Cedarwood Cemetery.

William A. Pence died 11 Mar 1916 at the age of 65. He was buried at the Cedarwood Cemetery with hs wife Mary R. She was born 5 Nov 1860 and died 11 Feb 1935.

Samuel E. Pence was a farmer at the time of his marriage on 16 Mar 1881 to Ellen Brumbaugh. Ellen was the daughter of Joseph and Elizabeth. Joseph Brumbaugh married Elizabeth Caldwell on 1 Sep 1840. Joseph and his family resided in **dwelling 1246**.

Virginia Frances Pence was born in 1854 and died in 1920. She was married on 23 Mar 1882 to Lemuel R. Foltz. Lemuel was born in 1850 and died in 1933. He was the son of John and Mary. John Walton Foltz was married to Mary J. Shaver on 30 Jan 1850. John W. Foltz and his family resided in **dwelling 556**. Virginia and Lemuel were buried in the Hawkinson United Methodist Church Cemetery in Mt. Jackson.

Lewis and Rebecca had a daughter Ella who was buried near her parents at Cedarwood. It is believed that she was the **Amanda E. Pence** in this household. She was born 27 Dec 1857 and died 21 Jul 1890.

There is a **David L. Pence** buried in the Gravel Springs Cemetery in Frederick County, Virginia. He was born 19 Feb 1860 and died 21 Nov 1899. This may have been the individual in this household.

Israel Dellinger was born ca. 1835. He enlisted on 18 Apr 1861 in Company Co the 10th Virginia Infantry. He was 6'2 with light complexion, light hair and blue eyes. He was a blacksmith and was transferred to Company F on 18 Apr 1862. In May of 1862 he was detailed as regimental blacksmith and was eventually made brigade blacksmith. Israel was taken prisoner on 2 Mar 1865 at Waynesboro. He was sent to Fort Delaware on 12 Mar 1865 and was released on 15 Jun 1865.

RELATED FAMILY:

Ambrose Fry, brother of Rebecca, married Julia Ann Gochenour on 10 Mar 1856 and resided in **dwelling 323**.

Lelia Virginia Fry, sister of Rebecca, married David Tisinger on 22 Feb 1854 and resided in **dwelling 1184**.

William H. Fry, brother of Rebecca, married Rosa Coffman on 6 May 1844 and resided in **dwelling 355**.

Susan Fry, sister of Rebecca, married Michael Patton on 12 Dec 1836 and resided in **dwelling 314**.

Matilda Fry, sister of Rebecca, married Dilman Estep on 12 Feb 1857 and resided in **dwelling 320**.

John A. Fry, brother of Rebecca, married Sarah Elizabeth Beasley on 27 Oct 1857 and resided in **dwelling 354.**

1850 CENSUS: Lewis Pence and family were present in dwelling 985 on page 69.

PAGE 12 EDINBURG   (Microfilm Page 590)

Dwelling 84   Family 84

Gustavus Lersner	30	Lumber Dealer	0	500	Germany
Edward Morrison	29	Lawyer			Virginia
Jacob Valentine	24	Laborer			"

Edward Morrison was 31 years old when he enlisted on 5 Apr 1862 in Company B of the Toms Brook Guard of the 33rd Virginia Infantry. He was reported to have been 6' with fair complexion, dark hair and blue eyes. On 3 May 1863 he was admitted to Chimborazo Hospital with constipation. He returned to duty 21 May 1863. He was readmitted to Chimborazo on 11 Oct 1863. He was taken prisoner at Winchester and was assigned to the U. S. Hospital with gunshot wounds to the left lung. He was sent to Point Lookout on 26 Oct 1864. He was exchanged on 30 Oct 1864. He obtained his parole on 4 May 1865 at Clarksburg, West Virginia.

1850 CENSUS: Jacob Valentine, a fourteen year old youth, was a resident in dwelling 1805 on page 130. He was a resident in the household of John and Mary Webb Lentz.

PAGE 12 EDINBURG   (Microfilm Page 590)

Dwelling 85   Family 85

William Allison	47	Collier 400	100	Virginia	
Ann Allison	44			"	
Perry J.Allison	21	Carpenter		"	
Marcus W. Allison	19	Laborer		"	
Joseph S. Allison	13			"	School
Elizabeth E. Allison	11			"	School

There is a marriage reported for **William Allison** and **Rosanna Hisey** on 23 Nov 1836. The bondsman for that marriage was John Sibert.

Perry Jefferson Allison was born 15 Nov 1838 and died 31 Jul 1912. He was a house painter when he married Martha Kibler on 27 Dec 1860. Martha resided in **dwelling 50**. She was born 2 Apr 1840 and died 25 Apr 1876. Martha was the daughter of John and Mary. John Kibler married Mary Wolverton on 1 Jun 1840. John Kibler and his family were residents of **dwelling 360**. Perry married 23 Sep 1877 to Sarah M. Coffman, the daughter of Levi and Elizabeth. Levi Coffman married Elizabeth S. Nichols on 12 Apr 1842. Levi Coffman and his family resided in **dwelling 1238**. Sarah M. Coffman Allison died 29 Aug 1895. Perry married for the third time to Anne E. Coffelt on 8 Dec 1897. She was the daughter of William and Katherine Fultz Coffelt. William and his family are believed to have resided in **dwelling 1217**. Perry was a merchant in Charlestown, West Virginia at the time of his third marriage. Perry Jefferson Allison and all three of his wives were buried in the Old Edinburg Cemetery. He had enlisted as a private in Company F of the 10th Virginia Infantry on 1 Mar 1862. He was wounded at Winchester on 14 Jun 1863. He was taken prisoner at Spotsylvania Courthouse on 12 May 1864. He was imprisoned on 21 May 1864 and was paroled on 7 Jun 1865.

Marcus W. Allison was reported to have been 5'7 1/2" with a dark complexion and brown eyes. He was a carpenter at the time he enlisted in Company C of the 10th Virginia Infantry on 18 Apr 1861. He transferred to Company F of the 10th Virginia Infantry on 18 Apr 1862. He was taken prisoner at Gettysburg on 3 Jul 1863. He was sent to Ft. McHenry in Jul 1863. He was then transferred to Fort Delaware and eventually arrived at Point Lookout on 26 Oct 1863. He was paroled at Staunton on 12 May 1865. It is reported he died in Hagerstown, Maryland where he was physician.

Joseph S. Allison was married on 11 Aug 1875 to Lucy A. Grandstaff, the daughter of Phillip Marcus and Sarah. Marcus and his family resided in **dwelling 62**. Lucy A. Grandstaff Allison died 16 Jun 1883 at the age of 30 years and 7 months. She was buried in the Old Edinburg Cemetery.

1850 CENSUS: No record of the Allison household in 1850.

99

PAGE 12 EDINBURG   (Microfilm Page 590)

Dwelling 86   Family 86

George W. Aughinbaugh	40	Clergyman Ger. Ref.	0	500
				Pennsylvania
Mary L. Aughinbaugh	35		Vermont	
Charles H. Aughinbaugh	10		Maryland School	
Martha L. Aughinbaugh	4		Maryland	
George W. Aughinbaugh	2m		Virginia	
Catherine N. Linder	26	Housegirl	Pennsylvania	

     George Aughinbaugh was a minister of the German Reformed Lutheran Church.

1850 CENSUS: No record of this family in 1850.

PAGE 13 WOODSTOCK   (Microfilm Page 839)

Dwelling 87   Family 87

William J. Supinger	36	Master Blacksmith	400	1700
				Virginia
Ann E. Supinger	34		"	
Sarah E. Supinger	11		"	School
William Supinger	10		"	School
Robert Supinger	5		"	
Laura V. Supinger	3		"	
Lewis J. Supinger	5m		"	

     William Jacob Supinger was born 5 Dec 1823 and died 22 Oct 1893. He was the son of Peter and Sarah. Peter Supinger and Sarah Kinsley were wed on 15 Mar 1820. William was married to **Ann E. Jordan** on 16 Apr 1849. Ann was the daughter of John Jordan and Barbara Wilkins. John and Barbara were married on 15 Dec 1813. Ann E. Jordan Supinger was born 13 Nov 1826 and died 28 Nov 1904.

     Sarah E. Supinger was born 21 Jul 1849 and died 7 Jul 1939. She was married on 5 Mar 1877 to Christopher Fansler. Christopher was a farmer and a carpenter. He was the son of William and Ellen. William Fansler married Nelly Walters on 28 Jan 1833. William and his family resided in **dwelling 2003**. Christopher Fansler was born 27 Jul 1844 and died 24 Nov 1910. He was a member of the Confederate army. He later served as Superintendent of the Shenandoah County Infirmary for a 10 year period. Christopher was buried in the Massanutten Cemetery.

William Jacob Supinger Jr. was born 20 Nov 1850 and died 10 Oct 1921. He did not marry.

Robert H. Supinger was born 20 Sep 1854. He married Anice Richie on 19 Sep 1879. Anice was born in Richey, a town in Scott County, Indiana on 21 Nov 1856. Robert spent much of his life farming in Deep Creek, Washington.

Laura V. Supinger was born 3 Aug 1857 and died 2 Sep 1921. She was married to Samuel M. Byrd. She was the third wife of Mr. Byrd. Samuel was born in Shenandoah County but was a resident of Washington County, Maryland. He was the son of Mountz and Doretha. He was and 18 year old carpenters apprentice in **dwelling 966** at the time of this census. He was a widower on 20 Dec 1877 when he married Virginia C. Koontz. Virginia was the daughter of Harrison and Susan. Harrison Koontz married Susan Ann Hisey on 6 Oct 1842. Harrison Koontz, the father of Virginia, resided in **dwellinig 91**. Virginia was born 9 Jun 1842 and died 27 Jul 1881. Laura V. Supinger and Samuel M. Byrd were married on 28 Oct 1889. Samuel M. Byrd was born 7 May 1839 and died 21 Sep 1907. Virginia C. Koontz and Samuel M. Byrd were buried at the St. Pauls Lutheran Church Cemetery in Woodstock.

Lewis Jordan Supinger was born 29 Jan 1860 and died 16 Sep 1919. He married Annie Taylor on 25 Oct 1899. Annie was born in Winchester of 26 Apr 1868. In Apr 1903 Lewis moved with his family to Braddock, Pennsylvania where he earned a living as a steam hammer man.

RELATED FAMILY:

        Elizabeth Jordan, sister of Ann, married David Gillock on 27 Jun 1857 and resided in **dwelling 126**.

        Charlotte Jordan, sister of Ann, married Jacob Keller on 2 Oct 1852 and resided in **dwelling 1971**.

        Peter and **Sarah Supinger**, brother and sister of William, were residents in the family homeplace **dwelling 88**.

        Louisa Supinger, sister of William, married David Fravel on 11 Jan 1860 and was a resident in **dwelling 200**.

1850 CENSUS: **William Jacob Supinger** resided with his parents in dwelling 266 on page 19.

        Ann E. Jordan resided in dwelling 267 on page 19.

PAGE 13 WOODSTOCK   (Microfilm Page 839)

Dwelling 88   Family 88

Sarah Supinger	25		3200 265	Virginia
Peter M. Supinger	23	Blacksmith		"

      Sarah R. Supinger, the daughter of Peter and Sarah, was born 21 Sep 1833 and died 17 Feb 1888. Peter Supinger married Sarah Kinsley on 15 Mar 1820. Sarah R. Supinger never married and is buried in the Emanuel Lutheran Church Cemetery in Woodstock.

      Peter M. Supinger, was the brother of Sarah. He was born 4 Mar 1837 and died 28 Sep 1906. He was married to Mary E. Bair (Bear) on 12 Nov 1861. Mary was born 8 Nov 1838 and died 29 May 1921. She was the daughter of Michael S. and Barbara Ann. Michael S. Bair married Barbara Ann Effinger on Oct 28 1835. Michael Bair and his family resided in **dwelling 99**. Peter Supinger is reported to have been a veteran of the Civil War. There was a Peter Supinger who enlisted as a private on 24 Sep 1862 at Berryville, Virginia in the 18th Virginia Cavalry. He was present on 26 Mar 1863. He was detailed as the regimental bugler during the period Jan 1864 to 31 Oct 1864. Peter Supinger and Mary E. Bair Supinger were buried in the Emanuel Lutheran Church Cemetery.

RELATED FAMILY:

      Louisa Supinger, sister of Peter and Sarah, married David Fravel on 11 Jan 1860 and resided in **dwelling 200**.

      William J. Supinger, brother of Peter and Sarah, married Ann E. Jordan 16 Apr 1849 and resided in **dwelling 87**.

1850 CENSUS: Peter and **Sarah Supinger** resided in the household of their parents in Dwelling 266 on page 19.

PAGE 13 WOODSTOCK   (Microfilm Page 839)

Dwelling 89 Family 89

Peter P. Ramey	43	Wagon Maker 1200	420	Virginia
Margaret A. Ramey	42			"
Francis A. Ramey	17			"
William H. Ramey	14			"

Phillip Peter Ramey was the son of John and Rebecca. John Ramey married Rebecca Baker on 30 Dec 1812. Phillip married **Margaret Ann Myers** on 18 Sep 1838. The bondsman for this marriage was Hiram Myers. Upon the death of Margaret he was reported to have married a woman named Kate Martin.

Francis Ashberry Ramey was born in 1842 and died in Jan 1924. Unofficial postwar service records for the 33rd Virginia Infantry indicate that he was a member of that unit. However, no official service record has been located. His wife was Lucretia Belt. She was born in 1846 and died 11 Aug 1824. Francis and Lucretia were buried in the Massanutten Cemetery in Woodstock.

William H. Ramey died 22 Jan 1920 at the age of 74. He married Mary Elizabeth Stewart on 21 Dec 1868. She was the daughter of William T and Susan. William and his family resided in **dwelling 140**. Mary Stewart Ramey, died 26 Jan 1933 at the age of 87. There is a tombstone for William H. Ramey in Massanutten Cemetery. William's tombstone reports that he was a member of Chews Battery of the Virginia Artillery. He was listed as a member of that unit but no additional details of service are known.

1850 CENSUS: Phillip Peter Ramey and his family were located in dwelling 268 on page 19.

PAGE 13 WOODSTOCK (Microfilm Page 839)

Dwelling 90   Family 90

Ellen Haun	25	Seamstress	0	50	Virginia
Ann V. Haun	3				"
Joseph L. Haun	1				"

Ellen Haun was the daughter of George of Henry and Catherine. George of Henry Haun married **Catherine Sheetz** on 12 Mar 1823. Ellen's parents resided in **dwelling 1813**. Ellen was not married at the time of this census. Her children eventually took the name of her husband. Ellen Haun married Reuben S. Allen on 25 Oct 1866. Reuben was the son of George and Catherine. There is a marriage reported for George Allen to Catherine Foland on 1 Dec 1834. Reuben's father George married a much younger woman on 7 Dec 1846. He married Christina Sine. In the 1850 census she was only eight years older than Reuben. They resided in dwelling 116 on page 78 of the 1850 census.

Christina Sine Allen the step-mother of Reuben resided in **dwelling 591.**

   Annie V. Allen daughter of Ellen and the step daughter of Reuben S. Allen, was married to Henry A. Menger on 19 Apr 1877. Henry was born in Liognitz, Prussia and was the son of William George and Mary Ann.

RELATED FAMILY:
   Rebecca Haun, sister of Ellen, married Jacob Fauber (Fauver) on 18 Oct 1855 and resided in **dwelling 972.**
   Catherine Haun, sister of Ellen, married William Golladay on 28 Jan 1857 and was located in **dwelling 988.**
   George Haun, brother of Ellen, married Elizabeth Ridenour on 17 Oct 1859 and resided in **dwelling 1814.**

1850 CENSUS: **Ellen Haun** was a resident in the household of her parents. They resided in dwelling 475 on page 34.

PAGE 13 WOODSTOCK (Microfilm Page 839)

Dwelling 91 Family 91

Harrison Koontz	46	Blacksmith 0	75	Virginia	
Emily F. Hisey	48			"	
Sarah V. Koontz	16			"	
Ann M. A. Koontz	12			"	School
John H. Koontz	10			"	School
Robert G. Koontz	6			"	

   Harrison Koontz was born in 1814 and died in 1900. He was buried in the Massanutten Cemetery. Harrison was married on 6 Oct 1842 to Susan Ann Hisey. The bondsman for the marriage was Lewis J. Hisey. Susan had died prior to this census.

   Emily F. Hisey is believed to have been the sister of Susan Ann Hisey Koontz. She probably came to the household to assist with the rearing of her sisters children. Emily appears in the household of her mother Jemima in 1850. It is believed that Emily and Susan were the children of John and Jemima. John Hisey married Jemima (Mima) Carrier on 4 Apr 1804.

Sarah V. Koontz is believed to have been listed as Virgina C. Koontz in marriage records. She was born 9 Jun 1842 and died 27 Jul 1881. She was married to Samuel M. Byrd on 20 Dec 1877. Samuel M. Byrd was the son of Mountz and Doretha. He had been widowed at the time of this marriage. He was born in Shenandoah County but was a resident of Washington County, Maryland. The identity of his first wife is not known. Samuel was born 7 May 1839 and died 21 Sep 1907. Samuel and Virginia were buried in the St. Paul's Lutheran Church Cemetery in Woodstock. Upon the death of Virginia, Samuel was married to Laura V. Supinger. Laura was born on 3 Aug 1857 and died 21 Sep 1907. She was the daughter of William and Ann. William Jacob Supinger married Ann E. Jordan on 16 Apr 1849. William and his family resided in **dwelling 87**. Laura was born 3 Aug 1857 and died 21 Sep 1907.

Annie M. Koontz was married to Lemuel F. Coffman on 25 Apr 1877. She was born in 1848 and died 2 Jul 1915. She is buried in the St. Paul's Lutheran Church Cemetery. Lemuel F. Coffman was the son of Reuben and Sarah. Reuben Coffman married Sarah Miller on 13 Dec 1847.

John H. Koontz was born in 1850 and died 11 Feb 1935. His wife was listed as Emma L. Riddelle. He married Emma on 8 Feb 1883. She was the daughter of James and Rebecca. Emma was born in 1853 and died 15 Aug 1927. They were buried in the Massanutten Cemetery.

Robert G. Koontz was born 16 Sep 1853 and died 7 Aug 1918. He was married to Betty S. Fravel on 27 Dec 1877. Betty was the daughter of John H. and Sarah J. Bettie S. Fravel Koontz was born 5 Oct 1854 and died 24 May 1887. They were buried in the St. Paul's Lutheran Church Cemetery. On 10 Oct 1890 Robert G. Koontz married Maggie C. Evans. Her parents were not listed.

1850 CENSUS: Harrison Koontz and his family resided in dwelling 274 on page 20.

Emily F. Hisey resided with her mother in dwelling 314 on page 23.

PAGE 13   WOODSTOCK   (Microfilm Page 839)

Dwelling 92   Family 92

John Hays	40	Day Labor	500	70	Ireland
Margaret Hays	40				"
Johanna Hays	16				"
Thomas Hays	14				"
James Hays	12				"
Margaret Hays	6				Va. Sch
Timothy Kniesly	47	Day labor			Ireland
James Whane	36	" "			"
Michael Laughland	24	" "			"
Owen Smith	23	" "			"
James McNance	28	" "			" C'tRd
James Flernice	32	" "			"
Patrick Nugent	30	" "			"
Cornelius Cavanaugh	45	" "			"

Johanna Hays, daughter of John and Margaret, was married on 6 Nov 1866 to Thomas Hays. It should be noted that this was not the same Thomas who appears in this household. Thomas was a laborer who had been born in Ireland but was residing in Alexandria, Virginia. He was the son of Patrick and Margaret.

1850 CENSUS: No record of this household in 1850.

PAGE 13   WOODSTOCK   (Microfilm Page 839)

Dwelling 93   Family 93

Henry Clower	60		400	100	Virginia
Mary Allington	74				"
Sarah C. Offner	49	Glove Maker			"

Henry Clower was the son of George and Susannah. He was born in 1800 and probably never married. He lived with his sister and her daughter.

Mary Clower died 5 Apr 1865. She had originally married Henry Offner on 13 Sep 1806. That marriage produced one child, **Sarah C. Offner.** Sarah never married and earned her living as a glove maker. Mary Clower Offner married for the second time in 1823 to Jacob Allington.

RELATED FAMILY:

        Peter Hounshour had married Elizabeth Clower in 1816. She was the sister of Henry and Mary. She was deceased at the time of this census. Her husband had remarried and resided in **dwelling 130.**

        Mary Everly had married Samuel B. Clower on 24 Mar 1816. Samuel was the brother of Henry and Mary. Samuel was deceased and Mary lived with her son in **dwelling 109.**

1850 CENSUS: **Henry Clower** and **Sarah C. Offner** resided in dwelling 281 on page 20.

PAGE 14 WOODSTOCK **(Microfilm Page 840)**

Dwelling 94 Family 94

```
Michael Sourbaugh   56  Saddle Toll Plater  500 60   Penn
Lucy Sourbaugh      47                                Va.
Mary E. Baggot      16                                "
Nancy Fetzer        97                                "
```

        Michael Sourbaugh was married to **Lucy McCon**, a widow, on 1 Feb 1832. The bondsman for the marriage was Mike Melhorn. In the 1850 census, Michael and Lucy had a set of twins. They were Mary E. and Thomas Sourbaugh. The twins were six years old. They are not present in this household. However, sixteen year old **Mary E. Baggot** is interesting.

1850 CENSUS: **Michael Sourbaugh** and his family resided in dwelling 284 on page 20.

PAGE 14 WOODSTOCK **(Microfilm Page 840)**

Dwelling 95 Family 95

John Haas 71 Commissioner in the Chancery 1800 9075 Va.

        John Haas was the Sheriff of Shenandoah County in the 1850. He had married Clara Gore on 21 Mar 1831. The bondsman for that marriage was Loring Sibert. John was a very prominent man in the county. On 10 May 1814 he was appointed an Ensign in the "Light Infantry", the 1st battalion, 13th regiment. John Haas was one of the men selected on 3 Mar 1834 to solicit funds in the Woodstock area for the Valley Pike. A road that would extend from Winchester to Harrisonburg. He was also appointed trustee of the Woodstock Female Seminary on 13 Mar 1847.

1850 CENSUS: **John Haas** and his family resided in dwelling 278 on page 20. He had a son Erasmus who would marry Elizabeth Irwin on 28 Nov 1866. Erasmus served in the 10th Virginia Infantry during the Civil War. He was not located in the 1860 census.

PAGE 14 WOODSTOCK   **(Microfilm Page 840)**

Dwelling 96 Family 96

Ephramin Grabill	47	Master Saddler	1550	1500	Virginia
Caroline Grabill	47				Virginia
John H. Grabill	21			"	School
Caroline Day	8			"	School

Ephramin Grabill was born 1 Feb 1813 and died 6 Jul 1882. He was the son of Henry Grabill, a soldier in the War of 1812. He was married to **Caroline Donaldson** on 18 Oct 1836. Caroline was the daughter of Elizabeth. Her father was reported to have been one of the first captains of a steamship in the United States. She was born 6 Nov 1812 and died 3 Mar 1893. They were buried in the Massanutten Cemetery.

John Henry Grabill was born 8 Feb 1839 and died in 1922. He was a teacher at the time he married Mary L. Hollingsworth on 19 Dec 1866. She was the daughter of Isaac and Mary. Isaac Milton Hollingsworth married Mary C. Pritchard on 20 Feb 1843 in Frederick County. Mary was born in 1846 and died in 1934. They were buried in the Massanutten Cemetery. John was a graduate of Dickinson College in Pennsylvania. He enlisted on 3 Jun 1861 in Company C of the 33rd Virginia Infantry as a Lt. He dropped out of that unit on 14 Jun 1862 and joined the 35th Battalion Virginia Cavalry. He enlisted in Company E on 30 Jul 1862. He was appointed Captain on 9 Sep 1862. He was in the Battle of Brandy Station and indicated that he had two horses shot from under him. He wrote and later published a "Diary of a Soldier of the Stonewall Brigade". He was captured on 9 Jun 1863 at Beverly Ford. He was in the Old Capitol Prison on 1 Jul 1863 and was sent to Johnson Island on 8 Aug 1863. John was paroled and sent to City Point on 24 Feb 1865. When he returned to Shenandoah County he served as a school principal and the editor and publisher of a newspaper. One of his most

108

important accomplishments occurred when he was appointed
the first Superintendent of Schools for Shenandoah County.
He worked closely with Dr. William H. Ruffner the State
Superintendent of Schools. Ruffner has been referred to
as the "Horace Mann of Virginia.

The identity of **Caroline Day** has not been established.

1850 CENSUS: **Ephramin Grabill** and family resided in
dwelling 279 on page 20.

PAGE 14 WOODSTOCK (Microfilm Page 840)

Dwelling 97 Family 97

George M. Borum	26	Dentist-Surgeon	0	2000	Virginia
Louisa C. Borum	27				Pennsylvania
Nannie K. Borum	2				Virginia
Mary L. Borum	1				Pennsylvania

George Michael Borum was born 1 Apr 1834 and died
in 1911. He was the son of Isaac and Scotta. Isaac Borum
was married to Scottie Keller on 8 May 1828. Isaac Borum
and his family resided in **dwelling 1656.** The date of George
Michael Borum's marriage to **Louisa C** has not been
established. Death records indicated that her maiden name
was Louisa C. Funk. Louisa died 1 Mar 1915 in Lynchburg.
George Michael Borum enlisted in the 11th Virginia Cavalry
on 26 Apr 1863. He applied for detail at Lynchburg on 28
Oct 1863 to the Medical Directors Office. He was detailed
by SO N 289 para 2 DANVI 21 Nov 1863. George was absent
sick from 31 Oct 1863 to 20 Apr 1864. He was paroled at
Winchester 17 Apr 1865. George was 6' with light
complexion, light hair and blue eyes. He was elected clerk
of the Board of Education on 8 Apr 1871. As an elected
official in this position he earned $2.50 a day for six
hours when there was work to do. Later in his life he
lived for a period of time in Bedford County.

Nannie K. Borum died 10 Sep 1861 at the age of one
year, 2 months and 27 days old. Ironically a year to the
day earlier her sister Mary had died.

Mary L. Borum died of dysentary on 10 Sep 1860.
George Michael Borum and his daughters were buried in the
Mt. Zion United Methodist Church Cemetery.

RELATED FAMILY:
Mary Rebecca Borum, sister of George, married Henry Setzer on 25 Feb 1850 and resided in **dwelling 1626**.

1850 CENSUS: George Michael Borum was a clerk. He resided in dwelling 1696 on page 122. He resided in the home of James L. and Frances C. Miller.

PAGE 14 WOODSTOCK (Microfilm Page 840)

Dwelling 98 Family 98

Mary Farra	53		0	100	Virginia
Lucippa Farra	21	Seamstress			"
James M. Farra	19	Blacksmith			"
Frances M. Farra	17				"

Mary Hockman was married to John W. Farrar on 29 May 1828. The bondsman for that marriage was Joseph Hockman. Mary was the daughter of Henry and Catherine. Henry Hockman married Catherine Ortz (Artz) on 27 May 1774. Upon the death of Catherine Ortz Hockman, Henry married Betsy Ortz on 24 Jul 1797. Mary Hockman was the daughter of Henry and Betsy. Mary Hockman Farrar was also known as "Polly".

On 29 May 1866, **Mary Lucippa Farra** was married to Derostas E. W. Myers, the son of John and Eliza. John Myers married Eliza Evans on 12 Jun 1841. John Myers and his family resided in **dwelling 1920**. The bondsman for the marriage was W. W. Magruder. D.E.W. Myers died 29 Jul 1908. His second wife was Rebecca Huffman. D.E.W. Myers married Rebecca Huffman on 24 Nov 1870. She was the daughter of Andrew and Rebecca. Rebecca Gochenour Miley married Andrew Hoffman on 20 Mar 1834. Andrew Huffman and his family resided in **dwelling 272**. He was a farmer at the time of his marriage to Lucippa.

RELATED FAMILY:
William H. Farrar, son of Mary, was married on 6 Nov 1856 to Elizabeth Catherine Cooper, the daughter of Joseph H. and Harriet Artz Cooper. William was reported to have been killed in combat during the Civil War. He is believed to have served in Company C of the 7th Virginia Cavalry. His widow later married Samuel Rinker in **dwelling 2**.

1850 CENSUS: **Mary Farrar** and family resided in dwelling 189 on page 14.

PAGE 14 WOODSTOCK **(Microfilm Page 840)**

Dwelling 99 Family 99

Michael Bair	49	Saddler	0 150	Maryland	
Barbara Bair	48			Virginia	
Mary E. Bair	20			"	
Virginia M. Bair	12			"	School
William H. Bair	18	Saddler		"	

Michael S. Bair was married on 28 Oct 1835 to **Barbara Ann Effinger**. Barbara was the daughter of Ignatious and Barbara. Barbara's mother was born in Pennsylvania and resided with Michael and his family in 1850.

Mary E. Bair was born 8 Nov 1838 and died 29 May 1921. She was married on 12 Nov 1861 to Peter M. Supinger. Peter resided in **dwelling 88**. He was the son of Peter and Catherine. Peter Supinger married Sarah Catherine Kniesly on 15 Mar 1820. Peter M. Supinger was born 4 Mar 1837 and died 28 Sep 1906. Peter and Mary were buried at Emanuel Lutheran Church Cemetery in Woodstock.

William H. Bair was 5'9" with light complexion, blue eyes and dark hair. He enlisted in Company F of the 10th Virginia Infantry as a Private. He was taken prisoner at Woodstock on 12 Dec 1863. He was sent to Athenum Prison in Wheeling, West Virginia and was transferred to Camp Chase in Ohio on 18 Dec 1863. He was released under the Oath of Allegiance on 16 Mar 1865. Federal records list him as a deserter.

1850 CENSUS: Michael S. Bair and family resided in **dwelling 285** on **page 20.**

111

PAGE 14 WOODSTOCK   (Microfilm Page 840)

Dwelling 100   Family 100

Name	Age	Occupation		
William H. Few	36	Master Tailor	1000	115
		Virginia		
Lucinda Few	25		"	
Lucy E. Few	4		"	
Hatta Few	1		"	
Without name	18days		"	
John W. Few	15	Tailors App.	"	
Mary A. Few	77		"	Blind
Elizabeth Reifsnider	45		Maryland	
Mary C. Reifsnider	22		Virginia	

William H. Few was the son of Samuel and Mary. He was born 8 Dec 1823 and died 13 Oct 1892. He was married to **Lucinda Boehm** on 13 Sep 1852. Lucinda was the daughter of David and Regina. David Boehm married Regina Swanie on 29 Aug 1828. Lucinda Boehm Few was born 2 Jul 1834 and died 3 Apr 1922. William and Lucinda were buried in the Emanuel Lutheran Church Cemetery.

Lucy E. Few died 7 May 1933. She was married to William P. Samuels, a railroad employee on 15 Aug 1887. He was the son of Joseph G and Sarah. This family resided in **dwelling 218.**

Hattie Howard Few was born 10 Aug 1858 and died 17 Aug 1878. She was buried near her parents in the Emanuel Lutheran Church Cemetery.

The 18 day old female is believed to have been **Bettie Few.** She was born in 1860 and died in 1928. She married Phillip Gray Fravel. Phillip was the son of Phillip J and Emma E. J. Phillip J. Fravel married Emma E. J. Koontz on 15 Mar 1854. They resided in **dwelling 111.** Phillip was born in 1860 and died in 1931. Phillip and Bettie were also buried at the Emanuel Lutheran Church Cemetery.

Mary A. Few was the mother of William H. Few. She was the wife of Samuel Few. On 28 May 1817 there was marriage in Frederick County for Samuel Few to Mary Ann Pritchard. Samuel was born 7 Jun 1852 and died 25 Oct 1859. He was buried in the family plot at the Emanuel Lutheran Church Cemetery. Mary was buried next to him but her tombstone was too deep to read. According to

112

Shenandoah County death records Mary Ann Few was born in Frederick County, Virginia. She was 79 years, 3 months and 18 days old when she died on 28 Oct 1860. The cause of death was pneumonia.

John W. Few appears to have been the nephew of William. He was an apprentice. He was born 22 May 1843 and died 6 Jan 1868. His tombstone records that he was the son of Stephen J. and Catherine. He is buried with other family members at the Emanuel Church.

Elizabeth Reifsnider and her daughter Mary Reifsnider resided with the Few family at the time of the 1850 census.

RELATED FAMILY

Lydia S. Boehm, sister of Lucinda, married David S. Rau on 7 Dec 1858 and resided in **dwelling 65**.

Abner Boehm, brother of Lucinda, resided in the home of George and Sarah Spiker. They were residents in **dwelling 1713**.

1850 CENSUS: William H. Few resided in the household of his father. They resided in dwelling 288 on page 21.

Lucinda Boehm resided in the household of her father David. They resided in dwelling 2025 on page 146.

PAGE 14 WOODSTOCK (Microfilm Page 840)

Dwelling 101   Family 101

John Keffer	57	Hatter	1000	100	Virginia	
Mary Keffer	53				"	
Mary E. Keffer	22				"	
Ann M. Keffer	20				"	
Susan E. Keffer	14				"	School
Addison Keffer	11				"	School

There was a marriage for **John Kiffer** to **Mary Byers** on 15 May 1828. The bondsman for that marraige was David Fravel.

RELATED FAMILY:

In the 1850 census John and Mary are reported to have had a son named William H. Keffer. He was a physician.   Dr. William H. Keffer resided in **dwelling 1683.**

1850 CENSUS: **John Keffer** and his family resided in dwelling 282 on page 20.

PAGE 15 WOODSTOCK   **(Microfilm Page 841)**

Dwelling 102   Family 102

Obed Coffman	37	Deputy Sheriff	1200	2052	Virginia
Catherine Coffman	33				"
Milton Coffman	13				" School
Alice Coffman	3				"

Obed Coffman was born 1 Jun 1823 and died 15 Oct 1872.   He was married to **Catherine Ann Snarr** on 27 Feb 1846.   Catherine was the daughter of John and Mary Hottel Snarr.   Catherine Ann Snarr Coffman was born 26 Jul 1824 and died 12 Aug 1897.   When Obed Coffman died Catherine Ann married Henry Hottel. Henry was a widower.   He had married Catherine Coffman on 18 Jun 1837. Henry's first wife died 10 Jan 1875.   Henry Hottel was born 5 Apr 1817 and died 10 Feb 1890.   He was the son of Joseph and Catherine.   Joseph Hottel married Catherine Snarr on 15 Jun 1815. Henry and his first wife were buried in the Pugh's Run Cemetery. Henry Hottel resided in **dwelling 1926** at the time of this census.   Obed Coffman was buried in the Emanuel Lutheran Church Cemetery in Woodstock.

Milton Coffman was born in 1846 and died in 1932. He was reported to have served in the Confederate army, although no record of his service has been located.   He was a merchant and a banker.   He is credited with reorganizing Shenandoah County Bank at the conclusion of the Civil War. He served as a cashier at the bank and was also the Superintendent of the Woodstock Lutheran Church Sunday School.   On 28 Jan 1869 Milton married Emma G. Heller. Emma was born in 1851 and died in 1916.   Milton and Emma were buried in the Massanutten Cemetery in Woodstock.   Emma was the daughter of Moritz and Elizabeth.   Moritz Heller married Emma Pitman on 19 Apr 1842.   Elizabeth Pitman Heller and family resided in **dwelling 118.**

Alice Cornelia Coffman was born 11 Jul 1857 and died 25 Jan 1916.   She was married on 3 Oct 1883 to the Reverend Peter L. Miller.   Peter was a Lutheran Minister and he died 14 Apr 1918.

114

1850 CENSUS: Obed Coffman and family resided in dwelling
                2072 on page 149.

PAGE 15 WOODSTOCK   (Microfilm Page 841)

Dwelling 103   Family 103

Charles A. Welch	46	Innkeeper	15850	6475	Maryland
Mary A. Welch	43				Virginia
Mary C. Welch	22				"
Mark Welch	21				" School
Richard Welch	18				" School
Robert P. Grove	43		0	600	"
					Deaf and Dumb
Thomas Pritchard	22	Mail Agent R.R.			"
Thomas Banks	32	(Mulatto) Barber			"

        Charles Welch was born in 1811 and died in 1892.
His wife Mary A. was born in 1816 and died in 1892. They
were buried in the Massanutten Cemetery in Woodstock.
Charles operated a hotel in Woodstock. It had originally
been owned by a man named Reamer and later an individual
named Shockley was the owner. It was the scene of a number
of historical events. President Andrew Jackson was a guest
of the hotel as he made the trip back to Tennessee.
President Millard Fillmore was reported to have held a
reception in the hotel.

        Mary Catherine Welch was born in 1838 and died in
1910. She was married on 23 Apr 1861 to Nehemiah Fountain.
Nehemiah was a lawyer from Caroline County, Maryland. He
was the son of Nehemiah and Lydia. Nehemiah was born in
1832 and died in 1876. He was a Captain in the 10th
Virginia Infantry during the Civil War. Mary Catherine and
Nehemiah were buried in the Massanutten Cemetery.

        Mark Welch was born in 1840 and died in 1862.
Mark enlisted in Company F of the 10th Virginia Infantry
and was commissioned a 2nd Lt. at Woodstock on 18 Apr 1861.
He was promoted to Captain on 18 Oct 1861. Mark died
during the war of typhoid fever. He was buried in the
Massanutten Cemetery.

        Richard Welch was born in 1841. The 1850 census
reports that he was born in Maine. Richard enlisted on 18
Apr 1861 as a private in Company F of the 10th Virginia
Infantry. He was transferred to Company D of the 18th
Virginia Cavalry on 17 Feb 1864. Richard Welch was killed

in action at Winchester in 21 Sep 1864. This may have
been the Third Battle of Winchester. He is buried with his
family in the Massanutten Cemetery.

1850 CENSUS: Charles A. Welch and family resided in
                   dwelling 286 on page 20.
                   Thomas Banks, resided in dwelling 834 on page
                   58. This was the residence of Rebecca
                   Moore. Rebecca was a black and was the
                   head of an independent household in 1850.

PAGE 15   WOODSTOCK   (Microfilm Page 841)

Dwelling 104   Family 104

Robert Cahoun	33	Carriage Maker	700	100	Virginia
Margaret Cahoun	57				Ireland
Margaret Hounshour	9				" School

      Robert H. Cahoun was the son of William and
Margaret. He died 14 Jul 1891. Robert married Mary E.
Snarr on 28 Nov 1872. She was the daughter of John and
Mary. Mary died 22 Jan 1909. Robert Cahoun enlisted in
Company D of the 18th Virginia Cavalry on 1 Apr 1864. He
joined the unit at Woodstock and was present from 1 May
1864 until 31 Oct 1864.

      Margaret Cahoun widow of William Cahoun. They were
both immigrants from Ireland. Margaret was born in 1789
and died 10 Jan 1862. She was buried in the St. Pauls
Lutheran Church Cemetery in Woodstock.

      Margaret Hounshour, the granddaughter of Margaret
Cahoun, was the daughter of Peter and Jane. Peter
Hounshour married Jane Cahoun on 5 May 1846. Peter
resided in **dwelling 116.** Jane Cahoun Hounshour died prior
to 1858 as Peter was described as a widower when he married
Frances "Fanny" Hamrick on 18 Mar 1858. Fanny was from
Rappahannock County, Virginia. She was the daughter of
Samuel and his wife Leah. Margaret Hounshour married
Thomas Gideon Hamrick on 29 Jul 1874. Thomas was the
brother of Fanny Hamrick Hounshour, the step-mother of
Margaret. Thomas resided in **dwelling 1855.** Margaret died
prior to 1892 as Gideon was married to Mary Ann Windle on
4 Feb 1892. Mary Ann was the daughter of Samuel and
Elizabeth. There was a marriage of Samuel D. Windle to
Elizabeth Lichliter on 28 Apr 1868. Mary Ann Windle

Hamrick died 28 Sep 1960. She was 92 years old. Gideon
Hamrick was a shoemaker. He died 29 Nov 1905.

1850 CENSUS: Robert Cahoun was a resident in dwelling 247
on page 18. This was the household of
Jacob and Ann Clinedinst. Robert may have
been an apprentice.

Margaret Cahoun was a resident in dwelling
283 on page 20. This was the household
of her daughter Jane and son-in-law Peter
Hounshour.

PAGE 15   WOODSTOCK   (Microfilm Page 841)

Dwelling 105   Family 105

Isiah Fetzer	30	Farmer	0	75	Virginia
Sarah Fetzer	26				"

1850 CENSUS: No record of this family has been located.

PAGE 15   WOODSTOCK   (Microfilm Page 841)

Dwelling 106   Family 106

George B. Rodeffer	25	Merchant	0	13000	Virginia
Samantha Rodeffer	23				"
Carrol L. Rodeffer	7m	(Male)			"

George B. Rodeffer was the son of David and Ann.
David Rodeffer married Ann Sager on 3 Sep 1830. David and
his family resided in **dwelling 139.** George's wife was
listed in some records as **Jerasha.** According to death
records she was the daughter of James L. Johnson and she
had been born in Frederick County, Virginia. Within months
of this census George and Jerasha were dead in an epidemic
of typhoid fever. George died 1 Aug 1860 at the age of 26
years, 6 months. Jerasha followed on 15 Nov 1860. She was
23 years and 6 months. David Rodeffer reported both of the
deaths. No evidence has been located regarding the fate
of the child in this household.

1850 CENSUS: **George Rodeffer,** was a 15 year old resident
in the household of his parents. They
resided in dwelling 257 on page 18.

PAGE 15   WOODSTOCK   (Microfilm Page 841)

Dwelling 107   Family 107

```
Joseph H. Clower    45  Merchant  800  19300      Virginia
Catherine Clower    35                               "
Phillip J. Hockman  22  Clerk                        "
```

Joseph H. Clower was born 19 May 1814 and died 1 Apr 1867. He was the son of John and Frances. John Clower married Frances Grove on 15 Jan 1809. Joseph, according to Clower family accounts, did not marry. That is probably true although a Frederick County, Virginia 6 Jun 1843 marriage record is of some interest. Joseph H. Clower married Eliza Pingley on that date. The primary problem with this household involves the identity of **Catherine Clower**. Clower family history contends that she married Isaac Bauserman on 29 Jan 1849. This does not appear to have a basis in fact. The Catherine Clower who married Isaac was the daughter of Samuel and Mary Everly Clower. Mary Everly Clower resided in **dwelling 109**. To further confuse the issue it appears that the name was actually Isaac Bowman not Bauserman. Catherine Clower Bowman resided in **dwelling 204** at the time of this census. Until further evidence is forthcoming it appears that the Catherine Clower listed in this household was the unmarried sister of Joseph H. Clower.

Phillip J. Hockman was the son of Joseph and Margaret. Joseph Hockman married Margaret Fravel on 20 Nov 1830. Phillip was born 11 Mar 1837 and died 29 Aug 1862. He had enlisted in Company F of the 10th Virginia Infantry on 18 Apr 1861 as a private. He was absent from the unit on 10 Jul 1861 as a result of illness. He was promoted to 3rd Sgt on 3 Apr 1862. Sgt Hockman was killed in action at Manassas on 29 Aug 1862.

RELATED FAMILY:
  Elizabeth Clower, sister of Joseph, married George Harrison Ott on 29 Nov 1841 and resided in **dwelling 125**.
  Isabella Clower, sister of Joseph, married Alexander Anderson on 19 Sep 1838 and resided in **dwelling 155**.
  Jacob B. Clower, brother of Joseph, married Julia Ann Haas and resided in **dwelling 176**.

1850 CENSUS: Joseph H. Clower and numerous brothers and sisters resided in the household of their mother Frances. They were residents of dwelling 277 on page 20.

PAGE 15 WOODSTOCK   (Microfilm Page 841)

Dwelling 108 Family 108

William Goladay   44 Merchant 0 100   Virginia
Susan J. Goladay   30   "
Otmay Goladay   6   "

1850 CENSUS: William Goladay was a 30 year old merchant residing in the hotel of Charles Welsh. They were located in dwelling 286 on page 20.

PAGE 15 WOODSTOCK   (Microfilm Page 841)

Dwelling 109 Family 109

Samuel V. R. Clower   26 Clerk 0 100 Virginia
Mary Clower   62   "

Mary Everly was born 17 Jan 1796 and died of "paralaes" on 23 Oct 1878. She was married to Samuel B. Clower on 24 Mar 1816. Samuel B. Clower was the son of George and Susannah Clower. He was born 25 Sep 1792 and died 7 Jan 1857.

Samuel Valentine Rigden Clower was born 1833 and died 17 Jun 1898. He was married to Mary J. Burner on 17 Jul 1865. Mary J. was born 1847 and died in 1924. She was the daughter of Joseph and Barbara. Joseph Burner married Barbara Richard on 26 May 1841. Joseph Burner and family resided in **dwelling 2006**. Samuel Valentine Rigden Clower enlisted as a private in Company F of the 10th Virginia Infantry on 18 Apr 1861. He was appointed Sgt. Major on 26 May 1861. He was absent sick and was eventually assigned to the hospital at Staunton on 1 May 1862. There is no further record of his service after the illness. Samuel and Mary were buried in the Massanutten Cemetery.

RELATED FAMILY:

Catherine Clower, the daughter of Mary Everly Clower, was married to Isaac N. Bowman on 29 Jan 1849. Shenandoah County marriage records refer to his

119

surname as Bauserman. However, Catherine and Isaac lived in the Clower household in 1850. They were listed as Bowman. In the 1860 census they are also listed as Bowman. They resided in **dwelling 204**.

Joseph H. Clower, nephew of Mary, resided in **dwelling 107**.

1850 CENSUS: **Samuel V. R. Clower** appears in dwelling 236 on page 17. He resided with his father and mother.

PAGE 15 WOODSTOCK **(Microfilm Page 841)**

Dwelling 110 Family 110

Bernadotte Schmitt	29	Druggist	700	3150	Virginia
Barbara S. Schmitt	27				Maryland
Nelson B. Schmitt	4				Virginia
Cooper D. Schmitt	6m				"
Lydia V. E. Bender	21				Maryland

Bernadotte Schmitt was born 28 Feb 1831 and died 30 Nov 1905. He was the son of John G. and Leah. John G. Schmitt married Leah Fry on 9 Jul 1821. John G. Schmitt was an immigrant from Switzerland. He was a merchant and physician in the town of Woodstock. Bernadotte married Barbara S. Bender. Barbara Bender Schmitt was 64 years, 8 months and 18 days old when she died on 1 Jul 1897. Bernadotte and Barbara were buried in the Massanutten Cemetery.

Nelson Bender Schmitt was born 3 Nov 1855 and died 29 Mar 1906. He never married.

Cooper Davis Schmitt was born in 1859 and died in 1910. He was a physician. Cooper married Rose Vernon Everly on 15 Jun 1885. She was the daughter of John F. and Susan. Rose Everly Schmitt was born in 1865 and died in 1915. Cooper was a professor at the University of Tennessee. He also came back to Shenandoah County to assist with running the family drug store. Cooper and Rose had a son Bernadotte E. Schmitt who was born on 19 May 1886. He earned his B.A. from the University of Tennessee where his father taught and then went to Oxford University as a Rhodes Scholar. During the first world war Bernadotte served as a 2nd Lt. with the field artillery. After the war he returned to the academic life at Western Reserve University. He published several historical works including **England and Germany 1740-1914.** Bernadotte was listed in **Who's Who in America.**

1850 CENSUS: Bernadotte Schmitt resided in the household of John Mumaw. They were residents of dwelling 109.

PAGE 15 WOODSTOCK (Microfilm Page 841)

Dwelling 111 Family 111

Phillip J. Fravel	30	Merchant	1700	20300	Virginia
Emma E. J. Fravel	29				"
Edward H. Fravel	5				"
Charles W. Fravel	3				"
Phillip G. Fravel	1				"
Frances Fravel	50				"

      Phillip James Fravel was born 22 Aug 1831 and died 28 Jan 1909. He was the son of David and Frances. David Fravel married Frances Miller on 1 Oct 1828. Frances Miller Fravel resided with her son in this household. Phillip was married to **Emma E. J. Koontz** on 15 Mar 1854. Emma was born 25 Jan 1830 and died 11 Feb 1899. She was the daughter of John and Mary. John Koontz had married Mary Thompson on 10 Sep 1818. John and his family resided in **dwelling 602.** Emeline "Emma" Koontz had been very well educated and was sent to a private school in Philadelphia for her training. Phillip and Emma were buried in the Emanuel Lutheran Church Cemetery in Woodstock. Phillip James Fravel had indicated in some family records that he served in the Confederate army. No record of service has yet been located.

      Edward Hutson Fravel was born 30 Mar 1855 and died 19 Oct 1918. He was educated as a physician at the Jefferson Medical College. He went to Poca, West Virginia as a specialist in eye, ear, nose and throat illness. On 2 May 1882 he married Bettie Stato Stewart, the daughter of James and Martha. Bettie was from Raymond City, West Virginia. Bettie was born 4 May 1855 and died in Jul 1925. Edward and his wife were buried at the Spring Hill Cemetery in Charleston, West Virginia.

      Charles William Fravel was born 18 Sep 1856 and died 29 Jul 1897. He was an accountant and was buried near his parents.

Phillip Gray Fravel was born in 1860 and died in 1931. His wife was Bettie Stackhouse Few. She was the daughter of William and Lucinda. William Few married Lucinda Boehm on 13 Sep 1852. William and his family including the new born Bettie resided in **dwelling 100**. Bettie was born in 1860 and died in 1928. Phillip followed in the footsteps of his father and grandfather and became a merchant. When his father gave up the business, Phillip went to Philadelphia and worked for the large Wanamakers Store. For 28 years he was employed by the Lit Brothers Store in that same city. He eventually moved back to Woodstock when his health became poor. Phillip and Bettie were buried in the Massanutten Cemetery.

Frances Miller was a descendant of Jacob Miller Sr. the founder of the town of Woodstock. She was the daughter of Phillip and Elizabeth. Phillip Miller married Elizabeth Grove on 1 Jan 1794. Frances was born 21 Apr 1807 and died 16 Feb 1888. She married David Fravel on 1 Oct 1828. David was the son of George and Elizabeth Bushong Fravel. Elizabeth had been born in York, Pennsylvania. George opened the first family store as one room in the family residence. David followed his father in the business. David was born 28 Jul 1796 and died 12 Oct 1833.

RELATED FAMILY:

          George H. H. Koontz, brother of Emma, resided in **dwelling 601**.

1850 CENSUS: **Frances Miller Fravel** resided in dwelling 300 on page 22. This was the household of Daniel Miller. He is believed to have been her brother. Her mother, 72 year old Elizabeth Grove Miller was also in the residence.

          Emma E. J Koontz was a resident in the household of her parents. They resided in dwelling 202 on page 15.

PAGE 16 WOODSTOCK   (Microfilm Page 842)

Dwelling 112   Family 112

| William Dosh | 47 Saddle/Harness Maker 1300 200 Virignia | |

Elizabeth A. A. Dosh	35	Virginia
Augusta A. Dosh	16	"
Virginia P. Dosh	12	" School
George F. Dosh	15	" School
William L. Dosh	10	" School
Thomas L. Dosh	8	" School
Mary W. Dosh	6	"
John L. Dosh	6m	"

William Dosh was born 24 Feb 1813 and died 25 Mar 1897. He was married to **Elizabeth Ware** on 25 Jun 1838. Elizabeth was the daughter of Gustavius and Mary Ann. Gustavius M. Ware married Anna Maria Fry on 17 Oct 1817. Mary Ann Fry Ware resided with this family in 1850. Elizabeth died 13 Aug 1877 at the age of 58 years, 9 months and 22 days old. William and Elizabeth were buried in the Emmanuel Lutheran Church Cemetery in Woodstock.

Augustus Ann Dosh was born 9 Oct 1842 and died 20 Jun 1891. She was buried near her parents.

Virginia Pamelia Dosh was born 23 Nov 1846 and died 27 Nov 1928. She was also buried in the Emmanuel Lutheran Church Cemetery.

George Fry Dosh was born 18 Jan 1845 and died 11 Jun 1906. He was buried near other family members.

William Linn Dosh was born in 1848 and died 16 Mar 1924. He was one of the few members of this family to have ever married. He married Ann Heller on 21 Mar 1883. Ann was the daughter of Moritz and Elizabeth. Moritz Heller married Elizabeth Pitman on 19 Apr 1842. Ann and her parents resided in **dwelling 118**. Ann Heller Dosh was born in 1852 and died 7 Feb 1931. William and Ann were buried in the Emmanuel Lutheran Church Cemetery.

Thomas L. Dosh was born 10 Aug 1850 and died 2 Sep 1923. He shares the same burial site as other members of this family.

Mary Ware Dosh was born 23 Mar 1855 and died 23 Sep 1913. She was buried at the Emmanuel Church Cemetery.

1850 CENSUS: **William Dosh** and his family were residents of dwelling 255 on page 18.

PAGE 16 WOODSTOCK   (Microfilm Page 842)

Dwelling 113 Family 113

John A. Krause	30	Boot and Shoemaker	0 50		Rodenburg
Ann E. Krause	21				Virginia
Eliza A. Krause	18Days				"
Moses Shifflet	17	Apprentice			"
Christina Barr	12				"

John A. Krause was born in Rodenburg, Germany. He was the son of Charley and Julia. He was married on 2 Aug 1859 to **Ann Elizabeth Barrow.** Ann was born in Frederick County. She was the daughter of Elijah and Alice. Elijah Barrow married Alice (Ally) L Steel on 10 Apr 1834. This marriage took place in Frederick County, Virginia.

The 1850 census reveals that Ann had a 2 year old sister in her household. The infants name was Christina. It is entirely possible that the Christina Barrow in that household was the 12 year old **Christina Barr** in this residence. If so she would be the daughter of Elijah and Alice.

1850 CENSUS: Ann Elizabeth Barrow Krause was a resident in dwelling 244 on page 66. This was the household of her parents. Her sister Christina was present in that household as well.

PAGE 16 WOODSTOCK   (Microfilm Page 842)

Dwelling 114 Family 114

James G. Fravel	52	Clerk in Chancery	2500 400 S Car	
Mary A. Fravel	51			Virginia
Sydney H. Fravel	23			"
James M. Fravel	22	Farmer		"
Catherine J. Fravel	20			"
Lucretia Fravel	14			" School
Robert J. Fravel	11			" School
Emma S. Fravel	8			" School

James Gregory Fravel was the son of John Bunyan and Mary Gregory Fravel. John and Mary were married in 1807. James was born 28 Sep 1808 and died 22 Aug 1875. He was born in Danville, Virginia and soon after moved with his family to South Carolina. The family eventually settled in Berkeley County, West Virginia. James was an attorney. On 6 Nov 1834 he married **Mary A. Fravel**. Mary was the cousin of James. She was the daughter of Henry Fravel and Barbara Fetzer. Henry and Barbara had married in 1808. John Bunyan Fravel and Henry Fravel were brothers.

Sydney Harris Fravel was born 31 Jan 1837 and died 19 Dec 1888. She was married to Josiah Hawes Davis on 11 Nov 1861. Josiah was born in Alexandria, Virginia. He was a mail agent and was the son of Josiah and Sarah M. Josiah was born in 1816 and died in 1871. Sydney and Josiah were buried in the Massanutten Cemetery.

James Marshall Fravel was born 2 May 1838. He enlisted on 3 Jun 1861 in Company C of the 33rd Virginia Infantry. He was absent sick in Jan and Feb of 1862. He was absent again in May of 1862 on sick leave. James was AWOL from Jun 1862 to May 1863. He was AWOL from Sep 1 to 13 Nov 1864. James was wounded in action at Bethel Church. He was paroled on 17 Apr 1865 at Winchester. James married Martha Stockwell on 29 Sep 1880. He was a tinsmith. Martha was from Barbour County, West Virginia. She was the daughter of Isaac and Mary.

Catherine Jane "Kate" Fravel was born 17 Mar 1840 and died 2 Apr 1906. She married George Christopher Hamman on 27 Jun 1869. He was the son of George and Catherine. George Hamman had married Catherine Schmucker 24 Mar 1827. George Christopher Hamman was born 8 Oct 1838 and died 11 Sep 1920. He was a 1st Lt. in Company F of the 10th Virginia Infantry during the Civil War. At the time of this census he was a resident of **dwelling 174.**

Lucretia Nesbit Fravel was born 24 Aug 1845.

Robert Gregory Fravel was born 5 May 1848 and died 16 May 1867.

Emmeline Susan Fravel was born 3 Nov 1851 and died 18 Aug 1921. She was married to William Henry Storm, a railway engineer, on 18 Nov 1878. He was the son of John C. and Ann E. William was born at Harpers Ferry, West Virginia on 8 Apr 1851 and died 15 Nov 1906. Emma and

William were buried in the Massanutten Cemetery.

RELATED FAMILY:

Catherine Fravel, sister of Mary, married George Rye on 2 Oct 1833 and resided in **dwelling 156.**

David Fravel, brother of Mary, married Louisa Supinger on 11 Jan 1860 and resided in **dwelling 200.** In addition, Mary's step-mother Catherine Lichliter Fravel and her half brother Joseph were in residence in that household.

George Fravel, brother of Mary, married Harriet Myers on 6 Nov 1833 and resided in **dwelling 177.**

Frederick Fravel, brother of Mary, married Ellen Catherine Miller on 24 Aug 1840. He was deceased. However, his widow was a resident of **dwelling 201.**

John Henry Fravel, brother of Mary, married Sarah Jane Bruce on 4 Jul 1848 and resided in **dwelling 145.**

Henry Clay Fravel, son of James and Mary, resided in **dwelling 199.**

1850 CENSUS: James G. Fravel and his family resided in dwelling 326 on page 24.

PAGE 16   WOODSTOCK   (Microfilm Page 842)

Dwelling 115   Family 115

Mary C. Spengler	41	0 126		Virginia
Samuel M. Spengler	19	Clerk		"
Alice A Spengler	17			"
Laura S. Spengler	14			" School
Ella E. Spengler	11			"
John J. Spengler	7			"
Mary C. Spengler	6			"
Amos L. Spengler	3			"
Sarah Preston	8	(Black)		"

Mary C. B. Redman, the daughter of John and Ann was born on 27 Sep 1817 in Westmoreland County, Virginia. She died 12 Apr 1883. Mary married **Cyrus Spengler**. Cyrus was the son of Anthony and Catherine. Anthony Spengler married Catherine Kendrick on 25 Feb 1796. Cyrus was born 10 Jan 1816. He was not in the household at the time of this census. He was reported to have enlisted in Company F of the 10th Virginia Infantry on 17 Jun 1862. He was a private. He transferred from Company F to the 3rd Virginia Militia on 1 Apr 1862. At the time Cyrus would have been

46 years old. Military records indicate at some point he provided a substitute. There is no record for Cyrus and the military after 31 Dec 1864 when he was reported "sick at home". He died prior to 1900 and Mary and Cyrus were both buried in the Emmanuel Lutheran Church Cemetery.

Samuel M. Spengler died at the age of 66 in North Carolina in May of 1906. He had resided for many years as a clerk in the city of Baltimore. He was 5'5" with light complexion, dark hair and dark eyes. He enlisted on 18 Apr 1861 as a private in Company F of the 10th Virginia Infantry. He was absent sick from 16 Aug until Oct 1861. He was promoted to 1st Corp. on 3 Apr 1862 and was detailed as a clerk on 7 Feb 1863. Samuel was taken prisoner at Spotsylvania Courthouse on 12 May 1864. He was sent to Fort Delaware on 20 May 1864. He was released on 15 Jun 1865. Samuel was married to Sarah Dosh on 6 Dec 1880. Sarah was the daughter of John G. and Rebecca. John and Rebecca resided in **dwelling 1718**. Sarah Dosh Spengler died at Washington, D.C. on 2 Feb 1938.

Laura S. Spengler was married to John F. Sheiry on 4 Sep 1872. John was a merchant from Franklin County, Pennsylvania. He was the son of Gideon and Elizabeth.

Emma Etheridge Spengler was married to William B. Lauck on 14 Sep 1876. He was born in Rockingham County, Virginia and was residing in Keyser City, West Virginia at the time of the marriage. He was the son of J. B. and Hanna J.

John Jett Spengler died at the age of 54 on 6 Apr 1906. Ford was the maiden name of his wife.

Amos Letcher Spengler was born in 1857 and died 7 Nov 1927. He was married to Emma Cornelia Balthis on 28 Oct 1896. Cornelia was the daughter of John Frederick and Mary. John F. Balthis and Mary Yost were married on 5 Apr 1848. John Frederick Balthis and his family resided in **dwelling 1716**. Cornelia was born in 1853 and died 24 Feb 1931. Amos and Cornelia were buried in the Riverview Cemetery in Strasburg.

RELATED FAMILY:
    Elizabeth B. Spengler, thought to have been the sister of Cyrus, married Henry Grove on 9 Mar 1829 and resided in **dwelling 1690**.

1850 CENSUS: **Cyrus Spengler** and family resided in dwelling 391 on page 28.

PAGE 16   WOODSTOCK   (Microfilm Page 842)

Dwelling 116   Family 116

Peter Hounshour	39	Jailer	20	873	Virginia
Frances Hounshour	19				"
Robert Hounshour	13				" School
Samuel Hounshour	9				" School
Ida E. Hounshour	1				"

       Peter E. Hounshour Jr. was the son of Peter E. Hounshour and his wife Elizabeth. Peter E. Hounshour Sr. resided in **dwelling 130.** Peter Jr. was married to Jane Cahoun on 5 May 1846. Jane was the daughter of Irish immigrants William and Margaret Cahoun. Margaret resided in **dwelling 104.** Jane Cahoun Hounshour was born 6 Mar 1826 and died 14 Nov 1855. She was buried at the St. Paul's Reformed Church in Woodstock. Upon the death of Jane, Peter was married to **Frances "Fanny" Hamrick** on 18 Mar 1858. She was the daughter of Samuel and Mary. In Stickley's obituary book, Sarah F. Hounshour died 28 Jan 1922 at the age of 84.

       Robert C. Hounshour was married on 29 Apr 1873 to Ophelia Clinedinst. She was the daughter of John and Martha. John and Martha resided in **dwelling 167.** Robert was a wagon maker at the time of his marriage to Ophelia. His name appears on the role of the Eighth Star Artillery during the Civil War.

       Samuel B. Hounshour was born in 1851 and died 25 Aug 1866. He was buried at the St. Paul's Reformed Church Cemetery in Woodstock.

       Ida Elizabeth Hounshour was the daughter of Peter and Frances Hamrick Hounshour. She was born in 1858 and died 5 Jul 1850. She married E. Scott Brown on 13 Jun 1884. Scott was born in 1853 and died 15 Apr 1904. Ida and Scott were buried in the Massanutten Cemetery.

RELATED FAMILY:
       Margaret Hounshour, daughter of Peter and Jane, resided with her Uncle Robert and grandmother in **dwelling 104.**

Susannah Hounshour, sister of Peter, married Phillip Miller on 30 Jul 1839 and resided in **dwelling 225.**

David Dinges Hounshour, brother of Peter, resided in **dwelling 224.**

Martha Hamrick and **Rebecca Hamrick**, believed to have been the sisters of Frances, resided in **dwelling 220.**

Nimrod Hamrick, believed to have been the brother of Frances, resided in **dwelling 239.**

Thomas Gideon Hamrick, believed to have been the brother of Frances, resided in **dwelling 1855.**

1850 CENSUS: **Peter Hounshour Jr.** and family resided in dwelling 283 on page 20.

PAGE 17 WOODSTOCK (Microfilm Page 843)

Dwelling 117 Family 117

Adolph Heller	46	Merchant	3000	15100	Austria
Mahala Heller	34				Virginia
Theresa E. Heller	16				" School
Charles H. Wiseman	6				"
Mary Gillock	21	Housegirl			"
Josepha Lowenback	25	Clerk			Austria
Adolph B. Heller	16				"
Moritz P. Heller	17				"

Adolph Heller was the son of Emanuel and Frances. He was born in Austria. However, the 1850 census indicates that he was born in Germany. Adolph was born 25 Nov 1814 and died 2 Mar 1875. **Mahala Heller** was born 6 Apr 1822 and died 24 Aug 1869. Adolph and Mahala were buried in the St. Paul's Reformed Church Cemetery in Woodstock. After Mahala's death Adolph Heller married Ellen S. Lichliter on 7 Sep 1870. Ellen was the daughter of Jacob and Elizabeth. Jacob Lichliter married Elizabeth Miller on 3 Mar 1841. Ellen S. Lichliter resided with her parent in **dwelling 123.** Ellen was born 1 Aug 1845 and died 25 Dec 1914. Historian John Wayland provides an account that Adolph Heller met and interviewed General George Custer. The interview took place during the Civil War when Custer and his troops were often in the vicinity of Shenandoah County.

Theresa Esther Heller was the daughter of Moritz and Elizabeth Heller. Moritz Heller married Elizabeth Pitman on 19 Apr 1842. Moritz Heller had died in 1856.

Elizabeth Pitman Heller and her family were located in **dwelling 118**. Theresa was born in 1844 and died 3 Sep 1864. She was married on 17 Feb 1862 to the Reverend Joseph A. Snyder. Joseph was a minister in the Evangelical Lutheran Church and was from Augusta County, Virginia. He was the son of Jacob and Elizabeth. The Reverend Joseph A. Snyder was born 25 Dec 1827 and died 22 May 1917. He was married two additional times after Theresa's death. His second wife was Virginia Allen. Virginia Allen was the daughter of Israel and Amanda. Israel Allen and his family resided in **dwelling 564**. Virginia Allen was born 9 Feb 1846 and died 22 Dec 1871. She was buried in the Old Union Church Cemetery in Edinburg. The third wife of Reverend Joseph Snyder was Georgia Warfield. Theresa Heller was buried at St. Pauls Reformed Church Cemetery while Reverend Snyder and Georgia Warfield Snyder were buried in the St. Mathews Lutheran Church Cemetery in New Market. In the short while that Theresa and Joseph were together their marriage produced a son. Adolph Heller Snyder became a very prominent editor in the Shenandoah Valley. He was the editor of newspapers in Strasburg, Woodstock and eventually Harrisonburg. He is credited with securing the land for the location of the teachers college in Harrisonburg. In addition he was elected to the Virginia House of Delegates. However, this occurred late in his life and he could not serve his term because of the deterioration of his health.

Joseph (Josepha) Lowenback was in the household of Adolph Heller in 1850. His brother Anthony Lowenback was also present at that time.

The two young men **Adolph and Moritz** who were in this household are definitely listed as having been born in Austria. They were likely nephews of Adolph who were sent to this country in search of opportunity. At the time of the census they were employed as clerks in his store. They are not believed to have permanently settled in the area.

RELATED FAMILY:
Moritz Heller's widow Elizabeth Pitman Heller, sister in law of Adolph, resided in **dwelling 118**.

1850 CENSUS: **Adolph Heller** and his family resided in dwelling 797 on page 56.

PAGE 17   WOODSTOCK   (Microfilm Page 843)

Dwelling 118   Family 118

Elizabeth Heller	45	2500	10000	Virginia	
Elizabeth M. Heller	15			"	School
Mary E. Heller	11			"	School
Martha C. Heller	9			"	School
Emma Heller	8			"	
Ann Heller	6			"	
Maretta Heller	4			"	
Sarah J. Orndorff	21	Housegirl		"	

Elizabeth Pitman was born 1 Oct 1818 and died 10 Dec 1904. She was married to Moritz Heller on 19 Apr 1842. Moritz was from Austria. He was born 7 Nov 1806 and died 5 Mar 1856. Moritz and Elizabeth were buried in the St. Paul's Reformed Church Cemetery in Woodstock.

Elizabeth Mahala Heller was married to Charles A. Holt on 29 Nov 1866.   Charles was from Augusta County, Virginia. He was the son of Thomas and Missouri. Charles was an attorney and eventually established a practice in Staunton, Virginia. He died 21 Oct 1908 in Staunton.

Martha C. "Mattie" Heller was born in 1851 and died 26 Jun 1927. She was married to Phillip A. Pitman on 16 Apr 1868. Phillip was a merchant from Frederick County, Virginia. He was the son of Solomon and Sarah C. Solomon Pitman married Sarah C. Longacre on 21 Feb 1835 in Frederick County, Virginia. Phillip is reported to have been a veteran of the Civil War. He was born in 1849 and died 23 Jan 1911. Martha and Phillip were buried in the Massanutten Cemetery.

Emma G. Heller was born in 1851 and died 12 Aug 1916. She was married on 28 Jun 1869 to Milton Coffman. Milton was the son of Obed and Catherine Ann. Obed Coffman married Catherine Ann Snarr on 27 Feb 1846. Obed and his family resided in dwelling 102. Milton was a merchant and a banker. He was a member of the Confederate army. Milton was born in 1846 and died in 1932. He and Emma were buried in the Massanutten Cemetery.

Ann Heller was born in 1852 and died 7 Feb 1931. She was married to William Linn Dosh on 21 Mar 1883. William was the son of William and Elizabeth. William Dosh married Elizabeth Ware on 25 Jun 1838. They resided in dwelling 112. William Linn Dosh was born in 1848 and died 16 Mar 1924. They were buried in the Emanuel Lutheran Church Cemetery.

M. Etta S. Heller was married on 13 Jun 1876 to R. Drake Haislip. He was a teacher from Louisiana. He was the son of C. W. and M. R.

Sarah J. Orndorff may have been the daughter of James. A 10 year old girl, Sarah J. was residing in the residence of James Orndorff at the time of the 1850 census.

RELATED FAMILY:
Susan Pitman, sister of Elizabeth, married Isaac Fisher on 14 Mar 1843 and resided in dwelling 2093.
Theresa Esther Heller, daughter of Moritz and Elizabeth, was a resident in dwelling 117. This was the household of her uncle.

1850 CENSUS: Moritz Heller and his family resided in dwelling 238 on page 17.
Sarah J. Orndorff appears to have resided with her father in dwelling 659 on page 47.

PAGE 17 WOODSTOCK (Microfilm Page 843)

Dwelling 119 Family 119

William Moreland	67	Farmer	26000	9762	Virginia
Margaret Moreland	63				"
Franklin T. Moreland	24				"

William Moreland was born 12 Aug 1793 and died 4 Apr 1863. His wife Margaret was born 1 Mar 1797 and died 15 Jan 1870. William was very active in his community. He served on the Valley Turnpike Committee and assisted in their effort to raise revenue for the road that would stretch from Winchester to Harrisonburg. He was also a charter member of Shenandoah Lodge 39 I.O.O.F that was organized on 15 Mar 1847.

Franklin T. Moreland was born 10 Oct 1832 and died 23 Jan 1877. He was buried at the Emmanuel Lutheran Church Cemetery.

RELATED FAMILY:
Virginia S. Moreland, daughter of William

and Margaret, married Samuel Stephenson on 15 May 1856 and was a resident of **dwelling 2062.**

1850 CENSUS: **William Moreland** and his family resided in dwelling 239 on page 17.

PAGE 17 WOODSTOCK **(Microfilm Page 843)**

Dwelling 120 **Family 120**

Moses Walton	34	Attorney 3800	10000	Virginia
Emily Walton	33			"
Annie Walton	8			" School
Morgan L. Walton	6			" School
Mary O. Walton	5			" School
Emma M. Walton	2			"
Samuel Walton	1			"
Ann M. Anderson	55			"

Moses Walton was born 14 Jan 1826 and died 15 Jun 1883. He was the son of Reuben Moore and Mary Harrison Walton. Reuben Moore Walton was located in **dwelling 165.** Moses was married on 5 Feb 1861 to **Emily M. Lauck.** The bondsman for the marriage was William C. Lauck. William C. Lauck was a minister from Frederick County, Virginia. Emily's parents were Morgan and Ann M. Morgan Lauck married Ann Marie Ott on 26 May 1824. Emily M. Lauck Walton was born 27 Mar 1826 and died 23 Feb 1908. Moses and Emily were buried in the Massanutten Cemetery. Moses Walton was a member of the Virginia House of Delegates from 1863 to 1865. He represented Page and Shenandoah Counties in the Constitutional Convention of 1867-1868.

Annie L. Walton was married on 24 Oct 1872 to I. S. Hendry of Frederick County, Virginia. He was the son of Charles and Eleanor. I. S. was a merchant residing in Cumberland, Maryland at the time of this marriage.

Morgan Lauck Walton was born 13 Oct 1853 and died 20 Oct 1935. He was married to Mary Alice March, the daughter of James H and Laura A. Eby March. James H. March was a minister. Mary "Mollie" Alice March Walton was born 23 Nov 1853 and died 12 Mar 1928. Morgan and Mollie were buried in the Massanutten Cemetery. Morgan was a graduate of Randolph Macon in 1872. He then went on to the University of Virginia to study law in 1875. He was a partner in the law practice of his father. Morgan was a member of the State Democratic Committee. In 1891 he began a four year term in the Virginia State Senate. Morgan was a member of the Knights of Pythias.

Mary O. Walton was born in 1855 and died on 4 Apr 1942. She was the wife of Judge Edgar Douglas Newman. Mary and Edgar were married on 20 Dec 1877. He was the son of Benjamin P. and Elizabeth. Benjamin P. Newman married Elizabeth Hockman on 6 May 1851. Benjamin and his family resided in **dwelling 1326**. Mary and Edgar were buried in the Massanutten Cemetery.

Emma Maria Walton died 8 Jan 1882. She was 24 years, 5 months and 26 days old. She was buried in the Emmanuel Lutheran Church Cemetery. Emma was married to John L. Keller on 28 Dec 1880. John was a grade school principal. He was the son of Jacob and Charlotte. Jacob Keller married Charlotte Jordan on 7 Oct 1852. Jacob and his family resided in **dwelling 1971**.

Ann Maria Ott was married to Morgan Lauck on 26 May 1824. She was reported to have been the daughter of Jacob Ott. When Morgan died, the widow Ann Maria Lauck was married to Samuel Anderson on 2 May 1833. She was the mother of Emily M. Lauck.

RELATED FAMILY:
        Anna M. Walton, the sister of Moses, married Dr. Josiah Campbell on 19 May 1858 and resided in **dwelling 226**.
        Elizabeth Walton, sister of Moses, married John W. Ott on 17 Dec 1850 and resided in **dwelling 159**.

1850 CENSUS: **Moses Walton** was in the household of his father. They resided in dwelling 240 on page 17.
                    Emily M. Lauck resided with her mother Maria in dwelling 303 on page 22.

PAGE 17   WOODSTOCK   (Microfilm Page 843)

Dwelling 121   Family 121

Name	Age	Occupation	Value	Birthplace	
Frederick Shaffer	40	Hotel Keeper	12000 8461	Hanover, Ger.	
Martha Shaffer	35			Virginia	
Theodore E. Shaffer	17			"	School
Mary M. Shaffer	12			"	School
Eliza L. Shaffer	9			"	School
Julia O. Shaffer	4			"	
Gilbert Vansickle	50			New Jersey	
Fanny Spengler	64			Virginia	
Henry Hardy	30	Teacher-Female		N Carolina	
Addison Borsh	22			New York	
James Kibler	21	Cabinet Maker		Virginia	
John Wilkins	22	Printers Journeyman		Virginia	
Charles Stoneburner	18	Printers Apprentice		"	
Richard Lee	15	Printers Apprentice		"	
Louisa Day	32	Housekeeper		"	
Benjamin Day	7			"	School
John Day	6			"	School
George Lillie	20			"	Can't Read
Ellen A. Alexander	23	(Mulatto)		"	
Robert Alexandria	6	(Mulatto)		"	
Samuel Hockman	25	Miller		"	

Frederick Shaffer died 19 Feb 1872. He was 52 years, 11 months and 21 days old. His wife **Martha** was born 11 Dec 1824 and died 30 Oct 1890. They were buried in the Emmanuel Lutheran Church Cemetery in Woodstock.

Theodore E. Shaffer was born 21 Oct 1843 and died 5 Mar 1865. He enlisted as private in Company E of the 11th Virginia Cavalry on 4 May 1862 at Port Republic. He was present from 1 Jan 1863 to 28 Feb 1863. He was absent 1 Sep 1863 to 31 Oct 1863. He was reported absent as a result of a wound from 31 Oct 1863 to 31 Mar 1864. On 14 Apr 1864 he was unable to bear arms due to a gunshot wound to the left wrist. He recovered on 13 Sep 1864. He was present and was involved in light duty on 30 Apr 1864. It is believed that he had been wounded a second time. Theodore Shaffer drowned while attempting to cross the river at Moore's Ford, near Mt. Jackson during a fight with the enemy. His death occurred on 5 Mar 1865. He was buried at the Emanuel Lutheran Church Cemetery.

Lila Shaffer, probably Elizabeth L in this census, was married to John Rutherford of Jefferson County, West Virginia on 3 Nov 1870. He was a clerk at the time of the marriage. John was the son of James and Elizabeth.

The Reverend **Henry Hardie** was born at Raleigh, North Carolina. He was the son of Henry and Marion. On 8 Aug 1860 he married Amelia Triplett. Amelia was the daughter of Leonidas and Matilda. Dr. Leonidas Triplett married Matilda Irwin on 24 Jun 1834. Leonidas Triplett and his family resided in **dwelling 606**. Reverend Hardie was born 18 Sep 1823 and died 23 Nov 1868. Ann Amelia Triplett was born in 1837 and died in 1907. They were buried in the New Mount Jackson Cemetery.

Addison Borsh enlisted as a Corporal in Company K of the 10th Virginia Infantry. He enlisted at Luray, Virginia. He entered the service as a 2nd Corporal but was reduced in rank on 23 Sep 1861. He entered the hospital at Culpepper on 18 Nov 1862 and remained there until 14 Feb 1863. He was AWOL on 17 Apr 1863 to 15 Jun 1863. He was assigned to the hospital on 23 Jul 1863 to 15 Oct 1863. He was AWOL in Oct 1863. He was taken prisoner at Spotsylvania Courthouse on 12 May 1864. He was assigned to Point Lookout, Maryland on 18 May 1864 and was taken to Elmira, New York in Aug 1864. He was exchanged on 29 Oct 1864. There was an individual in the same unit named John Borst. Military records indicate he was born in Middleburg, New York. He was a Sergeant. It is believed that he may have been the brother of Addison.

James Allen Kibler was born 7 Dec 1834 and died Feb 1929. He was the son of William and Catherine. William Kibler married Catherine Lineweaver on 26 Dec 1820. James was married to Amanda Louisa Fravel Hoover on 22 Nov 1866. In the book of marriages produced by Borden, James was listed as James A.Keller. Amanda was born 8 Dec 1849 and died in 1929. James and Amanda were buried in the Patmos Lutheran Church Cemetery. She was the daughter of Benjamin and Sarah. Benjamin Hoover married Sarah Walter on 29 Apr 1839. Benjamin Hoover and family resided in **dwelling 2063**. James was 5'8" with light complexion, gray eyes and dark hair. He enlisted on 18 Apr 1861 as a private in Company F of the 10th Virginia Infantry. He was promoted to 3rd Corporal on 3 Apr 1862. He was wounded on 3 May 1863 at Chancellorsville with a gunshot wound to the lumbar region. He was taken prisoner at Waynesboro on 3 Mar 1865. He was sent to Fort Delaware on 9 Mar 1865 and was released under the Oath of Allegiance on 15 Jun 1865.

Charles D. Stoneburner was born in Shenandoah County. He enlisted as a private in Company C of the 5th Virginia Infantry. He transferred to the Staunton Artillery. He is mentioned as having made application for membership in Stonewall Jackson Camp No. 25 of Staunton, Virginia on 21 Nov 1906. He was 64 years old at the time. He was recorded as having been a printer and he died in Staunton on 1 Dec 1919.

Louisa Vann Day was the daughter of Godfrey Vann and Nancy Clevenger. On 1 Oct 1814 Godfrey Vann married Nancy Clevenger in Frederick County, Virginia. Louisa married George Day on 2 Jan 1851. George was the son of Benjamin and Eveline. George Day was a forgeman at Columbia Furnace when he died on 19 Nov 1858. Birth records indicated that Louisa and George were the parents of at least two children. **John C. Day** was born 14 Aug 1853. A daughter, Caroline Day was born at Liberty Furnace on 26 Aug 1855. There is no information regarding the birth of **Benjamin Day**. Benjamin apparently was named in honor of his paternal grandfather.

Samuel P. Hockman is reported to have been born 22 Nov 1838. He enlisted as a Sergeant in Company C of the 33rd Virginia Infantry on 3 Jun 1861. He was killed in action at Manassas on 21 Jul 1861. He was the son of Abraham and Elizabeth. Abraham Hockman married Elizabeth Pennywitt on 7 Feb 1827. Abraham and other family members resided in **dwelling 625**.

RELATED FAMILY:
       Maria Kibler, sister of James A. Kibler, married Jacob Lineweaver on 30 Dec 1858 and resided in **dwelling 2053**.
       Sarah Vann, sister of Louisa Vann Day, married Jonathan Sine on 14 Sep 1836 and resided in **dwelling 1307**.
       John Henry Vann, brother of Louisa Vann Day, married Elizabeth Miller on 27 Feb 1858 and resided in **dwelling 1309**.
       Eli Vann, brother of Louisa Vann Day, married Elizabeth Dellinger on 4 Oct 1852 and resided in **dwelling 1311**.

Abraham Vann, brother of Louisa Vann Day, married Elizabeth Midinger on 30 Jul 1852 and resided in **dwelling 1318**.

Godfrey Vann, father of Louisa Vann Day, resided in **dwelling 1318** the home of Stephen Strawderman.

Jacob H. Hockman, brother of Samuel, married Sarah Ellen Haun and resided in **dwelling 621**.

Isaac Hockman, brother of Samuel, resided in **dwelling 1416**.

William Hockman, brother of Samuel, resided in **dwelling 12**.

1850 CENSUS: **Frederick Shaffer** and his family resided in dwelling 298 on page 21.

Gilbert Van Sickle was a resident in the household of Jacob Lichliter. They resided in dwelling 295 on page 21.

James A. Kibler was a resident in the household of his father. They resided in dwelling 1499 on page 107.

Samuel Hockman resided with his parents in dwelling 1347 on page 96.

PAGE 18 WOODSTOCK   (**Microfilm Page 844**)

Dwelling 122   Family 122

Conrad Lichliter	47	Master Tailor	1350	1140	Virginia
Elizabeth Lichliter	43				"
William F. Lichliter	15				" School
Jacob H. Lichliter	12				" School
David C. Lichliter	7				" School
Sarah E. Lichliter	5				"

Conrad Lichliter was born in 1813 and died in 1898. He was the son of Conrad and Sarah. Conrad Lichliter married Sarah Harman on 21 Apr 1804. Sarah Harman Lichliter was present in the household of her son Jacob at the time of this census. They were residents of **dwelling 123**. Conrad married **Elizabeth Jane Dinges** on 21 Mar 1844. (**Note:** Shenandoah County marriage records indicate that her surname was Dwyer. Her tombstone indicates that her name was actually Dinges.) The bondsman for the marriage was Joseph Fravel. Elizabeth Jane was born in 1817 and died in 1891. Conrad and Elizabeth were buried in the Massanutten Cemetery.

The Reverend **William F. Lichliter** was born in 1844 and died on 30 Jan 1926. He did not marry and was buried in the Massanutten Cemetery in Woodstock.

Jacob H. Lichliter was born in 1848 and died 22 Jul 1935. The obituary notice in the paper indicated that Jacob and his brother William both died in Pennsylvania. Jacob was buried with his brother in the Massanutten Cemetery.

Sarah Elizabeth Lichliter was born in 1854 and died 12 Mar 1934. She was married to the Reverend George A. Whitmore on 20 Oct 1880. George was born in Augusta County, Virginia and was residing in Dayton, Armstrong County, Pennsylvania at the time of the marriage. He was the son of Samuel and Sophia. George was born in 1848 and died on 22 May 1931. Although Sarah and George both died in the state of Pennsylvania, they were both buried in the Massanutten Cemetery.

RELATED FAMILY:
Jacob Lichliter, brother of Conrad, married Elizabeth Miller on 3 Mar 1841 and resided in **dwelling 123**.

1850 CENSUS: Conrad Lichliter and his family resided in dwelling 226 on page 16.

PAGE 18 WOODSTOCK (Microfilm Page 844)

Dwelling 123   Family 123

Jacob Lichliter	49	Master Hatter	2080	940	Virginia
Elizabeth Lichliter	40				"
Ann Lichliter	17				"
Samuel Lichliter	16				" School
Sarah E. Lichliter	14				" School
Daniel Lichliter	10				" School
Henry Lichliter	7				"
Sarah Lichliter	75				" C't Rd
Sarah Lichliter	54				"

Jacob Lichliter was the son of Conrad and Sarah. Jacob's mother Sarah is in this household. He was born 12 Mar 1811 and died 13 May 1884. Jacob was married to **Elizabeth Miller** on 3 Mar 1841. She was the daughter of Elizabeth. The bondsman for the marriage was Daniel Miller. Elizabeth was born in 1817 and died 27 Mar 1875.

Jacob and Elizabeth were buried in the St. Paul's Reformed Church in Woodstock.

Ann Lichliter was married on 20 Dec 1871 to George Lichliter of Jefferson County, West Virginia. He was the son of George and Jane. George was a farmer at the time of the marriage.

There was a **Samuel Lichliter** who enlisted in the Toms Brooks Guard, Company B of the 33rd Virginia Infantry. He enlisted on 1 Jun 1862 and was present thru December of 1864. He was paroled at Appomattox. It is not known if this military record was for the individual in this household.

Sarah E. Lichliter was born 1 Aug 1845 and died 25 Dec 1914. She was listed as Ellen S. Lichliter in her marriage record on 7 Sep 1870. She was married to Adolph Heller, a widower, residing in **dwelling 117**. Adolph Heller was born in Austria. He was the son of Emanuel and Frances. He was born 25 Nov 1814 and died 2 Mar 1875. His first wife, Mahala, died 24 Aug 1869. Ellen and Adolph were buried in the St. Paul's Reformed Church Cemetery in Woodstock.

Daniel Lichliter was born in 1850 and died 10 Feb 1922. Daniel B. was married to Virginia Miller on 18 Mar 1878. She was the daughter of Daniel and Barbara. Daniel Miller married Barbara Supinger on 8 Mar 1841. Daniel Miller and his family were residents of **dwelling 2293**. Virginia Miller Lichliter was born in 1857 and died in 1927. Daniel and Virginia were buried in the Massanutten Cemetery in Woodstock.

Henry Lichliter was born in 1852 and died in 1928. He was buried near his parents.

Sarah Harman Lichliter was born 26 Feb 1783. She was the daughter of Mathias and Eliza. Sarah married Conrad Lichliter on 21 Apr 1804. She was residing with her son Jacob at the time of this census.

Fifty-four year old **Sarah Lichliter** is believed to have been the daughter of Conrad and Sarah Harman Lichliter. However, the 1850 census lists this individual as a "widow". If that information is accurate there is the chance she was a daughter-in-law. It is known that she was born 14 Mar 1808.

RELATED FAMILY:

        Conrad Lichliter, brother of Jacob, married Elizabeth Jane Dinges on 21 Mar 1844 and resided in **dwelling 122.**

1850 CENSUS: Jacob Lichliter and his family resided in dwelling 295 on page 21.

PAGE 18 WOODSTOCK   **(Microfilm Page 844)**

Dwelling 124 Family 124

Joseph Bowman	56	Butcher	1800	1655	Virginia
Catherine Bowman	55				"
John Bowman	24				"
Sarah A. Linn	30				"
Catherine	9	(Black)			"

        Joseph Bowman was married to **Catherine E. Linn** on 13 Dec 1827.

        There were a number of **John W. Bowman's** listed in Civil War records for Shenandoah County. At this point specific information regarding the military record of the individual in this household has not been determined.

        Sarah A. Linn had, as of this writing, an undetermined relationship with the mistress of this household. She was listed as 30 years old in 1850.

1850 CENSUS: **Joseph Bowman** and his family resided in dwelling 296 on page 21.

PAGE 18 WOODSTOCK   **(Microfilm Page 844)**

Dwelling 125 Family 125

George H. Ott	47	Glove Maker	1200	1720	Virginia	
Elizabeth Ott	42				"	
George G. Ott	17				"	
John C. Ott	15				"	School
Lucy A. Ott	13				"	School
Frances J. Ott	11				"	School
Hugh G. Ott	9				"	
Mary A. Ott	7				"	
Frank Ott	4				"	

George Harrison Ott was born in 1812 and died 1887. He was married to **Elizabeth Clower** on 29 Nov 1841. She was the daughter of John and Frances. John Clower was the bondsman. John Clower married Frances Grove on 15 Jan 1809. Elizabeth Clower Ott was born in 1817 and died in 1884. George and Elizabeth were buried in the Massanutten Cemetery.

George Gordon Ott was born 29 Oct 1842. He was light complexed with dark hair and blue eyes. George was 6'. He enlisted at Woodstock in Company F of the 10th Virginia Infantry as a private on 18 Apr 1861. He appears on company rolls as a musician. He was the regimental drummer. He was wounded 3 Jul 1863 at Gettysburg. He was taken POW on 2 Mar 1865 at Waynesboro. He was sent to Fort Delaware on 7 Mar 1865 and was released under the Oath of Allegiance on 15 Jun 1865. He was a resident of Washington, D.C. in 1900 and died in Washington on 20 May 1908.

John C. Ott was born ca. 1845. He had a light complexion, blue eyes and light hair. He was 5'7". He enlisted in Company F of the 10th Virginia Infantry on 2 Mar 1863 as a private. John was wounded at Chancellorsville on 3 May 1863. He was arrested at Woodstock on 8 Nov 1863. He was sent to prison in Wheeling, West Virginia at the Atheneun Prison. On 15 Nov 1863 he was sent to Camp Chase, Ohio. He was sent to Fort Delaware on 4 Mar 1864 and was exchanged on 18 Sep 1864. He was taken POW again at Waynesboro on 2 Mar 1865. He was sent back to Fort Delaware on 12 Mar 1865. He was released under the Oath of Allegiance on 15 Jun 1865. John C. Ott died in Feb 1901 and was buried near his parents in the Massanutten Cemetery.

Lucy A. Ott was married to Richard C. Hughes, a widower, on 16 Feb 1874. Lucy died 8 Mar 1904 and is buried in the Massanutten Cemetery.

Frances "Fannie" J. Ott died at the age of 85 on 14 Jun 1934.

Hugh Garland Ott was born 17 Feb 1851 and died 26 Aug 1919. He was a glove manufacturer like his father. Hugh was married on 12 Dec 1876 to Annie W. Claxen of Washington, D. C. She was the daughter of Alfred and Joanna. Hugh was buried at Massanutten Cemetery.

Mary A. Ott was born in 1853 and died 8 Nov 1910. She was married on 4 Feb 1875 to Wright Gatewood Campbell. Wright was born in Shenandoah County but was residing in Franklin County, West Virginia. He was an editor and was later listed as a professor. He was the son of John F. and Martha C. John F. Campbell, a physician, was married to Martha C. Gatewood on 2 Jun 1846. Wright was born in 1849 and died 22 Jan 1925. Mary and Wright were buried in the Massanutten Cemetery.

RELATED FAMILY:

    Joseph H. Clower, brother of Elizabeth, resided in **dwelling 107.**

    Jacob B. Clower, brother of Elizabeth, married Julia Ann Haas and resided in **dwelling 176.**

    Isabella Clower, sister of Elizabeth, married Alexander Anderson on 19 Sep 1838 and resided in **dwelling 155.**

1850 CENSUS: **George Harrison Ott** and his family resided in dwelling 297 on page 21.

PAGE 19 WOODSTOCK   **(Microfilm Page 845)**

Dwelling 126 Family 126

David Gillock	33	Master Blacksmith	1200	645	Virginia
Elizabeth Gillock	32				"
Ann R. Gillock	6				"
Susan M. Gillock	5				"
David H. Gillock	2				"
Harvey Morris	20	Blacksmith Apprentice			"

In the 1850 census, **David Gillock** appears in the residence of John and Mary Gillock. John Gillock married Mary Fetzer on 10 Apr 1806. It is likely that David was their son. David Gillock was born 3 Jan 1824 and died 5 Mar 1899. He was married to **Elizabeth Jordan** on 27 Jan 1853. Elizabeth was the daughter of John and Barbara. John Jordan married Barbara Wilkins on 15 Dec 1813. Elizabeth Jordan Gillock was born 9 Nov 1829 and died 16 Nov 1901. David and Elizabeth were buried in the St. Paul's Reformed Church Cemetery in Woodstock. David Gillock enlisted on 14 Apr 1862 at New Market in Company H of the 2nd Virginia Infantry. He was a private and was detailed as a wagoner in the Quartermaster Department in Apr 1862. He remained on this detail until Mar/Apr 1864.

His last official entry shows him as a blacksmith in the Quartermaster Department from 30 Apr until 31 Oct 1864.

Ann Rebecca Gillock was born 20 Apr 1853 and died 9 Jul 1926. She was married to John Turner Haas on 25 Oct 1876. John was the son of Isaac and Sarah E. Isaac Haas married Sarah Elizabeth Coffman on 17 Oct 1838. Isaac Haas and his family were residents of **dwelling 137**. John Turner Haas was reported to have been a veteran of the Civil War. Ann Rebecca Gillock led the choir at St. Paul's Reformed Church in Woodstock and was President of the Ladies Aid Society. Ann and John were buried in the Massanutten Cemetery.

Susan M. Gillock was born 21 Oct 1855 and died 8 Jan 1875. She was buried near her parents at the St. Paul's Reformed Church Cemetery.

David Henry Gillock was born 15 Feb 1858 and died 21 Oct 1875.

RELATED FAMILY:
Ann E. Jordan, sister of Elizabeth, married William Jacob Supinger on 16 Apr 1849 and resided in **dwelling 87**.
Charlotte Jordan, sister of Elizabeth, married Jacob Keller on 2 Oct 1851 and resided in **dwelling 1971**.
Barbara Gillock, sister of David, resided in **dwelling 197**. She lived in the residence of **Harrison Gillock**. Quite likely, Harrison Gillock was the brother of David. Harrison had married Mary Jane Miller on 2 Apr 1851.

1850 CENSUS: **David Gillock** resided in the household of his father. They were residents of dwelling 225 on page 16.
Elizabeth Jordan resided in the household of her parents. They were located in dwelling 623 on page 44.

PAGE 19   WOODSTOCK   (Microfilm Page 845)

Dwelling 127   Family 127

John Bauserman	35	Blacksmith 90 2315	Virginia
Sarah C. Bauserman	34		"
Frederick Bauserman	4		"
John E. Bauserman	2		"
Emma C. Bauserman	1		"
Cora A. Bauserman	8m		"
Mary E. Fetzer	20		"
Michael Cullen	28	Fireman on R.R.	Ireland C'tRd

John W. Bauserman was the son of Frederick Bauserman. It is probable that the Frederick Bauserman and his wife Sarah residing in **dwelling 2041** were parents of John. He was married on 10 Aug 1854 to **Sarah Catherine Fetzer**. Catherine was the daughter of Samuel and Ann. Samuel Fetzer married Mary Ann Rye on 14 May 1829. Mary Ann Rye Fetzer, the widowed mother of Sarah, resided in **dwelling 195**.

Frederick Bauserman, named in honor of his paternal grandfather, was born 3 Sep 1855 and died 20 Oct 1861. He was buried in the Emanuel Lutheran Cemetery.

Emma C. Bauserman was born 20 Aug 1858 and died 7 Nov 1861. She was buried next to her brother in the Emanuel Lutheran Church Cemetery.

Mary Ellen Fetzer was the sister of Sarah Catherine Fetzer Bauserman. Mary Ellen married John F. Roberts on 14 Sep 1865. John was the son of Jesse and Maria. He was born in Pennsylvania but was a hotel keeper in Shenandoah County at the time of the marriage.

RELATED FAMILY:

Elizabeth Bauserman, believed to have been the sister of John, married Noah Wright on 26 Oct 1846 and resided in **dwelling 2040**.

1850 CENSUS: **John W. Bauserman** was a resident in the dwelling 990 on page 69. This was the residence of Jacob and Edith Pence.

Mary Ellen Fetzer resided with her mother in dwelling 217 on page 16. Sarah Catherine was not in the household.

145

PAGE 19 WOODSTOCK   **(Microfilm Page 845)**

Dwelling 128 Family 128

Martin Collins	27	Engineer R.R.	Maryland	
Amanda P. Collins	23		Virginia	
Maria V. Collins	3		"	
Margaret M. Collins	2		"	
Marietta Collins	11m		"	

1850 CENSUS: No record of this family has been located in 1850.

PAGE 19 WOODSTOCK **(Microfilm Page 845)**

Dwelling 129 Family 129

Joseph Bauserman	45	600	6400	Virginia	
Elizabeth A. Bauserman	36			"	
George R. Bauserman	9			"	School
Henry W. Bauserman	7			"	School
William P. Bauserman	3			"	

Joseph Bauserman was the son of Henry and Elizabeth. Henry Bauserman married Elizabeth Earhart on 30 Jul 1808. Henry was a resident with his daughter in **dwelling 132**. Joseph was born 30 Nov 1811 and died 14 Jan 1876. He was married to **Elizabeth Ann Wilson** on 3 Jan 1850. The bondsman for the marriage was William S. Arthur. Elizabeth was born 13 Jun 1823 and died 30 Jan 1892. Joseph and Elizabeth were buried at the St. Paul's Reformed Church Cemetery.

George R. Bauserman died 2 Dec 1923 at the age of 72 years, 10 months and 26 days old. He was married on 21 Dec 1871 to Susan E. Ruffner. Susan was the daughter of Reuben and Betsy Ann. Reuben Ruffner married Elizabeth Ann Shenk on 28 Aug 1848 in Page County, Virginia. George and Susan were also married in Page County, Virginia on 21 Dec 1871. Susan was born 4 Nov 1851 and died 17 Aug 1936. They were buried in the Ruffner-Bauserman Cemetery in Page County.

Henry W. Bauserman was born in 1853 and died in 1917. He was married on 28 Feb 1895 to Carrie A. Sine. He was a tinner at the time of the marriage. Carrie was the daughter of Daniel and Matilda. Daniel Sine married Matilda McDaniel on 26 Sep 1850. Daniel Sine and family resided in **dwelling 1258**. Carrie Sine Bauserman died on 12 Dec 1932 in Columbia Furnace, Virginia. She was 76 years old.

RELATED FAMILY:
> **Catherine Bauserman**, sister of Joseph, married Cornelius Palmer on 23 Feb 1842 an resided in **dwelling 132**.
> **Sarah Bauserman**, sister of Joseph, married Daniel Burner on 16 May 1840 and resided in **dwelling 133**.

1850 CENSUS: **Joseph Bauserman** and family resided in dwelling 205 on page 15.

PAGE 19 WOODSTOCK (Microfilm Page 845)

Dwelling 130   Family 130

Peter Hounshour	67	Plasterer	1000	2055	Virginia
Harriet Hounshour	56				" Cn't Rd
Rebecca A. Hounshour	35				"
Mary C. Hounshour	27				"

Peter Hoshour was married to Elizabeth Clower. Elizabeth was the daughter of George and Susannah. George Clower married Susannah Black on 29 Nov 1783. Elizabeth was born in 1794 and died 15 May 1822. Three children were born to their marriage. On 29 May 1823 Peter was married to **Harriet Boyer**. She was the ward of John Thompson. Harriet was mentioned in the 12 Feb 1844 Will of her sister Rebecca. Rebecca also mentions three children born to the union of Peter and Harriet. They were listed as Catherine, Rebecca and Samuel. Harriet Boyer Hoshour was born in 1804 and died 2 Feb 1872. She was buried in the St. Paul's Reformed Church Cemetery. Peter Hoshour died in 1879 at the age of 85.

Rebecca A. Hoshour was born 14 Sep 1821 and died 29 Jun 1860. She was buried at the St. Paul's Reformed Church Cemetery.

Mary Catherine Hoshour was born 10 Jan 1830 and died 17 Apr 1895. She was buried near her sister Rebecca.

RELATED FAMILY:
> **David D. Hoshour**, son of Peter and Elizabeth, and his wife Rebecca resided in **dwelling 224**.

Peter Hoshour Jr. son of Peter and
Elizabeth, married Frances Hamrick on 18 May 1858 and
resided in **dwelling 116.**

1850 CENSUS: Peter Hoshour Sr. and his family resided in
dwelling 300 on page 22.

PAGE 19 WOODSTOCK (Microfilm Page 845)

Dwelling 131 Family 131

Jacob Rodeffer	40	Shoemaker	190	50	Virginia
Ann C. Rodeffer	33				"
Mary E. Rodeffer	18				"
Phillip D. Rodeffer	17	Day Labor			"
Theodore Rodeffer	16				" School
Susan C. Rodeffer	10				" School
Sarah A. Rodeffer	7				"
David H. Rodeffer	1				"
Mary Grainton	70				" Cn't Rd

Jacob Rodeffer was married to **Ann Getz** on 18 Sep
1838. The bondsman for the marriage was Phillip Getz. The
1850 census lists this couple as approximately 10 years
older.

Phillip D. Rodeffer enlisted in Company D of the
33rd Virginia Infantry on 3 Jun 1861. He was present
through Sep 1862. He was wounded at Manassas on 30 Aug
1863. He was absent with his wound through Dec 1863. He
was admitted to Charlottesville Hospital on 26 Jan 1864
with a gun shot wound in the right thigh. He had his leg
amputated as a result of this wound and was furloughed on
8 Feb 1864.

Theodore Rodeffer was born 10 Mar 1845 and died 6
Jul 1912. He was a member of Chews Battery during the
Civil War. Theodore was married on 30 Sep 1872 to Mildred
Catherine Rodgers of Frederick County, Virginia. She was
the daughter of William and Catherine. Kate died 31 Jan
1932 at Stephens City, Virginia. Theodore was buried in
the Massanutten Cemetery.

Susan Catherine Rodeffer was born in 1851 and died
14 Dec 1927. She was married to John Franklin Brooks Jr.
on 22 Feb 1872. He was the son of John F. and Ann. The
Brooks family was originally from Hardy County, West
Virginia. However, they were residents of **dwelling 1250**

in Shenandoah County. John F. Brooks Jr. was born in 1848 and died 9 Aug 1924. John and Susan were buried in the Massanutten Cemetery.

Sallie A. "Rosa" Rodeffer was born in 1856 and died 15 Mar 1937. Her obituary lists her as Sara Rosa. She was the third wife of Robert H. Kibler, the son of Phillip and Elizabeth Haun Kibler. Phillip Kibler and his family resided in dwelling 1810. Robert was not in that household at the time of this census. Robert was twice a widower. He had married Mary Ann Elizabeth Ritenour on 20 Oct 1856. When Mary Ann died, Robert married Mary F. Miller on 20 Jun 1867. She was the daughter of Christian and Catherine. Robert H. Kibler was born in 1831 and died in 1907. Sallie and Robert were buried in the Patmos Lutheran Church Cemetery in Woodstock.

Mary Yager was the daughter of Jacob. She was married to John Weeks on 12 Oct 1822. When John died, Mary Yager Weeks married James Grantham on 10 Mar 1825. The bondsman for that marriage was Peter Hoshour. In the 1850 census, Mary Yager Weeks Grantham (Grainton) was listed as a shoemaker. In 1850 she was a neighbor of Jacob Rodeffer.

1850 CENSUS: Jacob Rodeffer and his family resided in dwelling 310 on page 22.
Mary Grantham and her husband James were residents of dwelling 315 on page 23.

PAGE 20 WOODSTOCK (Microfilm Page 846)

Dwelling 132 Family 132

Cornelius Palmer	48	Farming	1600	325	Ohio
Catherine Palmer	43				Virginia
Henry B. Palmer	13				"
Henry Bauserman	71				"
Jane Burner	16				"
Hizani Barber	49	(Black/Female)			"

Cornelius Palmer was married to Catherine Bauserman on 23 Feb 1842. Cornelius was the son of Frank. Catherine was the daughter of Henry and Elizabeth.

Henry Bauserman married Elizabeth Earhart on 30 Jul 1808.

Jane Burner has not been identified. Henry Bauserman's daughter Sarah married Daniel Burner on 16 May 1840. However no evidence has yet been discovered to establish this young lady as the grandchild of Henry Bauserman.

RELATED FAMILY:

      Sarah Bauserman, daughter of Henry Bauserman, married Daniel Burner on 16 May 1840 and resided in **dwelling 133.**

      Joseph Bauserman, son of Henry, married Elizabeth Ann Wilson on 3 Jan 1850 and resided in **dwelling 129.**

1850 CENSUS: Henry Bauserman and his wife were residents in dwelling 205 on page 15. This was the dwelling of Cornelius and Catherine Palmer.

PAGE 20 WOODSTOCK (Microfilm Page 846)

Dwelling 133 Family 133

Daniel Burner	46	Tanner	13525	4960	Virginia
Sarah Burner	40				"
Elizabeth C. Burner	18				" School
Henry B. Burner	13				" School
Mary E. Burner	9				" School
Charles W. Burner	6				" School
William Burner	4				"
Daniel F. Burner	2				"
Janes P. Burner	4m	(Female)			"
Catherine Orndorff	20				"

Daniel Burner was born 9 Oct 1813 and died 22 Apr 1873. He was married to **Sarah Bauserman** on 16 May 1840. Sarah was the daughter of Henry Bauserman. Henry was married to Eliza Earhart on 30 Jul 1808. Henry Bauserman resided in **dwelling 132.** Sarah Bauserman Burner was born 16 May 1818 and died 1 Mar 1896. Daniel and Sarah were buried in the Emanuel Lutheran Church Cemetery.

Elizabeth "Bessie" C. Burner was born 1842 and died 15 Aug 1919. She was married on 14 Nov 1866 to Edward Mark Bushong. Edward was a farmer at the time of the marriage. He had served in the 10th Virginia Infantry and the 12th Virginia Cavalry. Edward was the son of Henry and Mary Ann. Henry Bushong married Mary Ann Wendle on 4 Sep 1833. The Bushong family resided in **dwelling 1600.** Edward

Bushong was born 1839 and died 13 Nov 1922. **Bessie** and Edward were buried at the Massanutten Cemetery.

Henry B. Burner was born 1847 and died 23 Feb 1916. He did not marry. Henry was buried in the Massanutten Cemetery. Henry enlisted in Company D of the 18th Virginia Cavalry on 1 Mar 1864. He was present as of 31 Oct 1864. He was paroled 27 Apr 1865 at Winchester. Henry had a fair complexion, with fair hair, blue eyes and was 6'tall.

Mary Ellen Burner died 25 Jul 1895 at the age of 43 years, 2 months and 27 days old. She was married to John William Harvey Martin on 4 Nov 1873. John was a clerk at the time of the marriage. He was the son of Reverend George W. and Esther. John was born in Augusta County, Virginia in 1849 and died 1 Feb 1908. This couple was buried in the Massanutten Cemetery. John W. H. Martin married Mary Ellen Skyles, the daughter of Reverend N. H. and Mary Ellen Nycum Skyles on 2 Sep 1897. Mary Ellen Skyles Martin was born in 1867 and died in 1952.

Charles W. Burner was born in 1854 and died Jul 1916. He married Mary E. Hughes on 21 Nov 1882. Mary Ellen was the daughter of R. C. and Mary A. She was born in Clinton, Pennsylvania. Mary was born in 1858 and died 19 Aug 1908. Charles and Mary E. were buried in the Massanutten Cemetery. R. C. Hughes was the widower who married Lucy A. Ott of **dwelling 125** on 16 Feb 1874.

Dr. Daniel F. Burner was born 4 Jan 1858 and died 25 Aug 1897. His wife was Ophelia Wierman. They were married on 12 Dec 1894. Ophelia was the daughter of Benjamin and Catherine. Benjamin B. Wierman married Catherine A. Moore on 12 Mar 1857. Benjamin and family resided in **dwelling 1024**. Ophelia was born 3 Mar 1867 and died 10 Mar 1896. They were buried in the Emanuel Lutheran Church Cemetery.

J. Letcher Burner was born in 1860 and died on 28 Nov 1913. This individual was unmarried. The burial site was the Massanutten Cemetery next to Henry B. Burner. This may have been the individual listed as the 4 month old female in this household.

William Wilson Burner was listed as William Magruder on death records. He was born 9 Nov 1856 and died 29 Jul 1939. He was married to Birdie Marie Fadely on 12 Sep 1900. She was the daughter of Lorenzo and

Barbara. Lorenzo Fadely married Barbara Ann Will on 22 May 1840. Lorenzo and his family resided in **dwelling 1236**. Birdie was born 11 Jan 1871 and died 2 Feb 1847. They were buried at the Massanutten Cemetery.

A careful review of the 1850 census indicates that the individual listed as **Catherine Orndorff** may have been Mary C. Orndorff, the daughter of Lewis and Elizabeth. She was the 26 year old woman that married Mason D. Orndorff on 4 Oct 1866. Mason was the son of Phineas and Elinore Borden Orndorff. The age is correct. However individuals interest in the Orndorff family need to explore further.

RELATED FAMILY:

Joseph Bauserman, brother of Sarah, married Elizabeth Ann Wilson on 3 Jan 1850 and resided in **dwelling 129**.

1850 CENSUS: **Daniel Burner** and his family resided in dwelling 304 on page 22.

PAGE 20 WOODSTOCK **(Microfilm Page 846)**

Dwelling 134 Family 134

Phillip Rodeffer	40		340	73	Virginia
John Rodeffer	91				"
Amelia Rodeffer	58				"
Lydia McPherson	39	Housegirl			"
Sarah C. Dean	14				"
John L. Dean	6				"

In the 1850 census, 91 year old **John Rodeffer** was the head of the household. It is likely that he was the father of **Phillip** and **Amelia**.

John L. Dean and **Sarah C. Dean** were the children of Zedekiah and Mary Ann. They were grandchildren of John Rodeffer. Zedekiah Dean married Mary Ann Rodeffer on 7 Nov 1848. The bondsman for the marriage was William H. Rodeffer. Zedekiah and his family were neighbors of John Rodeffer and his family in 1850. Sometime during the decade of the 1850's Mary Ann Rodeffer Dean died. On 24 Jan 1860 Zedekiah Dean married Martha Barr. Zedekiah and Martha Barr Dean were residents in **dwelling 170**.

1850 CENSUS: **John Rodeffer** and family resided in dwelling 23 on page 15.

152

Sarah C. Dean resided with her parents in dwelling 204 on page 15.

PAGE 20   WOODSTOCK   (Microfilm Page 846)

Dwelling 135   Family 135

Sarah Lichliter   55   0 100   Virginia

     In the 1850 census, 45 year old **Sarah Lichliter** resided in a household with 10 year old David Lichliter. David has not been located in this census. There is no additional information available regarding this household.

1850 CENSUS: Sarah Lichliter was a resident in dwelling 210 on page 15.

PAGE 20   WOODSTOCK   (Microfilm Page 846)

Dwelling 136   Family 136

Lewis Kneisly   25   Tinner 0   70   Virginia
Frances Kneisly   20   "

     Lewis C. Kneisley was born in 1834 and died 7 Jul 1909. He was the son of Reuben and Susan. Reuben Kneisley was married on 3 Oct 1826 to Susan Majors. The bondsman for that marriage was Samuel Frew. On 14 Dec 1859 Lewis was married to **Frances Catherine Anderson**. Frances was born in 1840 and died 23 Jul 1915. Frances was the daughter of Alexander and Isabella. Alexander Anderson, an attorney, married Isabella Clower on 14 Sep 1838. Isabella Clower Anderson and some of her children were located in **dwelling 155**. Lewis and Frances were buried in the Massanutten Cemetery. Lewis enlisted on 18 Apr 1861 at Woodstock in Company F of the 10th Virginia Infantry. He was 4th Corporal. He was promoted to 2nd Sgt. on 3 Apr 1862. Lewis was wounded at Winchester on 25 May 1862. He was wounded in the shoulder in Jul 1862 at the Seven Days battle. He was wounded on 30 Aug 1862 at Manassas. Lewis was transferred to Company B on 31 Oct 1864. He was wounded in May of 1864 at Spotsylvania Courthouse. Lewis was taken prisoner on 25 Jan 1865 at Woodstock and was listed as a "guerilla". He was imprisoned at Fort McHenry on 18 Jan 1865 and was released on 5 May 1865.

153

RELATED FAMILY:

   Sarah Catherine Kniseley, sister of Lewis, married Daniel Smootz on 26 Dec 1850 and resided in **dwelling 138.**

   Luther B. Knisely, brother of Lewis, resided in **dwelling 169.** He was a printer in the household of John Gatewood, the editor of the **Tenth Legion.**

1850 CENSUS: **Lewis C. Kniseley** was a resident in the household of his father. They resided in dwelling 848 on page 59.

   Frances Catherine Anderson resided with her parents in dwelling 258 on page 19.

PAGE 20 WOODSTOCK **(Microfilm Page 846)**

Dwelling 137 Family 137

Isaac Haas	44	Post Master 1000 3500	Virginia
Mary E. Haas	27		"
William H. Haas	20	Mail Carrier (Route 1)	"
Mary H. Haas	18		"
John T. Haas	14		"
Sarah C. Haas	11		" School
Anna H. Haas	2		"
Christopher Snyder	27	Tailor	"

  Isaac Haas was born 2 Feb 1816 and died 8 Mar 1896. He was the son of John and Sarah. John Haas married Sarah Kurtz on 1 Apr 1815. Isaac was married to Sarah Elizabeth Hoffman on 17 Oct 1838. Sarah was born 6 Jun 1820 and died 18 Jun 1858. Sarah was listed in the will (Book 2, Page 450) of her brother Robert W. G. Hoffman. This will was proved on 10 Mar 1851. In that document Robert also indicated that his two slaves, Milton and Ambrose, were to go "to Liberia". This was an interesting characteristic of the period. The American Colonization Society had proposed that one solution to the controversial issue of slavery was to encourage slave owners to return their slaves to Africa. Apparently Robert W. Hoffman of Shenandoah County found this a desirable alternative. When Sarah Elizabeth Hoffman Haas died, Isaac Haas married **Mary Elizabeth Reed** on 15 Sep 1859. Mary was originally from Norfolk, Virginia. She was the daughter of Henry L. and Charlotte. Henry and Charlotte resided in **dwelling 158.** Mary Elizabeth Reed Haas was born 10 Apr 1833 and died 8 Nov 1896. Isaac and both of his wives were buried in the Emanuel Lutheran Church Cemetery.

154

William H. Haas was born in 1839 and died 27 Mar 1888. He was a merchant at the time of his marriage to Mary "Mattie" Grabill on 30 Jan 1873. Mattie C. Grabill Haas was born in 1852 and died in 1893. William H. Haas enlisted in Company F of the 10th Virginia Infantry. He was assigned to the Confederate States Mail Service. The parents of Mattie Grabill Haas have not been identified.

Mary H. Haas was born in 1841 and died in 1909. She was married on 26 Jun 1867 to William M. Hill. William was from Nelson County, Virginia. He was the son of Charles B and Martha. William was born in 1841 and died in 1893.

John Turner Haas was born in 1846 and died 15 Nov 1925. He was married to Annie R. Gillock on 25 Oct 1876. Annie was the daughter of David and Elizabeth. David Gillock married Elizabeth Jordan on 27 Jan 1853. David Gillock and family resided in **dwelling 126**. Annie R. Gillock Haas was born in 1853 and died in 1926. The Hottel family history reported that John T. Haas was a member of Imbodens Brigade of the 18th Virginia Cavalry. He was supposed to have been a member of Company D and was a courier for General Robert E. Lee. He later served in the Independent Cavalry. 18th Virginia Cavalry records indicate that he joined at Berryville, Virginia on 24 Sep 1862. He was present as of 26 Mar 1863. He was captured at Greencastle, Pennsylvania and sent to Fort Delaware on 7 Jul 1863. He was exchanged at City Point, Virignia on 31 Jul 1863. He was listed as AWOL during the period 1 Jan 1864 thru 31 Oct 1864.

Sarah C. "Kittie" Haas was born 9 Jan 1849 and died 21 Dec 1896. She was buried in the Massanutten Cemetery.

Annie Howard Haas was born in 1857 and died 2 Jun 1921. She was married to Luther Sommers Walker on 21 Oct 1884. Luther was a County Clerk and the son of Samuel L. T. Walker and Mary R. Sommers. Samuel and Mary were married on 21 Oct 1856. Samuel was the editor of the **Valley Democrat**. Luther Sommers Walker was born in 1857 and died 16 Aug 1907. Annie and Luther were buried in the Massanutten Cemetery.

Christopher Snyder was the son of John and Barbara. John B. Snyder married Barbara Artz on 23 Dec 1820 and resided in **dwelling 604**. John Snyder was a school teacher from Maryland.

1850 CENSUS: Isaac Haas and family resided in dwelling 294 on page 21.

Christopher Snyder resided with his parents in dwelling 1092 on page 76.

PAGE 20 WOODSTOCK (Microfilm Page 846)

Dwelling 138   Family 138

Daniel Smootz	32	Day Labor 0 125	Virginia	Can't Read
Sarah C. Smootz	27		"	
Cynthia A. Smootz	10		"	School
Charles Smootz	6	.	"	
Mary S. Smootz	4		"	

Daniel Smootz was married to **Sarah Catherine Knisley** on 26 Dec 1850. Daniel was the son of Abraham and Polly. She was the daughter of Reuben Knisley. At the time of Sarah's death Daniel was working as a railroad hand. Daniel A. Smootz was married to Anna A. Walters on 29 Dec 1868. Anna was the daughter of Leonard and Deborah. Leonard Walters and his family were located in **dwelling 603.** Anna was born in Wilmington, Delaware.

RELATED FAMILY:

Lewis Kniesly, brother of Sarah, was married to Frances Catherine Anderson on 14 Dec 1859 and resided in **dwelling 136.**

Luther B. Kniesly, brother of Sarah, resided in **dwelling 169.** He lived with John Gatewood the editor of the **Tenth Legion.**

1850 CENSUS: Daniel Smootz was in the household of his parents. They resided dwelling 2138 on page 153.

Sarah Catherine Kniesly resided with her parents in dwelling 848 on page 59.

156

PAGE 21 WOODSTOCK   (Microfilm Page 847)

Dwelling 139   Family 139

David Rodeffer	51	Farmer	4000	11,185	Virginia	
Ann Rodeffer	47				"	
William C. Rodeffer	25	Plasterer			"	
John H. Rodeffer	24	Brick Maker			"	
David Rodeffer	18	Cabinet Maker Appr.			"	
Mary V. Rodeffer	20				"	
Edward Rodeffer	17				"	School
Ann E. Rodeffer	15				"	School
Samuel A. Rodeffer	12				"	School
Ellen F. Rodeffer	10				"	
Catherine Rodeffer	72				"	
Elizabeth Black	68				"	
Mary Black	66				"	

David Rodeffer was born 28 Nov 1808 and died 17 Apr 1871.   He married **Ann Sager** on 3 Sep 1830.   Ann Sager Rodeffer died 16 Dec 1865 at the age of 51 years, 2 months and 11 days old.   They were buried in the Massanutten Cemetery.   On the tombstone of David Rodeffer there is an indication that he served in the Confederate Army.

Information regarding the Rodeffer family has been difficult to locate.   It is speculated that this was the family of George Rodeffer.   He was a veteran of the War of 1812.   George Rodeffer died on 26 May 1826.   He was married to **Catherine Swartz**.   She is believed to have been the 72 year old in this dwelling. Their marriage took place on 14 Jan 1807.   The marriage produced four children.
The children were James, Harrison, Elizabeth and David Mark.   Family history indicates that Catherine lived with the family of David Mark.

John Rodeffer died on 15 Aug 1860 of typhoid fever. He was 24 years and six months old at the time.

David Rodeffer, son of David and Ann, was born ca. 1843.   He enlisted at Woodstock on 18 Apr 1861 as a private in Company F of the 10th Virginia Infantry.   He was absent sick from 10 Oct 1862 to May 1863.   He was apparently employed as an army nurse after May 1863.   He was stationed at Camp Winder in Richmond.   David Rodeffer died at Denison, Texas in the late 1890's.

Edward Rodeffer enlisted in Company C of the 33rd Virginia Infantry on 2 Jun 1861. He was wounded on 21 Jul 1861 at Manassas. He was absent, wounded through February 1862. He was promoted to Corporal on 21 Apr 1862. He was present in April but was AWOL in Sep 1862. He was reduced in rank on 10 Sep 1862. He was present thru Dec 1862. Edward was on detached service thru Dec 1863. He was present in Feb 1865. Edward was paroled at Winchester on 17 Apr 1865. He was 5'7", fair complexion with light hair and grey eyes. Edward died 9 Mary 1926.

Annie Rodeffer was married to Dorsey Walters, a merchant from Frederick County, Virginia on 18 Dec 1867. He was the son of William and Margaret. William P Walters married Margaret Ewing on 10 May 1827 in Frederick County. Dorsey Walters and his parents resided in dwelling 562 in the town of Winchester at the time of the 1850 census. William P. Walters was a merchant.

Ella Frances Rodeffer was born 29 Jan 1850 and died 26 Apr 1930. She was buried in the Massanutten Cemetery.

Elizabeth Black resided with the family of David Rodeffer in 1850.

RELATED FAMILY:

George B. Rodeffer, the son of David and Ann, married Jerasha Johnson and resided in **dwelling 106.**

James Harrison Rodeffer, son of David and Ann, was not present in the household or Shenandoah County census. He was born 13 Nov 1836 and enlisted on 18 Apr 1861 as a private in Company F of the 10th Virginia Infantry. He was wounded on 3 May 1863 at Chancellorsville in the head and leg. He was transferred on 31 Oct 1864 to Thomson's Battery Horse Artillery on 7 Jan 1865. He was Mayor of Woodstock after the war. James Harrison Rodeffer died 26 Mar 1926 and was buried in the Massanutten Cemetery.

Mark M. Rodeffer, son of David and Ann, enlisted in Company F of the 10th Virginia Infantry and served with that unit from May 1862 to Aug 1862. He had originally enlisted inthe 10th Mississippi Rifles. He later transferred to Chew's Battery. He resided in Lovettsville in Loudoun County in 1900 and died in D.C. on 1 Apr 1928. He has not been located in this census.

1850 CENSUS: **David Rodeffer** and his family resided in dwelling 257 on page 18.

158

Mary Black resided with the family of Amos and Barbara Crabill. They resided in dwelling 949 on page 66.

PAGE 21 WOODSTOCK   (Microfilm Page 847)

Dwelling 140   Family 140

William T. Stewart	50	Cabinet Maker 2800 375	Virginia
Susan Stewart	47		Maryland
Margaret A. Hamaker	26	Common School Teacher	"
Mary E. Stewart	14		Va. Schl
Kate B. Stewart	8		"
John McMan	13		" School

William T. Stewart was 55 years, 11 months old at his death. His wife **Susan** died on 1 Jun 1878. She was 68 years of age. They were buried at the Emanuel Lutheran Church Cemetery.

Margaret A. Hamacker resided with the Stewart family in 1850. She was reported to have been the daughter of Stewart and Susan. Susan Stewart in this household was probably her mother. Margaret was born in Washington County, Maryland. She was married on 2 Sep 1862 to James S. Iden, a baggage master from Fauquier County, Virginia. He was the son of William and Elizabeth. William P. Iden married Elizabeth Glasscock on 13 Apr 1829 in Fauquier County. He was probably related to George Iden, the baggage master residing in **dwelling 142**. James S. Iden enlisted as a private in Company D of the 18th Virginia Cavalry.

Mary Elizabeth Stewart died 26 Jan 1933. She was married on 21 Dec 1868 to William Henry Ramey, the son of Phillip and Margaret Ann. Phillip Ramey married Margaret Ann Myers on 18 Sep 1838. William and his parents resided in **dwelling 89**. William H. Ramey died 22 Jan 1920. It indicates on his tombstone in the Massanutten Cemetery that he served with Chews Battery during the Civil War.

Kate Boyd Stewart was born 7 Jan 1852 and died 14 Feb 1925. She was listed as Kate Boyd Funk on her tombstone. Kate was the wife of George Frank Hupp Jr. George F. Hupp was born 27 Mar 1830 and died 12 Feb 1901. Kate and George were buried in the Riverview Cemetery.

John McMan was probably the John W. H. McMann who married Ella Knight on 25 Dec 1881. Ella was the daughter of William and had been born in Page County, Virginia. If this identification is correct John was the son of Michael and Nancy. Michael McMahon married Nancy Sharp on 3 Aug 1839. Nancy Sharp McMann was a resident in **dwelling 228.** John W. H. McMann, pronounced Mick Mann, married Lucy Burner on 3 Aug 1899. He died 23 Jun 1916 at the age of 76 and was buried in the Hutchinson Cemetery at Carmel in the Fort Valley.

RELATED FAMILY:

      Rebecca McMann, sister of John, resided in **dwelling 392.** She lived with the family of John and Sarah Pence.

1850 CENSUS: William T. Stewart and family resided in dwelling 243 on page 17.

PAGE 21 WOODSTOCK (Microfilm Page 847)

Dwelling 141   Family 141

Joseph S. Irwin	42	Physician 13,300 5300			Virginia
Sarah C. Irwin	25				"
Joseph S. Irwin	6				"
Franklin R. Irwin	1				"
William H. Triplett	26	Physician	0	150	"
Roberta Smootz	10				" School

    Joseph S. Irwin was born 30 Nov 1817 and died 16 Nov 1895. He was the son of Dr. Joseph J. Irwin and his wife Clarissa Mary. Dr. Joseph J. Irwin was born in Ireland. Joseph S. Irwin was originally married to Ellen Koontz Lantz on 1 May 1847. She was the widow of John D. Lantz. Ellen and John had married on 14 Oct 1844. George Grandstaff was listed as her guardian at the tim of this marriage. Ellen F. Lantz Irwin died 15 May 1849 at the age of 25. She was buried in the Pughs Run Cemetery at Maurertown. Joseph was then married to **Sarah Catherine Gochenour** on 13 Jan 1856. Sarah was the daughter of Henry of John Gochenour and Elizabeth Ann Knisely Gochenour. Sarah Catherine Gochenour Irwin was born 18 Dec 1833 and died 7 Dec 1914. Joseph and Sarah were buried in the St. Paul's Reformed Church Cemetery in Woodstock.

    Joseph S. Leonidas Irwin was born on 23 May 1857 and died 20 Jul 1886.

Franklin R. Irwin was born 5 Sep 1858 and died 10 Dec 1895. He is buried near his parents.

William H. Triplett was the son of Leonidas and Matilda. Dr. Leonidas Triplett married Matilda Berryhill Irwin on 24 Jan 1834. Matilda was the sister of Dr. Joseph S. Irwin who was the head of this household. Dr. Leonidas Triplett and his family resided in dwelling 606. William was born 16 Sep 1836 and died 27 Mar 1890. He was a member of the 10th Virginia Infantry for a brief period of time. He was Assistant Surgeon of his unit during Jul and Aug of 1861. William was married to Kathleen McKay on 5 Jun 1867. Kathleen was from Warren County, Virginia. She was the daughter of Robert and Nancy. Robert S. McKay married Nancy A. McKay on 24 Feb 1828 in Frederick County, Virginia. Kathleen was 27 years old when she died on 25 Apr 1871. William and Kathleen were buried in the Emanuel Lutheran Church Cemetery. William spent a number of years in London, England and studied under some of the most eminent surgeons in that nation. He was the author of an extensive treatise on microscopial anatomy entitled The Mechanics of Life.

Roberta A. Smootz was the daughter of William H. Smootz and Barbara Ann Gochenour. William and Barbara were married on 12 Nov 1849. Roberta's mother was the sister of Sarah C. Gochenour Irwin, the mistress of this household. Roberta was married on 20 Sep 1877 to William Perry Stultz. William was the son of Jacob H. and Lydia. Jacob H. Stultz married Lydia Naugle on 20 Nov 1841. Roberta died and was buried at the Stultz Cemetery in Alonzoville. The tombstone does not contain a death date. On 2 Mar 1882 William Perry Stultz married Sallie McCoy, the daughter of James and Elizabeth. James McCoy married Elizabeth Rosenberger on 4 Mar 1856. James McCoy and his family resided in dwelling 363. Sallie is believed to have been buried with Roberta in the Stultz Cemetery in Alonzoville William appears to have married for the third time. He was also married to Luella Short. Luella was born in 1859 and died in 1923. William Perry Stultz was born in 1850 and died in 1934. He and Luella were buried in the St. Luke Lutheran Cemetery at St. Luke.

RELATED FAMILY:

Mary Elizabeth Irwin, sister of Joseph S. Irwin, married William Smith Arthur on 30 May 1860 and resided in dwelling 198.

William H. F. Irwin, brother of Joseph S. Irwin, married Barbara Coffman on 8 Jun 1857 and resided in **dwelling 1284**. **John Irwin**, also a brother of Joseph, resided in the same household.

James Irwin, brother of Joseph S. Irwin, resided in **dwelling 157**.

Matilda Berryhill Irwin, sister of Joseph S. Irwin, married Leonidas Triplett on 24 Jan 1834 and resided in **dwelling 606**.

1850 CENSUS: **Joseph S. Irwin** was a resident with his parents in dwelling 229 on page 17.

William H. Triplett was a resident with his parents in dwelling 1087 on page 76.

Roberta Smootz resided in dwelling 766 on page 54.

PAGE 21 WOODSTOCK (Microfilm Page 847)

Dwelling 142 Family 142

Henry St. George Albert	48	Hotel Keeper 6300 3520	Va.
Emma E. Albert	42		"
Elvin F. Albert	23	Merchant	"
Mary V. Albert	23		"
James H. Albert	21		"
William H. Albert	18		"
Silas B. Albert	13		" Schl
Mary C. L. Albert	11		" Schl
Hugh M. Albert	8		" Schl
James N. Johnson	35	Conductor of Freight	Md.
William Heartshon	27	Engineer Gravel Train	"
Joseph Bowers	23	Day Labor	Va.
William Ludy	23	Day Labor	"
George Iden	22	Baggage Master	"

Elvin T. Albert was married to **Mary Virginia Miller** on 10 Nov 1859. She was the daughter of Thomas and Lydia. Thomas Miller was a minister from Pennsylvania. Lydia was reported to have been born in Madison County, Virginia.

James H. Albert was married on 7 Nov 1866 to Jane Gillock. Jane was the daughter of Henry Harrison and Rebecca. Henry and his family were located in **dwelling 197**. Jane was listed as Arabella Jane Gillock in that household. James H. Albert was born in Shenandoah County ca. 1840. He enlisted in Company F of the 10th Virginia Infantry as a private on 18 Apr 1861. He was reported as having a ruddy complexion, brown hair and hazel eyes. He was 6 foot tall. James was taken prisoner at Spotsylvania Courthouse on 12 May 1864. He was sent to Fort Delaware on 21 May 1864. He was released on 28 May 1864 under the Oath of Allegiance. He was a resident of Alvarado, Texas after the war.

William H. Albert was born 12 Feb 1842 and died 18 Feb 1906. He was married on 31 Dec 1874 to Mary Allen. Mary was the daughter of Reuben and Rebecca. Reuben Allen married Rebecca Peters on 21 Dec 1822. Rebecca Peters Allen and her family resided in **dwelling 634**. William was a carriage painter who was residing in Dayton, Ohio at the time of his marriage in 1874. Mary Peters Allen Albert was born 1 May 1845 and died 19 Apr 1917. They were buried in the Massanutten Cemetery. William H. Albert was of fair complexion with dark hair and hazel eyes. He was 5'11". William enlisted as a private in Company F of the 10th Virginia Infantry on 19 Jul 1861. He was detailed to a hospital near Chancellorsville on 3 May 1863. He was taken prisoner at Spotsylvania Courthouse on 12 May 1864. He was transferred to Fort Delaware on 20 May 1864. William was released on 28 May 1864 under the Oath of Allegiance.

Mary Catherine Leeper Albert was married on 9 Dec 1868 to Lemuel F. Burner. Lemuel was a carpenter. He was the son of Jacob and Sophia. Jacob Burner married Sophia Fravel on 19 Oct 1847. Lemuel Fravel Burner was born 28 Aug 1848 and died 23 Aug 1920. Mary was born 16 Oct 1849. She lived in Washington, D.C. with the family of her daughter.

There was a **Joseph Bowers** on the roll of the 33rd Virginia Infantry. No data positively identifies this individual as the man in this household. Joseph Bowers had joined the unit on 15 Jul 1861. He was wounded in action on 30 Aug 1862 at Manassas. He had a shoulder wound. He never returned to action and was retired to the Invalid Corp on 28 Apr 1864.

RELATED FAMILY:
Elizabeth Albert, daughter of Henry and Emma, married William Robinson on 5 Apr 1854 and resided in **dwelling 738.**

1850 CENSUS: **Henry St. George Albert** and family resided in dwelling 244 on page 17.

Mary Virginia Miller resided with her parents in dwelling 1051 on page 73.

PAGE 22 WOODSTOCK (Microfilm Page 848)

Dwelling 143 Family 143

Maria Dinges	49	2810 1775	Virginia	
John W. Dinges	15		"	School
Mary C. Dinges	14		"	School
Joseph B. Dinges	13		"	School

Maria S. Linn was married to Jacob Dinges on 15 Dec 1829. The bondsman for the marriage was Joseph Bowman.

John W. Dinges enlisted in Company F of the 10th Virginia Infantry as a private on 26 May 1861. He was the regimental drummer. John W. Dinges died 6 May 1863 of wounds received at Chancellorsville.

Joseph B. Dinges was born 27 Aug 1846 and died 6 Nov 1916. He is buried in the Massanutten Cemetery. On his tombstone there is an inscription which relates that he was a member of Rossner's Brigade of the 7th Virginia Cavalry.

1850 CENSUS: **Maria Linn Dinges** and her husband Jacob, resided in dwelling 299 on page 22.

PAGE 22 WOODSTOCK (Microfilm Page 848)

Dwelling 144 Family 144

Nathan Berricks	37	Laborer in Engine House 100 150	
			Maryland
Ann R. Berricks	33		"
Margaret A. Berricks	15		" School
George W. Berricks	13		" School
Laura V. Berricks	9		" School
Alice M. Berricks	6		" School

1850 CENSUS: No record of this family has been located in 1850.

164

Dwelling 145   Family 145

John H. J. Fravel	37	Painter O 90	Virginia	
Sarah J. Fravel	35		"	
George R. Fravel	9		"	School
Sarah B. Fravel	6		"	
Kate R. Fravel	4		"	
Charles F. Fravel	5m		"	

John Henry Fravel was born 11 Mar 1826 and died 13 May 1892. He was the son of Henry and Barbara. Henry Fravel III married Barbara Fetzer on 9 Aug 1808. John Henry Fravel was married to **Sarah Jane Bruce** on 4 Jul 1848. Sarah Jane was the daughter of Alexander Bruce. Alexander was from Scotland. He came to America in a party of 16 men to tour. He desired to remain and hid from other members of his party as they prepared to depart for Scotland. It is reported that he survived on berries until the group eventually gave up searching for him. Sarah Jane Bruce Fravel was born 21 Nov 1824 and died 5 Jun 1888.

George Robert Fravel was born 9 May 1849 and died 22 May 1904. He was a carpenter at the time he married **Eva C. Orndorff** on 30 May 1868. She was the daughter of James and Emily. Eva was born in 1845 and died 18 Jun 1870 at the age of 24 years and 8 months. George was then married to **Margaret Elizabeth "Maggie" Feller** on 27 Feb 1871. Maggie was the daughter of Samuel and Rachel. Samuel G. Feller married Rachel Snarr on 29 Mar 1840. Maggie was born 3 Sep 1849 and died 6 Apr 1910. George and Maggie were buried at Massanutten. George was a furniture dealer and mortician.

Sarah "Bettie" Fravel was married to Robert Gibson Koontz on 22 Dec 1877. Robert was the son of Harrison and Susan. Harrison Koontz married Susan Ann Hisey on 6 Oct 1842. Harrison Koontz and his family resided in **dwelling 91**. Robert Henry Koontz was born 16 Sep 1853 and died 7 Aug 1918. He was buried in St. Paul's Reformed Church Cemetery in Woodstock. Sarah "Bettie" Fravel Koontz was born 5 Oct 1854 and died 24 May 1877.

Kate Rye Fravel was born 20 Feb 1856 and died 31 Jan 1921. She was married to William Alexander Fox of Culpepper, Virginia. He was a shoemaker and was the son of Henry and Catherine. William was born 21 Sep 1852 and

died 2 Jul 1905. This couple was buried in Washington,
D.C.

     Charles Frederick Fravel was born 20 Sep 1859 and
died 12 Mar 1922. His wife was Ida Belle Hottel. They
were married on 23 Feb 1882. She was the daughter of
Abraham and Ann. Abraham Hottel married Ann Dirting on 22
Jun 1854. Ida Belle was born 22 Jun 1859 and died in Jun
1929. They were buried in the Massanutten Cemetery.
Charles was a furniture dealer, painter and paperhanger.

RELATED FAMILY:
     Mary Fravel, sister of John Henry Fravel,
married James Gregory Fravel on 6 Nov 1834 and resided in
dwelling 114.
     Catherine Fravel, sister of John Henry,
married George Rye on 2 Oct 1833 and resided in **dwelling
156.**
     David Fravel, brother of John Henry, married
Louisa Supinger on 11 Jan 1860 and resided in **dwelling 200.**
     George Fravel, brother of John Henry,
married Harriet Myers on 6 Nov 1833 and resided in **dwelling
177.**
     Frederick Fravel, brother of John Henry,
married Ellen Catherine Miller on 24 Aug 1840 and resided
in **dwelling 201.**

1850 CENSUS: John Henry Fravel and his family resided in
              dwelling 212 on page 15.

PAGE 22 WOODSTOCK   (Microfilm Page 848)

Dwelling 146   Family 146

John H. Fry	25	Day Labor	200	78	Virginia
Ellen F. Fry	24				"
George V. Fry	3				"
Charles R. Fry	1				"

     John H. Fry was the son of Phillip and Sarah.
Phillip Fry married Sarah Lineweaver on 12 Nov 1834.
John's father remarried when Sarah Lineweaver Fry died.
Phillip Fry and his second wife Leah Ann Dysert resided in
dwelling 1741. Phillip and Leah were married on 14 Feb
1845. John H. Fry married **Ellen Coffman** on 14 Apr 1856. He
was a collier at the time of the marriage. Ellen was the
daughter of John and Lucy. John Coffman married Lucy Jack

on 27 Feb 1832. John Coffman and his family resided in **dwelling 194.**

RELATED FAMILY:

> **Margaret Fry,** sister of John H. Fry, married John William Litten on 12 Jan 1860 and resided in **dwelling 1621.**

1850 CENSUS: **Ellen Coffman** and her parents were residents of dwelling 218 on page 16.

> **John H. Fry** appears as a 15 year old in the household of Samuel Fravel. They resided in dwelling 1183 on page 72. He may have left his father's household after the death of his mother.

PAGE 22 WOODSTOCK (Microfilm Page 848)

Dwelling 147 Family 147

Serena Blair	42	Washerwoman	1000	40	Virginia
James L. Blair	18	Printers Apprentice			"

Serena Proctor was married to Robert P. Blair on 6 Nov 1844. The bondsman for the marriage was John Blake.

James L. Blair enlisted in the 10th Virginia Infantry Company F on 4 May 1861. Unit records indicate that he deserted prior to Apr 1862. Shenandoah County records state that he was dismissed from the unit and was known to have died prior to 1900.

1850 CENSUS: **Serena Proctor Blair,** her husband Robert and family, resided in dwelling 215 on page 15.

PAGE 22 WOODSTOCK (Microfilm Page 848)

Dwelling 148 Family 148

Hugh Purvis	51	Conductor	0	50	Scotland
Ann Purvis	46				Virginia
Angus Purvis	18				" School
Robert H. Purvis	14				" School
Sarah A. Purvis	12				" School

Hugh Purvis was married to **Ann Reed** on 10 May 1841. The bondsman for the marriage was Phillip Miller.

1850 CENSUS: Hugh Purvis and his family resided in
              dwelling 313 on page 23.

PAGE 22 WOODSTOCK (Microfilm Page 848)

Dwelling 149 Family 149

Samuel Bauserman	40	Wagon Maker 100	671	Virginia
Catherine Bauserman	39			"
James H. Bauserman	16			" School
Sarah Bauserman	13			" School

   Samuel Bauserman was born 22 Dec 1819 and died 2
Feb 1907. He was married to **Catherine Artz** on 13 Nov 1843.
The bondsman for the marriage was Henry Artz. Catherine
was born 22 Mar 1820 and died 6 Sep 1907. They were buried
in the Culler Cemetery.

   James H. Bauserman enlisted in Company C of the
33rd Virginia Infantry on 15 Mar 1862. He was promoted to
Sgt. on 21 Apr 1862. James was wounded in his knee on 1
Jul 1862 at Malvern Hill. He returned to active duty in
Dec 1862. He was promoted to Lt. in 1864. On 19 Oct 1864
he was missing wounded in action. His wound was to his
left lung. The lung eventually collapsed and he died 31
Oct 1864.

   Sarah Elizabeth Bauserman was born 18 Oct 1846 and
died 17 Jun 1910. She was married on 8 Mar 1866 to Robert
Milton Cullers. Robert was born 12 Nov 1843 and died 10
Aug 1913. They were buried at the Cullers Cemetery near
Big Spring in Page County, Virginia. Robert was the son
of Henry and Catherine. Henry Cullers married Catherine
Huffman on 31 Aug 1835 in Page County, Virginia. Robert
was a blacksmith at the time of the wedding. He had served
in the Civil War. On 7 Mar 1862 he enlisted in Company K
of the 10th Virginia Infantry. He was a private and was
reported to have been wounded at Winchester on 25 May 1862.
He was absent sick in Sep 1862 through Dec 1862. He
transferred to the artillery on 3 Feb 1863.

1850 CENSUS: **Samuel Bauserman** and his family resided in
              dwelling 216 on page 16.

168

PAGE 22   WOODSTOCK   (Microfilm Page 848)

Dwelling 150   Family 150

John T. Hickman	65		3760	10,290	Virginia
Kitty R. Hickman	36				"
Emily Hickman	24				"
Joseph T. Hickman	23	Physician			"
Lucretia Reynolds	70				"
Martha Reynolds	25				"
Mary Harris	60				"

Samuel Kercheval, the Herodotus of the Shenandoah Valley, lists a John T. Hickman as one of the prominent citizens of the area. In the 1830's that individual was a resident of Hampshire County. It is not known if this is the individual who heads this household. The head of this household was in Shenandoah County at the time of the 1850 census. **John T. Hickman** was born 21 Apr 1795 and died 30 Mar 1884. He was buried in the **Emanuel Lutheran Church** Cemetery in Woodstock.

Kitty R. Hickman was born in 1827 and died in 1917. She was buried in the Mt. Jackson Cemetery.

Emma "Emily" Hickman died in 1884. She was buried near her father in the Emanuel Lutheran Church Cemetery.

Dr. Joseph T. Hickman was born in 1836 and died 17 May 1915. He was buried with his sister Kitty at Mt. Jackson. His wife was Mary Alice Moore. She was born in 1850 and died in 1911. Mary Alice was also buried there. Joseph T. Hickman enlisted in the 10th Virginia Infantry on 15 Jul 1861. He was in Company K with the rank of Lt. He was absent sick through Oct 1861 and was dropped from the ranks on 14 Jun 1862.

Lucretia Hickman, probably the sister of John, was married on 16 Mar 1813 to Benedict Reynolds in Frederick County, Virginia. Her name appears as Duoretia in the marriage record. Given the age variance, **Martha Reynolds** was probably a grandchild. The relationship of **Mary Harris** has not been established. However there was a very intriguing marriage on 25 Feb 1785 in Frederick County, Virginia. Benjamin Harris married Lucretia Hickman. The wife of Benjamin Harris may have been the aunt of John and Lucretia. If that assumption is correct Mary Harris may have been a cousin.

RELATED FAMILY:

                       Susan Mary Hickman, daughter of John T. Hickman, married William Donaldson on 14 Jan 1845 and resided in dwelling 175.

1850 CENSUS: John T. Hickman and his family resided in dwelling 223 on page 16. His wife was not present in the household. However, Lucretia and Martha Reynolds and Mary Harris were in the household at that time.

PAGE 23 WOODSTOCK   (Microfilm Page 849)

Dwelling 151 Family 151

Jacob C. Anderson	56	Blacksmith	1000	1040	Virginia C.R.
Rachel Anderson	53				"
Susan Gill	19	Housegirl			"
William Gill	14	Blacksmith Helper			"

    The Gill children resided in the household of Jacob and Rachel in 1850.

    Susan Gill was born in Frederick County, Virginia. She was the daughter of William and Catherine. On 11 Sep 1862 she was married to John W. Gordon, a merchant from Washington County, Maryland. He was the son of Jerome and Catherine. John W. Gordon was residing at Staunton, Virginia at the time of the marriage.

    George William Gill was born ca. 1843. He was a blacksmith. He enlisted on 18 Apr 1861 as a private in Company F of the 10th Virginia Infantry. He was detailed as a blacksmith in August of 1862 to the Ordnance Train, 1st Division. He later transferred to Company B on 31 Oct 1864. He was detailed to the Quartermaster Department of Gordon's Division as a blacksmith. He was taken prisoner at Appomattax in April of 1865. George William Gill is believed to have been married to Roberta Carr. He was 86 years old when he died on 10 Dec 1929 at Woodstock. He was buried in Pittsburgh, Pennsylvania.

1850 CENSUS: Jacob C. Anderson was living with his family in dwelling 224 page 16.

PAGE 23 WOODSTOCK   (Microfilm Page 849)

Dwelling 152   Family 152

```
Jacob Fogle        31 Day Laborer      0  160    Virginia
Martha Fogle       27                               "
Rachel A. Fogle    11m                              "
```

     Jacob Fogle was the son of Phillip and Mary.
Phillip Fogle married Mary "Polly" Burner on 10 Dec 1822.
Phillip and his family resided in **dwelling 449**. Jacob was
married on 28 Apr 1858 to **Martha Carrier**. Martha was
reported to have been the daughter of Elizabeth Carrier.
When the Civil War began Jacob Fogle enlisted on 8 Apr 1862
at Rudes Hill in Company G of the 2nd Virginia Infantry.
He was a private and was detailed as a teamster until
Jan/Feb 1863. He was permanently detailed to the Pioneer
Corp in Jan/Feb 1863. The last entry shows him present in
the Pioneer Corp Mar/Apr 1864. Jacob died soon after the
war. Martha Carrier Fogle later married Harvey Fogle on
27 Feb 1868. Harvey resided in **dwelling 469** at the time
of this census. He was the son of Valentine and Eva.
Martha Carrier Fogle was born 21 Jan 1833 and died 7 Feb
1912.

     Rachel A. Fogle was born 8 Feb 1860 and died 15 Jul
1940. She married William Homer Foltz on 18 Dec 1884.
William was the son of Robert and Mary. Robert W. Foltz
married Mary Lindamood on 26 Aug 1852. Robert W. Foltz and
his family resided in **dwelling 1583**. William Homer Foltz
was a widower. He had married Mattie C. Coffman on 25 Feb
1875. Mattie was the daughter of Robert and Sarah. Robert
R. Coffman married Sarah Eveline Rinehart on 17 Apr 1848.
Robert and his family resided in **dwelling 1224**. Mattie
Coffman Foltz died 9 Jun 1881. William Homer Foltz was
born 3 Mar 1853 and died 25 Nov 1929. They are buried in
the Christ Reformed Church Cemetery in Conicville.

1850 CENSUS: **Jacob Fogle** resided with his parents in
dwelling 1853 on page 133.
Martha Carrier was a 17 year old in residence
with the family of Jacob Anderson. They
resided in dwelling 224 on page 16.

171

PAGE 23 WOODSTOCK   (Microfilm Page 849)

Dwelling 153   Family 153

William F. Krebs	33	Physician	1810	2350	Penn.
Amanda Krebs	27				Virginia
William A. Krebs	8				"
Kate E. Krebs	6				"
Edgar W. Krebs	4				"
Laura V. Krebs	11m				"

William F. Krebs was a physician from Pennsylvania.
He was the son of Isaac and Esther. Dr. Krebs was born 8
Aug 1826 and died 13 Dec 1891. He was married to Sarah
Walton on 19 Nov 1850. Sarah was the daughter of Edward
and Catherine. Edward Walton married Catherine Byre on 6
May 1824. Edward Walton and his family resided in **dwelling
1415**. Sarah Walton Krebs was born 1 Aug 1829 and died 11
May 1856. Upon the death of Sarah, William F. Krebs
married **Amanda Taliferro**. Amanda was the daughter of Dr.
Edwin Taliferro and his wife Virginia. She was born 13 Dec
1830 in Augusta County, Virginia. Amanda resided in Mt.
Jackson at the time of the marriage. She died 26 Nov 1888.
Dr. Krebs and both of his wives were buried in the St.
Paul's Reformed Church Cemetery in Woodstock. William F.
Krebs was a respected breeder of thoroughbred horses.
According to Wayland's history he developed this interest
at about the time of the Civil War.

William A. Krebs was born 27 Sep 1851 and died 9
Aug 1861. He was buried at the St. Paul's Church Cemetery.

Kate Esther Krebs was born 24 Apr 1853 and died 16
Aug 1907. She was also buried at St. Paul's.

Edgar W. Krebs was born 8 Aug 1855 and died 17 Oct
1875. He was buried near his brothers and sisters.

Laura V. Krebs was born in 1858 and died 6 Feb
1862. She joined other members of her family in the
cemetery at St. Paul's.

RELATED FAMILY:
        Virginia Taliferro, probably the mother of
Amanda, married Whiting D. Farra in November of 1846 and
resided in **dwelling 598**. If this is so, she was the widow
of Dr. Edwin Taliferro.

172

1850 CENSUS: **Sarah Walton** appears in the household of her parents in dwelling 1348 on page 97.

PAGE 23 WOODSTOCK   (Microfilm Page 849)

Dwelling 154 Family 154

John H. Hunton	25	Clergyman/Lutheran 0 500	Just Mar.
			Virginia
Levinia P. Hunton	24		" Just Married

     John Henry Hunton was born 22 Apr 1833 and died 9 Mar 1907. He was the son of William Alexander and Anna Jayne Bayse Hunton. John's parents resided in **dwelling 774.** John Henry was reported to have been born in Fauquier County, Virginia. He married **Levinia Priscilla Baker** on 14 Dec 1859. She was the daughter of William and Elizabeth. William Baker married Elizabeth Hottel on 28 Mar 1822. Levinia was born in Warrenton, Virginia on 11 Oct 1834 and died 16 Jun 1908. John and Levinia were buried in Lima, Allen County, Ohio. John was ordained on 1 Sep 1857. He served the Friedens Church near Mt. Olive. This church was erected in 1824 on the site of the Hottel school. He moved to the mid-west and was 1st President of the Indiana Synod. He was also active in the Ohio Synod and was a mission Superintendent.

1850 CENSUS: **John Henry Hunton** resided with his parents in dwelling 1134 on page 80.
           Levinia Priscilla Baker resided with her parents in dwelling 617 on page 44.

PAGE 23 WOODSTOCK   (Microfilm Page 849)

Dwelling 155 Family 155

Isabella Anderson	48	1000	100	Virignia	
Mary E. Anderson	14			"	School
Robert G. Anderson	12			"	School
Laura A. Anderson	10			"	School

     Isabella Clower was born 21 Oct 1809 and died 24 Dec 1884. Isabella was buried at the Emanuel Lutheran Church Cemetery in Woodstock. She was the daughter of John and Frances. John Clower married Frances Grove on 15 Jan 1809. She married Alexander Anderson on 19 Sep 1838. Alexander was an attorney. The bondsman for their marriage was Alex Bowman.

Mary Ellen Anderson was married to Robert N. Gaw on 28 Jan 1869. Robert was a farmer. He was the son of Jacob and Sarah. His grandfather was an immigrant from Ireland. Robert N. Gaw and his family resided in dwelling 161.

Robert G. Anderson died 29 Oct 1926. He was a house painter and he never married. He was buried in the Emanuel Lutheran Church Cemetery. Robert's tombstone indicates that he was member of Imboden's Virginia Brigade. He enlisted in Company E of the 11th Virginia Cavalry. He was a private in that unit. He served as a musician in Imboden's Brigade. Post war rosters and pension records indicate that he transferred from the 7th Virginia Cavalry band to the 62nd Virginia Mounted Infantry Division on 17 Apr 1865. He was 5'6" with dark complexion, fair hair and hazel eyes.

RELATED FAMILY:

Frances Catherine Anderson, daughter of Alexander and Isabella, married Lewis C. Knisely on 14 Dec 1859 and resided in dwelling 136.

Joseph H. Clower, brother of Isabella, resided in dwelling 107.

Elizabeth Clower, sister of Isabella, married George Harrison Ott on 29 Nov 1849 and resided in dwelling 125.

Jacob B. Clower, brother of Isabella, married Julia Ann Haas and resided in dwelling 176.

1850 CENSUS: Alexander Anderson and his family resided in dwelling 258 on page 19.

PAGE 23 WOODSTOCK   (Microfilm Page 849)

Dwelling 156   Family 156

George Rye	50	Farmer	4500	700	Virginia
Catherine Rye	47				"
Rebecca Walker	22	Housegirl			"
John Moler	12	(Mulatto)			"

George Rye was born 19 Feb 1810 and died 24 Apr 1890. In the 1850 census he appears as a saddler from Maryland. He was married on 2 Oct 1833 to Catherine Fravel. Catherine was the daughter of Henry and Barbara. Henry Fravel III married Barbara Fetzer on 9 Aug 1808. Catherine was born 18 Jul 1813 and died 6 Mar 1888. George and Catherine were buried in the St. Paul's Lutheran Church

Cemetery in Woodstock. They did not have any children. George was a local surveyor. He became a judge. In addition, Judge Rye held the post of State Treasurer of Virginia from 1868 to 1871. During that period George and Catherine resided in the state capital at Richmond.

Rebecca Walker was born 10 Apr 1837 and died 23 May 1894. She was the daughter of Henry and Hannah. Henry Walker married Hannah Righman on 18 Sep 1824. Rebecca was married to Henry Eckard on 27 Apr 1867. Henry was born 14 Nov 1846 and died 24 May 1894. He was the son of Frederick and Elizabeth. His parents were born in Hesse, Germany. Henry was born in Rockingham County, Virginia. Henry Eckard and his family resided in **dwelling 1445**. Rebecca and Henry were buried in the Zion Lutheran Church Cemetery.

RELATED FAMILY:

David Fravel, brother of Catherine, married Louisa Supinger on 11 Jan 1860 and resided in **dwelling 200**.

George Fravel, brother of Catherine, married Harriet Myers on 6 Nov 1833 and resided in **dwelling 177**.

Frederick Fravel, brother of Catherine, married Ellen Catherine Miller on 24 Aug 1840. He was deceased at this time. His widow resided in **dwelling 201**.

John Henry Fravel, brother of Catherine, married Sarah Jane Bruce on 4 Jul 1848 and resided in **dwelling 145**.

Mary A. Fravel, sister of Catherine, married James Gregory Fravel on 6 Nov 1834 and resided in **dwelling 114**.

Mary Ann Rye, believed to have been the sister of George, married Samuel Fetzer on 14 May 1829 and resided in **dwelling 195**. She was a widow at the time of the census and George Rye had been executor of Samuel Fetzer's estate.

William Walker, brother of Rebecca, married Mary Ann Sheetz on 1 Dec 1853 and resided in **dwelling 947**.

Catherine Walker, sister of Rebecca, married James C. McKelvey on 15 May 1856 and resided in **dwelling 1156**.

1850 CENSUS: **George Rye** and his wife resided in dwelling 245 on page 18.

Rebecca Walker resided with her parents in dwelling 1369 on page 99.

PAGE 23 WOODSTOCK (Microfilm Page 849)

Dwelling 157 Family 157

James Irwin   33 Farmer   4100   160   Virginia

      James Irwin was the son of Dr. Joseph Irwin and his wife Clarissa Mary. Dr. Irwin was from Ireland. The record of his marriage and the surname of his wife has not been located.

RELATED FAMILY:

      William H. Irwin, brother of James, married Barbara Ann Coffman on 8 Jun 1857 and resided in **dwelling 1284**. Another brother, **John Irwin**, also resides in this household.

      Joseph S. Irwin, brother of James, married Sarah Catherine Gochenour on 12 Jan 1856 and resides in **dwelling 141**.

      Mary Elizabeth Irwin, sister of James, married William Smith Arthur on 30 May 1860 and resided in **dwelling 198**.

      Matilda Berryhill Irwin, sister of James, married Leonidas Triplett on 24 Jan 1834 and resided in **dwelling 606**.

1850 CENSUS: James A. Irwin was in dwelling 48 on page 4. He resided with his brother William H. Irwin.

PAGE 23 WOODSTOCK (Microfilm Page 849)

Dwelling 158 Family 158

Henry L. Reed	69	0 145	Mass.	
Charlotte L. Reed	53		"	
Thomas D. Reed	28		"	Idiotic
Charlotte P. Reed	18		Virginia	
Julia H. Reed	16		"	

RELATED FAMILY:

      Mary E. Reed, daughter of Henry and Charlotte, married Isaac Haas on 15 Sep 1859 and resided in **dwelling 137**. She was reported to have been born in Norfolk, Virginia.

1850 CENSUS: No record of this family has been located.

176

PAGE 23 WOODSTOCK   (Microfilm Page 849)

Dwelling 159   Family 159

John W. Ott	34	Deputy Sheriff	1200	1436	Virginia
Elizabeth H. Ott	31				"
William W. Ott	8				"
Charles F. Ott	6				"
Mary J. Ott	3				"
Ann V. Ott	9m				"

    John W. Ott was married on 17 Dec 1850 to **Elizabeth Walton**. Elizabeth was the daughter of Reuben Moore and Mary Harrison Walton. Reuben and his family resided in **dwelling 165**.

    Charles F. M. Ott was born 1854 and died in 1872. He was buried at the Emanuel Lutheran Church Cemetery in Woodstock.

RELATED FAMILY:
    Moses Walton, brother of Elizabeth, married Emily Lauck on 5 Feb 1851 and resided in **dwelling 120**.
    Anna Walton, sister of Elizabeth, married Josiah Lockhart Campbell on 19 May 1858 and resided in **dwelling 226**.

1850 CENSUS: Elizabeth Walton was a resident in the household of her parents. They resided in dwelling 240 on page 17.

PAGE 24 WOODSTOCK   (Microfilm Page 850)

Dwelling 160   Family 160

Willis Sullivan	64	0	4220	Virginia	
Ellenora Sullivan	57			"	
Frances A. Thompson	39			"	
Ellenore W. Thompson	18			"	School
Margaret M. Thompson	13			"	School
Fanny Thompson	9			"	School

    Willis Sullivan married **Eleanora Wiatt** on 27 Jul 1818. They were married in Fauquier County, Virginia.

    Frances Ann Sullivan, the daughter of Willis and Eleanora, married Thomas H. Thompson on 13 Mar 1838. They were married in Fauquier County, Virginia.

Margaret McGeorge Thompson, daughter of Thomas and Frances, married George H. Allen on 15 Mar 1865. George was a physician from Madison County, Virginia. He was the son of Thomas and Rebecca. Margaret was born in Fauquier County, Virginia.

1850 CENSUS: No record of this family has been located.

PAGE 24   WOODSTOCK   (Microfilm Page 850)

Dwelling 161   Family 161

Sarah C. Gaw	41	1400	400	Virginia	
Henrietta G. Gaw	19			"	School
Robert N. Gaw	13			"	School
Ann E. Gaw	10			"	School
Benjamin P. Gaw	7			"	

Sarah C. Gaw was the wife of Jacob R. Gaw. Jacob was the son of Robert Gaw and his wife Barbara Rinker Gaw. Robert Gaw was an immigrant from Ireland. The Hottel family history does not record him as the son of Robert. However, the 29 Aug 1829 will of Robert Gaw which was located in Will Book P on page 223 mentions his son Jacob R. Gaw. It states "the house and lot on which I now live in the town of Woodstock and 10 acres out lot adjoining Dr. Irwin and Abraham Fravel" will be left to Jacob. Jacob Gaw was buried with many members of his family in the St. Pauls Reformed Church Cemetery in Woodstock. Jacob R. Gaw was born in 1808 and died 18 Feb 1854.

Robert N. Gaw was a farmer at the time of his marriage to Mary Ellen Anderson on 28 Jan 1869. Mary Ellen was the daughter of Alexander and Isabella. Alexander Anderson married Isabella Clower on 19 Sep 1838. Isabella Clower Anderson and her family resided in dwelling 155. Robert N. Gaw, according to the Wayland history was a member of Company C of the 7th Virginia Cavalry.

Henrietta "Ettie" C. Gaw was married to Robert H. Moler on 27 Oct 1874. Robert was a farmer from Jefferson County, West Virginia. He was the son of Phillip and Susan.

1850 CENSUS: Jacob R. Gaw and his family resided in dwelling 207 on page 15.

PAGE 24   WOODSTOCK   (Microfilm Page 850)

Dwelling 162 Family 162

Curtis Neeb	31	Brakeman on Car	1000	200	Germany
Elizabeth Neeb	27				Virginia
George E. Neeb	8				"
Virginia Neeb	5				"

        Curtis Neeb was born in Germany in 1828. He died
in 1874.   Curtis was married to **Elizabeth Marshall** on 15
Aug 1850.   Consent for the marriage was provided by her
guardian Daniel Hisey. Elizabeth was born in 1830 and died
in 1893.   Curtis and Elizabeth were buried in the
Massanutten Cemetery.

        George E. Neeb was born in 1852 and died in 1869.

        Virginia Neeb was born in 1854 and died 9 Dec 1919.
She was married on 2 Jan 1872 to Michael Geary. Michael
was born in 1844 and died in 1891. He was an Irish born
engineer. He was the son of Michael and Mary and resided
in Alexandria, Virginia at the time of the marriage.
Virginia and Michael were buried in the Massanutten
Cemetery.

1850 CENSUS: Curtis Neeb was a confectionist at the time
                of the 1850 census. He was a resident in
                the household of George Rye. They resided
                in dwelling 245 on page 18.

PAGE 24   WOODSTOCK   (Microfilm Page 850)

Dwelling 163 Family 163

Flora Lutz   57 Washerwoman 0 80 Virginia Can't Read

1850 CENSUS: No record of this individual has been found
                in 1850.

PAGE   24   WOODSTOCK   (Microfilm Page 850)

Dwelling 164   Family 164

Mark Bird	49	Attorney 18,500	10,000	Virginia	
Sarah C. M. Bird	47			"	
Mark Bird	24	Law Student		"	
Ann H. Bird	19			"	School
Mary L. Bird	16			"	School
Isaac H. Bird	14			"	School
William M. Bird	12			"	School
Eitinge Bird	7			"	
Sallie M. Bird	4			"	
Cornelius W. Bird	1			"	
Rebecca H. Loder	25			"	
Ann Wanzer	40	Houseservant (Mulatto)		"	
Peggy Morton	35	Houseservant (Mulatto)		"	
Mary F. Morton	8	(Mulatto)		"	

Mark Bird was the son of Captain George Bird and
Hannah Allen Bird. George and Hannah were married on 25
Jan 1788. Mark Bird was a Commonwealth Attorney. He was
a representative of Hardy, Shenandoah and Warren Counties
to the Virginia Constitutional Convention of 1850-1851.
He was appointed Judge of the 18th Judicial District.
Judge Bird was born 23 Dec 1810 and died 2 Jan 1883. He
married **Sarah C. Macon Hite** on 18 Oct 1834. This marriage
took place in Frederick County, Virginia. The bondsman for
the marriage was Walker Hite. Sarah was born 7 Nov 1812
and died 5 Jul 1896. The Bird home in Shenandoah County
was called the "Birds Nest". Mark and Sarah and most of
their children were buried at the Massanutten Cemetery in
Woodstock.

Mark Bird Jr. was born 25 May 1836 and died 25 Feb
1903. He did not marry. Mark Jr was 5'6 3/4", fair
complexed with dark brown hair and gray eyes. He enlisted
n 18 Apr 1861 in Company F of the 10th Virginia Infantry.
Upon his enlistment at Woodstock he was appointed 2nd
Corporal. He appears as a 4th Corporal in October 1862.
He was promoted to 3rd Sergeant on 21 May 1863. Mark was
wounded at Gettysburg in Jul 1863. He returned to the
ranks in February 1864. He was transferred to Company B
of the 10th Virginia Infantry on 31 Oct 1864. He was taken
prisoner at Ft. Steadman near Petersburg on 25 Mar 1865 and
was send to Point Lookout on 28 Mar 1865. Mark was
released under the oath of allegiance on 23 Jun 1865.

Ann Hite Bird was born 28 Jan 1841 and died 15 Nov 1917. She did not marry and was buried at the Massanutten Cemetery.

Mary Louisa Bird was born 25 Jun 1843 and died 6 Jan 1904. She was married in Shenandoah County on 21 Nov 1872 to Smith S. Turner. Smith was an attorney in Warren County where he was born. He was the son of Robert and Lucy. Robert Turner married Lucy Green Long on 10 Feb 1825. Smith was born 21 Nov 1842 and died 8 Apr 1898. Mary and Smith were buried in the Prospect Hill Cemetery in Front Royal, Virginia. Smith S. Turner was a Captain in Company B of the 17th Virginia Infantry.

Isaac Hite Bird was born in 1845 and died in 1892. He was generally referred to as "Hite" Bird. Isaac was a member of the 7th Virginia Cavalry Company C. Hite married Lelia B. Zirkle. Lelia was born in 1854 and died in 1894. They were buried in the Massanutten Cemetery.

William Maury Bird was married to Rosella L. Culver.

Eitinge Fontaine Bird was married to Sarah Jordan.

Sallie Madison Bird was born in 1856 and died 11 Aug 1933. She was married to William Twyman Williams on 21 Feb 1883. William was the son of Samuel and Sarah. Samuel Crousden Williams married Sarah Carpenter Ott on 19 Jan 1833. Samuel C. Williams and his family resided in **dwelling 174**. The Williams family was very prominent in Shenandoah County and Samuel Crousden Williams was the organizer of the Muhlenberg Rifles at the outbreak of the Civil War. William Twyman Williams was an attorney and the Ruling Elder of the Presbyterian Church in Woodstock. He was born in 1849 and died in 1933. Sallie and William were buried in the Massanutten Cemetery.

Rebecca H. Loder lived with his family at the time of the 1850 census.

RELATED FAMILY:

Bettie Green Bird, daughter of Mark and Sarah, married Kenner B. Stephenson on 7 Dec 1859. They resided at Belle Grove. Although the couple was buried at Massanutten Cemetery they were not in Shenandoah County at the time of this census. Kenner B. Stephenson was an attorney and judge.

Reuben A. Bird, brother of Mark, married Hester Sigler on 12 Jun 1826 and resided in **dwelling 605**.

181

1850 CENSUS: Mark Bird and his family resided in dwelling
            328 on page 24.

PAGE 24   WOODSTOCK   (Microfilm Page 850)

Dwelling 165   Family 165

```
Reuben Walton       60 Farmer    11,250   8000  Virginia
Mary Walton         54                            "
David H. Walton     29 Attorney      0   1000    "
Elizabeth Walton    78                            "
Mary A. Walton      53                            "
Jonas Stephens      30 Farmhand (Black)          "
Mark More           16 (Black)                    "
```

     Reuben Walton was the county surveyor. He died 6
May 1874 at the age of 74 years, 10 months and 9 days old.
He was the son of Moses Walton and Elizabeth Moore. Moses
and Elizabeth were married in 1798 in Rockingham County,
Virginia. Elizabeth Moore Walton resided in this dwelling.
Reuben Walton was married at some point to **Mary Harrison.**
Mary Harrison Walton died 18 Dec 1872. She was 67 years,
4 months and 24 days old. Reuben and Mary were buried in
the Massanutten Cemetery.

     David Harrison Walton was born 21 Oct 1830 and died
7 Jul 1876. He was buried in the Massanutten Cemetery.
David attended Washington College and became an attorney.
He enlisted in Company K of the 33rd Virginia Infantry on
15 Jul 1861. He was a Captain at that time and eventually
attained the rank of Colonel. He was present thru Apr
1862. He was reduced in rank on 14 Jun 1862. David was
wounded at Cedar Run on 9 Aug 1862 and was wounded at
Manassas on 28 Aug 1862. He was paroled 9 Apr 1865 at
Appomattox.

     Elizabeth Moore was the daughter of Reuben R. Moore.
She married Moses Walton in 1798. Moses died 13 Mar 1847
and was buried in the Old Union Cemetery at Mt. Jackson.
Moses was a representative of Shenandoah County in the
Virginia House of Delegates from 1820 to 1823. He
represented Shenandoah and Rockingham County in the State
Senate from 1826 to 1830.

     Mary A. Walton, was the sister of Reuben. She died
25 May 1879 at the age of 79 years and 3 months old. She
was buried in the Massanutten Cemetery.

RELATED FAMILY:
> **Moses Walton**, son of Reuben and Mary, married Emily M. Lauck on 3 Feb 1851 and resided in **dwelling 120**.
> **Elizabeth Walton**, daughter of Reuben and Mary, married John W. Ott on 17 Dec 1850 and resided in **dwelling 159**.
> **Anna M. Walton**, daughter of Reuben and Mary, married Dr. Josiah Lockhart on 19 May 1858 and resided in **dwelling 226**.

1850 CENSUS: **Reuben Walton** and family resided in dwelling 240 on page 17.

PAGE 25 WOODSTOCK   (Microfilm Page 851)

Dwelling 166   Family 166

John W. Wolff	35	Meth. Minister	1200	305	Virginia
Mary C. Eakin	28				"
Catherine Wetzel	30				"
John C. Wolff	7				"
Virginia R. Wolff	5				"
Maria E. Eakin	5				"
Joseph J. Eakin	31	Meth. Minister	0	310	"

The configuration of this household is rather interesting. To list Rev. Joseph J. Eakin at the bottom was not a common practice unless an individual was deceased.

There was a John Wolff listed among the ministers of the county. However in the 1850 census 39 year old John G. Wolff and his wife Susan appear in dwelling 219. He was a minister of the German Reformed Church.

There was a James N. Eakin among the ministers who served the county. There is no mention of a Joseph J. Eakin.

1850 CENSUS: No record of members of this household has been located.

*Note: In the household of Christian Fauber, 18 year old Catherine Wetzel was listed in 1850. Nimrod Wetzel, apparently her brother, was also in the household. If this was her brother, it follows, that she is likely the daughter of John and Catherine.

PAGE 25 WOODSTOCK (Microfilm Page 851)

Dwelling 167 Family 167

John Clinedinst	48	Master Carriage Maker 4500 4000		
				Virginia
Martha A. Clinedinst	41			"
James A. Clinedinst	18	Carriage Maker Apprentice		"
Sarah C. Clinedinst	15		(School)	"
Ann O. Clinedinst	13		(School)	"
Ida F. Clinedinst	8		(School)	"
Barker N. Clinedinst	4			"
Jacob Mountz	25	Carriage Maker		"
John M. South	17	Carriage Maker Apprentice		"
William McDonald	22	Painter		"
Salus Mowery	13	(Black)		"

John Clinedinst is believed to have been a descendant of Jacob Clinedinst of Pennsylvania. John married **Martha Brady** on 21 Aug 1835 in Augusta County, Virginia.

James A. Clinedinst died in January of 1926 in Maryland. He was married on 29 Jan 1867 to Sally A. Belt. Sally was the daughter of James and Julia. She was a resident of **dwelling 751**. James was a coach maker at the time of his wedding. James had a dark complexion, brown eyes, dark hair and was 5'11". He enlisted at Woodstock on 18 Apr 1861 as a private in Company F of the 10th Virginia Infantry. He was promoted to 3rd Sergeant on 31 Oct 1861. He was reduced in rank on 3 Apr 1862 due to the reorganization of the unit. He was detailed as a clerk. James was taken prisoner at Woodstock on 12 Dec 1863 and sent to Wheeling, West Virginia (Atheneum Prison) on 16 Dec 1863. He was sent to Camp Chase, Ohio on 18 Dec 1863 and to Fort Delaware on 17 Mar 1864. James was paroled on 28 May 1865. He was a post war resident of Moorefield, West Virginia.

Ann Ophelia Clinedinst was married on 2 Apr 1873 to Robert C. Hounshour. Robert was the son of Peter and Jane. Peter E. Hounshour Jr. married Jane Cahoun on 5 May 1846. Robert was a wagon maker at the time of their wedding. Robert Hounshour and his family resided in **dwelling 116**.

John M. South was the son of Joseph and Jane. Joseph South married Jane McFee on 18 Nov 1837. John's sister Caroline had married Barnet Michael Clinedinst on

29 Jan 1857. Barnet was the son of John and Martha Clinedinst the heads of this household. John's mother Jane McFee South resided with the family of Barnet Clinedinst in **dwelling 168**. John M. South enlisted in the Eighth Star Artillery on 22 Apr 1861. He was with the 2nd section of the unit in Dec 1862. His re-enlistment resulted in a 60 day furlough and a $50 bounty. He was present on all remaining rolls. He was reassigned to the Danville Artillery in Sep 1862. He was courtmartialed per G.O. 88 10, Sep 1863. He was AWOL in Dec 1864. He was reported to have deserted to the enemy and there was no further record of his activity with the unit.

RELATED FAMILY:

   Barnet M. Clinedinst, son of John and Martha, married Caroline Mary South on 29 Jan 1857 and resided in **dwelling 168**.

   Jacob Clinedinst, believed to have been the brother of John, resided in **dwelling 792**.

1850 CENSUS: **John Clinedinst** and family resided in dwelling 246 on page 18.

PAGE 25 WOODSTOCK   (Microfilm Page 851)

Dwelling 168 Family 168

Barnet M. Clinedinst	23 Artist	600	800	Virginia
Carrie M. Clinedinst	20			"
Benjamin W. Clinedinst	8m			"
Catherine McFee	70			"
Jane South	40			"
Reuben Miller	10 (Black)			"

  Barnet Michael Clinedinst was the son of John and Martha. His parents resided in **dwelling 167**. Barnet was born in Lexington, Rockbridge County, Virginia. He was married on 29 Dec 1858 to **Caroline Mary South**. Caroline was the daughter of Joseph and Jane. Carrie's mother and grandmother were in this household. Barnet served in the 5th Virginia Infantry. He was listed as a musician. His postwar occupation was photography. He died in Washington, D. C. on 21 Dec 1904 and was buried in Rock Creek Cemetery in the District.

  Benjamin West Clinedinst was born in 1860 and died 12 Sep 1931. He was married to Emily G. Waters of Baltimore, Maryland on 5 Jun 1888. Benjamin attended Virginia Military Institute where his painting of VMI

Cadets at the battle of New Market would later be exhibited. Benjamin was named in honor of Benjamin West the famous artist. Barnet M. Clinedinst had seen an exhibit of West's painting "Death of the Pale Horse" when it was on exhibition at the Lutheran Church in Woodstock. Benjamin West Clinedinst seemed destined to succeed in the field of art and rose to prominence in that area. His specialties became genre pictures and portraits. He painted portraits of Theodore Roosevelt, Admiral Peary and General Custis Lee. He recieved numerous awards for his work. Benjamin and his family resided in Staunton, Virginia and Washington, D.C.

Catherine McFee was the mother of Jane McFee South and the grandmother of Carrie South Clinedinst. There was a marriage on 25 Nov 1815 for Catherine Coffman to John McAfee. It is not known for certain if this is the appropriate marriage.

Jane McFee married Joseph South on 18 Nov 1837. She was the daughter of Catherine McFee and the mother of Carrie South Clinedinst.

RELATED FAMILY:

       John M. South, son of Jane McFee, resided in **dwelling 167.**

1850 CENSUS: **Barnet M. Clinedinst** was a resident in the household of his father. They resided in dwelling 246 on page 18.
             Catherine McFee and her children resided in dwelling 259 on page 19.

PAGE 25 WOODSTOCK   **(Microfilm Page 851)**

Dwelling 169   Family 169

Name	Age	Occupation	Value		Place	
John Gatewood	41	Editor: Tenth Legion	1500	4920	Virginia	
Emily M. Gatewood	35				"	
Mary J. Gatewood	16				"	School
Julia M. Gatewood	14				"	School
Charles B. Gatewood	6				"	School
Samuel Gatewood	4				"	
Dewitt C. Gatewood	1				"	
Rebecca Bair	37				"	
Luther B. Kneisly	16	Printers Apprentice			"	
James M. Coburn	16	Printers Apprentice			"	

John Gatewood was a printer in Woodstock. In November of 1868 he retired from the **Shenandoah Herald**. Later he moved to Tazewell County, Virginia where he died. He represented Shenandoah County in the Virginia House of Delegates in 1857-1858 and 1861-1863. He was a Captain in Company C of the 33rd Virginia Infantry when the war broke out. He resigned on 23 Aug 1862 to serve in the legislature. John was married to **Emily M. Bare** on 22 Mar 1841. She was the daughter of Samuel. Emily was born in 1824 and died in 1886. She is buried in the Massanutten Cemetery.

Julia McCay Gatewood was born in 1845 and died 7 Nov 1927 in Gainesville, Virginia. She was married to Captain Henry C. Allen on 24 Jan 1867. He was a lawyer from Botecourt County, Virginia. He came to Shenandoah County to practice law in the birthplace of his father John James Allen. His mother was Mary. Henry became a judge and was Speaker of the Virginia House of Delegates in 1876 and 1877. Henry was born in 1838 and died 31 Oct 1889. Julia and Henry were buried in the Massanutten Cemetery.

Charles Bare Gatewood was appointed to the U. S. Military Academy at West Point ca. 1872. Upon graduation he was commissioned a 2nd Lt. in the 6th Cavalry. He was sent to take up duty on the frontier. Captain James H. Cook of Agate, Nebraska in his book **Fifty Years on the Old Frontier** indicates that Lt. Gatewood may be the man "who deserved the greatest credit for securing Geronimo and his band and bringing them where they could be placed on cars and taken to Florida." In written reports it is said that Geronimo referred to Lt. Gatewood as "Big Nose". Gatewood died at Fort Monroe, Virginia on 20 May 1896 at the age of 43.

Dewitt Clinton Gatewood died Apr 1937 in West Virginia.

Rebecca Bair (Bare) may have been the sister of Emily M. Bare Gatewood. In 1850 Rebecca resided with her mother Christina. She was also mentioned in the 17 Dec 1842 will of her father Samuel Bare.

Luther B. Kneisly was the son of Reuben and Susan. There are two marriages recorded for Reuben Kneisly. On 3 Oct 1826 Reuben Kneisly married Susan Majors. There was a second marriage of 28 Aug 1841 of Reuben Kneisly to Susan Lichliter. At this writing it is not clear if it was the same Reuben Kneisly or if either of these were the parents of Luther. Luther enlisted as a private in Company F of the 10th Virginia Infantry. He was promoted through the ranks to 3rd Corporal on 10 Jun 1863. He was a POW on 13 Dec 1863 and was sent to Wheeling, West Virginia and later to the Athenum Prison at Camp Chase Ohio. Luther was eventually sent to Fort Delaware on 17 Mar 1864 and was released on 15 Jun 1865. He died in March of 1890 in Kansas City, Missouri.

James M. Coburn was born ca. 1844. He enlisted on 18 Apr 1861 at Strasburg, Virginia. He joined Company A of the 10th Virginia Infantry. He appears in the hospital at Richmond on 13 Aug 1864. James died on 3 Jul 1927.

RELATED FAMILY:

Lewis Kneisly, brother of Luther B. Kneisly, married Frances Catherine Anderson on 14 Dec 1859 and resided in **dwelling 136.**

Sarah Catherine Kneisly, sister of Luther B. Kneisly, married Daniel A. Smootz on 26 Dec 1850 and resided in **dwelling 138.**

1850 CENSUS:
John Gatewood and his family resided in dwelling 249 on page 18.

Rebecca Bair resided with her mother in dwelling 250 on page 18.

Luther B. Kneisly resided with his father in dwelling 848 on page 59.

PAGE 25 WOODSTOCK (Microfilm Page 851)

Dwelling 170 Family 170

Zedekiah Dean	38	Farm Labor	0	100	Just Married Pennsylvania
Martha V. Dean	28				Virginia Just Married
Rachel Rudy	17	Housegirl			"

Zedekiah Dean was married on 7 Nov 1848 to Mary Ann Rodeffer. The bondsman for the marriage was William H. Rodeffer. It is probable that she was a descendant of John Rodeffer. John Rodeffer was located in **dwelling 134.** Upon the death of Mary Ann, Zedekiah was married to **Martha Barr** on 24 Jan 1860. She was the daughter of Michael and Elizabeth. Michael Barr married Elizabeth Koontz on 4 May 1830. Michael Barr and his family resided in **dwelling 1909.**

Rachel V. Rudy was the daughter of Isaac and Susan. Isaac Rudy married Susan Naggle on 16 May 1828. Isaac Rudy and his family resided in **dwelling 1857**. Rachel also appears in the household of her parents. She was listed twice in this census. Rachel was married on 6 Jan 1863 to Benjamin A. Orndorff. Benjamin was the son of Samuel and Rebecca. Samuel Orndorff married Rebecca Beeler on 21 Jul 1834 and resided in **dwelling 2292**.

RELATED FAMILY:

     Sarah C. Dean and **John L. Dean**, children of Zedekiah Dean and Mary Ann Rodeffer Dean, resided with their uncle Phillip Rodeffer in **dwelling 134.**

1850 CENSUS: **Zedekiah Dean** was present with his family in dwelling 204 on page 15.
      Mary Ann Rodeffer, deceased wife of Zedekiah Dean, resided with her father John Rodeffer in dwelling 203 on page 15.
      Martha Barr resided with her parents in dwelling 2059 on page 148.
      Rachel V. Rudy was located with her parents in dwelling 647 on page 46.

PAGE 26 WOODSTOCK **(Microfilm Page 852)**

Dwelling 171 Family 171

Jacob Hines	35	Plasterer	0	35 Maryland
Martha A. Hines	29			Virginia Cn't Rd
James J. Hines	5			"
Harriet H. Hines	4			"
Emanuel Hines	3m			"
Virginia C. Clower	7			" School

  Jacob Hines was born in Carroll County, Maryland. He was the son of Anthony and Magdalene. On 18 Sep 1857 he was married to **Martha A. Taylor** of Loudoun County, Virginia. She was the daughter of Samuel and Aceneth. Samuel Taylor married Alcinda McKim on 27 Feb 1832. On 5 Apr 1862, a Jacob Hines enlisted in Company B of the 33rd Virginia Infantry. He was taken POW at Woodstock on 2 Jun 1862 and was sent to Fort Delaware. He was exchanged on 5 Aug 1862 and was discharged on 7 Sep 1862. Jacob Hines was paroled at Winchester of 18 Apr 1865. According to military records he was 5'7" with fair complexion, dark hair and grey eyes. This member of the 33rd Infantry died in November of 1901. This individual was probably the head of this household. However there was a slight discrepancy

with the age. The Jacob Hines who enlisted in the service
was 31 at the time of his enlistement.

Emanuel Hines, according to his tombstone in the
village cemetery at Toms Brook, was born 12 Jan 1861 and
died 6 Jan 1926. However, he was in residence in this
household in 1860. He was a plasterer like his father.
Emanuel was married on 3 Jan 1888 to Mary Alice Miller.
Mary Alice was the daughter of Harrison and Rebecca.
Harrison Miller married Rebecca Kronk on 22 Mar 1860.
Harrison Miller and his family resided in **dwelling 1951.**
Mary Alice Miller Hines was born 3 Sep 1866 and died 15 Mar
1954. She was buried with Emanuél at the Toms Brook
Cemetery. Emanuel and Mary Alice had a son named Alva.
Alva served with the American Expeditionary Forces during
WWI. In John Wayland's **History of Shenandoah County** he
reproduced a poignant letter that Alva had written to his
parents from England in 1918.

1850 CENSUS: There is no evidence that Jacob Hines was
present in Shenandoah County in 1850. There
was an Emanuel Hines in dwelling 269 on
page 15. He was also from Maryland and may
have been a relative of Jacob. It may have
been a coincidence, but Jacob Hines named
one of his sons Emanuel. This suggests
there was a relationship.

PAGE 26 WOODSTOCK (Microfilm Page 852)

Dwelling 172 Family 172

James Wilson	50 Day Labor	0	25	Virginia	Cn't Rd
Elizabeth Wilson	40 Washer Woman		"		Cn't Rd
Rachel A. Wilson	14		"		
Evaline Wilson	11		"		
Mary S. Wilson	9		"		
Sarah E. Wilson	6		"		
Margaret C. Wilson	4		"		
Jacob Wilson	1		"		

James Wilson has not been identified. He was in
Shenandoah County in 1850. At that time his wife appears
as Lydia. Daughters **Rachel A. Wilson** and **Evaline Wilson**
appear in the household.

Jacob A. Wilson was born 19 Apr 1857 and died 14
Dec 1918. He was a teamster when he married Dorothea A.
Wood. They were married on 29 Apr 1880. She was the

daughter of Ephramin and Sarah. Ephramin Wood first wife
was named Dorothea. She died 22 May 1856. Ephramin then
married Elizabeth Bushong on 19 Aug 1858. Ephramin Wood and
family resided in **dwelling 684.** Dorothea "Dollie" A Wood
Wilson was born 14 Jun 1858 and died 21 Mar 1920. She was
buried at the Cedar Grove Brethren Church Cemetery in Mt.
Jackson.

Margaret "Maggie" Wilson married William Henry
Kingree on 25 Dec 1894. William was the son of Lemuel and
Sarah. Lemuel R. Kingree married Sarah C. Crider on 4 Mar
1867.

1850 CENSUS: James Wilson resided with his family in
dwelling 928 on page 65.

PAGE 26 WOODSTOCK (Microfilm Page 852)

Dwelling 173 Family 173

Margaret Myers	72	800	140	Va.	Cn't Rd
Mary C. Myers	36	Milliner		"	
Amanda J. Myers	34	Milliner		"	
Sarah J. Myers	33	Teacher Common School		"	

1850 CENSUS: **Margaret Myers** and her daughters resided in
dwelling 254 on page 18.

PAGE 26 WOODSTOCK (Microfilm Page 852)

Dwelling 174 Family 174

Samuel C. Williams	48	Clerk of Court 6200	10,000	
			Virginia	
Sarah C. Williams	51			"
Elizabeth S. Williams	22			"
Samuel C. Williams	17	(School)		"
George H. Williams	15	(School)		"
Mary J. Williams	13	(School)		"
William T. Williams	10	(School)		"
Charles C. Williams	9	(School)		"
Sarah White	63			"
William Wierman	26	Clerk and Salesman		"
George C. Hamman	21	Clerk 500	650	"
Samuel C. Samuels	18	Clerk 0	10,000	"

Samuel Croudson Williams was the son of Phillip and
Sarah. Phillip Williams married Sarah Croudson. He was
descended from William Williams the Justice of Stafford

County, Virginia in 1699. Samuel was born in 1811 and died in 1862. He was Deputy Clerk of the Court, a three times member of the House of Delegates and was the organizer of the Muhlenberg Rifles when the Civil War began. He served as Captain of that unit until he was incapacitated. Samuel married **Sarah Carpenter Ott** on 19 Jan 1833. Sarah was born in 1807 and died in 1886. She was the daughter of George and Elizabeth. George Ott married Elizabeth Offner on 11 Nov 1800.

Elizabeth "Bettie" Sarah Williams was born 26 Nov 1837 and died 13 Nov 1898. She was married to Thomas Marshall on 17 Oct 1860. Thomas was the son of Robert and Lucy. He was a civil engineer and he was born and was residing in Warren County, Virginia. Thomas enlisted in the 12th Virginia Cavalry on 13 Jan 1861. He enlisted in Company E at New Market, Virginia and was appointed 2nd Lt on 10 Apr 1862. On 11 Oct 1863 he was reported missing in action at the battle of Brandy Station. On 13 Oct 1863 he died. Thomas Marshall was buried in the cemetery near Happy Creek in Warren County, Virginia. Bettie was buried in the Massanutten Cemetery.

Samuel C. Williams enlisted on 18 Apr 1861 in Company F of the 10th Virginia Infantry. He was awarded the rank of 1st Corporal. He was reduced in rank on 3 Apr 1862 and was transferred to Chews Battery. Samuel married Sally F. Clower on 6 Oct 1869. Sally was the daughter of Jacob and Julia. Jacob B. Clower married Julia Haas and resided in **dwellling 176**. Sally died 30 Aug 1932 at Broadway, Virginia.

Mary Julia Williams was born in 1846 and died 27 Jul 1930. She was married in 1881 to Lewis Wagner. Lewis was born in 1836 and died in 1906. He was a veteran of the Civil War. Mary and Lewis were buried in the Massanutten Cemetery.

William Twyman Williams was married on 21 Feb 1883 to Sallie Madison Bird. Sallie was the daughter of Mark and Sarah. Mark Bird married Sarah Macon Hite on 18 Oct 1834. Mark Bird and family resided in **dwelling 164**. William was born in 1849 and died 17 Jun 1933. He was the ruling Elder of the Presbyterian Church of Woodstock. Sallie Madison Bird Williams was born in 1856 and died 11 Aug 1933. They were buried in the Massanutten Cemetery.

Charles Clayton Williams was 83 years old when he died 18 Feb 1935. He had never married.

George Henry Williams was born 5 Feb 1844. He was a member of Company E when he enlisted in the 12th Virginia Cavalry. He was reported to have been killed on 9 Jun 1863 at the battle of Brandy Station.

William L. Wierman was born 12 Jan 1829 and died 16 Apr 1920. He was in Winchester, Virginia at the time of his death. He was buried in the Mt. Hebron Cemetery in that city. He was the son of John R. Wierman. William was married to Anna L. McDonald. He enlisted in the 10th Virginia Infantry Company F. He was taken prisoner at Petersburg on 25 Mar 1865 and was sent to Point Lookout.

George Christopher Hamman was born 8 Oct 1838 and died 11 Sep 1920. He was the son of George and Catherine. George Hamman married Catherine Schmucker on 25 Mar 1827. When George died Catherine Schmucker Hamman married George Kibler. He was married on 27 Jun 1869 to Catherine "Kate" Jane Fravel. Kate was the daughter of James and Mary. James Gregory Fravel married Mary A. Fravel on 6 Nov 1834. James Fravel and family resided in **dwelling 114**. Kate was born 17 Mar 1840 and died 2 Apr 1906. George and Kate were buried in the Massanutten Cemetery. George Christopher Hamman had a florid complexion with dark hair and brown eyes. He was 5'5". He enlisted on 18 Apr 1861 in Company F of the 10th Virginia Infantry. He was 3rd Corporal. He was promoted to 4th Sergeant on 3 Apr 1862. He was wounded on 30 Aug 1862 at the battle of Second Manassas. He was wounded at Gettysburg on 3 Jul 1863. He was captured while at home on 16 Nov 1863 and was sent to Wheeling, West Virginia and eventually to the Athenum Prison at Camp Chase, Ohio on the 23 of Nov 1863. He was sent to Fort Delaware on 27 Mar 1864 and was paroled on 18 Apr 1865.

Samuel Coffman Samuels was the son of Green Berry and Maria. Green Berry Samuel married Maria Coffman on 7 Apr 1831. He was born ca. 1841 and died 6 May 1864. His father was a prominent man in the county and served as a member of Congress from 1839 to 1841. From 1852 until his death in 1859, Green Berry Samuels was a Justice of the Supreme Court of Appeals for Virginia. Samuel was educated at the University of Virginia. He enlisted as private in Company F of the 10th Virginia Infantry on 18 Apr 1861. He was detailed as a clerk. In June of 1861 he was taken prisoner at Front Royal and was exchanged at Aikens Landing on 5 Aug 1862. He was wounded at Chancellorsville on 3 Apr 1863 and died of wounds received on 5 May 1864 at the Wilderness. He was buried in the Lutheran Church in Woodstock.

RELATED FAMILY:

Ann Williams, sister of Samuel C. Williams, married Phillip Jones on 19 Nov 1818. She was a widow at the time of this census. She resided with her brother in law, William W. Magruder. William had married Mary Susan Williams on 20 Apr 1825. Mary Susan had died prior to the census. Ann Williams Jones and William W. Magruder, the brother in law of Samuel C. Williams, resided in **dwelling 209.**

Elizabeth Margaret Koontz, sister of Samuel C. Williams, resided in **dwelling 601** with her husband Dr. George Koontz.

John George Hamman, brother of George Christopher Hamman, married Lydia Maphis on 13 Apr 1854 and resided in **dwelling 47.**

Green Berry Samuels, brother of Samuel Coffman Samuel, resided in **dwelling 199.**

1850 CENSUS: Samuel Croudson Williams resided with his family in dwelling 324 on page 23.

Samuel Coffman Samuels resided with his father in dwelling 327 on page 24.

William L. Wierman resided with the family of Daniel Setzer in dwelling 334 on page 24.

George Christopher Hamman resided with his mother and step-father in dwelling 773 on page 54.

PAGE 26 WOODSTOCK (Microfilm Page 852)

Dwelling 175 Family 175

William Donaldson	44	Master Tinner	4500	9390	Md.
Susan M. Donaldson	40				Va.
Elizabeth R. Donaldson	14		(School)		"
Lucretia Donaldson	12		(School)		"
Caroline C. Donaldson	10				"
John W. Donaldson	8		(School)		"
Virginia Donaldson	3				"
Susan M. Donaldson	2m				"
Stephen H. Carder	18	Tinners Apprentice			"
George W. Helsley	14				"

William E. Donaldson was the son of Elizabeth. She resided in his household in 1850. William was married to Susan Mary Hickman on 14 Jan 1865. The bondsman for the marriage was John T. Hickman. Susan Mary Hickman Donaldson was 68 years old when she died on 6 Apr 1888. She was buried in the Emanuel Lutheran Church Cemetery in Woodstock. William E. Donaldson was one of the charter members of the Shenandoah Lodge #32 of the I.O.O.F when it began in Mar of 1847.

Elizabeth R. Donaldson was born in 1845 and died 5 Feb 1930. She was buried near her mother.

Mary Lucretia (Lou) Donaldson was born in 1847 and died 3 Apr 1919. She was married to John William Magruder on 10 Dec 1868. John was a farmer. He was the son of William and Mary. William W. Magruder and Mary Susan Williams were married on 20 Apr 1825. They were residents of **dwelling 209**. John was born in 1847 and died 2 Jul 1915. He was a member of the C.S.A. Their marriage produced one of the most important educators in the United States. Their son Frank Abbott Magruder wrote a textbook **American Government** which was used throughout this nation and is reported to have been the most widely used text in American high schools.

Caroline "Carrie" G. Donaldson was born in 1848 and died 15 May 1909. She was buried at the Emanuel Lutheran Church Cemetery.

John William Donaldson died 8 Dec 1931. He was married to Isabelle Lee Bruce the daughter of Robert Newhouse and Deborah Ann Bruce. Belle died 2 Jul 1932.

Minnie Susan Donaldson was born in 1860 and died 26 Sep 1942. "Miss Minnie" was buried in the Emanuel Lutheran Church Cemetery.

George W. Helsley probably was a participant in the Civil War. He may have been the Washington Helsley who was a member of Company C of the 7th Virginia Cavalry. There was also a George Helsley on the roll of the 33rd Virginia Infantry. He enlisted on 15 Jul 1861 in Company K and was taken POW at Gettysburg. It is not known if either of these individuals was the young man in this household.

RELATED FAMILY:
John T. Hickman, father of Susan Mary Hickman Donaldson, resided in **dwelling 150**.
Caroline Donaldson, sister of William Donaldson, married Ephramin Grabill on 18 Oct 1836 and resided in **dwelling 96**.

1850 CENSUS: **William Donaldson** resided with his family in dwelling 251 on page 18.

PAGE 27 WOODSTOCK (Microfilm Page 853)

Dwelling 176 Family 176

Jacob B. Clower	48	Carpenter	2600	425	Virginia	
Julia Ann Clower	42				"	
Sarah F. Clower	16				"	
James H. Clower	13				"	
Julia V. Clower	5				"	
Lewis B. Clower	1				"	
Sarah A. Haas	64				"	
Laura Warfield	25				"	Can't Read

Jacob B. Clower was the son of John and Frances. John Clower married Frances Grove on 15 Jan 1809. Jacob B. Clower died 12 Apr 1891 at the age of 76 years and 28 days old. He was married to **Julia Ann Haas.** Julia was the daughter of **Sarah A. Haas.** Sarah was also a resident of this household. Julia Ann Haas Clower died 6 Nov 1900 at the age of 82 years, 7 months and 10 days old. They were buried in the Emanuel Lutheran Church Cemetery in Woodstock.

Sarah Frances Clower died 30 Aug 1932 at Broadway, Virginia. She was married to Samuel Croudson Williams on 6 Oct 1869. Samuel was the son of Samuel and Sarah. Samuel Croudson Williams married Sarah Carpenter Ott on 19 Jan 1833. Samuel and his family resided in **dwelling 174.** Samuel was a veteran of the Civil War.

James Henry Clower died 8 Nov 1924. He was married to Antoinette Duboise Winfield. Antoinette died 30 Sep 1937.

Julia V. Clower was born 26 May 1856. She was married on 26 May 1880 to John R. Saum. John was the son of Elias and Delilah. Elias Saum married Delilah Sager on 7 Oct 1837. John R. Saum was a widower and resident of Rockingham County, Virginia at the time of the marriage.

RELATED FAMILY:
Isabella Clower, sister of Jacob B. Clower, married Alexander Anderson on 19 Sep 1858 and resided in **dwelling 155.**
Joseph H. Clower, brother of Jacob B. Clower, resided in **dwelling 107.**

Elizabeth Clower, sister of Jacob B. Clower, married George Harrison Ott on 29 Nov 1849 and resided in dwelling 125.

1850 CENSUS: Jacob B. Clower and family resided in dwelling 260 on page 19.

PAGE 27 WOODSTOCK   (Microfilm Page 853)

Dwelling 177 Family 177

George Fravel	51	Wheelwright 800	527	Virginia
Harriet E. Fravel	53			" Can't Read
Isabella Fravel	24			"
Caroline Fravel	22			" Insane
Mary Fravel	20			"
Jane Fravel	17			"
John Fravel	15	Wheelwright Apprentice		"
Robert Fravel	14			" School

George Fravel was the son of Henry and Barbara. Henry Fravel III married Barbara Fetzer on 9 Aug 1808. George Fravel was born 3 Oct 1808. George married **Harriet Ella Myers** on 6 Nov 1833. The bondsman for the marriage was Hiram Myers.

Isabella Fravel did not marry.

Mary Fravel was born 14 Mar 1838 and died 20 Mar 1914. She was married to Abraham J. R. Bauserman on 22 Nov 1855. Abraham was the son of Abraham and Margaret. Abraham Bauserman married Margaret Spiggle on 19 Oct 1822. Abraham J. R. Bauserman was born 15 Nov 1833 and died 18 Feb 1905. Mary and Abraham were buried in the Bowman-Wright Cemetery in Maurertown. It is not clear why Mary is listed in this household. She and her husband Abraham were listed in **dwelling 2029.**

John William Fravel was born in 1841 and died 16 May 1900. He was married on 22 Dec 1869 to Mary Magdaline Baker, the daughter of Benjamin Baker of Lost River, West Virginia. Mary Magdaline Baker Fravel was born in 1842 and died 29 Jan 1900.

Robert Fravel died 9 Apr 1915. He did not marry.

RELATED FAMILY:

Mary A. Fravel, sister of George, married James G. Fravel on 6 Nov 1834 and resided in **dwelling 114.**

John Henry Fravel, brother of George, married Sarah Jane Bruce on 4 Jul 1848 and resided in **dwelling 145**.

Catherine Jane Fravel, sister of George, married Judge George Rye on 2 Oct 1833 and resided in **dwelling 156**.

David Fravel, brother of George, married Louise Supinger on 11 Jan 1860 and resided in **dwelling 200**. When Barbara Fetzer Fravel died, Henry Fravel III was married on 23 Mar 1834 to Catherine Lichliter. Catherine Lichliter Fravel resided in this household with David.

Frederick Fravel, brother of George, had married Ellen Catherine Miller on 24 Aug 1840. Frederick was deceased. However, his widow was a resident of **dwelling 201**.

1850 CENSUS: George Fravel and his family resided in dwelling 262 on page 19.

PAGE 27 WOODSTOCK (Microfilm Page 853)

Dwelling 178 Family 178

Glover Hunt	70	Shoemaker	500	125	Penn Can't Read
Phebe Hunt	70				Virginia

Glover Hunt was married to **Phebe Fry** on 26 Aug 1823. The bondsman for the marriage was Peter Hounshour.

1850 CENSUS: **Glover Hunt** resided with his family in dwelling 263 on page 19. Their 23 year old daughter Rachel Hunt was also in the household. Rachel married Samuel R. Stirling on 8 Jul 1850.

PAGE 27 WOODSTOCK (Microfilm Page 853)

Dwelling 179 Family 179

Jacob Ott	57	Farmer	12,400	23,425	Virginia	
Susan Ott	46				"	
Ellenora Keller	24				"	Just Mar
Lawrence Keller	33	Miller			"	Just Mar
Ann E. R. Ott	22				"	
Emily S. Ott	20				"	
Sydney M. Ott	17				"	School
Margaret V. Ott	11				"	School
Lucy C. Ott	7				"	

Jacob Ott Jr. was born 18 Aug 1808 and died 24 May 1885. He was the son of Jacob and Mary. Jacob Ott married Mary Anderson on 11 Apr 1803. Jacob's father resided with him in 1850. Jacob Ott Sr. was born in Maryland. Jacob Ott Jr. was married to **Susanna Bowman** on 7 Apr 1835. The bondsman for their marriage was James N. Allen. Susanna was born 25 Mar 1814 and died 1 Oct 1893. They were buried in the Massanutten Cemetery.

Mary Ellen Ott was born 25 Jan 1836 and died 20 Dec 1905. She was married to **Lawrence Keller** on 24 May 1859. Lawrence was a miller and also served as County Supervisor for a number of years. Lawrence was born 24 Jan 1827 and died 1 May 1893. He was the son of Lawrence and Elizabeth. Lawrence Keller married Elizabeth Sibert on 3 Aug 1815. Mary Ellen and Lawrence were buried in the Emanuel Lutheran Church Cemetery in Woodstock.

Ann Eliza Ott was born 7 Aug 1837 and died 27 Jun 1905. She was married on 20 Feb 1862 to Phillip Wilson Magruder. Phillip was an attorney. He was born 16 Mar 1838 and died 4 Mar 1907. They were buried in the Massanutten Cemetery. Phillip was the son of William and Mary. William W. Magruder married Mary Susan Williams on 20 Apr 1825. They resided in **dwelling 209.**

Emily S. Ott was born 6 Aug 1840 and died 6 Feb 1916.

Sydney M. Ott was born 8 Jan 1844 and died 5 Feb 1932.

Margaret V. Ott was born 4 Mar 1850 and died 6 Oct 1910.

Lucy C. Ott was born 28 Feb 1858 and died 19 Jun 1925. None of these four women married and all were buried in the Massanutten Cemetery.

1850 CENSUS: Jacob Ott Jr. and his family resided in dwelling 241 on page 17.
Lawrence Keller resided with the family of Obed Coffman in dwelling 2072 on page 149.

PAGE 27 WOODSTOCK   (Microfilm Page 853)

Dwelling 180 Family 180

Jesse Orndorff	48 Farmer	0	25	Virginia	
Elizabeth Orndorff	43			"	
Walter E. Orndorff	19 Day Labor			"	
Minerva A. Orndorff	14			"	
Obed A. Orndorff	11			"	School
Israel A. Orndorff	8			"	School
Addison Orndorff	3			"	

Jesse Orndorff was born 29 Apr 1810 and died 24 Feb 1885. His wife **Elizabeth** was born 30 Jul 1817 and died 22 Aug 1891. They were buried in the Emanuel Lutheran Church Cemetery in Woodstock.

Walter E. F. Orndorff was a member of the 10th Virginia Infantry Company F. He was shot in battle at Chancellorsville on 2 May 1863 and died of his wounds on 21 May 1863. He was 22 years, 7 months and 2 days old. He is buried near his parents.

Minerva A. Orndorff was born 19 Nov 1845 and died 16 Jun 1901.

RELATED FAMILY:
Mary E. Orndorff, the daughter of Jesse, married John William Myers on 18 Nov 1858 and resided in **dwelling 1920.**

1850 CENSUS: Jesse Orndorff and his family resided in dwelling 942 on page 65.

PAGE 27 WOODSTOCK (Microfilm Page 853)

Dwelling 181 Family 181

Michael Melhorn	60 Saddletree Maker	500	156	Pa.
Susan Melhorn	59			Va.
Susan E. Melhorn	19			"
Henrietta F. Melhorn	15	(School)		"

Michael Melhorn was born 16 Jun 1799 and died 26 Jul 1870. He was married on 22 Mar 1826 to **Susan Burner**. The bondsman for the marriage was Adam Burner.

Susan E. Melhorn was married on 23 Jan 1863 to Thomas Spinks. Thomas was a railroad engineer who was born in Prince William County, Virginia. He was the son of Jared and Rebecca.

Henrietta Melhorn was married on 16 Oct 1865 to Alvin Stearns. Alvin was a farmer who had been born in Ohio. He was the son of Ebnezer and Tirzah.

1850 CENSUS: Michael Melhorn and his family resided in dwelling 265 on page 19. There were a number of other children in this family who resided in the household in 1850. One example was Mollie E. Melhorn, the daughter who married William H Hamrick on 29 Jan 1868. William was the Commissioner of Revenue for Rockingham County. Mollie and other children of Michael and Susan were not present in Shenandoah County in 1860.

PAGE 28   WOODSTOCK   (Microfilm Page 854)

Dwelling 182   Family 182

Harrison Fadely	29	Mulatto/Day Labor	400	183	Va.
Verinda Fadely	26	Mulatto			"
Lillie Dale Fadely	6	Mulatto			"
George C. Fadely	4	Mulatto			"
Ann A. Fadely	2	Mulatto			"

Harrison Fadely married Marinda Robinson on 20 Aug 1853. The married couple were both listed as a "free negro" in the marriage certificate.

Lillie Dale Fadely was married on 10 Oct 1874 to John William Bird. John was listed as a laborer and was the son of Harry and Sallie. When John died, Lillie Dale Fadely Bird married Joseph Harden in April of 1877. Joseph was a hostler from Fluvanna County, Virginia. A hostler was the person who has the care of horses at an inn. He was the son of James and Julia A.

George C. Fadely, a laborer, was married on 18 Feb 1877 to Alice Jackson. Alice was born in Rockbridge County, Virginia. Her parents were not recorded on the marriage certificate. Upon the death of Alice, George was married on 14 Sep 1884 to Virginia Williams. Her parents were not listed in the marriage record.

Annie Fadely was married on 3 Sep 1878 to Oscar Smith. Oscar was a hostler from Warren County, Virginia. He was the son of Oscar and Mary. Oscar Smith was a widower. He had originally married Cornelia Beal of Rockbridge County, Virginia on 4 Sep 1877.

1850 CENSUS: Harrison Fadely resided in the household of John Artz. They resided in dwelling 172 on page 13.

PAGE 28 WOODSTOCK (Microfilm Page 854)

Dwelling 183 Family 183

Rebecca Welden	33 Mulatto	0	78 Virginia
Caroline Welden	13 Black		"
Andrew Ralls	28 Mulatto		"

Rebecca Coffman was married to Newman Welden on 18 May 1846.

Caroline Welden was married to Wyatt Byes on 5 Oct 1869. Wyatt was a railroad hand from Cabell County, West Virginia. He was the son of David and Fanny.

1850 CENSUS: Rebecca Coffman Welden resided in dwelling 742 on page 52 with her husband Newman and family.

PAGE 28 WOODSTOCK (Microfilm Page 854)

Dwelling 184 Family 184

Margaret Myers	49	0	80	Virginia	
Angeline Myers	29			"	Dumb
James H. Myers	27 Wagon Maker			"	
Margaret G. W. Myers	20 Seamstress			"	

Margaret C. Wilson was married to George P. Myers on 4 Nov 1829. She was the daughter of Zachariah Wilson. Shenandoah County records reveal that Zachariah Wilson married Elizabeth Pinkley on 4 Apr 1791.

Angeline Myers in her obituary died on 14 Feb 1907 in Maurertown, Virginia. She was survived by her sister. Angeline did not marry.

Margaret G. W. Myers was born 23 Apr 1840 and died 7 Mar 1921. She was married to James H. Rosenberger on 1

Dec 1864. James was the son of Abraham T. W. and Mary Ann. Abraham T. W. Rosenberger married Mary Ann Fauver on 7 Apr 1832. James and his family resided in **dwelling 2034**. James was born 9 Aug 1834 and died 6 Jun 1910. They were buried in the Zion Christian Church Cemetery in Maurertown, Virginia.

1850 CENSUS: There is no record of the Myers family in 1850.

PAGE 28 WOODSTOCK (Microfilm Page 854)

Dwelling 185 Family 185

Henry Shaffer	45	Day Labor	0	110	Virginia
Delila Shaffer	30				"
Ann L. Shaffer	18				"
William T. Shaffer	15	Shoemakers Apprentice			"
Francis M. Shaffer	12				" School
Joseph H. Shaffer	9				" School
Marietta Shaffer	6				"
Mary Litten	61				"

This family is often recorded as Shaver in Shenandoah County records. **Henry Shaffer** was born in 1810 and died in 1900. His wife **Delila** was born in 1821 and died in 1896. Delila A. and Henry were buried in the Massanutten Cemetery in Woodstock.

On 28 Aug 1867 **Lucretia Shaver**, daughter of Henry and Delila, was married to James R. C. Fisher. James R. C. Fisher, the son of George and Mary, was from Augusta County, Virginia. It is probable that this was Ann L(ucretia) Shaffer.

William T. Shaffer was married on 18 Jun 1867 to Lucinda Day, the daughter of John and Ellen. John Day married Ellen Tanner on 4 May 1825. Ellen was 83 when she died on 15 Jan 1930. The Day family were in residence in **dwelling 1287**. William T. Shaffer was listed twice in this census. He was also an apprentice in **dwelling 744**. This was the residence of William A. Hunton.

Francis M. Shaffer was born in 1847 and died in 1895. He was a shoemaker at the time he married Ella Lonas. The marriage to Ella took place on 17 Aug 1876. She was the daughter of Joseph and Rachel. Joseph was listed as Frederick on this marriage certificate. Joseph Lonas was married to Rachel Huntsberger on 23 Apr 1832. They were located in **dwelling 1516** at the time of this census. Ella Lonas Shaffer was born in 1849 and died in 1934. They were buried at the Massanutten Cemetery.

Joseph H. Shaffer was married to Amanda Adelia Miller on 22 Mary 1886. Amanda was the daughter of Joseph and Evaline. According to obituary records Amanda Miller's mother Evaline was an Orndorff. Joseph was born 5 Aug 1850 and died 7 Sep 1934. Amanda A. Miller Shaffer was born 20 Feb 1863 and died 14 Jan 1960. They were buried at the Massanutten Cemetery.

Marietta Shaffer was married on 19 Sep 1872 to Jacob W. Rodeffer. He was a carpenter and the son of Jacob and Ann. Jacob Rodeffer married Ann Getz on 18 Sep 1838. They resided in dwelling 131.

1850 CENSUS: Henry Shaffer and his family resided in dwelling 674 on page 48.
Mary Litten was likely the wife of William Litten. They resided in dwelling 1826 on page 131.

PAGE 28   WOODSTOCK   (Microfilm Page 854)

Dwelling 186   Family 186

Henry T. Johnson	27 Shoemaker	0	150	England
Elizabeth Johnson	23			Virginia
Sarah C. Johnson	4			"

Henry T. Johnson was born in 1830 and died in 1911. He was born in London, England. Henry was married to Elizabeth Brown on 24 Oct 1854. Henry was the son of Thomas and Elizabeth. Elizabeth was the daughter of John and Catherine. There was a marriage of John Brown to Catherine Cramer on 13 Dec 1836. When Elizabeth Brown Johnson died, Henry T. Johnson was married to a widow, Mary Catherine Fry Kibler on 28 Sep 1863. Mary Catherine Fry was the daughter of Phillip and Sarah. Phillip Fry married Sarah Lineweaver on 12 Nov 1834. Phillip Fry and his family resided in dwelling 1741. Mary Catherine Fry had originally married George Kibler on 16 Feb 1860. George was the son of Phillip and Elizabeth. Mary Catherine was born in 1839 and died in 1910. Henry and Mary Catherine were buried in the Emanuel Lutheran Church Cemetery.

1850 CENSUS: Elizabeth Brown was a resident in dwelling 209 on page 15. This was the household of her father.

PAGE 28   WOODSTOCK   (Microfilm Page 854)

Dwelling 187   Family 187

Andrew Fitzpatrick	45	Master Mason	0	50	Ireland
Margaret Fitzpatrick	31				" Can't Rd
Mary A. Fitzpatrick	5				Virginia
Margaret E. Fitzpatrick	2				"
William H. Fitzpatrick	14 days				"

1850 CENSUS: There is no record of this family in 1850.

PAGE 28   WOODSTOCK   (Microfilm Page 854)

Dwelling 188   Family 188

Nancy W. Miller	53	Seamstress	300	100	Virginia
Lucy B. Miller	26				"
Margaret C. Miller	23				"
Gabriella J. Miller	19				"

Nancy Miller was the wife of Reuben Miller. She was listed as Ann W. Barber when she married Reuben on 13 May 1817. She was the daughter of John Barber. Reuben was the son of Christian Miller. This was reported in his will that was proved on 9 Apr 1849.

Gabriella J. Miller was married to J. Wesley Miller on 25 Feb 1875. J. Wesley was a widower. He was born and resided in Harrisonburg, Virginia. He was the son of George and Abigail. On 11 May 1826 George Miller married Abby Graham in Rockingham County, Virginia.

RELATED FAMILY:

Mary Jane Miller, daughter of Nancy and Reuben, married Harrison Gillock on 2 Apr 1851 and resided in dwelling 197.

Cassandra Miller, sister in law of Nancy Barber Miller, married Benjamin D. Hickman on 14 Apr 1847 and resided in dwelling 205.

1850 CENSUS: Nancy W. Miller was listed as Ann W. Miller in 1850. She resided with her husband Reuben in dwelling 234 on page 17.

205

PAGE 28   WOODSTOCK   (Microfilm Page 854)

Dwelling 189   Family 189

Joseph Fravel	71	1800	176	Virginia	
Rosanna Fravel	68			Maryland	Can't Read
Harvey C. Kneisley	11			Virginia	School

      Joseph Fravel   was born in 1795 and died on 18 Aug 1866.   He was the son of George and Elizabeth Bushong Fravel. On 5 Nov 1810 he was married to **Rosanna Gochenour**. Rosanna was the daughter of Jacob. Rosanna was born 5 May 1791 and died 3 Apr 1876. They were buried at St. Paul's Reformed Church Cemetery in Woodstock.

1850 CENSUS: **Joseph Fravel** and his wife Rosanna resided in dwelling 220 on page 16. Family records do not report any children in this family. However, in 1850 there was a young woman named Sarah Fravel living with this couple.
       Harvey C. Kneisley, even at the age of 2 appears to have been residing with individuals other than his parents. He was located in dwelling 854 on page 19. This was the family of William and Mary Ann Burner Copenhaver.

PAGE 28 WOODSTOCK   (Microfilm Page 854)

Dwelling 190   Family 190

Samuel Jones	24	Fireman on R.R.	Scotland
Catherine Jones	21		Maryland
William H. Jones	2		"

1850 CENSUS: There is no information on this family in 1850.

PAGE 29 WOODSTOCK (Microfilm Page 855)

Dwelling 191   Family 191

Charles Steel	33	Master Mason	0	400	Maryland	
Sarah J. Steel	28				Virginia	
Ann E. Steel	6				"	School
Walter Steel	5				"	
James E. Steel	3				"	
Claudia Steel	1				"	

206

1850 CENSUS: No record of this family in Shenandoah County in 1850.

PAGE 29 WOODSTOCK (Microfilm Page 855)

Dwelling 192 Family 192

Frank Fogle 22   Day Labor   0   100   Virginia
                                      Just Married/Can't Read
Mary Fogle   20   Va.   Just Married/Can't Read

         William Franklin Fogel was a blacksmith at the time of his marriage to **Mary Jane Santmeyer** on 22 Feb 1860. Her parents were not listed. John H. Fravel provided the affidavit for the marriage. He was the son of Michael Fogle and Mary Bushong. Michael and Mary were married on 28 May 1835.

         NOTE: There are no additional records for this family. However, their son Addison L. Fogle was a resident of Shenandoah County. According to his marriage record he was born in Hardy County, West Virginia. It may be that this family removed to West Virginia.

RELATED FAMILY:
         Jacob Fogle, brother of William Franklin Fogle, resided in **dwelling 448**. He was in the household of John McClanahan.
         Andrew Fogle and **Julia A. Fogle**, brother and sister of William, resided in **dwelling 1971**. This was the Shenandoah County Poor House. Julia A. Fogle was listed as an "idiot".

1850 CENSUS: William Franklin Fogel resided in dwelling 1854 on page 133. This was the household of his father Michael.

PAGE 29 WOODSTOCK (Microfilm Page 855)

Dwelling 193 Family 193

Daniel Feete   49 Clergyman   0   400   Maryland
Ann C. Feete   46   Pennsylvania
Louisa E. Feete   21   Maryland
Mary R. Feete   18   Virginia School
Albert Z. Feete   14   "   School
Caroline H. Feete   8   "

207

Daniel L. Feete was Pastor of the German Reformed Church.

1850 CENSUS: Daniel Feete and his family resided in dwelling 2212 on page 158 in Rockingham County. Ann C. Feete appears as Charlotte in the census.

PAGE 29 WOODSTOCK (Microfilm Page 855)

Dwelling 194 Family 194

John P. Coffman	53	Day Labor	0	74	Virginia	Can't Read
Lucy Coffman	52			"		
Mary Coffman	18			"		
Rebecca Coffman	15			"	School	
Eliza Coffman	9			"	School	

John P. Coffman, the son of Peter Coffman, was married to Lucy Jack on 27 Feb 1832.

Rebecca Coffman was married on 1 Jan 1866 to Stephen Burch of Oswego County, New York. Stephen was a painter and was the son of Robert and Jane.

RELATED FAMILY: Ellen Coffman, the daughter of John and Lucy, married John H. Fry on 14 Apr 1856 and resided in dwelling 146.

1850 CENSUS: John P. Coffman and family resided in dwelling 218 on page 16.

PAGE 29 WOODSTOCK (Microfilm Page 855)

Dwelling 195 Family 195

Ann Fetzer	40	400	700	Maryland

Mary Ann Rye was married to Samuel Fetzer on 14 May 1829. The marriage record indicates that she was the ward of Joseph Fravel. Samuel Fetzer died in the spring of 1843. Will book W indicates that Samuel's will was proved on 12 Jun 1843.

RELATED FAMILY: Sarah Catherine Fetzer, daughter of Samuel

and Mary Ann, married John W. Bauserman on 10 Aug 1854 and resided in **dwelling 127**. **Mary Ellen Fetzer**, another daughter of Mary Ann, resided with her sister.

George Rye was probably the brother of Mary Ann. In 1850 he was listed as a saddler from Maryland. He was executor of Samuel Fetzer's will. Judge George Rye and his wife Catherine Fravel Rye resided in **dwelling 156**.

1850 CENSUS: Mary Ann Rye Fetzer was residing in dwelling 217 on page 16.

PAGE 29 WOODSTOCK (Microfilm Page 855)

Dwelling 196 Family 196

Isaac Trout	58	Farmer	6150	6165	Virginia
Elizabeth Trout	50				Maryland
James I. Trout	22	Attorney			Virginia
Mary C. Trout	16				" School
Ruth E. Ambrose	24	Teacher of Latin			New Hampshire

Isaac Trout was married to **Elizabeth Donaldson** on 23 Oct 1832. She was reported to have been the daughter of Eliza.

James I. Trout enlisted on 3 Jun 1861 in the 33rd Virginia Infantry Company C as a Lt. He was present through Oct 1861. He was absent sick in Feb 1862. He was promoted to Captain on 21 Apr 1862. He resigned 6 Jan 1863. James died on 13 Dec 1905 at Richmond Soldiers Home at the age of 67. He was buried in the Hollywood Cemetery.

Mary E. Trout was married on 4 Jan 1866 to Joseph E. Norris. Joseph was born in Baltimore and was residing in Page County, Virginia. He was an artist. He was the son of James and Susan.

RELATED FAMILY:

William Donaldson, brother of Elizabeth, married Susan Mary Hickman on 14 Jan 1845 and resided in **dwelling 175**.

Caroline Donaldson, sister of Elizabeth, married Ephramin Grabill on 18 Oct 1836 and resided in **dwelling 96**.

1850 CENSUS: Isaac Trout and his family resided in dwelling 237 on page 17.

209

PAGE 29   WOODSTOCK   (Microfilm Page 855)

Dwelling 197   Family 197

Harrison Gillock	46	Carpenter	750	250	Virginia	
Mary J. Gillock	39				"	
Arabella J. Gillock	20				"	
Mary E. Gillock	17				"	
John H. Gillock	15				"	
Nancy F. Gillock	13				"	School
Edgar R. Gillock	8				"	School
Lelia Gillock	4				"	
Allelia Gillock	3				"	
Barbara Gillock	52				"	

Henry Harrison Gillock was married twice. His first wife was named Rebecca. Upon her death, Harrison was married to Mary Jane Miller on 2 Apr 1851. Mary Jane may have been the daughter of Reuben and Nancy W. Barber Miller. Nancy W. Barber Miller resided in dwelling 188. In the 1850 Census Reuben and Nancy had a 30 year old daughter named Mary. Harrison is believed to have been the son of John and Mary. John Gillock married Mary Fetzer on 10 Apr 1806. In 1850 Barbara Gillock, believed to have been the sister of Harrison, resided in the household of John and Mary.

Arabella Jane Gillock was married on 7 Nov 1866 to James Albert. James was a farmer and was the son of Henry St. George and Emma. James and his parents resided in dwelling 142. James was a private in Company F of the 10th Virginia Infantry. He and his family moved to Alvarado, Texas after the war.

Mary E. "Mollie" Gillock was married to George K. Lewis on 27 Aug 1872. George was a silversmith and was born in Rockingham County, Virginia. He was residing in Warren County at the time of the marriage. His parents were Charles and Nancy.

Definitive data on John H. Gillock has not been located. There was a John Gillock on the roll of Chew's Battery. In addition a John Gillock appears to have enlisted in Company F of the 12th Virginia Cavalry.

Edgar Randolph Gillock died at the age of 76 in Norfolk, Virginia on 16 Jan 1928. He was the husband of Hattie Bruce.

Luella Lelia Gillock was listed as Lelia Russell Gillock in her obituary notice. She was born 29 Jun 1852 and died 21 Nov 1924. She was married to Benjamin J. Hottel, a carpenter, on 25 Nov 1879. Benjamin was born 4 Mar 1854 and died 14 Mar 1929. They were buried in the Massanutten Cemetery. Benjamin was the son of John J. and Anna R. John J. Hottel married Anna R. Hudson in 1845. The Hottel family resided in **dwelling 1940**. Benjamin was a contractor-builder and a member of the Shenandoah County Fire Department at Woodstock.

Lou Gillock, believed to have been Allelia Gillock in this household, was married on 9 Oct 1887 to Erasmus C. Haas. Erasmus was the son of John and Clara. John Haas married Clara Gore on 21 Mar 1831. John Haas and his family resided in **dwelling 95**. Erasmus was a widower. He had married Elizabeth Irwin on 28 Nov 1866. Elizabeth was the daughter of Benjamin and Lucy. Benjamin Irwin married Lucy Coffelt on 7 May 1838. Benjamin Irwin and his family resided in **dwelling 1231**. Erasmus C. Haas was reported to have died on 23 Sep 1905.

RELATED FAMILY:

David Gillock, brother of Barbara Gillock, married Elizabeth Jordan on 27 Jan 1853 and resided in **dwelling 126**.

1850 CENSUS: Mary Jane Miller, resided with her parents in dwelling 234 on page 17.
Barbara Gillock resided with her parents in dwelling 225 on page 16.

PAGE 29 WOODSTOCK (Microfilm Page 855)

Dwelling 198 Family 198

William S. Arthur 52 Deputy Clerk 0 4500 Pennsylvania
Just Married
Mary E. Arthur 44 Virginia Just Md
William B. Arthur 12 " School

William Smith Arthur was born in Cumberland County, Pennsylvania. He married Susanna Margaret Druck (Trook) on 16 Aug 1847. The bondsman for the marriage was George Druck. Upon the death of Susannah, William married Mary Elizabeth Irwin on 30 May 1860. She was the daughter of Joseph and Clarissa Mary (surname unknown). Joseph Irwin was a physician and he was originally from Ireland.

William was the son of John and Margaret. William Smith
Arthur was born 18 Apr 1808 and died 29 Apr 1873. He was
buried in the St. Pauls Reformed Church Cemetery in
Woodstock.

RELATED FAMILY:
>>>>>>>**Joseph S. Irwin,** brother of Mary Elizabeth,
married Sarah Catherine Gochenour on 12 Jan 1856 and
resided in **dwelling 141.**
>>>>>>>**William Irwin,** brother of Mary Elizabeth,
married Barbara Ann Coffman on 8 Jun 1857 and resided in
dwelling 1281. Another brother **John Irwin** also resided in
that dwelling.
>>>>>>>**James Irwin,** brother of Mary Elizabeth,
resided in **dwelling 157.**
>>>>>>>**Matilda Berryhill Irwin,** sister of Mary
Elizabeth, married Dr. Leonidas Triplett on 24 Jan 1834 and
resided in **dwelling 606.**

1850 CENSUS:>>>**William Smith Arthur** and his wife Susannah
resided in dwelling 325 on page 23.
>>>>**Mary Elizabeth Irwin** resided with her father
Joseph in dwelling 229 on page 16.

PAGE 29 WOODSTOCK   (Microfilm Page 855)

Dwelling 199   Family 199

Green B. Samuels 20 Student at Law 0 10,500   Virginia
Henry C. Fravel   17   "

>>>>**Green Berry Samuels** was born 2 Nov 1839 and died
20 Feb 1901. He was the son of Green Berry and Maria.
Green Berry Samuels married Maria Coffman on 7 Apr 1831.
Green Berry Samuels Sr. was elected a member of Congress
from Virginia. He was also a prominent Judge in the
Virginia Supreme Court of Appeals. Green Berry Samuels Jr.
married Kathleen Boone on 19 Feb 1862. Kathleen was the
daughter of Abraham and Eliza. Abraham R. Boone married
Eliza Ann Van Nort on 25 Dec 1839. Kathleen was born 16
Nov 1842 and died 15 Mar 1925. She was buried in the
Prospect Hill Cemetery in Front Royal, Virginia. He died
in Front Royal and was buried in the Emanuel Lutheran
Church Cemetery in Woodstock with his parents. Green Berry
attained the rank of Captain in the 10th Virginia Infantry
Company F. He was captured twice and was a prisoner at
Fort Delaware. He served as an aide to General R. T. Colston.

GREEN BERRY SAMUELS
1839-1901 Captain: 10th Virginia Infantry Company F
Photo: Courtesy of Laura Virginia Hale Archives
Warren Heritage Society, Front Royal, Virginia

     Henry Clay Fravel was born 5 Oct 1842 and died 29
Nov 1894. He was buried in Luray, Virginia. Henry was a
jeweler by trade. He was the son of James Gregory Fravel
and Mary Fravel Fravel. James and Mary, cousins, were

married on 6 Nov 1834. James Gregory and his family were
located in **dwelling 114**. Henry was married to Almira
Virginia Weaver on 18 Jan 1870. She was born 14 Oct 1850
and died 10 Feb 1917 in Savannah, Georgia where she lived
with one of her children after Henry's death. Henry joined
the 10th Virginia Infantry Company F on 18 Apr 1861.   He
was a private and remained active on the roll until 23 Jul
1863 when he was listed as having deserted. However, in
July 1863 Henry Clay Fravel had joined Chew's Battery in
the Laurel Brigade.

RELATED FAMILY:
            Samuel C. Samuels, brother of Green Berry
Samuels, resided in **dwelling 174.**
            Elizabeth Margaret Samuels, sister of Green
Berry Samuels, married Dr. George Koontz and resided in
dwelling 601.

1850 CENSUS: **Green Berry Samuels** resided with his parents
            in dwelling 327 on page 24.
            Henry Clay Fravel resided with his family in
            dwelling 326 on page 24.

PAGE 30 WOODSTOCK   (Microfilm Page 856)

Dwelling 200   Family 200

David Fravel   39 Wheelwright & Farmer 5200   850   Va.
Catherine Fravel   54   (Can't Read)   "
Louisa Fravel   32   "
Sarah C. Fravel   3m   "
Joseph Fravel   18 Wheelwright Apprentice   "

        David Fravel was born 14 Dec 1820 and died 22 Mar
1902. He was the son of Henry and Barbara. Henry Fravel
III married Barbara Fetzer on 9 Aug 1808. Barbara Fravel
was born 22 Apr 1786 and died 4 Sep 1830 Henry was married
to **Catherine Lichliter** on 23 Mar 1834. The bondsman for
that marriage was Samuel Lichliter. Catherine was present
in this household. Catherine Lichliter Fravel was born 27
Nov 1802 and died 19 Aug 1881. Henry Fravel III was born
15 Mar 1781 and died 12 Jun 1851. His sons David and
Joseph followed him into the wheelwright trade. David was
married to **Louisa Supinger** on 11 Jan 1860. She was the
daughter of Peter and Sarah. Peter Supinger married Sarah
Catherine Kinsley on 15 Mar 1820. Louisa was born 5 Aug
1827 and died 22 Dec 1884. Members of this family were
buried in the St. Paul's Reformed Church Cemetery.

Sarah C. Fravel was born 12 Mar 1860 and died 22 Sep 1861.

Joseph Fravel was the son of Henry Fravel III and Catherine Lichliter Fravel. He was born 11 Feb 1842 and died 21 Aug 1909. Joseph eventually became employed in2 the building supply business. He was married to Catherine Victoria Hottel on 28 Feb 1872. Catherine was the daughter of John J. and Anna Hudson Hottel. Catherine was born 1 Jan 1844 and died 1 Jun 1892. Joseph and Catherine had 11 children and were buried in the St. Paul's Reformed Church Cemetery.

RELATED FAMILY:

William J. Supinger, brother of Louisa, married Ann E. Jordan on 16 Apr 1849 and resided in **dwelling 87.**

Peter and Sarah Supinger, brother and sister of Louisa, resided in **dwelling 88.**

Mary A. Fravel, sister of David, married James Gregory Fravel on 6 Nov 1834 and resided in **dwelling 114.**

John Henry Fravel, brother of David, married Sarah Jane Bruce on 4 Jul 1848 and resided in **dwelling 145.**

Catherine Jane Fravel, sister of David, married George Rye on 2 Oct 1833 and resided in **dwelling 156.**

Ellen Catherine Miller, married Frederick Fravel on 24 Aug 1840. Frederick was deceased. He was the brother of David. Ellen resided in **dwelling 201.**

George Fravel, brother of David, married Harriet Ella Myers on 6 Nov 1833 and resided in **dwelling 177.**

1850 CENSUS: David, Joseph and Catherine Fravel, resided with Henry Fravel III in dwelling 211 on page 15.

Louisa Supinger resided with her parents in dwelling 266 on page 19.

PAGE 30 WOODSTOCK (Microfilm Page 256)

Dwelling 201 Family 201

Ellen C. Fravel	42	1,000	180	Virginia
Mary Ann Fravel	7			"

Ellen Catherine Miller was married to Frederick Fravel on 24 Aug 1840. Ellen was born 6 May 1818 and died 23 Jan 1896. Frederick was born 19 Jun 1817 and died 27 Apr 1859. Ellen and Frederick were buried in the St. Paul's Reformed Church Cemetery in Woodstock. Frederick was the son of Henry and Barbara. Henry Fravel III married Barbara Fetzer on 9 Aug 1808.

Family records reveal that Ellen and Frederick did not have any children. If this is accurate **Mary Ann Fravel** may have been a neice. However, there is the possibility that she was their daughter.

RELATED FAMILY:

Mary Ann Fravel, sister in law of Ellen, married James Gregory Fravel on 6 Nov 1834 and resided in **dwelling 114.**

John Henry Fravel, brother in law of Ellen, married Sarah Jane Bruce on 4 Jul 1848 and resided in **dwelling 145.**

Catherine Jane Fravel, sister in law of Ellen, married George Rye on 2 Oct 1833 and resided in **dwelling 156.**

George Henry Fravel, brother in law of Ellen, married Harriet Ella Myers on 6 Nov 1833 and resided in **dwelling 177.**

David Fravel, brother in law of Ellen, married Louisa Supinger on 11 Jan 1860 and resided in **dwelling 200.**

1850 CENSUS: **Ellen Catherine Miller Fravel** and her husband were located in dwelling 213 on page 15.

PAGE 30 WOODSTOCK (Microfilm Page 856)

Dwelling 202 Family 202

Lewis Rosenbaum	46	Peddler of Dry Goods	0	200	
					Bohemia–Germany
Sarah Rosenbaum	32				Michigan
Charlotte Rosenbaum	10				" School
David E. Rosenbaum	7				" School

1850 CENSUS: There is no additional information on this family.

216

PAGE 30 WOODSTOCK (Microfilm Page 856)

Dwelling 203   Family 203

William Ott	58	Tanner and Farmer 16,530 32,080	
			Virginia
Eliza Ott	52		"
Sarah M. Ott	27		"
Virginia F. Ott	22		"
Mary J. Ott	20		"
Anna P. Ott	16		"
James E. Ott	14		" School
Emma C. Ott	12		"
Lewis P. Ott	10		"
Henry C. Ott	8		"
Samuel W. Ott	5		"
Catherine Smith	70		"

William Ott was married to **Eliza Bartman (Hartman)** on 28 Oct 1830. The minister for the marriage was Lewis Eichelburger. This marriage was registered in Frederick County, Virginia.

Very limited information on this family in Shenandoah County. Obituary records indicate that **Henry C. Ott** died in Winchester on 14 Nov 1932 at the age of 81. He never married.

1850 CENSUS: **William Ott** and his family resided in dwelling 208 on page 15.

PAGE 30   WOODSTOCK (Microfilm Page 856)

Dwelling 204   Family 204

Isaac N. Bowman	38	Miller	0	50	Virginia
Catherine M. Bowman	33				"
Mary C. Bowman	10				"
Alwilda T. Bowman	8				" School
Fritz C. Bowman	4				" School
Lucy E. Bowman	1				"

Isaac N. Bowman was married to **Catherine Meek Clower** on 29 Jan 1849. Isaac was listed as Isaac Bauserman in marriage records. Catherine was the daughter of Samuel and Mary. Samuel B. Clower married Mary Everly on 24 Mar 1816. Mary Everly Clower resided in **dwelling 109.**

Alwilda T. **Bowman** married John W. Hall on 10 Nov 1870. John was a railroad hand. He was the son of Templeton and Jane. John was originally from Alexandria, Virginia.

Lucy E. Bowman, daughter of Isaac and Catherine died 22 Jul 1935 in Woodstock. She was 77 years old and had never married.

RELATED FAMILY:
Samuel V. R. Clower, brother of Catherine, resided with his mother in **dwelling 109**.

1850 CENSUS: **Isaac N. Bowman** and his family resided with the family of Samuel Clower, his father in law, in dwelling 236 on page 17.

PAGE 30 WOODSTOCK   (Microfilm Page 856)

Dwelling 205   Family 205

Benjamin D. Hickman   59 Saddler   1400   1100   Virginia
Cassandra D. Hickman 53   "

Benjamin Hickman was married on 14 Apr 1847 to **Cassandra Miller**. The bondsman for the marriage was George M. Samuel. According to the will of Christian Miller (Will Book Y Page 481) she was his daughter.

RELATED FAMILY:
Nancy W. Barber married Reuben Miller on 13 May 1817. Reuben was deceased. He was the brother of Cassandra. Nancy W. Barber Miller, sister in law of Cassandra, resided in **dwelling 188**.

1850 CENSUS: **Benjamin Hickman** and his wife resided in dwelling 235 on page 17.

PAGE 30 WOODSTOCK   (Microfilm Page 856)

Dwelling 206   Family 206

Mary C. Hess   38   Virginia
Catherine J. Hess 12   "   School
Charles V. Hess   9   "

Mary C. Miller was married on 22 Sep 1845 to Wellington Hess. The bondsman for the marriage was Abraham Kager.

Catherine J. Hess was married on 22 Jul 1880 to 54 year old Alfred Miller. Alfred, a farmer, was the son of Jacob W. and Nellie. Jacob W. Miller and his wife Ellen were related to the founder of the town of Woodstock.

Charles V. Hess died 15 May 1896 at the age of 45 years, 9 months and 2 days old. He was buried in the Radar Evangelical Lutheran Church Cemetery at Timberville in Rockingham County, Virignia. Sarah, the wife of Charles, was buried near him. She died 15 Jul 1902 at the age of 57 years, 2 months and 20 days old.

1850 CENSUS: There was no record of this family in Shenandoah County.

PAGE 30   WOODSTOCK   (Microfilm Page 856)

Dwelling 207   Family 207

William H.Bargelt	33	Watch & Clock Maker	1700	2210
			Pennsylvania	
Catherine Bargelt	29		Virginia	
William F. Bargelt	6		"	
Laura E. Bargelt	1		"	
Mary Fravel	58		"	
Rebecca Fravel	31		"	

William Henry Bargelt was born in 1828 and died 24 Feb 1894. He was a jeweler from Hanover, Pennsylvania. He married Catherine Fravel on 25 Oct 1849. She was the daughter of Henry Fravel III and Mary Dinges Fravel. Catherine was born 11 Jan 1828 and died 26 Feb 1894. William was the Superintendent of the Sunday School of the Woodstock Reformed Church. William and Catherine were buried in the Massanutten Cemetery. William enlisted as a private in Company F of the 10th Virginia Infantry. He was a musician. On 8 Aug 1862 he was discharged on account of his age. There were reports that he sought to enlisted in Rossner's Cavalry late in 1862.

William Fravel Bargelt was born 5 Oct 1853 and died 24 Apr 1910. He was married to Sarah Catherine "Bettie" Few on 1 Dec 1884. Bettie was the daughter of William and

Lucinda. William H. Few (Fead) married Lucinda Boehm on 13 Sep 1852. William Few and family resided in **dwelling 100**. Bettie was born 2 Apr 1862 and died 26 Feb 1897. On 24 Oct 1900, William married Annie A. Litten, the daughter of John and Margaret. John Litten married Margaret Fry on 12 Jan 1860. John Litten and his family resided in **dwelling 1621**. Annie was born 13 Feb 1875 and died 29 Jan 1912. This family was buried in the Massanutten Cemetery.

Laura Elizabeth Bargelt was born 4 Jul 1858 and died 17 Aug 1897. She was married to Milton Hockman Hottel on 12 Dec 1894. The marriage was brief as a result of her early death. Milton was born 16 Nov 1857 and died 10 Jun 1928. He was the son of Isaac and Ann. Isaac Hottel married Ann Fravel on 8 Jun 1838. Isaac Hottel and family resided in **dwelling 1593**.

Mary Dinges Fravel was the mother of Catherine Fravel Bargelt. She married Henry Fravel III. Henry was born in Hardy County, West Virginia on 1 Nov 1787 and died 31 Aug 1848. He was the son of Henry Fravel II and Elizabeth Hockman. Henry and Elizabeth had married on 12 Dec 1786.

Rebecca Fravel was the sister of Catherine Fravel Bargelt. She was born in 1824 and died 18 Feb 1896. She resided with the families of William H. Bargelt and Milton Hockman Hottel.

RELATED FAMILY:
    Elizabeth Fravel, sister of Catherine Bargelt Fravel, married Josiah Heller on 21 Mar 1844. She died in Jan of 1857. Josiah Heller married Dorothy Allen on 22 Jun 1858 and resided in **dwelling 208**.

1850 CENSUS: **William Henry Bargelt** and his wife resided in dwelling 280 on page 20.
       Mary Dinges Fravel and her daughter **Rebecca** resided in dwelling 233 on page 17.

220

PAGE 31 WOODSTOCK   (Microfilm Page 857)

Dwelling 208 Family 208

Josiah Heller   42 Master Boot and Shoemaker 1800 1905
                                              Pennsylvania
Dorothea Heller   39   Virginia
Maria A. Heller   12   "   School
Rebecca C. Heller   9   "   School
William H. Heller   7   "
Nathan Huddle   14 Apprentice   "
Caroline Jackson   24 (Black)   "
Allen J. Heller   6m   "

Josiah Heller was married to Elizabeth Fravel on
21 Mar 1844. The bondsman for the marriage was Henry
Fravel. Elizabeth was the daughter of Henry Fravel III and
Mary Dinges Fravel. Mary Dinges Fravel resided in **dwelling
207.** Elizabeth was born 12 Jun 1822 and died in Jan 1857.
On 22 Jun 1858 Josiah was married to **Dorothy Allen.**
Dorothy was the daughter of Reuben and Rebecca. Reuben
Allen married Rebecca Peters on 21 Dec 1822. This family
was located in **dwelling 634.** Josiah Heller was the son of
William and Mary.

Maria A. Heller was born 18 Jan 1847 and died 19
Mar 1923 in Hanover, Pennsylvania. She was married on 2
Apr 1873 to Louis J. Bargelt, a tinner from Hanover,
Pennsylvania. Louis was the son of John and Lavinia. He
was born 12 Jan 1844 and died 3 Mar 1912 in Hanover,
Pennsylvania. The couple resided in Hanover during their
marriage. Louis was employed as a plumber.

Rebecca C. Heller is not mentioned in the family
information that has been located.

Allen J. Heller died 7 Sep 1860 and was buried in
the St Paul's Reformed Church Cemetery.

William H. Heller never married. He distinguished
himself as the manager of the **Chicago Tribune** job office.

Nathan Huddle was born 12 Sep 1844 and died 13 Jul
1924. He is listed twice in this census. He appears in
dwelling 366. This was the household of his father.
Nathan was the son of Elias and Margaret. Elias Hottel
married Margaret Walters on 25 Jul 1833. Nathan initially

married Mary E. Dewer. Mary was born in Augusta County,
Virginia on 7 Jan 1833. She died ca 1903. Nathan was
married for a second time to Lydia Shafer of Shadyside,
Ohio. He is believed to have served in Company K of the
7th Virginia Cavalry. He served for the duration of the
war without injury. Nathan preferred the name **Huddle**. He
moved to Armstrong Mill, Ohio. It is believed that he was
known as "**Dock**".

1850 CENSUS: **Josiah Heller** and his family resided in
                    dwelling 292 on page 21.
                    Dorothy Allen resided with her family in
                    dwelling 1117 on page 78.
                    Nathan Huddle resided with his parents in
                    dwelling 966 on page 67.

PAGE 31 WOODSTOCK   (Microfilm Page 857)

Dwelling 209   Family 209

William W. Magruder	56 Physician	9025	18,000	Maryland
George Magruder	25 Physician			Virginia
Phillip W. Magruder	22 Attorney			"
John W. Magruder	16			" School
Henry C. Magruder	11			" School
Mary E. Magruder	19			"
Ann Jones	63			"
Caroline V. Lee	44			Maryland
Elizabeth J. Jones	29			Virginia

William Wilson Magruder was the son of George Beall
Magruder of Georgetown, Maryland. He died 11 May 1867 at
72 years of age and was buried in the Emanuel Episcopal
Church Cemetery in Woodstock. William had served as a
member of the House of Delegates from Shenandoah County in
1829 and 1830. He was married to Mary Susan Williams on
20 Apr 1825. She was the daughter of Phillip Williams.
The bondsman for the marriage was Robert Turner. Her
mother was Sarah Coudson Williams.

George Williams Magruder was as physician. He was
a 2nd Lt. in the 10th Virginia Infantry Company F. He was
a surgeon in that unit. George went to Texas after the
conflict and died in Ft. Worth.

Phillip Wilson Magruder was born 16 Mar 1838 and
died 4 Mar 1907. He was an attorney and married Ann Eliza
Ott on 20 Feb 1862. She was the daughter of Jacob and

Susan. Jacob Ott Jr. married Susanna Bowman on 7 Apr 1835. Jacob and his family resided in **dwelling 179**. Ann Eliza Ott Magruder was born 7 Aug 1837 and died 22 Jun 1905. They were buried in the Massanutten Cemetery. Phillip enlisted in the 10th Virginia Infantry Company F on 18 Apr 1861 as 3rd Sgt. He was commissioned as a 2nd Lt. on 8 Oct 1861. He was not re-elected and was reduced in ranks on 3 Apr 1862. He was wounded on 3 May 1863 at Chancellorsville in the spine and knee. He was then detailed as a clerk in Dec 1863 to Staunton.

John William Magruder was born in 1847 and died 2 Jul 1915. He was a farmer at the time of his marriage to Mary Lou Donaldson on 10 Dec 1868. Mary Lou was the daughter of William and Susan Mary. William E. Donaldson married Susan Mary Hickman on 14 Jan 1845. William and his family resided in **dwelling 175**. Mary Lou was born in 1847 and died 3 Apr 1919. This family was buried in the Massanutten Cemetery. There was a John Magruder who served with the 7th Virginia Cavalry Company C. It has not been established that this was the same individual. John William Magruder and his wife were the parents Frank Abbott Magruder. Frank was the author of **American Government** the most widely used textbook in high schools in the United States.

Henry C. Magruder did not marry. He died 29 Jan 1906 in Woodstock.

Mary E. Magruder was married on 7 Jul 1864 to Holmes Conrad, an attorney from Frederick County, Virginia. He was the son of Robert and Elizabeth. Holmes was a Major in the Confederate army. He compiled a distinguished record of service. He was born 31 Jan 1840 and attended Winchester Academy. In 1854 he enrolled at VMI. Holmes taught school at White Sulphur Springs, West Virginia. He eventually graduated from the University of Virigina. He initially served in Company A of the 1st Virginia Cavalry. He assisted in the capture of Sir Percy Wyndham near Harrisonburg. He transferred to Company D of the 11th Virginia Cavalry. He was appointed 1st Lt on 2 Oct 1862. He was appointed Adjutant of that unit and was recommended for Inspector of the Cavalry by General L. L. Lomas. Lt. Col M. D. Ball wrote of Conrad on 6 Dec 1863. He "always conducted himself most gallantly stimulating his regiment to brave deeds by his worthy example of fearlessness in the face of danger." He distinguished himself at Ashland. In 1864 he served as an aide to General Rosser. Promoted in

the field to rank of Major. He was 6' with dark
complexion, black hair and gray eyes. Holmes practiced law
in Winchester and Washington, D.C. He was a member of the
Virginia House of Delegates in 1878 to 1882 and in 1892.
He served on the Board of Visitors of the University of
Virginia for 12 years. He was appointed Assistant United
States Attorney General in Jun 1893. He was appointed
Solicitor General of the United States from 1894 to 1897.
He was a professor of law at Georgetown University and died
in Winchester on 4 Sep 1915.

Ann Williams Jones was the sister of Mary Susan
Williams Magruder. She continued to live with the family
after the death of Mary Susan. She married Phillip ap
Catesby Jones on 19 Nov 1818. It is believed that
Elizabeth J. Jones was her daughter.

Caroline V. Lee lived with the family of W. W.
Magruder in 1850. She died 11 May 1881 at the age of 53.
She was buried in the Emanuel Lutheran Church Cemetery.

RELATED FAMILY:
Samuel Croudson Williams, brother of Mary
Susan Williams Magruder and Ann Williams Jones, resided in
dwelling 174.

1850 CENSUS: **William W. Magruder** and his family resided
in dwelling 322 on page 23.

PAGE 31 WOODSTOCK (Microfilm Page 857)

Dwelling 210 Family 210

Eliza Robinson	22	(Mulatto)	Virginia
Robert J. Robinson	3	(Mulatto)	"
Charles E. Robinson	10m	(Mulatto)	"

There is limited information on this family. There
was a 9 year old **Eliza Robinson** located in dwelling 1178
on page 83 in the 1850 census. She was in the residence
of Joshua Nichols, an ordinary keeper. Her mother Emily
Robinson was present in that dwelling.

1850 CENSUS: This family was not located in the 1850
census.

PAGE 31 WOODSTOCK   (MIcrofilm Page 857)

Dwelling 211   Family 211

Samuel Baker	31	Tailor	Virignia
Mary Baker	31		"
William T. Baker	6		"
Charles H. Baker	2		"
Mary Baker	53	0 100	"

The first name of the head of this household is difficult to read. There is no record of this family in Shenandoah County records. They do not appear to have been present in Shenandoah County in 1850.

1850 CENSUS: This family was not located in the 1850 census.

PAGE 31 WOODSTOCK   (Microfilm Page 857)

Dwelling 212   Family 212

John J. Davis	44	Master Foundry Man 0 50	D.C.
Catherine J. Davis	40		Virginia

John Davis married Catherine Kingree on 23 Oct 1851. Nathaniel Rinker provided the affidavit for the marriage.

1850 CENSUS: Catherine Kingree resided in dwelling 1677 on page 121. This was the household of Henry and Elizabeth Henry Pearson. They were married on 30 Oct 1838. There was also a Catherine Kingree in dwelling 1263 on page 90.

PAGE 31 WOODSTOCK   (Microfilm Page 857)

Dwelling 213   Family 213

David B. Shirk	25	2500	95	Pennsylvania
Mary C. Shirk	25			Virginia
James R. Shirk	3			"
Virginia Shirk	1			"

There is no additional information available on this family.

1850 CENSUS: This family was not located in the 1850 census.

PAGE 31 WOODSTOCK (Microfilm Page 857)

Dwelling 214   Family 214

Nancy Lewis	54	50 75	Virginia
Isaac Lewis	20 Day Labor		"
Jacob Lewis	16 Day Labor		"

Nancy Roller was married to Isaac Lewis on 11 Jun 1832. The bondsman for the marriage was James Dysart.

Jacob Lewis, a laborer, married Eliza A. Fry on 2 Jan 1868. She was the daughter of Elias and Susan. Elias Fry married Susan Fry on 1 Dec 1851. Elias and his family resided in **dwelling 1492**. Eliza A. Fry was not in the household at the time of this census. She is believed to have been a resident in the household of her uncle Reuben. Reuben Fry and his family resided in **dwelling 628**. It is possible that Jacob Lewis died prior to 1874. Marriage records for 24 Dec 1874 indicate that Eliza Fry, the daughter of Elias and Susan was married on that date to John J. Long. John was the widowed son of George and Barbara. George Long married Barbara Bowman on 11 Aug 1834. John J. Long had married Rebecca Funkhouser on 28 Jan 1858. Military records for Company B of the 18th Virginia Infantry show a Jacob Lewis on the roll of that unit. It has not been established that this was the individual in this household.

RELATED FAMILY:

William Lewis, son of Isaac and Nancy, married Mary Sigler on 2 May 1858 and resided in **dwelling 1499**.

1850 CENSUS: Nancy Roller Lewis and her family resided in dwelling 272 on page 19.

PAGE 31   WOODSTOCK   (Microfilm Page 857)

Dwelling 215   Family 215

Athferrath Firrel	49	0 20	Virginia
Ottwell Firrel	17 Day Labor		"
Harriet H. Firrel	7		"

Otway **(Ottwell) P. Ferrell** was born ca. 1842. He was a resident of Shenandoah County at the time he enlisted in Company B of the 10th Virginia Infantry. Otway was a private and a musician (fifer) when he enlisted at Harrisonburg, Virginia. He was transferred to Company F on 18 Apr 1862 and was pressent for duty thru 29 Feb 1864. He transferred to the 7th Virginia Cavalry band. He was taken POW on 11 Jan 1865 at Woodstock. He was ordered by General Phillip Sheridan not to be exchanged as he was branded a "guerilla". Otway was sent to Fort McHenry in January of 1865. He was paroled and released under the Oath of Allegiance on 1 May 1865. Otway died at Woodstock in 1868. The name Ferell was spelled in many ways. In Shenandoah County the name is found as **Ferl, Firrel, Farrell** and **O'Farrell**.

1850 CENSUS: **Alcinda (Athferrath) Ferrell** and her husband Joseph resided with their children in dwelling 919 on page 64.

PAGE 32 WOODSTOCK (Microfilm Page 858)

Dwelling 216 Family 216

Peter Zimmer   38 Carpenter   0   40 Virginia
Sarah C. Zimmer   14   "

   Simon Peter Zimmer was the son of Peter and Catherine. He was born in Washington County, Maryland. Peter was married to Nancy Ponser on 10 Mar 1835. The bondsman for the marriage was Michael S. Baird. In the 1850 census his wife was listed as Ann M. Zimmer. Simon Peter was married to Edith Ridenour on 13 Dec 1860. Edith was the daughter of Adam and Barbara. Adam Ridenour married Barbara Utz on 23 Sep 1804. Edith Ridenour and her mother resided in **dwelling 482.**

   Sarah C. Zimmer was born 14 Apr 1846 and died 4 Jan 1916. She was married on 27 Mar 1870 to John L. Lichliter, the son of James and Elizabeth. James M. Lichliter married Elizabeth Dellinger on 13 Jan 1846. John and his parents resided in **dwelling 1878.** John L. Lichliter was born 21 Oct 1848 and died 10 Jul 1920. They were buried in the Riverview Cemetery at Strasburg.

1850 CENSUS: **Simon Peter Zimmer** and family resided in dwelling 261 on page 19.

PAGE 32 WOODSTOCK   (Microfilm Page 858)

Dwelling 217   Family 217

Barbara Elick	47 Seamstress	400	50	Virginia Cn't Rd
Mary Elick	18			"
John W. Elick	8			"

Barbara Good was married to Godlove Frederick Elick on 31 Jan 1829. Barbara was the daughter of Samuel Good. Frederick was born in Germany.

Mary Elick did not marry. She died on 3 Feb 1907.

John W. Elick was married on 4 Apr 1880 to Mary Ida Costello Storm. She was the daughter of John and Frances. Mary Ida was from Jefferson County, West Virginia. She died 25 Mar 1919.

1850 CENSUS: Frederick Elick and his family resided in dwelling 273 on page 20.

PAGE 32 WOODSTOCK   (Microfilm Page 858)

Dwelling 218   Family 218

Joseph G. Samuels	39	610	3309	Virginia
Sarah A. Samuels	41			"
Mary C. Samuels	9			" School
William P. Samuels	4			"
Joseph B. Samuels	2			"
Joseph H. Samuels	74	30,000	3386	"

Joseph H. Samuels was the father of **Joseph G. Samuels.** His wife was named Catherine. Catherine P. Samuels was born 19 Apr 1793 and died 21 May 1850. She was buried in the Emanuel Lutheran Church Cemetery in Woodstock.   Joseph H. Samuels was an Attorney at Law. Joseph G. Samuels was a merchant at the time his wife Sarah died. On 3 Oct 1872, Joseph G. Samuels was married to Martha A. Hamrick. Martha Ann Hamrick resided in **dwelling 220.** She was the daughter of Samuel and Sarah. Samuel Hamrick married Sarah E. Priest on 2 Feb 1831. Mattie Hamrick Samuels was born 22 Dec 1831. She was born in Rappahannock County, Virginia. Joseph G. Samuels was born in Wood County, West Virginia.

Mary K. Samuels was born 6 Nov 1856 and died 22 May 1933. She was buried at the Emanuel Lutheran Church Cemetery.

William P. Samuels, an employee of the railroad, married Lucy E. Few on 15 Aug 1887. Lucy was the daughter of William and Lucinda. William H. Few married Lucinda Boehm on 13 Sep 1852. William H. Few and his family resided in dwelling 100. Lucy E. Few Samuels died 7 May 1933 at Woodstock.

1850 CENSUS: Joseph H. Samuels and family resided in dwelling 1004 on page 70.

PAGE 32 WOODSTOCK   (Microfilm Page 858)

Dwelling 219 Family 219

Thomas J. Rinker	32	2400	296	Virginia
Ann H. Rinker	32			"
Edward H. Rinker	4			"
Sallie E. Rinker	2			"
Anna L. Rinker	1			"

Thomas J. Rinker was a laborer. He was the son of Jacob and Elizabeth. There was a marriage on 8 Sep 1821 for Jacob Rinker and Elizabeth Frantz. Thomas J. Rinker joined Company D of the 18th Virginia Cavalry on 1 Mar 1864 at Woodstock. He was captured on 11 Jan 1865 at Woodstock and sent to Fort McHenry. He was listed as a guerilla and was not exchanged according to an order by General Phillip Sheridan. His first wife died and Thomas was married on 23 Nov 1876 to Elizabeth Fisher Brubeck. Elizabeth had married Phillip Brobeck on 15 Mar 1860. He was the son of Phillip and Mary. Elizabeth was the daughter of George and Catherine. George Fisher married Catherine Sine on 10 Apr 1816.

Sallie E. Rinker was born in 1855 and died 9 Jun 1861. She was buried at the St. Paul's Reformed Church Cemetery at Woodstock.

1850 CENSUS: This family has not been located in the 1850 census.

229

PAGE 32 WOODSTOCK   (Microfilm Page 858)

Dwelling 220 Family 220

| Martha Hamrick | 25 Seamstress 0 100 | Virginia |
| Rebecca E. Hamrick | 18 | " |

     Martha Ann "Mattie" Hamrick was born 22 Dec 1831. She was the daughter of Samuel and Sarah. Samuel Hamrick married Sarah E. Priest on 2 Feb 1831. She was born in Rappahannock County, Virginia. On 3 Oct 1872 she was married to Joseph G. Samuels. Joseph was born in Wood County, West Virginia. He was the son of Joseph and Catherine. The Samuels family resided in **dwelling 218**. Joseph was a merchant. He was a widower. At the time of this census he resided with his first wife Sarah and their children.

     Rebecca Elizabeth Hamrick was the sister of Mattie Hamrick. She was born 2 Apr 1843 and died in 1923. Rebecca was also born in Rappahannock County. She married John Edward Mankin on 9 Jul 1861. John was a painter. He was born and resided in Alexandria, Virginia. He was the son of John and Elizabeth. She later married James Payne Garner. He was a proof reader with the Government Printing Office until he retired in 1923. James died on 3 Mar 1942.

RELATED FAMILY:
     Sarah Frances "Fanny" Hamrick, sister of Martha and Rebecca, married Peter E. Houshour Jr. on 18 Mar 1858 and resided in **dwelling 116**.
     Nimrod Farrow Hamrick, brother of Martha and Rebecca, married Lydia C. Myers on 17 Mar 1857 and resided in **dwelling 239**.
     Thomas Gideon Hamrick, brother of Martha and Rebecca, resided in **dwelling 1855**.

1850 CENSUS: No record of this family has been located in Shenandoah County.

PAGE 32 WOODSTOCK (Microfilm Page 858)

Dwelling 221 Family 221

| Elizabeth Freet | 54 Weaver 416 | 65 Virginia |
| William H. Freet | 18 Carpenter | " |

Elizabeth Freet was born 24 Oct 1803 and died 26 Sep 1885. She was buried in the St. Paul's Reformed Church Cemetery in Woodstock. Elizabeth was the daughter of Joseph and Susannah. Joseph Freet married Susanna Rife on 15 Oct 1799. This name sometimes appears as Fried in Shenandoah County records.

William H. Freet may have been the son of Elizabeth or her sister Rebecca. They were residents in the household of Susannah Rife Freet in 1850.

1850 CENSUS: Elizabeth Freet resided in dwelling 317 on page 23. Her mother was the head of this household.

PAGE 32 WOODSTOCK (Microfilm Page 858)

Dwelling 222 Family 222

Mary Grantham	64	0	20	Virginia

Mary Yager was the daughter of Jacob Yager. She was married on 12 Oct 1822 to John Weeks. The marriage was of short duration. The will of John Weeks was proved on 10 Feb 1824. Upon the death of John, Mary was married on 10 Mar 1825 to James Grantham. The bondsman for this marriage was Peter Houshour. In the 1850 census Mary was listed as a shoemaker. It is probable that Mary Yager Weeks Grantham was listed twice in the 1860 census. She also appears in the household of Jacob Rodeffer. They resided in dwelling 131. In that household her name was spelled Grainton. Jacob Rodeffer was a shoemaker.

1850 CENSUS: Mary Grantham and her husband James resided in dwelling 315 on page 23.

PAGE 32 WOODSTOCK (Microfilm Page 858)

Dwelling 223 Family 223

Robert Stidley	51	Teacher Common School	500	100	Va.
Mary J. Stidley	18				"
Rebecca F. Stidley	16				"

Robert Stidley was married on 27 Oct 1835 to Eliza Ann Burke. She was the daughter of John.

Mary Jane Stidley was married on 23 Dec 1869 to John R. Gill. John was a blacksmith. He was born in Winchester, Virginia. He was the son of William and Catherine.

Rebecca Frances Stidley was born in 1847 and died in 1919. She was married to John W. Wiley on 23 Nov 1873. John was born in Rockbridge County, Virginia. He was a laborer at the time of the marriage. John was born in 1830 and died in Front Royal on 23 Mar 1906. He was the son of Adam and Elizabeth. John and Rebecca were buried in the Massanutten Cemetery.

RELATED FAMILY:
James W. Stidley, son of Robert, resided in **dwelling 545.** He was a farmhand.

1850 CENSUS: Robert Stidley and his family resided in dwelling 146 on page 11.

PAGE 32 WOODSTOCK (Microfilm Page 858)

Dwelling 224   Family 224

David D. Hounshour	38	Master Mason	900	240	Virginia
Rebecca J. Hounshour	35				"
John S. Hounshour	9				" School
Emma C. Hounshour	7				"
Cornelius Hounshour	5				"
Martha J. Hounshour	2				"
Harriet P. Hounshour	6m				"

David Dinges Hoshour was born 13 May 1822 and died 25 Jul 1901. He was the son of Peter and Elizabeth Clower Hoshour. Peter Hoshour resided in **dwelling 130.** Marriage records for David and **Rebecca** were not discovered. She was born in 1824 and died in 1870. Rebecca was buried in the St. Paul's Reformed Church Cemetery. On 27 Feb 1879 David was married to Ellen Virginia Hurn. She was the daughter of Isaac Hurn. Ellen was born in 1824 and died in Front Royal on 2 Jul 1910. David and Ellen were buried in the Prospect Hill Cemetery in Front Royal, Virginia. David Dinges Hoshour was born in Augusta County, Virginia. He was a member of the 18th Virginia Cavalry. He enlisted in Company D on 1 Feb 1864 at Woodstock. He claimed 2,800 dollars for a horse that was killed in action at Bunker Hill, West Virginia on 1 Sep 1864. He was wounded in an accident in October of 1864.

John Samuel Hoshour was born in Augusta County, Virginia on 16 Sep 1850. He died on 23 Feb 1925. John was married to Virginia "Jennie" Isabella Carper on 26 Nov 1871. Jennie was born 29 Jul 1851 and died 6 Sep 1931. She was the daughter of William and Mary. Virginia and her parents resided in **dwelling 1625**. She was born in Frederick County, Virginia. John and Virginia were buried in the Massanutten Cemetery.

Martha J. Hoshour was born in 1857 and died in 1862.

Harriet P. Hoshour was born in 1858 and died in 1862. She was buried with her sister Martha and her mother in the Massanutten Cemetery.

RELATED FAMILY:

Peter Hoshour Jr., brother of David, resided in **dwelling 116**.

Susannah Hoshour, sister of David, married Phillip Miller on 30 Jul 1839 and resided in **dwelling 225**.

1850 CENSUS: There is no record of David D. Hoshour in this census. It may be that he was a resident of Augusta County at that time.

PAGE 32 WOODSTOCK (Microfilm Page 858)

Dwelling 225   Family 225

Phillip Miller	48	Butcher	0	100	Virginia
Susan Miller	42				"
Elizabeth Miller	19				"
Ellen F. Miller	16				"
Harriet H. Miller	13				" School
Maria D. Miller	5				"
Alice E. Miller	3				"
Edward Howe	30	Boss on R.R.			Massachusetts

The parents of **Phillip Miller** are not known. It is believed that he may have been the son of Jacob W. Miller and his wife Ellen. If this is accurate, John Wayland reports that Phillip Miller died as a prisoner at the Point Lookout Prison Camp in Maryland during the Civil War. Phillip married **Susannah Hoshour** on 30 Jul 1839. The bondsman for the marriage was Christian Miller. Susannah was the daughter of Peter and Elizabeth Clower Hoshour. Peter Hoshour was a resident in **dwelling 130**. She was born

15 Feb 1818 and died 24 Sep 1891. Susannah was buried in St. Paul's Reformed Church Cemetery in Woodstock.

Elizabeth Clower Miller was married on 2 Jan 1861 to **Edward Howe**. Edward was a resident in this household at the time of the census. He was a manager on the railroad. Edward was from Worchester County, Massachusetts and was the son of Francis and Hannah.

Ellen F. Miller was born in 1844 and died 20 Jan 1912. She was married on 15 Mar 1866 to John H. Hoover. John was a farmer and a veteran of the Civil War. He served as a private in Company F of the 10th Virginia Infantry. He was the son of Benjamin and Sarah. Benjamin Hoover married Sarah Walters on 29 Apr 1839. John and his family resided in **dwelling 2063**. John was born in 1842 and died 12 Sep 1915. John and Ellen were buried in the Massanutten Cemetery.

Harriet H. Miller was born 16 Sep 1846 and died 21 Jul 1935. "Hattie" was married on 11 Jun 1872 to Alvin Bemis. Alvin was a carpenter. He was the son of Cheney and Martha. Alvin was born in Spencer, Massachusetts and resided in Brookfield, Massachusetts at the time of the wedding. He was born 16 Oct 1839 and died 19 Apr 1919.

Maria Dinges Miller was born in 1855 and died 30 Mar 1931. She was married to William Worth Logan on 10 Feb 1876. William was born in Washington County, Maryland in 1853 and died 22 Oct 1938. He was the son of Hugh and Mary. William was a school teacher. William and Maria were buried in the Massanutten Cemetery.

Alice E. Miller was born in 1857 and died 17 Feb 1924 in Washington, D.C. She was married on 14 Oct 1875 to Mahlon G. Feller, the son of Samuel and Rachel. Mahlon was a carpenter. He was reported to have been a veteran of the Civil War. Mahlon was born in 1845 and died 1 Nov 1925 in Washington, D.C. Alice and Mahlon were buried in the Massanutten Cemetery.

RELATED FAMILY:

      Peter Hoshour Jr., brother of Susannah, resided in **dwelling 116**.

      David Dinges Hoshour, brother of Susannah, resided in **dwelling 224**.

If Phillip Miller was the son of Jacob W. and Ellen Miller, his brother **Dr. Thomas J. M. Miller** was located in **dwelling 1630.**

1850 CENSUS: **Phillip Miller** and his family resided in dwelling 227 on page 16.

PAGE 33   WOODSTOCK   (Microfilm Page 859)

Dwelling 226   Family 226

Josiah L. Campbell	26	Physician	2000	1000	Virginia
Annie M. Campbell	26				"
Reuben W. Campbell	1				"
Labin J. Campbell	20	Student of Medicine			"

Josiah Lockhart Campbell was born 5 Apr 1834 and died 12 Feb 1912. He was the son of Robert and Rebecca. Robert M. Campbell married Rebecca A. Lockhart on 4 Jun 1833 in Frederick County, Virginia. Josiah was born in Frederick County. He was married on 19 May 1858 to **Anna M. Walton.** Anna was the daughter of Reuben and Mary Harrison Walton. Reuben Walton, father of Anna, resided in **dwelling 165.** Anna died 23 Apr 1878 at the age of 41 years, 5 months and 8 days old. Anna M. Walton Campbell was one of a group of women who protested to General George A. Custer when he captured Davy Getz. Davy was a harmless, half-witted man of 30 who had the misfortune of hunting in the woods. Despite the pleas of the women, Davy was marched 45 miles to Bridgewater in Rockingham County, forced to dig his own grave and was shot by General Custer's men. Josiah married a second time to Gertrude B. Baxter. She was born in 1852 and died in 1936. Josiah was reported to have died in Nowata, Oklahoma. Josiah and both of his wives were buried in the Massanutten Cemetery. Josiah Lockhart Campbell served as a surgeon in the Confederate forces. He was in the 33rd Virginia Infantry, the 10th Virginia Infantry and the 7th Virginia Cavalry.

Reuben W. Campbell died 6 Mar 1860. He was buried near his parents.

Labin J. Campbell was probably a cousin of Josiah. In the 1850 census of Frederick County, 9 year old Labin Campbell resided in the household of William Campbell. William Campbell married Eliza Bell Cartmell on 7 Mar 1833. There was a Joseph L. Campbell, a surgeon, in the 10th Virginia Infantry. It is possible that this was Labin.

RELATED FAMILY:

Elizabeth Walton, sister of Annie, married John W. Ott on 17 Dec 1850 and resided in **dwelling 159.**

Moses Walton, brother of Annie, married Emily Lauck on 5 Feb 1851 and resided in **dwelling 120.**

1850 CENSUS: **Josiah Campbell** resided with his father in Frederick County. They were located in dwelling 205 in District 16.

Anna M. Walton resided with her parents in dwelling 240 on page 17.

Labin J. Campbell appears in the household of William and Eliza in Frederick County. They are believed to have been his parents. They resided in dwelling 208 in District 16.

PAGE 33 WOODSTOCK   (Microfilm Page 859)

Dwelling 227   Family 227

Alexander Bowman	50	Master Mason	7250 5218	Virginia
Barbara Bowman	43			"
Ann Maria Bowman	21	Teacher Common School		"
Virginia Bowman	15			" School
Ellenora Bowman	13			" School
Samuel Bowman	11			" School
Elizabeth Bowman	9			"
Lucy A. Bowman	6			"
William L. Bowman	3			"
Howard A. Bowman	1			"
Caloub Robinson	23	(Black)		"

Alexander Bowman was married on 1 Dec 1837 to **Barbara Bare.** She was the daughter of Samuel Bare.

RELATED FAMILY:

Emily and **Rebecca Bare** resided in **dwelling 169.** Emily Bare had married John Gatewood on 22 Mar 1841. She was also the daughter of Samuel Bare. It has not been established but these women may have been sisters of Barbara Bare Bowman.

1850 CENSUS: **Alexander Bowman** and his family resided in dwelling 320 on page 23.

236

PAGE 33 WOODSTOCK   (Microfilm Page 859)

Dwelling 228   Family 228

Nancy McMahon   36 Washerwoman 0   10 Virginia Can't Read

        Nancy Sharp married Michael McMahon on 3 Aug 1839.
The bondsman for the marriage was John G. Smith.

RELATED FAMILY:
                Rebecca McMahon, daughter of Nancy Sharp
McMahon, resided in **dwelling 392**. This was the household
of John and Sarah Pence.

1850 CENSUS: There is no record of this individual in
                1850.

PAGE 33 WOODSTOCK   (Microfilm Page 859)

Dwelling 229   Family 229

Rebecca Martin   70   0 20   Virginia Can't Read

        There is no other record of this individual in
Shenandoah County.

1850 CENSUS: There is a 60 year old **Rebecca Martin**
                residing with her 29 year old daughter
                Louisa in the 1850 Frederick County census.

PAGE 33 WOODSTOCK   (Microfilm Page 859)

Dwelling 230   Family 230

Andrew J. Cullers   40 Carpenter   1000   1165   Virginia
Mary L. Cullers   38   "
Sarah C. Cullers   13   " School

        Andrew J. Cullers was married to **Mary Bader** on 13
Jul 1843. She was the sister of Samuel. The bondsman for
the marriage was Daniel Burner. It is reported that this
couple may have been buried in the Massanutten Cemetery.
However, there is no record of their burial in the Borden
cemetery books.

        Sarah "Sallie" C. Cullers is reported to have wed
George W. Rabb. She may have been buried in Newton, North
Carolina.

1850 CENSUS: Andrew Culler and his family resided in dwelling 846 on page 59.

PAGE 33 WOODSTOCK (Microfilm Page 859)

Dwelling 231   Family 231

Jacob Teeter	59	150	90	Virginia
Mary Teeter	54			"
Joseph Teeter	20 Day Labor			"
Barbara A. Teeter	17			"
Rachel C. Teeter	15			"

Jacob Teeter married Mary Stover on 27 Mar 1832. The bondsman for the marriage was Henry Horey.

Joseph C. Teeter (Teater), a farmer, married Elizabeth Baker on 5 Dec 1861. Elizabeth was the daughter of Isaac Baker. She was born in Ohio. Joseph C. Teeter was a twin. His sister Mary resided in dwelling 232. Joseph enlisted on 18 Apr 1861 in Company F of the 10th Virginia Infantry. He was a private. He was frequently ill of typhoid fever while he was in the service. He was present until 25 Apr 1862. Sometime after this date records indicate that he died while in the hospital.

RELATED FAMILY:

Mary Teeter, daughter of Jacob and Mary, married Alfred McInturff on 24 May 1855 and resided in dwelling 232.

Rebecca Teeter, daughter of Jacob and Mary, married Samuel Fogel on 30 Jun 1853 and resided in dwelling 266.

1850 CENSUS: Jacob Teeter and family resided in dwelling 302 on page 22.

PAGE 33 WOODSTOCK (Microfilm Page 859)

Dwelling 232   Family 232

Alfred McInturff	25 Carpenter	0	125	Virginia
Mary McInturff	20			"
William H. McInturff	2			"
Emily W. McInturff	6m			"

Alfred R. McInturff was married on 24 May 1855 to Mary Teeter. Mary was the daughter of Jacob and Mary.

Jacob Teeter married Mary Stover on 27 Mar 1832. Jacob
Teeter and family resided in **dwelling 231**. Alfred was the
son of Henry and Elizabeth. Henry McInturff (Mountain
Henry) married Elizabeth Ridenour on 28 Feb 1821.
Elizabeth Ridenour McInturff resided in **dwelling 455**.

RELATED FAMILY:

        Rebecca Teeter, sister of Mary Teeter
McInturff, married Samuel Fogle on 30 Jun 1853 and resided
in **dwelling 266**.

        Nancy Ann McInturff, sister of Alfred,
married Elanson Reynard on 5 Dec 1848 and resided in
dwelling 250.

        Eliza Miller McInturff, sister of Alfred,
married Jacob Lichliter on 3 Mar 1841 and resided in
dwelling 542.

        Julia Ann McInturff, sister of Alfred,
married Elias Hottel on 25 Feb 1854 and resided in **dwelling
371**.

        Marcus M. McInturff, brother of Alfred,
married Mary E. Long on 16 Feb 1858 and resided in **dwelling
456**.

        Lewis McInturff, brother of Alfred, married
Margaret Ann Edwards on 16 Nov 1852 and resided in **dwelling
1944**.

1850 CENSUS: **Alfred R. McInturff** was a resident in
                dwelling 2049 on page 148. This is believed
                to have been his sister Ann McInturff
                Reynard and her husband Elanson.
           Mary Teeter resided with her parents in
                dwelling 302 on page 22.

PAGE 33 WOODSTOCK   **(Microfilm Page 859)**

Dwelling 233   **Family 233**

Mary Hill	57 Millener	700	290	Virginia
Susan Grey	76 (Black)			"

      Mary Ott was born 9 May 1803 and died 13 Jan 1873.
She was buried in the St. Paul's Reformed Church Cemetery
in Woodstock. Mary was married to Joseph Hill on 11 May
1824. The bondsman for the marriage was John Haas. Mary
Ott Hill was a resident in the household of her mother,
Mary Ott, in 1850. Mary Ott was born 21 Feb 1783 and died
20 Jul 1853. She was buried next to her daughter Mary.

1850 CENSUS: **Mary Ott Hill** resided with her mother in dwelling 316 on page 23.

PAGE 33 WOODSTOCK **(Microfilm Page 859)**

Dwelling 234 **Family 234**

George Bennicks	32	Blacksmith	300	100	Maryland
Levina Bennicks	30				"
Emma J. Bennicks	11				"
Levina A. Bennicks	6				"
Ida A. Bennicks	4				"
Benjamin F. Bennicks	1				Virginia

       There is no additional information available on this household.

1850 CENSUS: This family was not in Shenandoah County in 1850.

PAGE 34 WOODSTOCK **(Microfilm Page 860)**

Dwelling 235 **Family 235**

Neetow Luckins	24	(Black/Female) Washer	0	25	Virginia
Mary Luckins	4	(Black)			"
Martha E. Luckins	3	(Black)			"
Laura L. Luckins	1	(Black)			"

       There is no additional information available on this household.

1850 CENSUS: This family was not in Shenandoah County in 1850.

PAGE 34 WOODSTOCK **(Microfilm Page 860)**

Dwelling 236 **Family 236**

Talisandra Schmitt	31	Farmer	300	500	Virginia	
Elizabeth Rudy	49				"	Can't Read

       There is no additional information available on this household.

1850 CENSUS: This family was not located in the 1850 census.

PAGE 34 WOODSTOCK   (Microfilm Page 860)

Dwelling 237 Family 237

Atwell Conner	34 Farmer	1100	726	Virginia
Catherine Conner	33			"
William H. Conner	4			"
Rebecca J. Conner	2			"
Thomas B. Conner	10m			"
Catherine Conner	24			"

Atwell Conner was married on 14 Jan 1852 to Catherine Reeser. John Reeser was the bondsman for the marriage.

William H. Conner was born 30 Jan 1856 and died 12 Jun 1860. He was buried at St. Paul's Reformed Church Cemetery in Woodstock.

1850 CENSUS: Atwell Conner resided in dwelling 835 on page 58. This was the household of Daniel and Mary Fravel.

PAGE 34 WOODSTOCK (Microfilm Page 860)

Dwelling 238 Family 238

Samuel Clanahan	27 Farmer	800	360	Virginia
Catherine E. Clanahan	27			"
---------- Clanahan	10days	(No sex listed)		"

This family was listed as McClanahan in other records. Samuel Clanahan was born 20 Apr 1831 and died 26 Aug 1909. He was the son of Jacob and Mary. Jacob Clanahan married Mary Burner on 20 Sep 1827. Samuel Clanahan was married to Catherine Elizabeth Golladay on 7 Nov 1858. Catherine was born 24 Apr 1832 and died 10 Apr 1910. Samuel and Catherine were buried in the Bethel Lutheran Church Cemetery in Hamburg, Virginia. Catherine was the daughter of Abraham and Mary. Abraham Golladay married Mary Burner on 28 Feb 1826. A Samuel Clanahan enlisted on 14 Apr 1862 in Company H of the 2nd Virginia Infantry. He was detailed as a teamster on 30 Jun thru 31 Oct 1862. He was taken prisoner of war at Strasburg on 22 Sep 1864. Samuel was sent to Point Lookout and was eventually paroled on 18 Feb 1865. Additional information is needed to establish the head of this household as the member of the 2nd Virginia Infantry.

Mary Elizabeth Clanahan was probably the 10 day old infant in this household. She was born in 1860 and died in 1926. She was married on 25 Mar 1880 to James B. Hamman. James was the son of Samuel and Christina. Samuel Hamman married Christina C. Lantz on 1 Apr 1850. James B. Hamman is occasionally listed as James B. Hammond in county records. He was born in 1859 and died in 1910. James and his family resided in **dwelling 1403**. Mary Elizabeth and James were buried in the Bethel Lutheran Church Cemetery.

RELATED FAMILY:

Delilah Golladay, sister of Catherine, married Alexander Clem on 18 Dec 1856 and resided in **dwelling 517**.

David Golladay, brother of Catherine, resided in **dwelling 422**. His sisters Marilla and Mary were also in that household.

1850 CENSUS: Catherine Elizabeth Golladay resided with her mother in dwelling 1864 on page 134.

Samuel Clanahan resided with his parents in dwelling 1895 on page 136. The family was listed as McClanahan at that time.

PAGE 34   WOODSTOCK   (Microfilm Page 860)

Dwelling 239   Family 239

Nimrod F. Hamrick	25	Boot & Shoemaker	0	75	Virginia
Lydia G. Hamrick	26				"
Mary F. Hamrick	2				"
John S. Hamrick	3m				"

Nimrod F. Hamrick was born in Little Washington in Rappahannock County, Virginia. He was born 8 Oct 1833 and died 23 Jul 1910. He was the son of Samuel and Sallie. Samuel Hamrick married Sarah "Sallie" Elizabeth Priest on 2 Feb 1831. Nimrod was married to **Lydia Susan Myers** on 17 Mar 1857. She was the daughter of John and Delilah. John Myers married Delilah Leadley on 30 Jun 1821. John Myers and his family resided in **dwelling 1920**. Nimrod enlisted in Company C of the 33rd Virginia Infantry on 3 Jun 1861. He was AWOL in Sep and Oct 1861. He was absent Aug thru Dec of 1862 as a result of a wound in the heel that was received in the second battle for Manassas. He was later wounded in action at Spotsylvania on 12 May 1864. He was paroled on 18 Apr 1865. Nimrod was 5'10". Lydia Myers Hamrick died in 1868. Upon her death he was married to

Virginia Catherine Rittenour on 22 Feb 1872. Virginia was born 14 Oct 1853 and died 19 Dec 1901. Catherine was the daughter of Isaac and Christina. Isaac Rittenour married Christina Lickliter on 7 Nov 1853. Isaac Rittenour resided in **dwelling 2037**. Nimrod and Virginia were buried in the Massanutten Cemetery.

Mary F. Hamrick does not appear in Hamrick family records. She probably died in childhood.

John Samuel Hamrick was born 18 Feb 1859 and died Jan 1927. He was reared by his mother's sister Mary Myers and her husband Samuel Bowman. Samuel and Mary resided in **dwelling 1941**. John was a charter member of the Woodstock Christian Church and taught schools in Shenandoah County. He later worked for the Norfolk and Western Railroad and was transferred to Norfolk, Virginia. John married Annie Marie Kite. She was born at Marksville in Page County, Virginia on 31 Aug 1862 and died 3 May 1923.

RELATED FAMILY:

Martha Hamrick and **Rebecca Hamrick**, sisters of Nimrod, resided in **dwelling 220**.

Sarah Frances "Fanny" Hamrick, sister of Nimrod, married Peter E. Houshour Jr. on 18 May 1858 and resided in **dwelling 116**.

Joel Thomas Myers, brother of Lydia, married Mary Jane McFarling on 22 Apr 1858 and resided in **dwelling 2239**.

Mary M. Myers, sister of Lydia, married Samuel Bowman in Jul of 1854 and resided in **dwelling 1941**.

1850 CENSUS: **Lydia G. Myers** was located with her father in dwelling 836 on page 58.

PAGE 34 WOODSTOCK (Microfilm Page 860)

Dwelling 240 Family 240

Rachel A. Moore   33 (Black) Cook 0 10 Virginia
William Moore   6 (Black)   "

No additional information has been located on this family.

1850 CENSUS: **Rachel Moore** was a resident in dwelling 307 on page 22. She appears to have had a son Albert. He was 4 years old at the time.

PAGE 34 WOODSTOCK (Microfilm Page 860)

Dwelling 241 Family 241

Malinda Grant	35 (Black)	0	10 Virginia
Emma Grant	3 (Black)		"
Milton Turner	20 (Black)		"

Malinda Grant was the daughter of Thomas and Allie. She was married on 27 Dec 1866 to Orange Christy of Botetourt County, Virginia. He was the son of David and Maria.

1850 CENSUS: There is no record of this family in 1850.

PAGE 34 WOODSTOCK (Microfilm Page 860)

Dwelling 242 Family 242

Rebecca Becket	65 (Black)	0	10 Virginia
Isaac Moore	44 (Black)		"
Maria Moore	19 (Black)		"
Joseph Rickerson	9 (Black)		"

1850 CENSUS: **Isaac Moore** appears in the household of Dr. John G. Schmitt. Dr. Schmitt was a merchant in addition to being a physician. They resided in dwelling 319 on page 23.

PAGE 34 WOODSTOCK (Microfilm Page 860)

Dwelling 243 Family 243

Cornelius Hammack	27 Minister U.B.	0	200	Virginia
Mary E. Hammack	28			"

No additional information has been located on individuals in this household.

1850 CENSUS: This family has not been located in 1850.

PAGE 34 WOODSTOCK   (Microfilm Page 860)

Dwelling 244   Family 244

Jacob Maphis	36	Farmhand 0	109	Virginia	
Julia C. Maphis	32			"	
Lucy J. Maphis	12			"	School
Mary C. Maphis	10			"	School
Emma B. Maphis	9			"	School
Amonia E. Maphis	6			"	School
Henrietta S. Maphis	3			"	
Sarah U. Maphis	8m			"	

Jacob Maphis was married on 14 May 1846 to **Julia C. Hutchinson**. She was the daughter of Charles.

Lucy J. Maphis was married on 8 Apr 1869 to Joseph W. Newland. Joseph was a farmer. He was the son of Isaac and Elizabeth. Isaac Newland married Elizabeth Roof on 5 Feb 1833. The Newland family resided in **dwelling 583**.

Mary "Mollie" C. Maphis was born in 1849 and died 13 Mar 1930. She was married on 21 Apr 1870 to William Homer Ruby. William was born in 1843 and died in 1921. He was the son of Jacob and Diana. Jacob Ruby married Diana Brinker on 9 Jun 1831. The Ruby family resided in **dwelling 565**. Mollie and William were buried in the New Mount Jackson Cemetery.

Emma B. Maphis was married on 15 Oct 1874 to George W. Furry. George was born in Augusta County, Virginia and resided in Rockingham County at the time of the marriage. He was a painter. George was the son of William and Ellen. Emma B. Maphis died 3 May 1922 at Mount Jackson. George W. Furry died 5 Oct 1912 at Rinkerton.

Amonia E. Maphis was married on 21 Dec 1875 to George W. Foltz. George was the son of John and Pierce. There was a marriage on 10 May 1854 for John Foltz to Pearly Walters. The family of John Foltz resided in **dwelling 1386**. George W. Foltz is believed to have been buried in the St. Marys Pine Church Cemetery. He was born 1 Feb 1855 and died 25 Jul 1921.

Henrietta "Nettie" S. Maphis was married on 2 Jan 1877 to William F. Allen. William was the son of Isaiah and Mary. Isaiah Allen married Mary Jane Henkle on 6 Apr 1846. Isaiah Allen and his family resided in **dwelling 646**.

1850 CENSUS: There is no record of this family.

PAGE 34 WOODSTOCK (Microfilm Page 860)

Dwelling 245 Family 245

```
Lawrence Donovan     27 Day Labor   0  25 Ireland
Elizabeth Donovan    27                    Virginia Cn't Rd
John T. Donovan       5                    "
William C. Donovan    1                    "
```

Lawrence Donovan was born in 1828 and died 23 Jul 1896. He was married to **Elizabert Bussey** on 25 Aug 1853. Johnson Burk provided the affidavit for the marriage. Elizabeth died 30 Apr 1884 at the age of 50. Lawrence and Elizabeth were buried at the Union Forge Cemetery.

William C. Donovan was born 18 Aug 1860 and died 3 Jul 1923. He was married on 25 Sep 1885 to Nannie M. Shay. Nancy was the daughter of William and Allie. William Shay married Allie Ann Martin on 7 Oct 1854. William Shay and his family resided in **dwelling 8**. William and Nannie were buried in the Cedarwood Cemetery. This family was also listed as Dunnavan and Dunivan.

RELATED FAMILY:

Johnson T. Burke, the bondsman for the marriage of Lawrence and Elizabeth, resided in **dwelling 1737**. He had married Catherine Bussey on 8 Feb 1842. At the time of this census Catherine had apparently died. There was a Margaret Burke in residence. It may be that Margaret Burke was Johnson's sister in law. Johnson T. Burke married Margaret Bussey on 17 Feb 1863. It is probable that Catherine and Margaret were sisters of Elizabeth Bussey Donovan. Margaret's wedding certificate, like her sister Elizabeth, indicates that the parents were "not known".

1850 CENSUS: Elizabeth Bussey resided in the household of George and Frances Clower. They were located in dwelling 1371 on page 99.

PAGE 35 WOODSTOCK (Microfilm Page 861)

The last two members of the Lawrence Donovan household were listed on this page. No other households were listed.

PAGE 36 WOODSTOCK   (Microfilm Page 862)

This is the actual final page of the 1860 **Shenandoah County** Census. There were no households listed on this page.

PAGE 37   EDINBURG DISTRICT   (Microfilm Page 561)

Dwelling 246   Family 246

Nathaniel Q. Humston	75		11,900	8900	Virginia
Margaret Humston	68				"
Benjamin F. Humston	29	Farmer			"
Rebecca F. Humston	21				"
Emma A. Humston	3				"
Ann M. Humston	1				"

Nathaniel Q. Humston was reported to have been the son of Edward Humston Sr. Nathaniel was married 5 Dec 1826 to **Margaret Stephenson**. The bondsman for the marriage was Robert Stephenson. Margaret was the daughter of James and Hannah. James Stephenson married Hannah Watson on 9 Jan 1775. Margaret is mentioned in the 12 Feb 1829 will of her mother (Will Book U - page 279).

Benjamin Franklin Humston was born 12 Jan 1830 and died 21 Sep 1904. He was married to **Rebecca Frances Hockman** on 29 May 1856. She was the daughter of Isaac and Maria. Isaac Hockman married Maria Saum on 4 Nov 1834. Isaac Hockman and his family were residents of **dwelling 1930**. Rebecca was born 28 Aug 1838 and died 1 Mar 1907. Benjamin and Rebecca owned several farms. One of their farms was in Jefferson County, West Virginia. This couple is reported to have been buried in Winchester, Virginia.

Emma Adelia Humston, daughter of Benjamin and Rebecca, was born 19 Sep 1856. She was married on 16 Sep 1874 to William Gaunt. William was born in Rappahannock County, Virginia on 17 Feb 1848.

Anna Maria Humston, was born 23 Dec 1858. She was married on 28 Nov 1882 to E. Ashby Humston. Ashby was born at New Castle, Kentucky. He attended Home College at Campbellsburg, Kentucky and was a physician in Winchester, Virginia.

RELATED FAMILY:

Note: N. Q. Humston was the son of Nathaniel and Margaret. He was born in 1832 and died in 1906. He was a prominent physician in Shenandoah County. He was probably away at school at the time of this census. He married Louise E. Bowman on 12 Nov 1872. She was the daughter of David and Rebecca. David Bowman married Rebecca Cline on 4 Nov 1833. David Bowman and his family resided in **dwelling 350.**

1850 CENSUS: **Nathaniel Q. Humston** and his family resided in dwelling 2035 on page 174. They were listed as Humpston.

Rebecca Frances Hockman resided with her parents in dwelling 922 on page 64.

PAGE 37 EDINBURG DISTRICT (Microfilm Page 561)

Dwelling 247 Family 247

Phillip Pitman	63	Farmer	18,500	2458	Virginia
Mary S. Pitman	59				"
Viola L. Pitman	21	Teacher Common School			"
Emma A. Pitman	17				" School
Nathan J. Pitman	15				" School
Catherine Pitman	24	Teacher of Music (Listed as Male)			
Sarah Evans	35	Housewoman			"

Phillip Pitman was born 22 Jan 1797 and died 26 Mar 1876. His father Lawrence was a man of some importance in Shenandoah County affairs. Lawrence was manager of the Red Bank Mill and his tavern was a popular stopping place for teamsters and stage coaches. Phillip married **Mary Susan Houston**, daughter of Captain George Houston. George was from Rockingham County and served as an officer in the Revolutionary War. Mary Susan was born 23 Aug 1800 and died 8 Aug 1863. Phillip and Mary were buried in the Snapp Cemetery near Edinburg. Phillip served as a soldier in the War of 1812. He also enlisted on 20 Apr 1861 at Edinburg as a private in Company C of the 10th Virginia Infantry. He transferred to Company F on 18 Apr 1862. He was eventually discharged on 18 Jul 1862 due to age and infirmity. From 1848 to 1861 he served as a member of the Virginia State Senate. Through his efforts the Manassas Gap Railroad was extended through Shenandoah County. Phillip was a large slave holder and engaged in farming and lumbering.

Viola Lavinia Pitman was married to William H. Gould on 22 Apr 1868. William was born and resided in Frederick County, Virginia. He was the son of Daniel and Mary. Daniel Gold married Phoebe Scott on 9 Jan 1827. This name was also written as Gold. William was a farmer and a widower. William H. Gold married Margaret Ann Hood on 19 Jan 1847.

Emma A. Pitman was married on 10 Nov 1868 to Elisha Phelp Payne. Elisha was born in Berkley County, West Virginia and resided in Frederick County, Virginia at the time of his marriage. He was a farmer. His parents were John and Mary.

Nathan J. Pitman was born 9 Jul 1844 and died 12 Mar 1883. He was buried near his parents in the Snapp Cemetery. Nathan enlisted on 20 Apr 1861 at Harpers Ferry as a private in Company C of the 10th Virginia Infantry. He transferred to Company F of the 10th Infantry on 18 Apr 1862. He was taken prisoner at Gettysburg on 3 Jul 1863. Nathan was sent to Fort McHenry on 12 Jul 1863 and eventually to Point Lookout, Maryland on 27 Oct 1863. Prior to that he was taken for a period of time to Fort Delaware. Nathan was exchanged on 17 Jan 1865 and was paroled at Mt. Jackson on 21 Apr 1865. Phillip Pitman had two other sons in the Confederate Army. Sons John and Archibald also served.

Sarah Evans is believed to have been Sarah Freeman, the wife of David Evans. Sarah and David were married on 2 Mar 1859. The bondsman for the wedding was Kesha Evans. Sarah and David were neighbors of the Pitman family in 1850.

RELATED FAMILY:

John L. Pitman, son of Phillip, resided in dwelling 598.

Mary Laura Pitman, has not been located in this census. She married Robert B. Snapp on 27 Dec 1855. The association with the Snapp family may account for the fact that members of this family were buried in the Snapp Cemetery.

1850 CENSUS: Phillip Pitman and his family resided in dwelling 2036 on page 147.

Sarah Freeman Evans resided with her husband David in dwelling 2033 on page 147.

PAGE 37 EDINBURG DISTRICT   (Microfilm Page 561)

Dwelling 248   Family 248

William H. Ort	26	Day Labor	0	75	Virginia	Can't Read
Rebecca J. Ort	20				"	Can't Read
Mary E. F. Ort	1				"	

      William H. Ort (written Ortt on his tombstone) was born 21 Dec 1834 and died 16 Sep 1908. He was the son of Jacob and Eliza. William was married to **Rebecca J. Pence** on 6 Jan 1857. Rebecca was the daughter of Joseph and Mahala. Joseph Pence married Mahala Grim on 8 Sep 1836. Joseph Pence and his family resided in **dwelling 305.** Rebecca had a twin sister named Martha. Martha has not been located in this census. Rebecca J. Pence was born 1 May 1839 and died 31 Jan 1922. William and Rebecca were buried in the Cedarwood Cemetery in Edinburg. William H. Ort was a member of Myers Company of the 7th Virginia Cavalry. He enlisted at Hawkinstown on 5 Apr 1862. He was a private at the time of his transfer to the 12th Virginia Cavalry on 1 May 1862. He was detailed as a teamster in Sep and Oct of 1862. The roll for Nov and Dec of 1863 show him as AWOL. He was present in early 1864 but was listed as AWOL in Jul and Aug of 1864. William was paroled at New Market on 20 Apr 1865.

1850 CENSUS: Rebecca J. Pence resided with her parents in dwelling 992 on page 69.

PAGE 37 EDINBURG DISTRICT   (Microfilm Page 561)

Dwelling 249 Family 249

Daniel Sibert	48	Day Labor	0	132	Virginia	
Mary A. Sibert	43				"	
Joseph W. Sibert	17				"	
John H. Sibert	16				"	
Martha J. Sibert	14				"	School
Elizabeth M. Sibert	11				"	School
Sarah C. Sibert	7				"	School
James H. Sibert	3				"	

      Daniel Sibert was married on 27 Jan 1841 to **Mary Ann Evans**. The bondsman for the marriage was David Evans.

      Joseph W. Sibert was born 9 May 1842 and died 5 Apr 1920. He was married on 12 Jan 1873. In his marriage certificate to Sophia Bowers he was listed as a farmer born in Warren County, Virginia. Sophia was the daughter of Reuben and Mary. Reuben Bowers married Mary Holler on 8 Aug 1832. Reuben Bowers and his family resided in **dwelling 1207**. Sophia Bowers Sibert was born 3 Feb 1848 and died 1 Mar 1929. Joseph and Sophia were buried in the Cedarwood Cemetery in Edinburg. Joseph W. Sibert was listed as a veteran in his obituary. There was a Joseph W. Sibert on the roll of Company B of the 2nd Virginia Infantry.

John H. Sibert was married on 14 Nov 1872 to Amanda E. Bowman. Amanda was listed as the daughter of Reuben and Sarah.

Martha Jane Sibert was married on 1 Jan 1871 to George W. Barton. George was a farmer. He was the son of Levi and Catherine. Levi Barton married Catherine Clinedinst on 1 Mar 1827. Levi and his family resided in **dwelling 318**.

Elizabeth M. Sibert was born 28 Jul 1849 and died 25 May 1908. She was married to John W. Carper on 26 Dec 1872. John was a farmer. He was the son of Henry and Elizabeth. Henry Carper married Elizabeth Koontz on 1 Aug 1849. Henry and his family resided in **dwelling 259**. John W. Carper was born 4 Mar 1850 and died 22 Jan 1927. Elizabeth and John were buried in the Snapp Cemetery near Edinburg.

Sarah Catherine Sibert was born 29 Apr 1853 and died in Aug 1924. She was married to James H. Hoover on 3 Jan 1882. James was listed as the son of Reuben and Catherine. Reuben Hoover married Catherine Huddle on 8 Dec 1824. In the Hottel family history Catherine was listed as Catherine Riddelle. James H. Hoover was born 7 Oct 1828 and died 11 Aug 1913. James and his parents resided in **dwelling 283**. Sarah and James were buried in the St. Paul's Reformed Church Cemetery in Woodstock.

1850 CENSUS: **Daniel Sibert** and his family resided in dwelling 851 on page 59.

PAGE 37   EDINBURG DISTRICT   (Microfilm Page 561)

Dwelling 250   Family 250

Elanson Reynard	46	Farmer	1000	230	Virginia	
Nancy Reynard	35				"	
Eliza J. Reynard	10				"	School
Sarah A. Reynard	8				"	
Franklin P. Reynard	7				"	School
Alfred R. Reynard	6				"	
Emma A. Reynard	4				"	
Mary A. Reynard	2				"	

Elanson Reynard was born 22 Oct 1812 and died 9 Jul 1888. On the muster roll of 1835, Elanson was a private in the Grenadiers. He was in the 13th Regiment of the 2nd Battalion of the Virginia Militia. Elanson married **Nancy Ann McInturff** on 5 Dec 1848. The bondsman for the marriage was Levi McInturff. Ann was the daughter of Henry and Elizabeth.   Henry "Mountain Henry" McInturff married Elizabeth Ridenour on 28 Feb 1821.   Elizabeth Ridenour McInturff resided in **dwelling 455.**

Eliza Jane Reynard was married to Ezra C. Armentrout, a farmer from Rockingham County, Virginia on 9 Sep 1873. Ezra was the son of Michael and Mary. Michael Armentrout married Mary Horler on 4 Nov 1830 in Rockingham County, Virginia. These may have been the parents of Ezra.

Sarah Ann Reynard was born in 1851 and died in 1931.   She was married to James Bowman on 3 Nov 1872. James was a blacksmith. He was born in 1849 and died in 1934. James was the son of Jacob and Sophia. Jacob Bowman married Sophia Armentrout on 19 Aug 1841. Jacob and his family resided in **dwelling 1465.** James Bowman was not in his parents household at the time of the census. Sarah and James were buried in the New Mount Jackson Cemetery.

Franklin P. Reynard was reported in obituary notices to have died in New Jersey at the age of 78 on 9 Jul 1931. He was survived by his wife Anna.

Almira L. Reynard (known as Mollie Lee) was born in 1857 and died 30 Dec 1930. It is believed that this was the Mary A. Reynard listed in this household. She married Daniel D. Downey on 13 Dec 1877. Daniel was the son of Andrew and Mary. Andrew Jackson Downey married Mary Ann Bowman on 28 Jan 1839. They resided in **dwelling 1779.**

Daniel D. Downey was born in 1853 and died 17 Sep 1912. Mollie and Daniel were buried in the Hawkinson United Methodist Church Cemetery near Mount Jackson.

Note: Elanson and Ann had a son Joseph Henry, who was born in 1859 and died in 1932. He was not in this household. He married Mary Catherine Sibert. They were also buried in the Hawkinson United Methodist Church Cemetery.

RELATED FAMILY:

    Elanson Reynard was undoubtedly related to Reynard families in **dwellings 251** and **252**. However, the exact relationship has not been determined.

    Alfred McInturff, believed to have been the brother of Ann, resided in **dwelling 232.** He married Mary Teeter on 24 May 1855. Alfred resided with Elanson and Ann in 1850.

    Julia Ann McInturff, sister of Nancy, married Elias Hottel on 25 Feb 1854 and resided in **dwelling 371.**

    Eliza Miller McInturff, sister of Nancy, married Jacob Lichliter on 3 Mar 1841 and resided in **dwelling 542.**

    Marcus M. McInturff, brother of Nancy, married Mary E. Long on 16 Dec 1858 and resided in **dwelling 456.**

    Lewis McInturff, brother of Nancy, married Margaret Ann Edwards on 16 Nov 1854 and resided in **dwelling 1944.**

1850 CENSUS: Elanson Reynard and his family resided in dwelling 2049 on page 148.

PAGE 37   EDINBURG DISTRICT   (Microfilm Page 561)

Dwelling 251   Family 251

Elizabeth Reynard	63	300	125	Virginia
Susan Reynard	61		"	

    There is no additional information available for this household.

RELATED FAMILY:

    Precise relationships have not been established but there must have been some relationship to families in **dwellings 250** and **252**.

253

1850 CENSUS: Elizabeth Reynard resided in dwelling 2048 on page 148. 24 year old Sarah Reynard was also in residence.

PAGE 37 EDINBURG DISTRICT (Microfilm Page 561)

Dwelling 252   Family 252

Abraham Reynard	58	Day Labor	350	220	Virginia	Cn't Rd
Mary Reynard	55				"	Can't Read
Susan C. Reynard	30				"	Can't Read
Rebecca J. Reynard	25				"	
George H. Reynard	19				"	
Sarah F. Reynard	13				"	School
Jackson Reynard	9				"	School
Mary A. Reynard	7				"	School
George A. Reynard	1				"	

     Abraham Reynard was a private in the 13th Regiment, 2nd Battalion of the Virginia Militia in 1835. He was married to **Margaret Ort** on 24 Aug 1825. Margaret was the daughter of John Ort.

     George H. Reynard was a farmer at the time of his marriage to Elizabeth Estep on 23 Dec 1862. Elizabeth was the daughter of Jacob and Mary. Elizabeth is believed to have been a resident of **dwelling 254**. George enlisted in the 10th Virginia Infantry as a private on 18 Apr 1861. He transferred to Company F on 18 Apr 1862. He served in the Cavalry after 27 Feb 1863. George was taken prisoner at Spotsylvania Courthouse on 12 May 1864. He was sent to Fort Delaware on 21 May 1864. George died at Fort Delaware on 14 Feb 1865 of chronic diarrhea. Elizabeth Estep Reynard was married in May of 1872 to William Marston. William was a widowed farmer who had been born in Spotsylvania County. He was the son of Jacob and Mary. William had married Elizabeth Newland on 29 Apr 1843. He resided in **dwelling 585**.

RELATED FAMILY:
     Elizabeth Reynard, daughter of Abraham and Mary was married to William Koontz on 14 Jan 1858 and resided in **dwelling 253**.
     The **Reynard** families in **dwelling 250** and **251** are thought to have been related. The relationship at this writing has not been determined.

1850 CENSUS: Abraham Reynard and his family resided in dwelling 2051 on page 148.

PAGE 38   EDINBURG DISTRICT   (Microfilm Page 562)

Dwelling 253   Family 253

William Koontz	24 Day Labor	Virginia	
Elizabeth J. Koontz	23	"	Can't Read
John W. Koontz	2	"	
Rebecca A. Koontz	1	"	

     William Koontz was the son of Moses and Mary. Moses Koontz married Nancy Ort on 27 Jun 1820. William Koontz married **Elizabeth Reynard** on 14 Jan 1858. Elizabeth was the daughter of Abraham and Mary. Abraham Reynard married Margaret Ort on 24 Aug 1825. Abraham Reynard and family resided in **dwelling 252.** William Koontz enlisted in Company B of the 33rd Virginia Infantry on 10 Aug 1862. He was wounded at Manassas on 28 Aug 1862. He was on leave through December of 1862. William was paroled on 20 Apr 1865 at Mt. Jackson. He was reported to have been 5'10" with dark complexion, gray eyes and brown hair. He was living in Edinburg in 1900.

     Rebecca Koontz was married on 3 Jun 1906 to James W. Minnick. James was a laborer from Rockingham County, Virginia. He was the son of James and Elizabeth. James was a widower. He had originally married Jennie Sissler on 6 Feb 1883. Jennie died 30 Oct 1905 at the age of 38 years, 3 months and 20 days old. She was buried in the Cedar Grove Cemetery in Mt. Jackson. Jennie was the daughter of Joseph and Lydia. Joseph was a forgeman from Cente County, Pennyslvania. He had married Lydia Hopewell on 1 Nov 1860.

RELATED FAMILY:

     Harriet Frances Koontz, sister of William, married Joseph Erasmus Newland on 27 Oct 1859 and resided in **dwelling 554.**

1850 CENSUS: Elizabeth Reynard resided with her parents in dwelling 2051 on page 148.

PAGE 38   EDINBURG DISTRICT   (Microfilm Page 562)

Dwelling 254   Family 254

Daniel S. Bowman	40	Farmer	700	3335	Virginia	
Francis M. Bowman	37				"	
Erasmus R. Bowman	5				"	
Mary M. Bowman	2				"	
Viola K. Bowman	11m				"	
Mary A. Bowman	75				"	Can't Read
Elizabeth Estep	21				"	
John Fox	18	Farmhand			"	

Daniel Snyder Bowman was born 21 Dec 1819 and died 12 Oct 1900. He was the son of Christian and Mary. Christian Bowman married Mary Snyder on 3 Apr 1812. She was the daughter of Peter. Daniel married **Francis M. Hess (Nehs)** on 8 Jun 1854. Francis was born 14 May 1822 and died 2 Jan 1916. She was the daughter of William and Mary. Daniel and Francis were buried in the Cedarwood Cemetery with other members of the household.

Erasmus R. Bowman was born 17 May 1855 and died 9 Oct 1919. He was married on 14 Sep 1876 to Edgar Florence Bowman. Edgar was the daughter of Joseph and Sarah. Joseph Bowman married Sarah A. Johnson on 21 Nov 1821. Edgar and her parents resided in **dwelling 258**. Edgar Florence Bowman was born 26 Dec 1853 and died 13 Jun 1920. Erasmus and Edgar were buried in the Cedarwood Cemetery in Edinburg.

Mary Virginia (Jennie) Bowman was born in 1857 and died 26 Oct 1943. She was married on 13 Nov 1895 to Charles E. Keller. Charles was born in Ohio. He was the son of Abram and Harriet. Abraham Keller married Harriet Sibert. They resided in **dwelling 2007**. Charles E. Keller was born in 1866 and died in 1935.

Elizabeth Estep was probably the daughter of Jacob and Mary. She married George H. Reynard on 23 Dec 1862. He was the son of Abraham and Mary. Abraham Reynard married Margaret Ort on 24 Aug 1825. George and his parents resided in **dwelling 252**. George served the Confederacy during the Civil War. He was taken prisoner at Spotsylvania Courthouse and was sent to Fort Delaware. While in prison he died on 14 Feb at Fort Delaware of chronic diarrhea. Elizabeth married William Marston in May of 1872. William was the son of Joseph and Mary. He was

born in Spotsylvania County. William was a widower. He
had originally married Elizabeth Newland on 29 Apr 1843.
William and his wife resided in **dwelling 585**.

        John A. Fox was the son of Samuel and Elizabeth.
His mother died sometime after 1850 and his father
remarried. Samuel Fox resided in **dwelling 255**. John A.
Fox served in the 10th Virginia Infantry during the Civil
War. He enlisted on 18 Apr 1861 as a private in Company
C. He was absent from 15 Aug through 29 Sep 1861. He died
on 29 Sep 1861 at Camp Blair, Fairfax Station of typhoid
fever.

RELATED FAMILY:
        Joseph and **Nancy Fox**, the brother of and
sister of John, resided in **dwelling 259**.

1850 CENSUS: **Daniel S. Bowman** resided with his parents in
                 dwelling 1002 on page 70.
                 Francis M. Hess resided in dwelling 1007 on
                 page 70. This was the household of
                 Christina Hawkins.
                 John A. Fox resided with this parents in
                 dwelling 2038 on page 147.

PAGE 38 EDINBURG DISTRICT   **(Microfilm Page 562)**

Dwelling 255 Family 255

Samuel Fox	39	Day Labor	0	100	Virginia
Catherine Fox	21				"
Barbara J. Fox	13				"
Mary J. Fox	10				"
Harvey F. Fox	5m				"
William Rinker	2				"

        Samuel Fox was originally married to a woman named
Elizabeth. She was alive in 1850. His second wife was
named Catherine. When he married Catherine several of his
children left the household and went to live with
neighbors.

        Harvey F. Fox was born 25 Dec 1860 and died 3 Feb
1935. He was married to Alberta V. Reynard on 29 Apr 1888.
Alberta was born 1 Sep 1862 and died 23 Sep 1934. Alberta
was the daughter of Jackson and C.A. Harvey and Alberta
were buried in the Cedarwood Cemetery. There was a Jackson
Reynard and his wife Mary Ann in **dwelling 553**. They had

a daughter Alberta who married George L. Grim on 13 Mar 1881. She was 19 at the time of the wedding. If this is the correct family Alberta appears to have been married twice.

RELATED FAMILY:

        John A. **Fox**, son of Samuel and Elizabeth, resided in **dwelling 254**.

        Joseph and **Nancy Fox**, the son and daughter of Samuel and Elizabeth, resided in **dwelling 259**.

1850 CENSUS: **Samuel Fox** and his family resided in dwelling 2038 on page 147.

PAGE 38 EDINBURG DISTRICT (Microfilm Page 562)

Dwelling 256 Family 256

John Scroggins	48	Farmhand	0	100	Virginia	Can't Read
Ann Scroggins	51			"		Can't Read
Martha E. Scroggins	17			"		

       John Scroggins was born in Rappahannock County, Virginia. He was the son of William and Polly. Frederick County marriage records reveal the John Scroggins married Mary Ann Piggins on 11 Feb 1836. The bondsman for the marriage was Thomas Lake. After Ann died, John Scroggins married Isabella (Belle) Grandstaff Pence on 4 Jan 1877. Isabella was a widower. She was the daughter of Benjamin and Elizabeth. Benjamin Grandstaff married Elizabeth Clinedinst on 14 Oct 1820. Benjamin and his family resided in **dwelling 324**. Isabella had married Jacob Pence on 19 Aug 1858. Jacob was the son of Joseph and Martha Beach Pence. Jacob and Isabella resided in **dwelling 337**. Isabella was born in 1842 and died in 1885. She was buried in the Old Edinburg Cemetery.

1850 CENSUS: **John Scroggins** and his family have not been located in 1850.

PAGE 38 EDINBURG DISTRICT   (Microfilm Page 562)

Dwelling 257   Family 257

Dorilas J. Martz	34 Farmer	5320	1135	Virginia
Susan E. Martz	27			"
Andrew J. Martz	8			"
Elizabeth F. Martz	6			"
Henrietta I. Martz	4			"
Emma J. Martz	1			"
Sarah Miller	48 Housewoman			"

Dorilas J. Martz was born in 1825 and died in 1906. It is likely that he came from Rockingham County, Virginia as the Martz name was rather common in that county. There was a Dorilus Henry Lee Martz from Rockingham County who joined Company G of the 10th Virginia Infantry. He rose to the rank of Lt. Colonel and served as a member of the House of Delegates after the war. Dorilas J. Martz of Shenandoah County married **Elizabeth Susan Grandstaff** on 8 May 1848. The bondsman for the marriage was John Grandstaff. Elizabeth was the daughter of John and Elizabeth. John I Grandstaff married Elizabeth Liggett on 27 Feb 1826. Elizabeth Liggett Grandstaff resided in **dwelling 46**. Elizabeth Susan was born in 1829 and died in 1904. Dorilas and his wife were buried in the Old Edinburg Cemetery.

Henrietta I. Martz was born in 1855 and died in January of 1921. She was buried near her parents in the Old Edinburg Cemetery.

Emma J. Martz was born 5 Feb 1859 and died 22 Jun 1939. She was married on 27 Jul 1880 to Joseph E. Newland. Joseph Erasmus Newland was the son of William and Mary. He was a widower at the time of his marriage to Emma. Joseph had originally married Harriet Francis Koontz on 27 Oct 1859. Joseph and Harriet resided in **dwelling 554**. Emma was buried in the Old Edinburg Cemetery.

Sarah Miller is thought to have been the widow of Joseph Miller. Sarah Hausenfluke married Joseph Miller on 28 Mar 1831. Joseph was the son of Peter and Christina Hisey Miller. Sarah was the daughter of John Hausenfluke.

RELATED FAMILY:
      Robert Henry Grandstaff, the brother of Elizabeth, married Elizabeth Johnson on 15 Sep 1856 and

resided in **dwelling 45.**
         Eveline B. Grandstaff, sister of Elizabeth, married John H. Rau on 11 Jan 1854 and resided in **dwelling 64.**

1850 CENSUS: **Sarah Hausenfluke Miller** resided in dwelling 141 on page 11.
          Dorilas Martz and his wife resided in dwelling 1650 on page 119 in Rockingham County.

PAGE 38 EDINBURG DISTRICT   **(Microfilm Page 562)**

Dwelling 258   Family 258

Joseph Bowman	49	Farmer	2400	677	Virginia
Sarah A. Bowman	36				"
Cumberland M. Bowman	11				"
Laura V. Bowman	10				"
Sarah J. Bowman	9				"
Edgar F. Bowman	6				"
_____ Bowman	3m	(Male)			"

    Joseph Bowman was 72 years old at his death on 21 Jul 1883. He was born on 16 Nov 1810 to Jacob and Sarah Fravel Bowman. Joseph Bowman was married on 20 Oct 1847 to **Sarah A. Johnson,** the daughter of Cumberland Marshall and Sarah Jennings Johnson. She was born in Rappahannock County, Virginia on 21 Nov 1821. Sarah died 4 Jul 1892. Joseph and Sarah were buried in the Old Edinburg Cemetery.

    Marshall Cumberland Bowman was born 24 Jul 1848 and died 25 Feb 1904. He was married on 21 Oct 1875 to Mollie E. Ritenour of Rappahannock County. Mollie was the daughter of John Henry and Mary. She was born 16 Nov 1849.

    Laura Virginia Bowman was born 29 Aug 1849 and died 30 Apr 1924. She was buried in the Old Edinburg Cemetery.

    Sarah Alice Bowman was born 19 Dec 1850 and died 7 Mar 1919. She was married on 11 Nov 1880 to William O. Coates. William was born at Louisa Court House on 23 Jun 1849 and died 6 May 1908. William and Sarah were buried in the Cedarwood Cemetery in Edinburg.

    Edgar Florence Bowman was born 26 Dec 1853 and died 13 Jun 1920. Edgar Florence was married to Erasmus R. Bowman on 14 Sep 1876. He was the son of Daniel Snyder and

Francis M. Hess Bowman. Daniel Snyder Bowman and his family resided in **dwelling 254**. Erasmus was born 17 May 1855 and died 9 Oct 1919. They were buried in the Cedarwood Cemetery in Edinburg.

The unnamed infant in the household was **Burder B. Bowman**. Burder was born 27 Feb 1860 and died 27 Apr 1951. He never married. Burder served two terms as a member of the Virginia House of Delegates. He was buried in the Old Edinburg Cemetery.

RELATED FAMILY:

Isaac R. Bowman, brother of Joseph, resided in **dwelling 11**.

1850 CENSUS: Joseph Bowman and family resided in dwelling 2037 on page 147.

PAGE 38 EDINBURG DISTRICT (Microfilm Page 562)

Dwelling 259 Family 259

Henry Carper	32	Farmer	3640	580	Virginia
Elizabeth Carper	32				" Can't Read
John W. Carper	10				" School
Emma G. Carper	7				" School
Joseph H. Carper	5				"
Edward H. Carper	2				"
Joseph Fox	21	Farmhand			" Can't Read
Nancy Fox	15	Housegirl			"

Henry Carper was born 9 Oct 1824 and died 27 Apr 1899. He was married to **Elizabeth C. Koontz** on 1 Aug 1849. The bondsman for the marriage was Moses Koontz. Elizabeth was born 29 Sep 1826. Tombstones recording their lives are located in the Cedarwood Cemetery.

John H. Carper was born 4 Mar 1850 and died 22 Jun 1927. He was married to Elizabeth M. Sibert on 26 Dec 1872. Elizabeth was born 28 Jul 1849 and died 25 May 1908. Elizabeth was the daughter of Daniel and Mary Ann. Daniel Sibert married Mary Ann Evans on 27 Jan 1841. Elizabeth Margaret Sibert resided with her parents in **dwelling 249**. John and Elizabeth were buried in the Snapp Cemetery near Edinburg.

Edward H. Carper was born 25 Oct 1857 and died 24 May 1892. He was buried at Cedarwood Cemetery.

Joseph Fox was the son of Samuel and Elizabeth. Samuel Fox resided with his second wife in **dwelling 255**. Joseph Fox married Elizabeth Wetzell on 30 Dec 1862. Elizabeth was born in Page County, Virginia. Her parents were not listed in marriage records. Joseph Fox is believed to have joined the 10th Virginia Infantry at Edinburg on 18 Apr 1861. He was a laborer. John was described as 5'6", with dark hair and dark complexion. He was a private when he transferred from Company C to Company F. on 18 Apr 1862. He was in the hospital at Winchester on 5 Oct 1862. John was assigned duty with the cavalry on 17 Feb 1863. He returned to the ranks and deserted on 4 Jul 1863. He was confined to the brigade guard house in the winter of 1863 until Feb 1864. He was confined to Lynchburg Prison Hospital in March of 1864 and was paroled 20 Apr 1865. John was later a resident of Oak Ridge in Rockingham County, Virginia.

Nancy C. Fox was the sister of Joseph. There is no indication that she ever married. However, Minnie M. Fox, the daughter of Nancy C. Fox, married John S. Clinedinst on 20 Nov 1887. No father was listed in the marriage record.

RELATED FAMILY:
        John A. Fox, brother of Joseph Fox, resided in **dwelling 254**.

1850 CENSUS: Joseph Fox was located in dwelling 2038 on page 147. This was the household of his father Samuel Fox.

PAGE 39 EDINBURG DISTRICT   (Microfilm Page 563)

Dwelling 260   Family 260

Perry Pence	33 Farmer	0	355	Virginia
Catherine Pence	29			"
Jacob P. Pence	5			"
Lydia C. Pence	2			"
Erasmus M. Pence	9m			"

Perry Pence was born 15 Mar 1827 and died 29 Aug 1888. He was married to **Catherine Boehm**. Catherine was born 20 Oct 1830 and died 5 Oct 1910. They were buried in the Union Forge Cemetery in Edinburg.

Jacob **Perry** Pence was born 24 May 1855 and died 15 Mar 1940. He was married to Meta Gray Shaffer on 6 Jan 1880. In the marriage record Meta's parents were not listed. However in the obituary notice she lists her parents as Duralis and Fannie Proctor. Jacob and Mettie were buried in the Union Forge Cemetery.

There was a marriage recorded for **Lydia C. Pence** to Robert S. Tysinger on 9 Oct 1879. Her parents were listed as John and Katie. There is no record of a marriage for this couple unless Perry was John Perry Pence. Of interest is the fact that Lydia and her husband were buried in the same plot with other members of this family in the Union Forge Cemetery. Lydia was born in 1857 and died in 1921. Robert S. Tysinger was born in 1854 and died in 1927. Robert was the son of David and Seatta. David Tysinger married Seatta Virginia Fry on 22 Feb 1854. Robert and his parents resided in **dwelling 1184.**

Erasmus Marion Pence was born 17 Sep 1859 and died 10 Dec 1948. He was married on 3 Feb 1909 to Mary Catherine Thompson. Mary Catherine was the daughter of James and Sarah. James H. Thompson married Sarah Haun on 23 Dec 1852. James Thompson and his family resided in **dwelling 1823.** Erasmus was buried in the Sheetz Cemetery. Nancy C. Pence was buried next to him. This may have been Mary Catherine. She was born 19 Oct 1863 and died 25 Nov 1911.

1850 CENSUS: **Perry Pence** resided with his parents, Jacob and Edith, in dwelling 990 on page 69.

PAGE 39 EDINBURG DISTRICT (Microfilm Page 563)

Dwelling 261   Family 261

John Clinedinst   30 Master Mason 400 335 Va. Cn't Rd
Catherine Clinedinst 21   "

John "Jack" Clinedinst was born 5 Jan 1831 and died 19 Dec 1905. He was the son of Isaac and Lydia. Isaac Clinedinst married Lydia Holler on 7 Mar 1825. Lydia Holler Clinedinst resided with several of her children in **dwelling 322.** Jack married **Sarah Catherine Bowman** on 30 Sep 1858. She was the daughter of Samuel and Elizabeth Colbeck Bowman. Sarah was born 8 Dec 1839 and died 11 Mar 1915. Jack and Sarah were buried in the Bowman Cemetery in Edinburg.

RELATED FAMILY:

Michael Clinedinst, brother of John, married Lydia Miller on 27 Sep 1853 and resided in **dwelling 2064.**

Caroline Clinedinst, sister of John, married Charles W. Hutchinson on 6 Apr 1850 and resided in **dwelling 78.**

George Bowman, brother of Catherine, resided in **dwelling 329.**

Mary Frances Bowman, sister of Catherine, resided in **dwelling 267.**

1850 CENSUS: John Clinedinst resided with his parents in dwelling 678 on page 48.

Sarah Catherine Bowman resided with her parents in dwelling 1675 on page 120.

PAGE 39 EDINBURG DISTRICT (Microfilm Page 563)

Dwelling 262 Family 262

Thomas Leacount	44	Day Labor	0	50 Virginia Cn't Rd
Mary Leacount	35			"
Frances Leacount	15			"
Commodore Leacount	10			"
Joseph Leacount	8			"
Rebecca Leacount	5			"

Thomas Leacount was married on 12 Jan 1846 to **Mary Bun.** The bondsman for the marriage was George Keller. Courthouse records reveal that her name was actually **Burner.** In Oct 1906, 93 year old Mary Leacount died in the Union Forge area.

Frances "Fannie" Leacount was married on 6 Jan 1897 to Ambrose B. Jenkins. Ambrose was a carpenter. He was the son of Cornelius and Rebecca. Cornelius Jenkins married Rebecca Cave on 25 Jun 1831 in Rockingham County, Virginia. Ambrose resided with his parents in **dwelling 843.** Ambrose was a widower at the time he married Fannie. Ambrose had married Elizabeth Williams on 7 Oct 1873. Elizabeth Williams was the daughter of Henry and Sarah. Henry Williams married Sarah Burner on 10 Aug 1852. Elizabeth Williams and her parents resided in **dwelling 263.** Mrs. Ambrose Jenkins died 2 Apr 1916 at the age of 71.

Commodore Decatur Leacount was married on 10 Jul 1873 to Sophia Fogle Branner. Sophia was the daughter of

Phillip and Mary. Phillip Fogle married Mary "Polly"
Burner on 10 Dec 1822. Sophia and her parents resided in
dwelling 449. Sophia had originally been married to Andrew
Jackson Branum (Branner) on 6 Mar 1862. Andrew was born
in Rockingham County. He was the son of Paul and Polly.
Paul Brenner married Mary Monger on 27 Dec 1830 in
Rockingham County. Andrew Jackson Branum was a member of
the 10th Virginia Infantry and was imprisoned in Jul of
1863 at Camp Chase, Ohio.

    Joseph L. Leacount was born in 1851 and died 31
Oct 1931 in West Virginia. He was married on 11 Feb 1886
to Sarah Etta Barb. Sarah was the daughter of Noah and
Rebecca. Noah Barb married Ann Rebecca Miller on 11 Oct
1855. Sarah was born in 1865 and died in 1930. Noah Barb
resided in **dwelling 1313.** Joseph and Sarah were buried in
the Union Forge Cemetery near Edinburg.

    Rebecca R. Leacount was married on 23 Aug 1877
to William R. Henson of Page County, Virginia. William was
the son of Tapley J. and Mildren.

1850 CENSUS: **Thomas Leacount (Lacount)** and his family
resided in dwelling 975 on page 68.

PAGE 39 EDINBURG DISTRICT   **(Microfilm Page 563)**

Dwelling 263 Family 263

Henry Williams	42	Carpenter	0	50	Virginia Cn't Rd
Sarah Williams	27				"
Catherine Williams	8				"
Elizabeth Williams	6				"
Eliza Williams	3				"

    Henry Williams was married to **Sarah Burner** on 10
Aug 1852.

    Sarah Catherine Williams was born in 1851 and died
in 1936. She was married to John A. Patton on 7 Oct 1873.
John was the son of Michael and Susan. Michael Patton
married Susan Fry on 12 Dec 1836. John A Patton and his
parents resided in **dwelling 314.**

    Elizabeth Williams was married on 7 Oct 1873 to
Ambrose Jenkins. Ambrose was the son of Cornelius and
Rebecca. Cornelius Jenkins married Rebecca Cave on 25 Jun
1831 in Rockingham County, Virginia. Elizabeth died prior

to 1897 as Ambrose Jenkins was married on 6 Jan 1897 to Frances "Fannie" Leacount. Fannie was the daughter of Thomas and Mary. Thomas Leacount married Mary Burner on 12 Jan 1846. Fannie and her parents were the neighbors of Elizabeth Williams. They resided in **dwelling 262**.

1850 CENSUS: **Sarah Burner** resided in dwelling 976 on page 68. This was the household of Thornton Downey and his family.

PAGE 39 EDINBURG DISTRICT **(Microfilm Page 563)**

Dwelling 264 Family 264

Andrew J. Artz	40	Farmer	5430	2009	Virignia
Bathsheba J. Artz	41				"
Samuel J. Artz	23	Farmhand			"
Mary S. Grandstaff	14				"

Andrew J. Artz was born in Oct 1818 and died Jun 1861. He was buried in the Old Edinburg Cemetery. Andrew was married in Frederick County, Virginia on 21 Dec 1847 to **Bathsheba Martz**. Andrew was the son of John and Mary. John Artz married Mary "Polly" Hoffman on 25 Mar 1805.

Samuel Jefferson Artz was probably the nephew of Andrew. He was the son of Mary. Mary Artz is believed to have been the sister of Andrew. In 1850 she appears to have had two children. These two children were twins. Samuel's twin sister Elizabeth married George W. Grandstaff on 18 Jun 1856 and resided in **dwelling 13**. There is no evidence that Mary was married. Samuel married Mary Louise Miley on 30 Jul 1862. Mary Louise was the daughter of Abraham and Sarah. Abraham Miley married Sarah Roads on 17 Feb 1834. Mary Louise and her parents resided in **dwelling 30**. Mary Louise was born 26 Feb 1842 and died 15 Feb 1912. Samuel and Mary Louise were buried in the Zion Christian Church Cemetery in Maurertown. Samuel Jefferson Artz enlisted in Company C of the 10th Virginia Infantry on 21 Apr 1861. He enlisted at Harpers Ferry. He was present in Jan and Feb of 1862. There was no additional record of his activities in this unit. It is believed that he later enlisted in the 23 Virginia Cavalry.

Mary S. Grandstaff was the neice of Andrew J. Artz. Andrew's sister Flora married William B. Grandstaff. Flora Artz Grandstaff died in Oct 1853. Mary's father William has not been located in this census. Mary's brother

John Pustal Grandstaff resided with his grandfather Phillip in **dwelling 267**. Phillip Grandstaff Jr. had married Mary Cooper on 6 Aug 1816. They were the parents of William B. Grandstaff.

1850 CENSUS: **Mary S. Grandstaff** resided with her parents in dwelling 733 on page 52.
Andrew J. Artz and his nephew **Samuel J. Artz** resided in the household of John Artz. They resided in dwelling 172 on page 13.

PAGE 39 EDINBURG DISTRICT (Microfilm Page 563)

Dwelling 265   Family 265

George Tharp	35	Farmhand	0	18	Virginia	Can't Read
Susan Tharp	40				"	Can't Read
Jerry Tharp	7				"	
Isabella Tharp	5				"	

George Tharp was married to **Susan Evans** on 3 Nov 1852.

Jeremiah Tharp was married on 13 Jan 1881 to Mary Frances Keller. Mary Frances was the daughter of Abraham and Harriet W. Sibert Keller. The Keller family resided in **dwelling 2007**.

Virginia B. Tharp, daughter of George and Susan, was married in Aug 1875 to Joseph William Evans. It is believed that she was the Isabella listed in this household. Joseph was the son of David and Sarah. David Evans married Sarah Freeman on 2 Mar 1849. Joseph and his parents resided in **dwelling 1743**.

1850 CENSUS: **George W. Tharp** resided in dwelling 582 on page 309 in Page County.

PAGE 39 EDINBURG DISTRICT (Microfilm Page 563)

Dwelling 266   Family 266

Samuel Fogle	31	Farmhand	0	40	Virginia
Rebecca Fogle	24				"
Viola B. Fogle	5				"
Virginia F. Fogle	2				"
Julia A. Hoffman	12				"

Samuel Fogle was married to Rebecca Teater on 30 Jun 1853. Rebecca appears to have been the daughter of Jacob and Mary. Jacob Teeter married Mary Stover on 27 Mar 1832. Rebecca's parents resided in dwelling 231. Samuel was 86 years old when he died 2 Sep 1907. Rebecca Teeter Fogle was born 22 Jul 1835 and died 20 Jun 1899. They were buried in the Massanutten Cemetery in Woodstock.

Viola B. Fogle married Luther H. Jackson on 25 Jul 1876. Luther was a farmer who had been born in Frederick County, Virginia and resided in Hampshire County, West Virginia. He was the son of Samuel A. and Mary.

RELATED FAMILY:
Mary Teeter, sister of Rebecca, married Alfred R. McInturff 24 May 1855 and resided in dwelling 232.

1850 CENSUS: Rebecca Teeter resided with her father in dwelling 302 on page 22.

PAGE 39 EDINBURG DISTRICT   (Microfilm Page 563)

Dwelling 267 Family 267

Phillip Grandstaff   67 Farmer   9940 0 Virginia
Mary Grandstaff   64   "
Mary F. Bowman   17   "
John P. Grandstaff   8   " School

Phillip Grandstaff Jr. was the son of Phillip and Elizabeth. Phillip Grandstaff Sr. married Elizabeth Haas on 21 Dec 1784. Phillip Jr. married Mary Cooper on 6 Aug 1816. She was the daughter of George Cooper.

Mary F. Bowman was the daughter of Samuel Bowman. She married Joseph R. Miley on 30 Nov 1865. Joseph was the son of Abraham and Sarah. Abraham Miley married Sarah Roads on 17 Feb 1834. Abraham Miley and his family were residence in dwelling 30. Joseph R. Miley resided in dwelling 35. He served in the Confederate Army. His name appears on the roll of the 10th Virginia Infantry and the 12th Virginia Cavalry. Joseph died in 1902. Mary died 19 Jan 1910.

John Pustal Grandstaff was the grandson of Phillip and Mary. He was the son of William B. and Flora Artz Grandstaff. Flora died in Oct 1853. John's sister Mary

S. Grandstaff resided in **dwelling 264** with her uncle Andrew J. Artz.

RELATED FAMILY:

        Jacob B Snapp, brother in law of Phillip, had married Rebecca Grandstaff 4 Apr 1831 and resided in **dwelling 44.**

        Elizabeth Liggett, sister in law of Phillip, had married John I. Grandstaff on 27 Feb 1827 and resided in **dwelling 46.** John I. Grandstaff died in 1852.

        George P. Grandstaff, brother of Phillip, married Mary Reedy on 3 Oct 1810 and resided in **dwelling 63.**

        Benjamin Grandstaff, brother of Phillip, married Elizabeth "Betsy" Clinedinst on 14 Oct 1820 and resided in **dwelling 324.**

        Catherine A. Grandstaff, sister of Phillip, married John A. Fry on 10 Jun 1815 and resided in **dwelling 353.**

        Joseph F. Grandstaff, son of Phillip, married Louisa C. Riddleberger on 25 Oct 1851 and resided in **dwelling 54.**

        Jane E. Grandstaff, daughter of Phillip, married William H. Hisey on 7 Feb 1842 and resided in **dwelling 69.**

        Branson Grandstaff, son of Phillip, married Evaline Liggett on 9 Jun 1842 and resided in **dwelling 313.**

1850 CENSUS: **Phillip Grandstaff** and his family resided in dwelling 695 on page 49.

PAGE 40 EDINBURG DISTRICT **(Microfilm Page 564)**

Dwelling 268   Family 268

Jacob Wetzel	56	Day Labor	0	110	Virginia	
Delila Wetzel	51				"	
Benjamin Wetzel	16	Day Labor			"	School
Jesse Wetzel	13				"	School
David Wetzel	11				"	School
Clarisa Wetzel	8				"	
Martha Wetzel	6				"	

    The **Wetzel** family may have been from Hardy County in present day West Virginia. Children in this family report their birth in that county.

There is a **Benjamin Wetzel** reported on the roll of the 33rd Virginia Infantry. He enlisted on 10 Aug 1862 in Company G. He was wounded at Manassas on 30 Aug 1862 and died of the wounds received in that battle. There is no conclusive evidence that this was the individual located in this household.

Martha J. Wetzel, daughter of Jacob, was married on 12 Jun 1873 to Ambrose Miller. Ambrose was a widower. He was a collier and was the son of Phillip and Mary. Martha was born in Hardy County, West Virginia.

RELATED FAMILY:
Martin M. Wetzel, son of Jacob and Delila, resided in **dwelling 43** with his wife Mary A. Vines.

1850 CENSUS: Jacob Wetzel and his family resided in dwelling 545 on page 306 in Page Co.

PAGE 40 EDINBURG DISTRICT (Microfilm Page 564)

Dwelling 269 Family 269

Samuel Painter	54 Farmer	11,000	6314	Virginia
Ann Painter	59			N. Carolina
James Painter	26 Farmer	2,916	150	Virginia
Isabelle V. Painter	22			"
Sarah C. Painter	24			"
Joseph H. Painter	3			"
Samuel A. Painter	9m			"
Mary J. Spengler	18			"

Samuel Painter was born 23 Jul 1805 and died 6 Feb 1883. He was married to **Susanna Ruddell** on 16 Jan 1833. Susanna, listed as Ann in this census, was the daughter of George. She was born 9 Aug 1799 in North Carolina and died 27 Apr 1870. Samuel and Susanna were buried in the Lantz-Bowman Cemetery.

James M. Painter was born in 1833 and died 8 Sep 1915. He was married to **Isabella V. Hoffman** on 16 Jan 1856. Isabella was the daughter of Andrew and Rebecca. Andrew Hoffman married Rebecca Miley on 20 Mar 1834. Rebecca Miley Hoffman was a widower at the time of this census and resided in **dwelling 272**. Isabella V. Hoffman Painter was born in 1837 and died 10 Feb 1910. James and Isabella were buried in the Cedarwood Cemetery in Edinburg. James was 5'10" with a ruddy complexion, hazel eyes and brown hair. He enlisted on 28 Aug 1862 at Edinburg in Company K of the 12th Virginia Cavalry. He was captured by the 12th Illinois Cavalry at Bunker Hill on 5 Sep 1862. He was sent to Cairo, Illinois for exchange. He was absent throughout much of the period and persumed to have been in prison. In Bruce's History of Virginia Vol. IV he is mentioned. "He went through the war as a private, but everyone knew him as Captain Painter." In the postwar, he was a county supervisor of Shenandoah County. He was a Republican in his politics. James belonged to no specific church, but stood for the finest moral principles of Christianity. James and Isabella were the parents of 10 children.

Sarah Catherine Painter was the sister of James M. Painter. She was married to Isaac B. Sheetz on 21 Dec 1865. Isaac was the son of George and Elizabeth. George Sheetz married Elizabeth Kibler on 22 Mar 1836. George and Elizabeth resided in **dwelling 2163**. However Isaac was not in the household of his parents. There were two members of the Sheetz family named Isaac B in Shenandoah County during this period. One of these gentlemen was a member of the 10th Virginia Infantry and the 7th Virginia Cavalry. He was wounded in action while a member of the cavalry and died in 1904. The other Isaac B. Sheetz died 3 Jul 1917 at Bridgewater, Virginia.

Joseph Henry Painter was born in 1857 and died 3 Apr 1942. He was the first son of James and Isabella and he married Dora E. Kelley on 22 Dec 1880. Dora was the daughter of Patrick and Isabella. Patrick H. Kelley married Isabella Hockman in Decemeber of 1855. The Kelley family resided in **dwelling 296**. Dora E. Kelley Painter was born in 1860 and died 1 Dec 1937.

Samuel Andrew Painter was born in 1862 according to his tombstone. However, this data appears to have been incorrect as he is reported in the 1860 census. Samuel died 18 Jul 1929. Samuel was married on 13 Oct 1901 to Annie Walton Creighton. Annie was born and resided in Washington, D.C. She was born in 1875 and died in 1947. She was the daughter of John and Sarah. Samuel and Annie were buried in the Cedarwood Cemetery.

Mary Jane Spengler was also a resident in the Painter household at the time of the 1850 census. She was born 25 Apr 1840 and died 21 Nov 1896. Mary Jane was the daughter of Amos Spengler. Amos resided in **dwelling 2096**.

He had originally married Margaret Stewart on 4 Dec 1832. Margaret died 8 Oct 1841 at the age of 33. It is probable that Mary Jane was given to the Painter family to rear at the time of her mothers death. Mary Jane married Robert William Burk, the son of John and Mary. Robert resided with his widowed father in **dwelling 309**. Robert died in 1914. He had a distinguished military career and served as a Lt. in the 11th Virginia Cavalry during the war. He was a merchant and a banker after the conflict.

1850 CENSUS: **Samuel Painter** and his family resided in dwelling 174 on page 13.
Isabella V. Hoffman resided with her mother in dwelling 167 on page 12.

PAGE 40 EDINBURG (Microfilm Page 564)

Dwelling 270 Family 270

Daniel Keller	40	Farmer	5895	822	Virginia	
Sarah J. Keller	39				"	
Elezar L. Keller	12				"	School
Frances A. Keller	11				"	School
Thornton D. Keller	6				"	School

Daniel C. Keller was born 25 Aug 1819 and died 23 Oct 1899. He was married to **Sarah Jane Downey** on 15 Jan 1845. The bondsman for the marriage was Eleazer Downey. Sarah is believed to have been the daughter of Eleazer and Frances. Eleazer Downey Sr. married Fannie Hoffman on 30 Aug 1811. Sarah's mother Frances resided in **dwelling 275**. Sarah was born 12 Feb 1821 and died 10 Mar 1901. Daniel and Sarah were buried in the Cedarwood Cemetery in Edinburg.

Lewis Eleazar Keller was married to Virginia E. Keller on 16 Feb 1871. She was the daughter of Aaron and Elizabeth. Aaron C. Keller married Elizabeth E. Funkhouser on 27 Dec 1849. Virginia was born in Rockingham County, Virginia and resided in Page County at the time of this marriage. Virginia E. Keller and her parents resided in **dwelling 1573**.

Frances A. Keller was born 5 Dec 1848 and died prior to 1898. She was buried in the Cedarwood Cemetery near her parents. Frances married William C. Alther on 16 May 1872. He was born in Page County and was the son of Jacob and Elizabeth. Page County marriage records reveal that Jacob Alther married Elizabeth Clem on 16 Jan 1837. Shenandoah County marriage records indicate that Jacob Alther married Elizabeth Kibler on 3 Nov 1820. It may be that this was the same Jacob Alther. William C. Alther resided in Page County at the time of his marriage to Frances. On 16 Nov 1898 William C. Alther married Minerva J. Funkhouser. She was the daughter of Phillip and Elizabeth. Phillip Funkhouser married Elizabeth Hottel on 11 Mar 1841. Minerva was born 1 Oct 1855 and died 20 Jan 1907. She resided with her parents in **dwelling 1935**.

RELATED FAMILY:

Eleazer Downey Jr., brother of Sarah Jane, married Lydia Haun on 4 Dec 1848 and resided in **dwelling 274**.

Andrew Jackson Downey, brother of Sarah Jane, married Mary Ann Bowman on 28 Jan 1839 and resided in **dwelling 1779**.

Thornton Downey, brother of Sarah Jane, married Amelia Ann Miley on 12 Dec 1838. He was deceased at the time of this census. His widow Amelia resided in **dwelling 76**.

Barbara Ellen Downey, sister of Sarah Jane, married Abraham C. McInturff on 9 Sep 1844. She was deceased at the time of this census. Her husband Abraham resided in **dwelling 409**.

1850 CENSUS: Daniel Keller was listed as David. He was in dwelling 541 on page 41 in Page County.

PAGE 40   EDINBURG DISTRICT   (Microfilm Page 564)

Dwelling 271   Family 271

Madelene Huddle	60	0	100	Virignia	Can't Read
Martin Huddle	52			"	Idiot
Nancy Myers	48			"	

Information obtained regarding this household is derived from the **Hottel Family History**. All of these individuals are believed to have been the children or grandchildren of Solomon Hottel and Frances Blosser Hottel.

Magdalene Hottel never married. She resided in her fathers home and used a room upstairs. She also used the garden and had a sufficient quality of fruit. She took care of her brother Martin and and a sister Elizabeth until they died. Magdalene is reported to have died in 1875.

Family records indicated that she was 105 at the time of her death. She is reported to have been one of only two members of this very large family to have been a centenarian. However, the 1850 census indicates that she was 60 years old in 1850. Evidence from these two census reports suggests that she may not have been as old as the family history reports.

Martin Hottel was under the guardianship of his sister Magdalene. He is thought to have died during the Civil War.

Nancy Myers may have been the sister of Magdalene. Barbara Hottel, sister of Magdalene, married Jacob B. Myers on 12 Feb 1827. Jacob was a wagon master and died as a result of foul play. He was found dead in his shop with his head crushed. Barbara died in 1860. They are supposed to have two children with very long hair that hung almost to their feet. When the Hottel family home burned down in 1840, the Myers children moved in with the family of Samuel Painter. Samuel Painter resided in **dwelling 269.** Family records indicate that the Myers children died shortly after the fire.

1850 CENSUS: **Magadalene Hottel** and her brother **Martin** resided in dwelling 173 on page 13. An indivudal named Barbara Hines was also in the household.

PAGE 40 EDINBURG DISTRICT (Microfilm Page 564)

Dwelling 272   Family 272

Rebecca Hoffman	61		3390	255	Virginia Cn't Rd
Rebecca F. Hoffman	23				"
Andrew J. Hoffman	19	Farmhand			"
Flora J. Hoffman	17				"

Rebecca Gochenour was married to Joseph Miley on 12 Aug 1818. Upon the death of Joseph, Rebecca married Andrew Hoffman on 20 Mar 1834. She was 81 years old when she died on 31 Mar 1880. Rebecca Gochenour Miley Hoffman was buried in the Cedarwood Cemetery.

Rebecca F. Hoffman was married to Derostus E. W. Myers on 24 Nov 1870. Derostus was a widower. He had married Mary Lucippa Farra on 29 May 1866. Mary was the daughter of John W. and Mary Hockman Farra. Mary and her

parents resided in **dwelling 98.** Derostus died at
Strasburg, Virginia on 29 Jul 1908. He was the son of John
and Eliza. John Myers married Eliza Evans on 12 Jun 1841.
Derostus and his parents resided in **dwelling 1920.**

    Andrew J. Hoffman was born 3 Jul 1840 and died 10
Oct 1877. He was buried at Cedarwood Cemetery in Edinburg.
Andrew J. Hoffman enlisted in the 10th Virginia Infantry
Company C on 18 Apr 1861. He went into the hospital with
brochitis in January of 1862. 10th Virginia Infantry
records indicate that he transferred to the 7th Virginia
Cavalry. However, it appears that he actually was in the
11th Virginia Cavalry. He was 4th Sgt in Company E. He
enlisted at Swift Run Gap on 1 May 1862. He was captured
at Strasburg on 22 Apr 1863. He was at a number of prisons
including Fort McHenry in Baltimore, Maryland. He was
eventually exchanged at City Point on 2 May 1863. He was
described as 5'6" with dark complexion, black hair and
hazel eyes.

    Flora J. Hoffman was born 12 Oct 1842 and died 1 May
1927. She was married to William H. Evans on 2 Oct 1879.
William was born 22 Mar 1845 and died 19 Jun 1914. He was
the son of John and Susan. William resided with his
father in **dwelling 277.** Flora and William were buried in
the Cedarwood Cemetery.

RELATED FAMILY:

    Isabella V. Hoffman, daughter of Rebecca,
married James M. Painter on 16 Jan 1856 and resided in
dwelling 269.

1850 CENSUS: **Rebecca Hoffman** and family resided in
    dwelling 167 on page 12.

PAGE 40 EDINBURG DISTRICT (Microfilm Page 564)

Dwelling 273 Family 273

Ezra Coffman	42	Farmer	0	575	Virginia	
Mary Coffman	39				"	
William H. Coffman	18	Farmhand			"	
Ann E. Coffman	16				"	
Mary E. Coffman	12				"	School
Absolum Coffman	8				"	
Barbara E. Coffman	5				"	
Amos L. Coffman	6m				"	

Ezra Coffman was the son of Adolph and Barbara. Adolph Coffman married Barbara Rinker on 31 Mar 1803. Adolph Coffman resided in **dwelling 1764**. Ezra was born 17 Feb 1818 and died 15 Feb 1865. He married **Mary Haun** on 2 Nov 1840. Mary was the daughter of Jacob and Catherine Kibler Haun. Jacob Haun and his family resided in **dwelling 1769**. Ezra enlisted in the 5th Virginia Infantry on 14 Mar 1862 at Rude's Hill. He was AWOL on 20 Apr 1862 and was listed as deserted. According to the **Hottel** family history, one day while crossing a river, the Yankees called for him to halt. Being somewhat deaf he failed to hear their command and continued his crossing, whereupon they shot him to death. Ezra was buried in the Downey Cemetery. Mary's father purchased a home for her near Calvary where she lived until her death. She is buried in the Haun Cemetery.

William H. Coffman was born 14 Nov 1844 and died 18 May 1864. He was buried in the Downey Cemetery.

Ann E. Coffman died 28 Oct 1925. She was married to James Jehu Coffman on 12 Dec 1867. James was the son of Joseph and Catherine. Joseph M. Coffman married Catherine Kessler on 3 Oct 1829. James and his parents resided in **dwelling 1324**. James was born 3 Apr 1837 and died 24 May 1917. James and Annie were buried in the Coffman Cemetery near Edinburg.

Mary E. Coffman may have been Kate C. Coffman. She was born 14 May 1849 and died 30 Jul 1923. In the 1850 census Mary's middle name was listed as "C". She married William Henry Hoover on 24 Sep 1868. William was the son of Abraham and Rebecca. Abraham Hoover married Rebecca Marshall on 16 Nov 1840. William and his family resided in **dwelling 1874**. William was born 6 Sep 1841 and died 28 Jun 1920.

Absolom Coffman was born 21 Mar 1852 and died 4 Jul 1936. He was married to Mary C. Evans on 17 Sep 1876. Mary was the daughter of Joseph and Hannah Via Evans. Mary and her parents were located in **dwelling 38**. Mary C. Evans Coffman was born 27 Jul 1854 and died in 1927. They were buried at Cedarwood Cemetery.

Barbara Ellen Coffman was born 18 Dec 1859 and died 17 Nov 1930. She was married on 17 Sep 1875 to Daniel W. Copenhaver. He was a shoemaker. Daniel was the son of William and Mary Ann. William Copenhaver married Mary Ann

Burner on 8 Oct 1839. Daniel and his family resided in **dwelling 1866**. Daniel was born 9 Nov 1853 and died 7 Aug 1925. They were buried in the Mt. Calvary United Church of Christ in Woodstock.

RELATED FAMILY:

      Henry H. Haun, brother of Mary Haun Coffman, married Catherine Coffman, sister of Ezra, on 8 Nov 1847. They resided in **dwelling 1771**.

      Jacob Haun, brother of Mary Haun Coffman, married Elizabeth Coffman, sister of Ezra, on 11 Jan 1852. They resided in **dwelling 1770**.

      Lydia Haun, sister of Mary Haun Coffman, married Eleazaer Downey on 4 Dec 1848 and resided in **dwelling 274**.

      Sarah Ellen Haun, sister of Mary Haun Coffman, married Jacob Hockman on 20 Feb 1855 and resided in **dwelling 621**.

      Susan Haun, sister of Mary Haun Coffman, married David Sheetz on 11 Dec 1851 and resided in **dwelling 1796**.

      Reuben Coffman, brother of Ezra, married Rebecca Holler on 11 Feb 1852 and resided in **dwelling 1765**.

      Levi and **Henry Coffman**, brothers of Ezra, resided in **dwelling 1550**.

      Joseph Coffman, believed to have been the brother of Ezra, married Elizabeth Coffelt on 20 Aug 1828 and resided in **dwelling 1282**.

1850 CENSUS: **Ezra Coffman** and his family resided in dwelling 1338 on page 110.

PAGE 41 EDINBURG DISTRICT (Microfilm Page 565)

Dwelling 274 Family 274

Eleazar Downey	34	Farmer	660	767	Virginia	
Lydia Downey	31				"	
Jacob H. Downey	9				"	
Martha E. Downey	7				"	School
Mary E. Downey	6				"	
Thornton Downey	4				"	
Eleazar Downey	2				"	
Ann E. Downey	6m				"	
CAN'T READ	12	(Male)			"	School

      Eleazer Downey Jr. was the son of Eleazer Downey Sr. and Frances "Fannie" Hoffman. Eleazer Sr. had married

Fannie on 30 Aug 1811. Fannie Hoffman Downey resided in **dwelling 275**. Eleazer was born 6 Aug 1825 and died 6 Jul 1863. He married **Lydia Haun** on 4 Dec 1848. Lydia was the daughter of Jacob and Catherine Kibler Altarfer Haun. Lydia was born in Nov 1828 and died 2 Jul 1906. Eleazer and Lydia were buried in the Downey Cemetery.

Jacob Henry Downey was born in 1850 and died 2 Mar 1929. He married Virginia B. Newland on 26 Dec 1872. Virginia was the daughter of Isaac and Frances. Isaac Newland married Frances Barricks on 25 Jun 1850. Virginia and her family resided in **dwelling 583**. Virginia was born in 1854 and died 19 Aug 1920. They were buried in the New Mount Jackson Cemetery. Jacob was a constable and served as Deputy Sheriff in Shenandoah County.

Martha E. "Mattie" Downey was married to Asher M. Strole on 20 Mar 1872. Asher was born in Page County, Virginia. He was the son of William and Sarah. Page County marriage records report that William A. Strole married Sarah Ann Kibler on 11 Aug 1845. Asher resided in Newton, Indiana at the time of the marriage.

Mary Elizabeth "Mollie" Downey was married on 3 Aug 1871 to Hiram Newton Liskey of Rockingham County, Virginia. He was the son of Abraham and Diana. After the death of Hiram, Mollie married Albert H. Liskey of Bridgewater, Virginia.

Thornton Jackson Downey was born 17 Oct 1855 and married Lillian M. Barritt on 28 Dec 1884 in Wellington, Illinois.

Eleazer Downey was a shoemaker. He was residing in Rockingham County when he married Mabel C. Irwin. Mabel was the daughter of E.L. and Sarah.

Ann Elizabeth Downey was reported to have been born 10 Dec 1860. However, Shenandoah County records indicate she was born in October of 1859. She was married to Edward Gold Echard. Edward was born in Rockbridge County, Virginia on 5 Apr 1852. They resided in Wellington, Illinois.

RELATED FAMILY:
    Sarah Jane Downey, sister of Eleazer, married Daniel Keller on 15 Jan 1845 and resided in **dwelling 270**.

Andrew J. Downey, brother of Eleazer, married Mary Ann Bowman on 28 Jan 1839 and resided in **dwelling 1779**.

Thornton Downey, brother of Eleazer, married Amelia Ann Miley on 12 Dec 1838. Thronton was deceased at the time of this census. Amelia Ann Miley Downey resided in **dwelling 76**.

Barbara Ellen Downey, sister of Eleazer, married Abraham C. McInturff on 9 Sep 1844. She was deceased at the time of this census. Abraham C. McInturff resided in **dwelling 409**.

Mary Haun, sister of Lydia, married Ezra Coffman on 2 Nov 1840 and resided in **dwelling 273**.

Henry H. Haun, brother of Lydia, married Catherine Coffman on 8 Nov 1847 and resided in **dwelling 1771**.

Sarah Ellen Haun, sister of Lydia, married Jacob Hockman on 20 Feb 1855 and resided in **dwelling 621**.

Jacob Haun, brother of Lydia, married Elizabeth Coffman on 11 Jan 1852 and resided in **dwelling 1770**.

Susan Haun, sister of Lydia, married David Sheetz on 11 Dec 1851 and resided in **dwelling 1796**.

1850 CENSUS: Eleazer Downey and his family resided in dwelling 974 on page 68.

PAGE 41 EDINBURG DISTRICT   (Microfilm Page 565)

Dwelling 275   Family 275

Frances Downey	70	0	135	Virginia Can't Read
Mary A. Downey	18		"	School

Frances "Fannie" Hoffman married Eleazer Downey Sr. on 30 Aug 1811. Frances was the daughter of Christian Hoffman. Eleazer was the son of Darby Downey and his wife Lythia. Will Book R on page 382 lists other members of this family. Darby Downey married Sythe Evans on 25 Sep 1798. This suggests that Darby Downey may have been married prior to his 1798 marriage. Darby was an immigrant from Ireland. Eleazer died 28 Jun 1858.

Mary Ann Elizabeth Downey is believed to have been the granddaughter of Frances Downey. It is probable that she was taking care of her grandmother. Mary Ann appears to have been listed twice in this census. She was the daughter of Andrew J. and Mary Ann. Andrew Jackson Downey married Mary Ann Bowman on 28 Jan 1839. Mary Ann and her parents resided in **dwelling** 1779. Mary Ann Elizabeth Downey married Gideon Coffelt on 18 Apr 1861. He was the son of George and Elizabeth. George Coffelt married Elizabeth Foltz on 13 Dec 1814. Gideon resided with his father in **dwelling** 1196. Mary Ann was born 21 Feb 1844 and died 18 Dec 1871. She was buried in the Coffelt-Maphis Cemetery near Edinburg. Gideon remarried on 30 Jan 1875 to Mahala Haas, the daughter of Regina and Jonathan. Jonathan Haas married Regina Coffman on 30 Mar 1830. Mahala and her mother resided in **dwelling 1825.** Gideon was born 28 Mar 1827 and died 6 Oct 1894. He was buried near Mary Ann Elizabeth in the Coffelt-Maphis Cemetery. Mahala Haas Coffelt was born 28 Mar 1838 and died 16 Feb 1917. She was buried in the Bethel Lutheran Church Cemetery in Woodstock.

RELATED FAMILY:

        Eleazer Downey Jr., son of Frances, married Lydia Haun on 4 Dec 1848 and resided in **dwelling 274.**

        Sarah Jane Downey, daughter of Frances, married Daniel Keller on 15 Jan 1845 and resided in **dwelling 270.**

        Barbara Ellen Downey, daughter of Frances, married Abraham McInturff on 9 Sep 1844. Barbara Ellen died prior to this census. Abraham and a number of grandchildren resided in **dwelling 409.**

        Thornton Downey, son of Frances, married Amelia Ann Miley on 12 Dec 1838. Thornton died prior to this census. His widow resided in **dwelling 76.**

1850 CENSUS: Frances Downey resided with her husband in dwelling 974 on page 68.

PAGE 41 EDINBURG DISTRICT (Microfilm Page 565)

Dwelling 276 Family 276

John Vena	37 (Black)	Day Labor	0	70	Virignia
Mary A. Vena	26 (Black)				"
James H. Vena	7 (Black)				"
Robert Vena	6 (Black)				"

1850 CENSUS: No record of this family has been located.

PAGE 41 EDINBURG DISTRICT   (Microfilm Page 564)

Dwelling 277   Family 277

John Evans	34	Farmhand 200	245	Virginia	Cn't Rd
Barbara A. Evans	70			"	
Mary Evans	38			"	Can't Read
William H. Evans	14			"	School
Charles W. Keiffer	8			"	School

       Barbara A. Daley was married to Jesse Evans on 27 Aug 1814. The bondsman for this marriage was John Daley.

       In 1850 **John Evans** resided in a household with 48 year old Susan Evans. **Mary Evans** was also in the household. The relationship of this family is not clear. There was a marriage of John Evans to Mary M. Shank on 20 Feb 1843. Mary was the daughter of Henry Shank. It is not clear that this was the same family.

       The relationship of **William Henry Evans** is not clear. He was born 22 Mar 1845 and died 19 Jun 1914. He was reported in marriage records to have been the son of John and Susan. There is no marriage record reported for John and Susan. It is possible that William may have been the son of Susan Evans, the sister of John. On 3 Nov 1852 a Susan Evans married George Tharp. Susan Evans Tharp was the same approximate age as the Susan Evans residing in this household in 1850. Susan Evans Tharp and her husband George were residents of **dwelling 265** in this census. William Henry Evans married Flora E. Hoffman on 2 Oct 1879. Flora was the daughter of Andrew and Rebecca. Andrew J. Hoffman married Rebecca Gochenour Miley on 20 Mar 1834. Flora resided with her mother in **dwelling 272**. Flora was born 12 Oct 1842 and died 1 May 1927. William and Flora were buried in the Cedarwood Cemetery in Edinburg.

       Charles W. Keiffer has not been indentified. However a two year old male with the surname Keefer was in this household in 1850.

1850 CENSUS: John Evans and other members of this family resided in dwelling 2124 on page 152.

281

PAGE 41 EDINBURG DISTRICT   (Microfilm Page 565)

Dwelling 278   Family 278

Nimrod M. Hoffman	38	Farmer	4100	462	Virginia
Mary C. Hoffman	35				"
Thomas A. Hoffman	14				"
Phillip S. Hoffman	11				"
Frances C. Hoffman	9				"
Samuel J. Hoffman	7				"
James Hoffman	6				"
Mary S. Hoffman	3				"
Christian A. Hoffman	1				"

Nimrod Milton Hoffman was the son of Andrew Jackson Hoffman and Frances Stover Hoffman. Andrew and Frances were married on 1 Apr 1820. Nimrod was born 14 Jul 1822 and died 19 Apr 1885. He was buried in the Hoffman Cemetery near Edinburg. Nimrod was married to **Mary C. McCord** on 5 Feb 1845. Mary was the daughter of Catherine. She was born 27 Feb 1825 and died 7 Apr 1862. She was buried near Nimrod in the Hoffman Cemetery. On 27 Jan 1864 Nimrod was married to Lydia Ann Clinedinst. Lydia was the daughter of Isaac and Lydia. Isaac Clinedinst married Lydia Holler on 7 Mar 1825. Isaac and his family resided in **dwelling 322**. Lydia Ann Clinedinst Hoffman died prior to 1870. Nimrod's third wife was Mary Laura Pitman Snapp. Mary Laura was a widow. She had married Robert B. Snapp on 27 Dec 1855. Robert was a farmer who was born in Augusta County, Virginia. Mary Laura was the daughter of Phillip and Mary Susan. Phillip Pitman was married to Mary Susan Houston. Robert B. Snapp may have been deceased at the time of this census as Mary Laura resided with her parents in **dwelling 247**.

Thomas Andrew Hoffman was born in 1846 and died 25 Jun 1924. He was originally married to Katie A. Balthis. Katie was born in 1850 and died in 1890. She was buried with Thomas in the Cedarwood Cemetery. On 23 Jul 1896 Thomas A. Hoffman married Lucy Ellen Evans Downey. Lucy was the daughter of Joseph and Hannah Via Evans. She resided with her parents in **dwelling 38**. Lucy Ellen had married Joseph W. Downey on 24 Dec 1874. Joseph was born 4 Jun 1849 and died 17 Jul 1892. Joseph and Lucy Ellen were buried in the Cedarwood Cemetery.

Phillip Stover Hoffman was born in 1848 and died 17 Dec 1919. He was married on 21 Dec 1899 to Alberta

"Bertie" Catherine Gay. Bertie was born in 1864 and died on 11 Mar 1916. She was the daughter of Albert and Annie. Albert E. Gay married Ann C. Strickler on 11 Mar 1850. The Gay family resided in **dwelling 797**. Phillip and Bertie were buried in the Cedarwood Cemetery.

Frances C. Hoffman married Andrew J. Hoffman on 18 Dec 1873. Andrew was the son of Thornton and Amelia. Thornton Downey married Amelia Ann Miley on 12 Dec 1838. Thornton Downey died 24 Mar 1853 and his widow Amelia Ann Miley Downey resided with her family in **dwelling 76**. Andrew J. Hoffman resided with his uncle and namesake Andrew J. Downey in **dwelling 1779**.

Samuel J. Hoffman was born in 1852 and died 1 Nov 1914. Samuel was a physician. He married Margaret Virginia Rinker on 10 Apr 1878. Margaret was the daughter of Samuel and Rachel C. Vance Rinker. Samuel Rinker and his family resided in **dwelling 2**. Margaret was born 4 Feb 1853 and died in 1932. Samuel James Hoffman served two terms as a representative of Shenandoah County in the Virginia State Legislature. Samuel and Margaret were buried in the Massanutten Cemetery.

James O. Hoffman was born in 1855 and died in 1935. He was married to Laura A. Hoover on 31 Dec 1890. Laura was born in 1855 and died in 1920. She was the daughter of Silas and Martha E. Silas Hoover married Martha E. Nihiser on 21 Mar 1860. Silas and Martha resided in **dwelling 282**. Laura A. Hoover Hoffman was born in 1869 and died in 1920. James and Laura were buried in the Cedarwood Cemetery.

Mary S. Hoffman died 22 Feb 1890. She was 32 years, 10 months and 12 days old. Mary was buried at Mt. Zion United Methodist Church Cemetery near Strasburg, Virginia. Mary had married Thomas William Ritenour on 7 Dec 1881. Thomas was the son of Amos and Sarah. Amos Ritenour married Sarah Ann Long on 14 Sep 1833. Amos Ritenour and his family resided in **dwelling 1707**. Thomas was born 21 Jun 1848 and died 21 Mar 1908. Thomas was buried near Mary in the Mt. Zion Cemetery. According to his obituary, Thomas had married Bertie Lee Maphis. Bertie Lee was the daughter of Joseph and Thursa. Frederick County marriage records report a marriage for Jacob M. Maphis and Theresa W. Swartz on 2 Mar 1848. Joseph Maphis and his family resided in **dwelling 302**. Bertie Lee Maphis Ritenour died 19 Apr 1927.

283

RELATED FAMILY:

     Rebecca Gochenour Miley Hoffman, step-mother of Nimrod, resided in **dwelling 272**.

     Joseph W. Hoffman, believed to have been the brother of Nimrod, married **Eveline V. McCord**, thought to be the sister of Mary, on 24 Nov 1849 and resided in **dwelling 34**.

     Isabella V. Hoffman, step sister of Nimrod, married James Painter on 16 Jan 1856 and resided in **dwelling 269**.

1850 CENSUS: **Nimrod Milton Hoffman** and his family resided in dwelling 168 on page 13.

PAGE 41   EDINBURG DISTRICT   (Microfilm Page 565)

Dwelling 279   Family 279

John Reeser	36	4120	588	Virginia
Martha Reeser	25			"
William H. Reeser	6			"
Ann E. Reeser	3			"
Mary F. Reeser	1			"

  John W. Reeser was born 24 Mar 1824 and died 2 Apr 1902. He was married to **Martha Copp**. Martha may have been the daughter of Jacob and Rebecca. There was a marriage for Jacob Copp to Rebecca Hamman (Huffman) on 21 Feb 1839 in Page County, Virginia. There is an age discrepancy for Martha as she was reported to have been born in 1834. This family was located in **dwelling 1886**. Martha Copp Reeser was born 6 Jun 1834 and died 6 Aug 1912. John and Martha were buried in the Cedarwood Cemetery.

  William H. Reeser was born 9 Aug 1853 and died 6 Sep 1931. He was married to Nancy C. Downey on 3 Apr 1873. Nancy was the daughter of Andrew J. and Mary Ann. Andrew Jackson Downey married Mary Ann Bowman on 28 Jan 1839. Andrew and his family resided in **dwelling 1779**. Nancy Catherine "Kate" Downey died 11 Mar 1903 at the age of 48 years and 15 days old. She was buried in the Hawkinson United Methodist Church Cemetery near her parents. William was buried in the Cedarwood Cemetery with his brother and sister.

  Annie E. Reeser was born 6 Dec 1857 and died 19 Mary 1936. She was buried next to William. Another brother, Joseph M. Reeser was buried in the same grave site. Joseph M. Reeser was born 24 Apr 1864 and died 13 Apr 1940.

Mary Frances "Fannie" Reeser was born 31 May 1859 and died 16 Apr 1925. She was married on 21 Feb 1912 to Morgan F. Schmucker in Winchester, Virginia. Morgan was the son of Ferdinand and Catherine. Ferdinand Schmucker married Catherine Funkhouser on 7 Oct 1839. Morgan was a widower at the time of his marriage. Morgan had married Ann Elizabeth Bauserman on 1 Oct 1868. Ann was the daughter of Noah and Sarah. Noah Bauserman married Sarah Saum on 8 Jul 1846. Noah and his family resided in **dwelling 1978**. Ann Bauserman Schmucker was born in 1849 and died in 1909. Morgan F. Schmucker was born in 1845 and died in 1936 at the age of 90. Morgan and both of his wives were buried in the Toms Brook Cemetery.

1850 CENSUS: **John W. Reeser** resided with Moses and Mary Fravel in dwelling 930 on page 65.
Martha Copp apppears in the household of her parents in dwelling 183 on page 13.

PAGE 41 EDINBURG DISTRICT (Microfilm Page 565)

Dwelling 280 Family 280

Isaac Bowman	30	Farmer	18,538	3218	Virginia
Eve E. Bowman	27				"
Joseph S. Bowman	4				"
Rebecca J. Bowman	2				"
Emily Sibert	19				"

Isaac Bowman was born 5 May 1830 and died 12 Oct 1891. He is thought to have been the son of Steven and Elizabeth Hockman Stover Bowman. Isaac married **Eve Elizabeth Sheetz** on 15 Sep 1852. Eve was the daughter of Joseph M. and Rebecca. Joseph M. Sheetz married Rebecca Haun on 23 Jun 1830. Eve's parents resided in **dwelling 1776**. Isaac's father Stephen resided in **dwelling 28**. Eve Elizabeth Sheetz Bowman was born 9 Dec 1832 and died 31 Aug 1876. Isaac and Eve are reported to have been buried in the Willow Grove Cemetery.

Joseph Steven Bowman was born in 1855 and died 23 Feb 1912. He was married to Emma C. Hutcheson on 20 Jan 1885. She was the daughter of Charles and Caroline. Charles W. Hutcheson married Caroline Clinedinst on 6 Apr 1850. Emma and her family resided in **dwelling 78**. Emma

C. Hutcheson Bowman was born in 1857 and died in 1941. They were buried in the Cedarwood Cemetery in Edinburg.

Rebecca Jane Bowman was born 10 Aug 1857 and died 5 Feb 1907. She was married to John Fadely, the son of Joseph and Sallie, on 30 Aug 1885. John was born 18 Dec 1865.

RELATED FAMILY:

Cassandra Sheetz, sister of Eve, married William Hoover on 13 Feb 1855 and resided in **dwelling 1818.**

1850 CENSUS: Eve Elizabeth Sheetz resided with her parents in dwelling 79 on page 6.
Isaac Bowman appears in the household of Stephen Bowman. They resided in dwelling 711 on page 50.

PAGE 42 EDINBURG DISTRICT (Microfilm Page 566)

Dwelling 281 Family 281

Elizabeth Tusing	35	(Mulatto)	Washerwoman 0	80	Va.
Samuel Tusing	16	(Mulatto)	Day Labor		"
Sarah C. Tusing	13	(Mulatto)			"
William Tusing	11	(Mulatto)			"
Caroline Tusing	9	(Mulatto)			"
George H. Tusing	3	(Mulatto)			"

1850 CENSUS: There is no record of this family in 1850.

PAGE 42 EDINBURG DISTRICT (Microfilm Page 566)

Dwelling 282 Family 282

Silas Hoover	21	Blacksmith	0	50 Virginia	Just Mar.
Martha E. Hoover	21			"	Just Married

Silas B. Hoover was born in 1833 and died in 1914. He was the son of Joseph and Elizabeth. Joseph Hoover married Elizabeth Burner on 20 May 1828. Joseph Hoover and his family resided in **dwelling 1869.** Silas was married to **Martha E. Nihiser** on 21 Mar 1860. Martha was the daughter of John and Harriet. John Nihiser married Harriet Proctor on 25 Aug 1817. The widow Harriet Proctor Nihiser resided in **dwelling 1974.** Martha E. Nihiser Hoover was born in 1838 and died in 1896. Silas and Martha were buried in the Hoover Cemetery near Woodstock. Silas B. Hoover was 6'0"

286

with fair complexion, light hair and blue eyes. He enlisted in the 10th Virginia Infantry Company F at Woodstock as a private on 10 Dec 1862. He was originally detailed as a teamster. In December of 1863 he was detailed as a blacksmith with the ordnance train. Silas was paroled on 17 Apr 1865 at Winchester.

1850 CENSUS: Silas Hoover resided with his parents in dwelling 180 on page 13.

PAGE 42 EDINBURG DISTRICT (Microfilm Page 566)

Dwelling 283   Family 283

James Hoover	30	Farmer	Virginia	
Reuben Hoover	58		"	Insane
Rachel Hoover	53		"	
Sarah C. Hoover	18		"	School
Joseph Fravel	16	Farmhand	"	
Barbara A. Kern	23	Housegirl	"	

James H. Hoover, was the head of this household as a result of his fathers disability. He was born 6 Oct 1829 and died 1 Aug 1913. He married Sarah Catherine Sibert on 3 Jan 1882. She was born 29 Apr 1853 and died in Aug 1924. This couple was buried in the St. Paul's Reformed Church Cemetery in Woodstock.

Reuben Hoover was the son of John and Elizabeth Fravel Hoover. He was born 17 May 1801 and died 9 Aug 1866. He was married to Catherine Huddle (Riddelle) on 8 Dec 1824. Reuben was buried in the old cemetery of the Reformed Church in Woodstock. On 6 Nov 1838 Reuben Hoover married Rachel Kern. The bondsman for that marriage was William Moreland. Rachel died 23 Nov 1898 at Ogden in Boone County, Iowa. She resided with her daughter Sarah C. Hoover Rinker.

Sarah Catherine Hoover was born 25 May 1845 and died 23 Nov 1898. She married Jonathan Henry Rinker on 15 Feb 1865. Jonathan was born 9 May 1841. He was the son of Henry St. John and Mary. Henry St. John Rinker married Mary Fravel on 6 Jul 1840. Jonathan and Sarah removed to Ogden in Boone County, Iowa.

Barbara A. Kern may have been listed twice in this census. She is also believed to have appeared in **dwelling**

2265. If so, her parents were Jacob and Rebecca. Jacob
Kern married Peggy Ann Rosenberger on 23 Jan 1833.

1850 CENSUS: James Hoover and other members of this family
                resided in dwelling 163 on page 12.

PAGE 42 EDINBURG DISTRICT (Microfilm Page 566)

Dwelling 284 Family 284

Patrick Riley	37	Laborer on R.R.	Ireland
Mary Riley	32		"
Kesura Riley	12		" School
Daniel A. Riley	8		Virginia School
Patrick Riley	6		"
John Riley	4		"
Mary Riley	3		"
Bridget Riley	1		"

1850 CENSUS: There is no evidence of this family in
                Shenandoah County in 1850.

PAGE 42 EDINBURG DISTRICT (Microfilm Page 566)

Dwelling 285 Family 285

Edward Sullivan	33	Boss on R.R.	500	50	Ireland
Catherine Sullivan	29				"
Patrick Sullivan	10				Virginia
James Sullivan	6				"
Julia Sullivan	2				"
Edward Sullivan	1				"
John Collins	35	Laborer on R.R.			Ireland C/R
Thomas Walsh	17	Laborer on R.R.			"

1850 CENSUS: There is no evidence of this family in
                Shenandoah County in 1850.

288

PAGE 42   EDINBURG DISTRICT   (Microfilm Page 566)

Dwelling 286   Family 286

Washington Grayson	46 (Mulatto)	Day Labor	Virginia	
Malinda Grayson	41 (Mulatto)	Washerwoman	"	
Robert Allen	15 (Mulatto)		"	Idiot
Ann E. Allen	14 (Mulatto)		"	
Silas Grayson	12 (Mulatto)		"	
Arabella Grayson	6 (Mulatto)		"	
Rebecca Blanhour	45 (Black)		"	
Lucy A. Richards	21 (Mulatto Seasmstress		"	
Benjamin Blanhour	6 (Black)		"	
Mary Blanhour	4 (Black)		"	

1850 CENSUS: **Washington Grayson** and his family resided in dwelling 2118 on page 152. In that census it was reported that he was born in Maryland. His wife was listed as Winney Grayson.

PAGE 43   EDINBURG DISTRICT   (Microfilm Pge 567)

Dwelling 287   Family 287

Ann Weldon	40 (Black)	400	50 Virginia	
Elanson Wanzer	21 (Mulatto)		"	

1850 CENSUS: There is no record of this family in the 1850 census. However, the **Weldon** and **Wanzer** names were common among black and mulatto families in Shenandoah County in this period.

PAGE 43 EDINBURG DISTRICT   (Microfilm Page 567)

Dwelling 288   Family 288

William Smith	44 (Black)	Blacksmith	1000	175	Va.
Mary Smith	32 (Black)				"
Samuel Smith	21 (Mulatto)	Farmhand			"
Sarah C. Smith	18 (Mulatto)				"
Amanda Smith	9 (Mulatto)				"
Hattie Johnson	68 (Mulatto)				"
Albert Smith	10 (Mulatto)				"

1850 CENSUS: There is no record of this household in 1850.

289

PAGE 43 EDINBURG DISTRICT   (Microfilm Page 567)

Dwelling 289   Family 289

Eliza Mars	46 (Black)	0 20	Virginia
William Mars	9 (Black)		"
Samuel Mars	7 (Black)		"
Mary E. Mars	5 (Mulatto)		"
Margaret Mars	19 (Mulatto)		"

1850 CENSUS: There is no record of this household in 1850.

PAGE 43   EDINBURG DISTRICT   (Microfilm Page 567)

Dwelling 290   Family 290

William A. Wightman	33 Merchant 2000	400	Pennsylvania
Julia A. Wightman	26		Virginia
Samuel E. Wightman	6		"
William H. Wightman	4		"
Mary E. Wightman	3		"

William A. Wightman was born 8 Jun 1826 and died 7 Mar 1876. According to census data he was born in Pennsylvania. William married **Julia Skyrock Grandstaff** on 20 Jul 1852. Julia was the daughter of John and Isabella. John Jackson Grandstaff married Isabella A. Murray on 5 Mar 1835.   John J. Grandstaff and his family resided in **dwelling 328**. Julia was born 9 Jan 1834 and died 1 Apr 1910.   William and Julia were buried in the Old Edinburg Cemetery.

Samuel E. Wightman was born 15 Jun 1853 and died 16 Jun 1922. According to obituary records he was married to Kate Dunbar. Samuel was buried in the Old Edinburg Cemetery.

William H. Wightman was born in 1856 and died 14 Jul 1905. He was married on 23 Dec 1879 to Cora Belle Holtzman. Cora was the daughter of Benjamin and Sarah. Benjamin B. Holtzman married Sarah Elizabeth Riddleberger and resided in **dwelling 56**. Cora Belle Holtzman Wightman was born in 1860 and died 21 Dec 1945. William and Cora were buried in the Cedarwood Cemetery in Edinburg.

Mary E. Wightman was born 5 Apr 1857 and died 9 Apr 1924. She was married on 6 Dec 1883 to Frederick M. Hisey. Frederick was the son of Robert and Amelia. Robert

F. Hisey married Amelia Riddleberger on 9 May 1852. Robert and his family were located in **dwelling 21**. Frederick was born 30 May 1855 and died 22 Dec 1926. Mary and Frederick were buried in the Cedarwood Cemetery.

RELATED FAMILY:

Mary Margaret Grandstaff, sister of Julia , married Reuben Lee Allen in November of 1855 and resided in **dwelling 325**.

1850 CENSUS: **William A. Wightman** resided in dwelling 723 on page 51.

Julia A. Grandstaff resided with her parents in dwelling 712 on page 50.

PAGE 43 EDINBURG DISTRICT   **(Microfilm Page 567)**

Dwelling 291   Family 291

Richard Miller	60	Shoemaker	1600	1425	Virginia
Artemisia L. Miller	44				"
George M. Miller	17	Clerk			"
William K. P. Miller	16	Mail Messenger			"
Alice A. Miller	14				" School
Marshall M. Miller	12				" School
Luela M. Miller	8				"
Adesta Fidelas Miller	2				"

Richard Miller was born 28 Feb 1798 and died 17 Apr 1871. He was married at least three times. His first wife was Elizabeth Kingree. They were married 9 Oct 1823. She was the daughter of Solomon and Elizabeth Jones Kingree. Elizabeth was born 27 Nov 1802 and died 27 Mar 1825. Elizabeth was buried in the Old Union Church Cemetery in Mt. Jackson. Richard's second wife was Mary Allen. Mary was the daughter of Israel and Sarah Pifer Allen. She was born 28 Oct 1811 and died 21 Dec 1841. She is also buried in the Old Union Cemetery. Richard married **Artemisia L. Grandstaff** on 25 Jan 1842. Artemisia was the daughter of George P. and Mary Reedy Grandstaff. Artemisia was born 27 Jun 1816 and died 25 Jan 1892. Richard and Artemisia were buried in the Old Edinburg Cemetery.

George Marcus Miller was born ca. 1843 and was a painter. He enlisted at Edinburg on 18 Apr 8161 as a private in Company C of the 10th Virginia Infantry. George transferred to Company F of the 10th on 18 Apr 1862. He was wounded in the hand on 8 May 1862 at McDowell. He was AWOL

from 2 Jun 1862 until September of 1862. He eventually
transferred to the 7th Virginia Cavalry. George was
married on 16 Jun 1869 to Frances "Fanny" Cornelia Vincent.
Fanny was born in Clarke County, Virginia. Fanny died 20
Nov 1892. George died 17 Aug 1919 in Iowa. Fanny was the
daughter of Joseph W. and Eliza.

William K. Polk Miller died at the age of 78 on
25 Jan 1923 in West Virginia. His first wife, Elizabeth
Denio Miller died in 1917. He was survived by his second
wife Ella C. Hansberger Miller.

Alice Adele Miller was born 31 Aug 1846 and died
31 Aug 1926. She married John Samuel Hutcheson on 17 Mar
1869. John had a distinguished military career as a member
of the 10th Virginia Infantry. In later life he was a
respected editor and minister. He was the son of Charles
and Elizabeth. Charles Hutcheson married Eliza B. Whissen
n 15 Mar 1827. Charles Hutcheson and his family resided
in **dwelling 68**. John was born 29 Mar 1842 and died 20 Mar
1911.

Marshall Orland Miller married Mary Wharton.

Louella Miller married George Wharton.

Adesta Fidelas "Addie" Miller was born in 1857 and
died in 1927. She was married to Frank Dewitt Jennings on
29 Aug 1880. Frank was the son of Henry and Mary. Frank
and his parents resided in **dwelling 1**. Frank was born in
1855 and died in 1922. Addie and Frank were buried in the
Cedarwood Cemetery.

RELATED FAMILY:

   Mary Frances Grandstaff, sister of
Artemisia, married William J. Dinges on 25 May 1847 and
resided in **dwelling 58**.
   Elizabeth Ann Grandstaff, sister of
Artemisia, married William J. Koontz on 12 Aug 1837 and
resided in **dwelling 60**.
  Milton M. Grandstaff, brother of Artemisia,
married Emily J. A. Frye on 19 Nov 1846 and resided in
dwelling 61.
   Phillip Marcus Grandstaff, brother of
Artemisia, married Sarah Miller and resided in **dwelling 62**.
  Ellen M. Grandstaff, sister of Artemisia,
married John R. Miller and resided in **dwelling 53**.

John Jackson Grandstaff, brother of Artemisia, married Isabella Murray on 5 Mar 1835 and resided in **dwelling 328**.

Richard Miller, believed to have been the son of Richard, resided in **dwelling 586**.

1850 CENSUS: Richard Miller and his family resided in dwelling 713 on page 50.

PAGE 43 EDINBURG (Microfilm Page 567)

Dwelling 292 Family 292

Ebenezer Caruthers	27	Stonecutter 0	150	Scotland
Martha A. Caruthers	29			Virginia
Ida F. Caruthers	2			"
Leona P. Caruthers	8m			"
Adda C. Jacobs	10			"

Ebenezer Caruthers was a stonecutter. He created a number of tombstones for individuals in the Strasburg area prior to the Civil War. He was the son of James and Jess. Ebenezer married on 1 Jan 1857 to **Martha Ann Hockman**. Martha was the daughter of Jacob and Elizabeth. Jacob F. Hockman married Elizabeth Zimmerman on 9 Nov 1816. Jacob F. Hockman and his family resided in **dwelling 293**. Ebenezer was born ca. 1833. He enlisted at Edinburg on 18 Apr 1861 as a member of the 10th Virginia Infantry Company F. In May of 1862 he joined Company K of the 12th Virginia Cavalry. Ebenezer was 5'6" with dark complexion, blue eyes and black hair. He was wounded at the battle of Brandy Station on 9 Jun 1863. He was present in September and October of 1863 through August of 1864. His horse was killed in action near Warrenton Springs on 12 Oct 1863 and was appraised at $700. Ebenezer was paroled at Mt. Jackson on 3 May 1865. He entered the Soldiers Home at Richmond on 13 May 1898 and was sent to an asylum from the Soldiers Home on 5 Sep 1898.

Leona P. Caruthers was married on 29 May 1878 to John H. Ott. John was a carpenter and bridge builder. He was born and resided in Jefferson County, West Virginia. He was the son of Martin and Catherine.

RELATED FAMILY:

William M. Hockman, brother of Martha, married Rebecca Frances Matthews on 9 Feb 1860 and resided in **dwelling 295**.

Mary Hockman Artz, believed to have been the sister of Martha, married Henry Artz on 5 Jul 1851 and resided in **dwelling 294**.

Isabella Hockman, sister of Martha, married Patrick Kelly in December of 1855 and resided in **dwelling 296**.

1850 CENSUS: There was no record of this family in the 1850 census.

PAGE 43 EDINBURG DISTRICT (Microfilm Page 567)

Dwelling 293   Family 293

Jacob F. Hockman	73	1500	190	Virginia	
Elizabeth Hockman	62			"	Can't Read
Sarah J. Hockman	24			"	Can't Read
Amelia C. Hockman	19			"	

According to Daniel Bly, **Hockman** family historian, **Jacob Hockman** the son of Joseph Hockman, removed to Hampshire County. It appears that Jacob actually remained in Shenandoah County and settled near Edinburg. He was married to **Elizabeth Zimmerman**, the daughter of Christian Zimmerman of Woodstock on 9 Nov 1816. Jacob and Elizabeth had a large number of children. Elizabeth died on the 80th anniversary of her birth on 9 Jan 1797. She was buried in the Cedarwood Cemetery. Her son Dr. Christian Hockman appears to have been buried near her. Christian was born 25 Jul 1830 and died 27 Nov 1894. Christian resided with the family in 1850. He was probably named after his paternal grandfather Christian Zimmerman.

Sarah J. Hockman did not marry. She died at the age of 80 on 1 Nov 1915 in Edinburg.

RELATED FAMILY:

Martha Ann Hockman, daughter of Jacob, married Ebenezer Caruthers on 1 Jan 1857 and resided in **dwelling 292**.

William M. Hockman, son of Jacob, married Rebecca Frances Matthews on 9 Feb 1860 and resided in **dwelling 295**.

Isabella Hockman, daughter of Jacob, married Patrick Kelly in December of 1855 and resided in **dwelling 296**.

Mary Hockman, believed to have been the daughter of Jacob, married Henry Artz on 5 Jul 1851 and resided in **dwelling 294.**

1850 CENSUS: Jacob F. Hockman and his family resided in dwelling 2043 on page 147.

PAGE 43 EDINBURG DISTRICT (Microfilm Page 567)

Dwelling 294 Family 294

Mary Artz	34	Virginia	
John W. Artz	14	"	School
Henrietta E. Artz	8	"	School
Frances L. Artz	6	"	School

Henry Artz married **Mary Hockman** on 5 Jul 1851. It is believed that Mary was the daughter of Jacob and Elizabeth. Jacob Hockman married Elizabeth Zimmerman on 9 Nov 1816. 24 year old Mary Hockman resided with her parents in 1850. Jacob Hockman and his family resided in **dwelling 293.**

Note: There was a Henry Artz and his wife Elizabeth residing near the Hockman family in 1850. He resided in dwelling 2046 and the Hockman's lived in dwelling 2043. It is probable that his wife died and he took Mary as his second wife. However, Henry and Elizabeth did not have a son John W. In the Hockman household in 1850 there was a 4 year old John W. Hockman. John may have been the son of the unmarried Mary.

RELATED FAMILY:

William M. Hockman, brother of Mary, married Rebecca Frances Matthews on 9 Feb 1860 and resided in **dwelling 295.**

Isabella Hockman, sister of Mary, married Patrick Kelly in December of 1855 and resided in **dwelling 296.**

Martha Ann Hockman, sister of Mary, married Ebenezer Caruthers on 1 Jan 1857 and resided in **dwelling 292.**

1850 CENSUS: Mary Hockman resided in dwelling 2043 on page 147.

PAGE 44 EDINBURG DISTRICT   (Microfilm Page 568)

Dwelling 295   Family 295

William M. Hockman	38 Shoe & Boot Maker Va.		Just Mar.
Rebecca F. Hockman	16	"	Just Married

William M. Hockman was the son of Jacob and Elizabeth. Jacob F. Hockman married Elizabeth Zimmerman on 9 Nov 1816. Jacob and his family resided in **dwelling 293**. William was married to 16 year old **Rebecca Frances Mathews** on 9 Feb 1860. Rebecca was born in Prince William County, Virginia. She and her family resided in Shenandoah County at the time of the marriage. She is listed in marriage records as the daughter of William and Emily. There is a family in **dwelling 903** that may have some relationship to Rebecca. The mistress of the household was Emily Mathews. However, her husband was named Thomas. William M. Hockman died 11 Jan 1897 at the age of 75 years, 11 months and 12 days old. Rebecca Frances Mathews Hockman died 21 Jun 1890 at the age of 45 years, 10 months and 3 days old. They were buried in the Cedarwood Cemetery.

RELATED FAMILY:
        Mary Hockman, sister of William, married Henry Artz on 5 Jul 1851 and resided in **dwelling 294**.
        Isabella Hockman, sister of William, married Patrick Kelly in December of 1855 and resided in **dwelling 296**.
        Martha Ann Hockman, sister of William, married Ebenezer Caruthers on 1 Jan 1857 and resided in **dwelling 292**.

1850 CENSUS: William M. Hockman resided with his parents in dwelling 2043 on page 147.

PAGE 44 EDINBURG DISTRICT (Microfilm Page 568)

Dwelling 296   Family 296

Patrick H. Kelly	29 Stone cutter	0	50 Virginia	
Isabella F. Kelly	27		"	
Charles W. Kelly	3		"	
Elenora Kelly	2		"	
Dora E. Kelly	3m		"	

        Patrick Kelly was born 17 Mar 1831 and died 29 Oct 1906. He was married to **Isabella F. Hockman** in December

of 1855. Isabella was born 21 Jan 1833 and died 9 Sep
1911. She was the daughter of Jacob and Elizabeth. Jacob
F. Hockman married Elizabeth Zimmerman on 9 Nov 1816.
Jacob and his family resided in **dwelling 293**. Patrick and
Isabella were buried in the Cedarwood Cemetery in Edinburg.
Patrick Henry Kelly was born in Richmond, Virginia. He
enlisted on 2 Aug 1862 at New Market, Virginia in Company
E of the 12th Virginia Cavalry. He was a private and was
present from Sep 1863 through Apr 1864. Unofficial sources
indicate that he was wounded in the hip. The battle and
the date he was wounded are not recorded.

Elenora Kelly was born in 1858 and died in 1927.
She was buried near her parents.

Dora Elizabeth Kelly was born in 1860 and died 1
Dec 1937. She was married to Joseph Henry Painter on 23
Dec 1880. Joseph was the son of James M. and Isabella.
James M. Painter married Isabella V. Hoffman on 16 Jan
1856. James M. Painter and his family resided in **dwelling
269**. Joseph Henry Painter was born in 1857 and died 9 Apr
1942. Dora and Joseph were buried in the Cedarwood
Cemetery.

RELATED FAMILY:
Martha Ann Hockman, sister of Isabella,
married Ebenezer Caruthers on 1 Jan 1857 and resided in
dwelling 292.
Mary Hockman, sister of Isabella, married
Henry Artz on 5 Jul 1851 and resided in **dwelling 294**.
William M. Hockman, brother of Isabella,
married Rebecca Frances Mathews of 9 Feb 1860 and resided
in **dwelling 295**.

1850 CENSUS: Isabella F. Hockman, resided with her parents
in dwelling 2043 on page 147.

PAGE 44 EDINBURG DISTRICT (Microfilm Page 568)

Dwelling 297 Family 297

Lovett Knight	38	0 40	Virginia Can't Read
Timothy Knight	16	Day Labor	"
Lydia Ann Knight	12		"
John H. Knight	9		"
Alpha Knight	9m		"

Lovett Knight is believed to have been **Louisa Jenkins**. Louisa Jenkins married Timothy Knight in Page County, Virginia on 1 May 1840. She is thought to have been the daughter of Zachariah and Alpha. Zacaraiah Jenkins married Alpha Robertson on 9 Mary 1821. Zacariah and Alpha were residents in **dwelling 298**. Timothy Knight Sr. has not been located in this census.

There was a marriage on 23 Jul 1871 for Joseph H. Knight to Polena Elick. He was 21 years old at the time of the wedding. This may actually have been the John H. Knight who appears in this household. Joseph was listed as the son of Timothy and Alpha. Further research on this matter is required.

Alpha Knight, named in honor of her maternal grandmother, was married on 8 Dec 1874 to Frank Henry Steinnecke. Frank was the son of Christian and Mary. He was a cigar maker from Hanover, Germany.

RELATED FAMILY:

> **Oliver Perry Jenkins,** brother of Louisa Jenkins Knight, married Elizabeth Rudy on 3 Nov 1859 and resided in **dwelling 1772.**

1850 CENSUS: Timothy and **Louisa Knight** and family resided in dwelling 273 on page 286 in Page County.

PAGE 44 EDINBURG DISTRICT   (Microfilm Page 568)

Dwelling 298   Family 298

Zachariah Jenkins	61	0	50	Virginia	Can't Read
Alpha Jenkins	55			"	
Julius Jenkins	32			"	Can't Read
James W. Jenkins	20 Farmhand			"	

Zachariah Jenkins was the son of James and Elizabeth. James Jenkins married Elizabeth Parks on 28 Feb 1798. Zachariah married **Alpha Robertson** on 9 Mar 1821. The bondsman for the marriage was James Jenkins. Alpha Robertson Jenkins died sometime after this census. Zachariah Jenkins was married on 14 Aug 1873 to Anna Sunafrank. Anna was 50 years old and her parents were not listed.

A number of **James W. Jenkins** are reported to have fought in the Civil War. There is no precise evidence but

Company G of the 12th Virginia Cavalry had a James W. Jenkins in service. Other men from Shenandoah County served with this unit.

RELATED FAMILY:
                    Lovett Knight, believed to have been Louisa Jenkins, daughter of Zachariah, married Timothy Knight on 1 May 1840 and resided in **dwelling 297.**
                    Oliver Perry Jenkins, son of Zachariah, married Elizabeth Rudy on 3 Nov 1859 and resided in **dwelling 1772.**

1850 CENSUS: **Zachariah Jenkins** and his family resided in dwelling 272 on page 286 in Page County, Virginia.

PAGE 44 EDINBURG DISTRICT   (Microfilm Page 568)

Dwelling 299 Family 299

John Robinson	34	Farmer	100	200	Virginia	
Mahala Robinson	33				"	
William C. Robinson	9				"	School
Sanford A. Robinson	8				"	School
John H. Robinson	6				"	School
Akin E. Robinson	4				"	
Belerocous Robinson	2				"	

       John Robinson was married to **Mahala J. Burke** on 21 Feb 1848.   The bondsman for the marriage William H. Linkins.

       Akin E. Robinson was a salesman at the time of his marriage on 13 Aug 1884 to Sarah Bell Conn.   Sarah was the daughter of Rafael and S. A. Conn.   Rafael Conn and his family resided in **dwelling 362.**   Sarah was born in 1851 and died 23 Mar 1927.   She was buried in the Lebanon Church Cemetery.

       John and Mahala had a daughter Mary M. Robinson who was born 30 Oct 1859 and died 17 Jul 1877.   She was buried in the Cedarwood Cemetery.

1850 CENSUS: **John Robinson** and his family resided in dwelling 105 on page 8.

299

PAGE 44 EDINBURG DISTRICT   (Microfilm Page 568)

Dwelling 300   Family 300

William Ripley	60	Farmer	29,350	8216	Virginia	
Mary J. Ripley	27				"	
Jackson Lindamood	19	Farmhand			"	
George Webster	8				"	School

   William Ripley was born 10 Aug 1801 and died 17
Feb 1884.   He was originally married in Orange County,
Virginia to Elizabeth Eve on 20 May 1832.   Upon the death
of Elizabeth, William was married on 2 Nov 1846 to Mary L.
Pitman, the daughter of Lawrence Pitman.   Mary L. Pitman
Ripley was born 20 Nov 1815 and died 19 Jun 1855.   William
and Mary were buried in the Old Union Church Cemetery at
Mt. Jackson.   The union of the Ripley and the Pitman family
enabled William to purchase Red Banks from his father in
law.   Redbanks, an historic home, was located midway
between Mt. Jackson and Edinburg on the Valley Pike.   It
was situated at a site near the banks of the Shenandoah.
It was a favored stopping place for stage coach drivers.
In fact, John Wayland indicates that William may have been
a stage driver at some point.   Andrew Jackson and Madame
Jerome Bonaparte were guests at Red Bank and Stonewall
Jackson may have used the house as his headquarters for a
period of time.   Confederate troops camped near the house
and the area was referred to as Camp Buchanan.

   Mary Jane Ripley was born 22 Mar 1833 and died 26
Dec 1872.   She was married to John L. Pitman on 20 Sep
1860.   John was a resident in **dwellling 598**.   He was the
son of Phillip and Mary.   Phillip Pitman, the brother of
William's late wife Mary L., married Mary Susan Houston and
resided in **dwelling 247**.   John L. Pitman was born 10 Oct
1829 and died 26 Oct 1896.   When Mary Jane died in 1872,
John L. married the widowed wife of his brother-in-law
Valentine Ripley.   Valentine had married Mary Elizabeth
Allen on 9 Dec 1858.   Valentine and Mary Elizabeth resided
in **dwelling 301**.   Valentine died 17 Oct 1869.   Mary
Elizabeth Allen Ripley and John L. Pitman were married on
26 Oct 1875.   Mary Elizabeth was born 27 Jan 1837 and died
16 May 1900.   All members of this family were buried in the
Old Union Church Cemetery.

RED BANKS
Located on the Valley Pike and north fork of the Shenandoah
Midway between Mt. Jackson and Edinburg

Photo: Courtesy of John Walter Wayland Collection,
Winchester-Frederick County Hist. Society Archives
Winchester, Virginia

Jackson Lindamood appears to have been listed twice in this census. He also appears in **dwelling 570**. He resided with Samuel Lindamood. Andrew Jackson Lindamood enlisted in Company C of the 10th Virginia Infantry on 18 Apr 1861 at Harpers Ferry. Private Lindamood died 27 Jan 1862 at Mt. Jackson of pneumonia.

RELATED FAMILY:
Valentine Ripley, son of William, married Mary Elizabeth Allen on 9 Dec 1858 and resided in **dwelling 301.**

Samuel Lindamood, believed to have been the brother of Jackson, married Barbara Ann Ryan on 25 Mar 1856 and resided in **dwelling 570**.

Phillip Pitman, brother in law of William, married Mary Susan Houston and resided in **dwelling 247**.

1850 CENSUS: William Ripley and his family resided in dwelling 1003 on page 70.

Jackson Lindamood resided in dwelling 1326 on page 95. It appears that he and his mother resided with his grandmother Mary.

PAGE 44 EDINBURG DISTRICT (Microfilm Page 568)

Dwelling 301 Family 301

Valentine Ripley	25 Farmer	19,000	18,950	Virginia
Mary E. Ripley	22			"
Frances A. Ripley	1m			"

Valentine Ripley was born 21 Aug 1835 and died 17 Oct 1869. Valentine was born in Orange County, Virginia. He was the son of William and Elizabeth. William Ripley married Elizabeth Eve on 20 Mar 1832. William Ripley resided in **dwelling 300**. Valentine Ripley married **Mary Elizabeth Allen** on 9 Dec 1858. Mary Elizabeth was the daughter of John and Frances. John J. Allen married Frances M. Moore on 13 Oct 1834. John J. Allen's widow Catherine Kingree Allen resided in **dwelling 586**. John had married Catherine on 23 Feb 1854. Mary Elizabeth was born 27 Jan 1837 and died 16 May 1900. After Valentine died, Mary Elizabeth married her brother-in-law, John L. Pitman. John L. Pitman had married Valentine's sister Mary Jane Ripley on 20 Sep 1860. Mary Jane resided with her parents in **dwelling 300**. Mary Jane was born 22 Mar 1833 and died 26 Dec 1872. John was the son of Phillip and Mary Susan Houston Pitman. Phillip and his family resided in **dwelling 247**. At the time this census was taken John L. Pitman resided in **dwelling 598**. John L. Pitman was born 10 Oct 1829 and died 26 Oct 1896. Mary Elizabeth Allen Ripley Pitman, Valentine Ripley, John L. Pitman and Mary Jane Ripley Pitman were all buried in the Old Union Church Cemetery at Mt. Jackson. Valentine Ripley enlisted on 18 May 1861 in Company G of the 33rd Virginia Infantry. He rose to the rank of Lieutenant but was dropped from the rolls of that unit in 1862 for unknown reasons.

Frances Allen Ripley was born 13 Apr 1860 and died 4 Jan 1929. She was married on 3 Nov 1881 to Dr. Jacob Garner Paxton Williamson, the son of Jacob D and Mary. Jacob D. Williamson was referred to in family records as Major Williamson. Dr. Williamson was born in Rockingham County, Virginia on 19 May 1857 and died 27 Mar 1894. Dr. and Mrs. Williamson were buried in the Lutheran Reformation Church Cemetery in New Market, Virginia.

1850 CENSUS: **Valentine Ripley** resided with his parents in dwelling 1003 on page 70.
Mary Elizabeth Allen resided with her parents in dwelling 1020 on page 71.

PAGE 44 EDINBURG DISTRICT **(Microfilm Page 568)**

Dwelling 302 Family 302

Joseph Maphis	33 Miller	6600	4550	Virginia	
Theresa W. Maphis	34			"	
Barbara L. Maphis	9			"	School
Emma J. Maphis	3			"	
James D. Maphis	9m			"	
James H. Swartz	23 Sawyer			"	

Joseph Maphis was born 2 Feb 1827 and died 2 Dec 1906. He was reported to have been the son of David and Barbara. Joseph was married in Frederick County, Virginia to Theresa W. Swartz on 2 Mar 1848. Joseph was listed as Jacob in the marriage record of that county. Theresa was born 18 Aug 1825 and died 8 Feb 1886. Joseph and Theresa were buried in the Old Union Church Cemetery at Mt. Jackson. Joseph Maphis married again after Theresa's death. He married Mary C. Wenck on 24 Jan 1888. Mary was the daughter of Andrew and Catherine Elizabeth. Mary's father was from Hesan, Germany. Captain Andrew Wenck and his family resided in **dwelling 952.**

Barbara Lavenia Maphis was born 19 May 1851 and died 20 Aug 1886. Barbara was buried in the Old Union Church Cemetery. She was married to J. P. Lonas. John P. Lonas was the son of Joseph and Rachel. Joseph Lonas married Rachel Huntsberger on 23 Apr 1832. Joseph Lonas and his family resided in **dwelling 1516.** John P. Lonas appears on the roll of Company C of the 7th Virginia Cavalry. When Barbara died, John was married to E. French Tanqueary of Rockbridge County, Virginia on 24 Sep 1890. She was the daughter of Alfred and Laura. John P. Lonas was born in

1836 and died in 1917. He was buried in the New Mt.
Jackson Cemetery.

Emma Jane Maphis was born 13 Apr 1857 and died 11
Jun 1936. Emma was married on 4 Jul 1878 to Madison Monroe
Funkhouser. Madison was the son of Noah and Anna. Noah
Funkhouser married Anna Elizabeth Hockman on 24 Nov 1846.
Noah and his family resided in **dwelling 2077**. Emma Jane
Maphis Funkhouser and her husband were buried in the
Riverview Cemetery in Strasburg. Madison Monroe Funkhouser
was born 30 Dec 1852 and died 1 Dec 1932.

James H. Swartz is believed to have been the
brother of Theresa. There is a good possibility that they
were the children of James and Mahala. James Swartz
married Mahala McDonald on 3 Jan 1825 in Frederick County,
Virginia. James Swartz Sr. was also a miller. Twelve year
old James H. Swartz appears in the household of his parents
in 1850. They resided in dwelling 1333 in Frederick County
at that time.

1850 CENSUS: **Joseph Maphis** resided in dwelling 869 on page
61.

PAGE 44   EDINBURG DISTRICT   (Microfilm Page 568)

Dwelling 303   Family 303

William Maphis	69 Farmer	Virginia	
Catherine Maphis	64	"	Can't Read

William Maphis died 16 Mar 1860 in the 69th year
of his life. He is believed to have married **Catherine
Painter** on 25 Jan 1817. She was the daughter of Phillip
Painter. Catherine Maphis died 11 May 1868. William and
Catherine were buried in the Lantz-Bowman Cemetery.

RELATED FAMILY:
        George Maphis, son of William and Catherine,
married Anna Elizabeth Cline on 18 Mar 1843 and resided in
dwelling 304.

1850 CENSUS: **William Maphis** and his family resided in
        dwelling 993 on page 69.

PAGE 45   EDINBURG DISTRICT   (Microfilm Page 569)

Dwelling 304   Family 304

George Maphis	40	Farmer	8356	2077	Virginia
Elizabeth Maphis	39				"
William H. Maphis	13				" School
Ira A. Maphis	9				" School
Mary C. Maphis	7				" School
Luther M. Maphis	4				"
Linden P. Maphis	2				"
Catherine Bowman	18	Housegirl			"

George Maphis was born 18 Aug 1819 and died 5 Apr 1911. He was the son of William and Catherine. William Maphis married Catherine Painter on 25 Jan 1817. William and Catherine were residents in **dwelling 303**. George was married to **Anna Elizabeth Cline** on 18 Mar 1843. Anna was born 26 Jun 1820 and died 28 Sep 1907. George and Anna were buried in the Lantz-Bowman Cemetery near Edinburg. George Maphis enlisted as a private in Company E of the 11th Virginia Cavalry. He only appears on the post war roster of that unit. No other information is available regarding his service.

There was a **William H. Maphis** on the roll of the 12th Virginia Cavalry. He was born in 1844 and was 5'6" with dark complexion, blue eyes and dark hair. He enlisted 28 Aug 1862 at Edinburg as a private in Company K. He was present from Sep 1863 through Apr 1864. He was wounded at Todds Tavern on 5 May 1864 and was absent with his wounds in July and August of 1864. He was paroled at Winchester on 19 Apr 1865. It is not known for certain if this is the individual who appears in this household.

Mary C. Maphis was married on 14 Apr 1874 to David B. Stiles of Rockingham County, Virginia. He was the son of Christian and Hannah.

Luther M. Maphis was born 8 Oct 1855 and died 25 Jan 1933. His wife, Cora P. Wotring Maphis, was born 1 Apr 1865 and died 25 Feb 1929. They were buried in the St. Johns Lutheran Church Cemetery in Frederick County, Virginia.

Catherine Bowman was probably Mary Catherine Bowman. She was 8 years old at the time she appears in the household of Henry and Catherine Cline in 1850. Henry

Cline married Catherine Wiseman on 27 Nov 1802. Henry and
Catherine resided in **dwelling 1569**. It may be that they
were the parents of Anna Elizabeth Cline Maphis.

1850 CENSUS: George Maphis resided with his parents in
dwelling 993 on page 69.

PAGE 45 EDINBURG DISTRICT (Microfilm Pge 569)

Dwelling 305 Family 305

Joseph Pence	52	Farmer	800	390	Virginia Can't Read
Mahala Pence	49				" Can't Read
James H. Pence	19	Wagoner			"
Robert Pence	17	Farmhand			"
Mary C. Pence	16				"
William H. Pence	13				"
Annie E. Pence	12				"
Ellen Pence	9				"
Beale Pence	7				"
Sarah J. Pence	3				"

Joseph Pence was born 30 Jun 1807 and died 16 Apr
1880. Joseph may have been the son of George Pence, as 70
year old George was in the household in 1850. There was
a marriage on 17 Feb 1802 of George Pence to Elizabeth
Bear. Joseph may have been married originally to Martha
Beach. That marriage took place on 5 Jan 1835. Joseph's
son Jacob specifically indicates in his marriage that he
was the son of Joseph and Martha Beach. This needs to be
checked. It is known that he was married to **Mahala Grim** on
8 Sep 1836. The bondsman for the marriage was Peter Green
(Grim?). Mahala Grim Pence was born 16 Jun 1811 and died
1 Apr 1882. They were buried in the Old Union Church
Cemetery in Mt. Jackson.

James M. Pence was born 16 Mar 1841 and died 26 Apr
1915. James was married to Emily Virginia Crawford on 8
Feb 1862. Emily was the daugther of Edward and Elizabeth.
Edward Crawford married Elizabeth Smith on 2 Apr 1844.
Emily Crawford and her family resided in **dwelling 931**.
James and Emily divorced prior to 1876. On 27 Feb 1876
Emily Crawford married John M. Fadely. James married
Rebecca Fry on 25 May 1867. Rebecca was the daughter of
Absalom and Christina Fry. Rebecca was born 9 Jul 1826 and
died 11 Dec 1897. She resided with her parents in **dwelling
1359**. Rebecca was buried in the St. Marys Pine Church
Cemetery near Mt. Jackson. James M. Pence then married

Catherine Click on 9 Mar 1898. Sarah Catherine was the daughter of Samuel and Sallie. She died 3 Apr 1934 at the age of 74. James and Sarah C. Pence were buried in the New Mount Jackson Cemetery.

Robert Pence died 29 Nov 1899 at the age of 55 years and 5 months. He was married to Rebecca Chilcott on 29 Dec 1864. Rebecca was the daughter of Jonathan and Rosena Wolverton Chilcott. Jonathan and his family resided in **dwelling 1214**. Rebecca Chilcott Pence died 9 Oct 1892 at the age of 46 years and 1 month old. They were buried in the Union Forge Cemetery.

Mary Catherine Pence was married on 31 Dec 1863 to Charles M. Stratton. Charles was a sugar planter from Louisiana. He was the son of Archie and Mary.

Annie Elizabeth Pence was born 2 Mar 1849 and died 21 Oct 1922. She was married on 19 Mar 1868 to Joseph Thomas Grim. Joseph was the son of Phillip and Elizabeth. Phillip Grim married Elizabeth "Betsy" Ann McCullough on 12 Oct 1838. Phillip Grim and his family resided in **dwelling 587**. Joseph Thomas Grim was born 1 Sep 1844 and died 24 Apr 1906. Ann and Joseph were buried in the New Mount Jackson Cemetery.

Barbara Ellen Pence was born in 1851 and died in 1929. She was married to George W. Ward on 4 Jun 1878. George was the son of Arthelia Ward. He was born in 1850 and died in 1906. George and Barbara were buried in the New Mount Jackson Cemetery.

Beale Pence was married on 17 Jun 1873 to Rebecca F. Rush. Rebecca was the daughter of Wellington and Catherine. Wellington Rush married Catherine Dellinger on 7 Dec 1840. Rebecca F. Rush and other members of this family resided in **dwelling 560**.

RELATED FAMILY:

   Rebecca J. Pence, daughter of Joseph and Mahala, married William H. Ort on 6 Jan 1857 and resided in **dwelling 248**.

   Jacob Pence, son of Joseph and Mahala, married Isabella Grandstaff on 19 Aug 1858 and resided in **dwelling 337**.

   Martha Pence, believed to have been the daughter of Joseph and Mahala and twin of Rebecca, married George E. Bowman and resided in **dwelling 329**.

1850 CENSUS: Joseph Pence and his family resided in dwelling 992 on page 69.

PAGE 45 EDINBURG DISTRICT (Microfilm Page 569)

Dwelling 306   Family 306

Jacob Fultz	41 Farmer	0	1145	Virginia	
Rachel Fultz	40			"	
William A. Fultz	20 Farmhand			"	
John E. Fultz	15			"	
Isaac E. Fultz	10			"	Deaf & Dumb
Isabella F. Fultz	8			"	

Jacob Fultz, the son of John Fultz, was born 20 Dec 1817 and died 21 Jun 1901. Jacob is believed to have been the son of John and Margaret. John Fultz (Foltz) married Mary Margaret Pence on 14 May 1815. John Fultz and his family resided in **dwelling 577**. Jacob was married to **Rachel Shaver** 18 Jun 1838. She was the daughter of Frederick. Rachel Ellen Shaver was born 28 Oct 1819 and died 23 23 May 1887. Jacob, Rachel and other members of this family were buried at the Hawkinson United Methodist Church Cemetery in the vicinity of Mt. Jackson.

William A. Fultz was married to Amanda Kerlin on 21 Mar 1861. She was the daughter of Gasner and Anna. Gasner Kerlin married Anna Jones on 12 Feb 1834. Gasner Kerlin and his family resided in **dwelling 559**. William A. Fultz was 5'11" with dark complexion and dark hair and eyes. He enlisted at Hawkinstown in Captain Myers company of the 7th Virginia Cavalry. He later enlisted in Company K of the 12 Virginia Cavalry on 1 May 1862. He was detailed as a teamster in Sep of 1862. William was wounded at Upperville on 21 Jun 1863. He was absent with his wounds in September, October, November and December of 1863. He returned to service in January of 1864. On 24 Jul 1864 he was assigned to the Invalid Corp. He received his parole at Winchester on 20 Apr 1865.

John Effiah Fultz was born in 1841 and died in 1914. John married Sarah Jane Fultz on 10 Dec 1868. Sarah was born in Rockbridge County, Virginia in 1845 and died in 1926. She was the daughter of Uriah and Anna. Uriah Foltz married Ann Hoover on 25 Oct 1841 in Shenandoah County, Virginia. Ann Hoover Foltz resided in **dwelling 572**. John and Sarah were buried in the Hawkinson United Methodist Church Cemetery. There is a record which indicates that John E. Foltz enlisted on 1 May 1862 at Woodstock in Company K of the 12 Virginia Cavalry. This is the same date of enlistment as his brother William. John was present in September and October of 1863. He was reported as AWOL on the 11 of November of that year. He was present at the 31 December 1863 muster. He was wounded at Todds Tavern on 6 May 1864 and was admitted to the general hospital in Charlottesville on 8 May 1864 with his wound. He was transferred to the hospital at Staunton on 13 May 1864.

        Isaac E. Fultz was listed as being deaf. He was born 27 Oct 1843 and died 16 May 1894. He probably did not marry as a result of his handicap. Isaac was buried near his parents.

RELATED FAMILY:
        Walton Foltz, brother of Jacob, married Jane Shaver on 30 Jan 1850 and resided in **dwelling 556**.
        Margaret Foltz, sister of Jacob, married Simon Woods on 6 Nov 1855 and resided in **dwelling 686**.

1850 CENSUS: Jacob **Fultz** and his family resided in dwelling 991 on page 69.

PAGE 45 EDINBURG DISTRICT (Microfilm Page 569)

Dwelling 307 Family 307

Susan Myers	55	0	55	Virginia Deaf & Dumb
Mary C. Myers	26			"
Hetty Myers	16			"
John Ireland	33	Saddler		Ireland
Elizabeth Ireland	19			Virginia
Susan E. Ireland	6m			"
Mary E. Myers	1m			"

        Susan Pence married Abraham Myers on 8 Jan 1827. There was a Susannah Myers listed in the Old Union Church Cemetery. She was born 31 May 1805 and died 20 May 1888. She was listed as the wife of Jonathan Myers. There is some evidence that this may have been the same individual who was head of this household. She was buried next to Mary Lucas, the daughter of Abraham and Susan. Susan was the daughter of Jacob Pence. Susan is mention in the will of her father as recorded in Will Book W on page 312. In this will her father indicates that his daughter Susan was deaf and dumb. He also indicates in this will dated 12 Jun 1843 that her husband Abraham Myers had left her.

Mary C. Myers appears to have been listed as Leah Myers in a 1 Nov 1860 marriage to George Washington Patton. George was the son of Michael and Susan. Michael Patton married Susan Fry on 12 Dec 1836. Michael Patton and his family resided in **dwelling 314**. George Washington Patton died 30 Nov 1920. Mary C. Myers died prior to her husband and he was remarried to Mary Shank. George lived in **dwelling 353** at the time of this census.

John Ireland was the son of John and Alice. At the time he married **Elizabeth Myers** he was a superintendent on the railroad. Their marriage took place on 14 Oct 1858. Elizabeth was born 20 Apr 1840 and died 10 Jul 1929. She was buried in the New Mount Jackson Cemetery. John Ireland took up the cause of the Confederacy and enlisted in Company G of the 33rd Virginia Infantry on 24 Mar 1862. He was present in Dec of 1862 but was AWOL in Dec of 1863. John was admitted to Chimborazo Hospital with typhoid fever on 6 Apr 1863 and died 14 Apr 1863. On 5 Jan 1865 Elizabeth Myers Ireland married Patrick Higgins. Patrick was also born in Ireland. He was the son of Thomas and Mary and resided in New Orleans.

Henrietta "Hetty" Myers was married on 27 Nov 1862 to James L. Johnson. James was a widower from Sullivan County, Tennessee. He was a baker and was the son of Thomas and Elizabeth.

RELATED FAMILY:

Mary Myers, daughter of Susan, married Jacob Lucas on 15 Nov 1847 and resided in **dwelling 663**.

Isaac Myers, son of Susan, married Elizabeth Martz on 24 Feb 1859 and resided in **dwelling 1449**.

Missouri Barnes Pence, sister in law of Susan, was the widow of David Pence. She had married David Pence on 12 Mar 1832. Missouri resided in **dwelling 571**.

Mary Margaret Pence, sister of Susan, married John W. Foltz on 14 May 1815 and resided in **dwelling 577**.

1850 CENSUS: **Susan Pence Myers** and other members of her family resided in dwelling 1036 on page 72. Jacob and Mary Myers Lucas were also in the household.

PAGE 45   EDINBURG DISTRICT   (Microfilm Page 569)

Dwelling 308   Family 308

Beale S. Pence	35	Farmer	2900	737	Virginia	
Rebecca Pence	27				"	
Mary S. Pence	5				"	
John Pence	4				"	
Selena Pence	3				"	
Luela Pence	2				"	
Sarah Estep	22				"	
Samuel Drummond	40	Farmhand			"	Can't Read

Mary S. Pence was married to William B. Firth of Jefferson County, West Virginia on 27 Jan 1881. William was the son of John N. and Phebe A. On 22 Aug 1910 William B. Firth was a widower at the time he married Sarah C. Sheffer. Sarah was the daughter of Jonas and Edith Catherine Golladay Shaffer. Sarah and her parents resided in **dwelling 671**. She was born 9 Oct 1846 and died 22 Feb 1923. Sarah was buried at the New Mount Jackson Cemetery.

John L. Pence was married on 20 Oct 1887 to Dolly Virginia Wilkin. John was born 10 Apr 1856 and died 16 Jan 1930. Virginia was born 8 Dec 1868 and died 26 Aug 1934. They were buried in the Hawkinson United Methodist Church Cemetery. Dolly Virginia was the daughter of Solomon and Rebecca. Solomon Wilkins married Rebecca J. Clem on 2 Jun 1853. Solomon and his family resided in **dwelling 2306**.

Sarah Estep may have been the daughter of Thomas and Mary. Thomas Estep married Mary Ann Betz on 17 Nov 1836. Thomas and his family resided in **dwelling 1575**.

Samuel Drummond was the son of Thomas and Lovinia. He was born in Prince William County, Virginia. He married Lydia Dotson on 12 Apr 1842. He was divorced from Lydia when he married Ellen Frances Burner on 26 Sep 1867. Ellen was the daughter of Henry and Elizabeth. Henry Burner married Elizabeth Kneisley on 28 Mar 1838. Henry and his family resided in **dwelling 531**. Lydia Dotson, the first wife of Samuel, later married Henry Roomsburg.

1850 CENSUS: **Samuel Drummond** resided in dwelling 984 on page 69.
Sarah Estep appears in dwelling 1289 on page 92. This was the home of her father Thomas Estep.

PAGE 46 EDINBURG DISTRICT   (Microfilm Page 570)

Dwelling 309   Family 309

John Burke	82	1860	2670		Virginia
Robert W. Burke	28	Clerk			"
Susan Pence	25	Housegirl	0	35	"
Sarah A. Berry	39				"

NOTE: The ages for individuals in this household were difficult to read.

John Burke was originally married to a woman named Mary. There was a marriage of John Burke to Polly Coffman on 8 Sep 1811. Her guardian was Edmond Carver. On 21 Jun 1866 90 year old John Burke married **Susannah Pence**. He was listed as the son of Thomas and Sarah. Susannah was the 49 year old daughter of Isaac.

Robert William Burke was the son of John and Mary. He was married to Mary Jane Spengler. Mary Jane was the daughter of Amos Spengler. She resided with her father in **dwelling 269**. Mary Jane Spengler Burke was born 25 Apr 1840 and died 21 Nov 1896. She was buried at the Cedarwood Cemetery in Edinburg. Robert enlisted on 18 Apr 1861 as a private in Company F of the 10th Virginia Infantry. He was detached as an orderly to Colonel Gibbons. He was absent in December of 1861. He was elected as a Lt. with the Hess Cavalry about Apr 1862. He was dropped from the roll of that unit in Oct 1862. Robert was born in Augusta County, Virginia and had originally enlisted at Mt. Jackson. He was appointed Brevet 2nd Lt. in Company E of the 11 Virginia Cavalry. He was absent in November and December of 1862 and was on sick furlough until Feb of 1863. His illness was such that he was forced to appear before the examining board at Staunton General Hospital in May of 1863 regarding his poor health. It was determined that he was unable to perform his duties and he resigned at Edinburg on 23 May 1863. He was a merchant and banker in the post war years in Edinburg. He died in that city in 1914.

RELATED FAMILY:
         Lewis Burke, son of John and Mary, married Mary Estep on 19 Sep 1858 and resided in **dwelling 1850.**

1850 CENSUS: John Burke and his family resided in dwelling 686 on page 48.

Sarah A. Berry appears to have resided with her sister in dwelling 724 on page 51.

PAGE 46 EDINBURG DISTRICT   (Microfilm Page 570)

Dwelling 310   Family 310

Rosanna Newman	35 (Black)	Washerwoman 0	20 Virginia
William Newman	15 (Black)	Farmhand	"

1850 CENSUS: This family does not appear in 1850.

PAGE 46 EDINBURG DISTRICT   (Microfilm Page 570)

Dwelling 311 Family 311

John Turner	35 Day Labor	0	75 Ireland	Can't Read
Mary Turner	24		Virginia	
John D. Turner	6		"	
James W. Turner	4		"	
Michael Turner	2		"	
Charles Turner	6m		"	

NOTE: This was very difficult to read and the researcher does not have a high degree of confidence that this is the correct surname.

PAGE 46 EDINBURG DISTRICT   (Microfilm Page 570)

Dwelling 312   Family 312

James Gumby	59 (Black)	0	20 Virginia
Mary C. Gumby	37 (Black)		"
Ashberry Gumby	12 (Black)		"
William A. Gumby	10 (Black)		"
Milton S. Gumby	8 (Black)		"
Alicia Gumby	6 (Black)		"
James A. Gumby	4 (Black)		"
Victoria Gumby	2 (Black)		"

James Gumby was present in the 1850 census. He resided in the household of **Mary C. Strother**. It appears that James and Mary were formally married sometime during the decade of the 1850's. **Ashberry C. Gumby** and **William Arthur Gumby** were listed in the household at that time. However both of these young males had the surname of Strother. The names of children in this family are very interesting. Names such as **Milton, Alicia** and **Victoria**

were not characteristic of families so recently unshackled
from the bondage of slavery.

1850 CENSUS: **Mary C. Strother** was the head of household
170 on page 12. **James Gumby** resided in the
household.

PAGE 46   EDINBURG DISTRICT   (**Microfilm Page 570**)

Dwelling 313   Family 313

Branson Grandstaff	40	Day Labor	0	150	Virginia
Evaline Grandstaff	42				"
Phillip B. Grandstaff	16				" School
Cemantha Grandstaff	8				" School

Branson Grandstaff the son of Phillip and Mary.
Phillip Grandstaff married Mary Cooper on 6 Aug 1816.
Phillip and his family resided in **dwelling 267**. Branson
was married on 9 Jun 1842 to **Elizabeth Evaline Liggett**.
The bondsman for the marriage was Samuel Bochy. Branson
enlisted on 15 Apr at Keezletown in Company H of the 12th
Virginia Cavalry. He was listed as Bransome in company
records. He was absent on detail at the horse hospital in
September and October of 1863. He was present through
January of 1864. He was reported as AWOL on 18 Feb 1864.
He returned to service in March of the same year. Branson
died prior to 1880.

Phillip Broadus Grandstaff was reported to have
enlisted in Company K of the 12th Virginia Cavalry on 23
May 1862. He was reported as present in the last months
of 1863. Phillip was wounded in action in late January of
1864 at Moorefield, West Virginia. He died of his wounds
on 15 Feb 1864.

Mary Cemantha Grandstaff was married on 8 Dec 1871
to Benjamin F. Parker. Benjamin was a woolen manufacturer
from Yorkshire, England. He was the son of Peter and Mary
and was born ca. 1840.

RELATED FAMILY:
    Joseph F. Grandstaff, brother of Branson,
married Louisa Riddleberger on 28 Oct 1851 and resided in
dwelling 54.
    Jane Grandstaff, sister of Branson, married
William Hisey on 7 Feb 1842 and resided in **dwelling 69**.

Amanda Grandstaff, sister of Branson, married Isaac H. Ritter on 7 Mar 1848 and resided in **dwelling 14.**

1850 CENSUS: **Branson Grandstaff** and his family resided in 691 on page 49.

PAGE 46 EDINBURG DISTRICT (Microfilm Page 570)

Dwelling 314 Family 314

Michael Patton	45	Collier	500	50 Virginia	Can't Read
Susan Patton	40			"	Can't Read
Mary E. Patton	21			"	
John Patton	17	Collier		"	
Ida Patton	12			"	

Michael Patton was married to **Susan Fry** on 12 Dec 1836. Susan was the daughter of John and Catherine. John A. Fry married Catherine Grandstaff on 10 Jun 1815. John A. Fry and his family resided in **dwelling 353.** Michael and Susan's son, George W. Patton resided with his grandparents at the time of this census.

John A. J. Patton was married on 7 Oct 1873 to Sarah Catherine Williams. Sarah was the daughter of Henry and Sarah. Henry Williams married Sarah Burner on 10 Aug 1852. Sarah Catherine and her parents resided in **dwelling 263.** John A. J. Patton appears on the roster of Company C of the 7th Virginia Cavalry.

Sarah Ida V. Patton was born 25 Dec 1857 and died 5 Mar 1938. She was married to Isaac Clinedinst on 12 Nov 1874. Isaac was the son of Isaac and Lydia. Isaac Clinedinst Sr. married Lydia Holler in March of 1825. Lydia Holler Clinedinst and her family resided in **dwelling 322.** Isaac Clinedinst was born 12 Oct 1832 and died 5 Dec 1911. He was a member of Company C of the 7th Virginia Cavalry. Ida and Isaac were buried in the Hawkinson United Methodist Church Cemetery in the vicinity of Mt. Jackson.

RELATED FAMILY:

John A. Fry Jr., brother of Susan, married Sarah Beasley on 27 Oct 1857 and resided in **dwelling 354.**

William Harrison Fry, brother of Susan, married Rosa Coffman on 6 May 1844 and resided in **dwelling 355.**

Ambrose B. Fry, brother of Susan, married Julia Ann Gochenour on 25 Mar 1856 and resided in **dwelling 323**.

Rebecca Fry, sister of Susan, married Lewis Pence on 21 May 1849 and resided in **dwelling 83**.

Matilda Fry, sister of Susan, married Dilman Estep on 12 Feb 1857 and resided in **dwelling 320**.

Seatta Fry, sister of Susan, married David Tisinger on 27 Feb 1854 and resided in **dwelling 1184**.

1850 CENSUS: Michael Patton and his family resided in dwelling 690 on page 49.

PAGE 46 EDINBURG DISTRICT   (Microfilm Page 570)

Dwelling 315   Family 315

Joseph Barton	25	Carpenter	300	75	Virginia
Sarah C. Barton	19				"
William D. Barton	1				"
Mary E. Miller	17				"

Joseph M. Barton was born 29 Jan 1831 and died 2 Sep 1892. He was the son of Levi and Catherine. Levi Barton married Catherine Clinedinst on 1 Mar 1827. Levi Barton and his family resided in **dwelling 318**. Joseph was married on 27 Aug 1857 to **Sarah Catherine Miller**. Sarah was the daughter of Joseph and Sarah. Joseph Miller married Sarah Hausenfluke on 28 Mar 1831. Sarah Hausenfluke Miller is believed to have been a resident of **dwelling 257**. Sarah Catherine was born 22 Sep 1841 and died 12 Apr 1914. Joseph and Sarah were buried in the Union Forge Cemetery in Edinburg.

William D. Barton was born in 1858 and died 21 Jun 1936. He married Mary E. Kelley on 28 Dec 1884. Mary E. Kelley was born in 1862 and died in 1927. William and Mary were buried in the Cedarwood Cemetery. Mary was the daughter of Patrick and Isabella. Patrick Henry Kelly had married Isabella Hockman in December of 1855. Patrick and his family resided in **dwelling 296.**

Mary Elizabeth Miller was the sister of Sarah Catherine Miller Barton. She was married on 28 Dec 1865 to Isaac O. Barton. Mary Elizabeth Miller Barton was born 4 Apr 1842 and died 30 Jun 1897. Isaac O. Barton was a member of the 10th Virginia Infantry. He died 23 Nov 1912. The family is believed to have been buried in the Union

316

Forge Cemetery. Isaac O. Barton was the brother of Joseph
M. Barton.

NOTE: Joseph M. Barton is also thought to have been a
member of the 10th Virginia Infantry. However there are
discrepancies in the data as it is reported in Terrence V.
Murphy's history of that unit.   According to that
information Joseph was born 26 Mar 1835. He was 5'5" with
fair complexion, gray eyes and light hair.   He was a
carpenter. He enlisted in Company C on 18 Apr 1861. He
was elected 3 Cpl on 25 Dec 1861.   He transferred to
Company F on 18 Apr 1862. According to Murphy, Joseph was
discharged on 18 Jul 1862 as a result of his age. Further
the record indicates that he died 16 Aug 1920 and was
buried in Mt. Hebron Cemetery in Winchester. While is it
probable that he was a member of the 10th, his brother also
being a member, it does not seem likely that he would be
discharged as a result of age.   At the time of his
discharge he had not yet reached the age of 30. There is
also a question regarding his burial at the Mt. Hebron
Cemetery.   These two factors place Murphy's data in
question.   Members of the Barton family will have to sort
this out.

PAGE 46 EDINBURG DISTRICT (Microfilm Page 570)

Dwelling 316   Family 316

John W. Heaton	32	Teacher of Music	500	120	Virginia
Julia A. Heaton	32				"
Joseph S. Heaton	3				"
Lucy M. Heaton	2				"
Martha F. Heaton	11m				"

Jonathan W. Heaton was married on 19 Jul 1853 to
Julia Ann Barton. Julia Ann was the daughter of Levi and
Catherine.   Levi Barton married Catherine Clinedinst on 1
May 1827.   Levi and Catherine resided in **dwelling 318.**
Jonathan W. Heaton was commissioned on 18 Apr 1861 as a 1st
Lt. in Company C. He was killed in action on 21 Jul 1861
at Manassas. Jonathan was born 3 Oct 1827 and was buried
in the Union Forge Cemetery in Edinburg. His tombstone
indicates that he "fell at the Battle of Bull Run". Julia
Ann Barton Heaton was married on 24 May 1870 to Phillip
Ruby. Phillip was born 15 Aug 1806 and died 20 Feb 1881.
He was buried at the Ruby Cemetery near Edinburg. Phillip
had originally married Mary Ann Sibert on 2 Dec 1833.
Phillip was the son of Henry and Catherine. Henry Ruby

married Catherine Rodeffer on 9 Jan 1802. Phillip Ruby and his first wife resided in **dwelling 1171**. Julia Ann Barton Heaton Ruby was born 26 Dec 1827 and died 15 Jan 1887. She was buried near Jonathan in the Union Forge Cemetery. In some Shenandoah County records this family name appears as **Eaton**.

Lucy M. Heaton was married on 25 May 1882 to Charles L. Coffman. In marriage records his parents were listed as Reuben and Sarah. Charles was a farmer.

Martha F. Heaton was born 29 Jun 1859 and died 7 Jun 1889. She was married to John Osceola Grandstaff on 23 Oct 1877. Osceola was a laborer at the time of his marriage. He was the son of Milton M. and Emma. Milton M. Grandstaff married Emily "Emma" Roundtree on 19 Nov 1846. Milton Grandstaff and his family resided in **dwelling 61**. Osceola J. Grandstaff was born 4 Apr 1852 and died 13 Dec 1925. Martha and Osceola were buried in the Union Forge Cemetery.

RELATED FAMILY:

Joseph Barton, brother of Julia Ann, married Sarah Catherine Miller on 27 Aug 1857 and resided in **dwelling 315**.

Mary C. Barton, sister of Julia Ann, married George W. Windle on 26 Mar 1854 and resided in **dwelling 317**.

1850 CENSUS: Julia Ann Barton resided with her parents in dwelling 687 on page 49.

PAGE 47 EDINBURG DISTRICT (Microfilm Page 571)

Dwelling 317 Family 317

George Windle	30	Millwright	500	100	Virginia
Mary C. Windle	30				"
William A. Windle	5				"
Samuel R. Windle	1				"

George W. Windle was the son of George and Sarah. George Wendle married Sally Borden on 20 Mar 1807. He was born at North Mountain and died 25 Feb 1904 at the age of 76 years, 5 months and 3 days old. He was married to **Mary C. Barton** on 26 Mar 1854. Mary was the daughter of Levi and Catherine. Levi Barton married Catherine Clindedinst on 1 May 1827. Levi and his family resided in **dwelling**

318. Mary C. Barton Windle was 76 years, two months and 2 days old when she died on 10 Nov 1900. George and Mary were buried in the Cedarwood Cemetery in Edinburg. George Washington Windle enlisted in the Eighth Star New Market Artillery on 4 Mar 1862. He was present for all rolls. He was reassigned to the Danville Artillery in Sep 1862. He was absent sick at Staunton on 15 Jun 1863. He returned to active service on 31 Aug 1863. There is no further record related to his military service.

NOTE: There is a potential problem with this household. Readers are encouraged to view information on **dwelling 32.** It will demonstrate that there was another George W. Windle in this census. He was a resident of the town of Edinburg. Both individuals were approximately the same age and married woman named Mary. The primary confusion involves the record of military service and burial information. It is not clear which of these two couples were buried in Cedarwood Cemetery. The George W. Windle who died on 25 Feb 1904 and is buried in Cedarwood Cemetery lies next to Robert Windle the son of George Windle in **dwelling 32.** Data regarding these two families may be confused. There may be a simple explanation. However, it will necessitate clarification by researchers interested in the Windle.

       William A. Windle was married on 11 Sep 1878 to Caroline Coffelt. He was a farmer. Caroline was the daughter of Israel and Isabella. Israel Coffelt married Isabella Corbin on 3 Jun 1856. Israel and his family resided in **dwelling 1222.**

       Samuel R. Windle was born 27 Jun 1858 and died 7 Apr 1891. He was married on 13 Sep 1881 to Laura V. Artz, the daughter of Samuel A. and Mary. Samuel A. Artz married Mary Lou Miley on 30 Jul 1862. Laura was born 9 Mar 1863 and died 10 Jul 1920. Samuel and Laura were buried in the Union Forge Cemetery in Edinburg. Upon the death of Samuel, Laura V. Artz Windle married William Rhodes. William was the son of Abraham and Sarah. Abraham Rhodes married Sarah Haun on 1 Jun 1849. Abraham and William resided in **dwelling 1877.** William Rhodes was a farmer. He was born 23 Mar 1853 and died 9 Oct 1935. He was buried in the Zion Christian Church Cemetery in Maurertown.

RELATED FAMILY:
       Joseph Windle, brother of George, married Rebecca Ann Newland on 29 Dec 1859 and resided in **dwelling 1450.**

Joseph Barton, brother of Mary, married Sarah Catherine Miller on 27 Aug 1857 and resided in **dwelling 315**.

Julia Ann Barton, sister of Mary, married Jonathan W. Heaton on 19 Jul 1853 and resided in **dwelling 316**.

1850 CENSUS: George Windle was an apprentice millwright. He resided in dwelling 124 on page 9. This was the residence of Jacob Ludwick.

Mary C. Barton resided with her parents in dwelling 687 on page 49.

DRAWING by

Robert Thibodeau

PAGE 47   EDINBURG DISTRICT   (Microfilm Page 571)

Dwelling 318   Family 318

Levi Barton	58	Farmer	3900 400	Virginia
Catherine Barton	61			"
George W. Barton	26	Farmhand		"
Sarah Miller	23			"
Isaac O. Barton	31			"
Emily F. Barton	16			"

Levi Barton was married on 1 May 1827 to Catherine Clinedinst.

George W. Barton was 5'6" with dark complexion, dark eyes and hair. He enlisted on 16 Apr 1862 at Rude's Hill in Company K of the 2nd Virginia Infantry. He was AWOL on 10 Jun 1862 and was fined one months pay. He was absent sick in July and August of 1863. He returned to service in September. George was detailed as an ambulance driver for the brigade from March through August of 1864. He was detailed as a teamster in October and November of 1864. He was admitted to Chimborazo #2 on 11 Feb 1865 with the "camp itch". He was transferred to Chimborazo #1 on 5 Mar 1865. He was taken POW at Richmond Hospital on 3 Apr 1865. He was assigned to the Jackson Hospital at Libby Prison in Newport News and was administered the Oath of Allegiance at Newport News 15 Jun 1865. George returned to Shenandoah County and married Martha Jane Sibert on 1 Jan 1871. She was the daughter of Daniel and Mary Ann. Daniel Sibert married Mary Ann Evans on 27 Jan 1841. Daniel Sibert and his family resided in dwelling 249.

Sarah J. Barton was married on 11 Feb 1858 to Peter E. Miller, the son of Joseph of Peter Miller and Sarah Hausenfluke Miller. Sarah Hausenfluke is believed to have been a resident of dwelling 257. Peter was not in the household at the time of this census. He was the brother of Joseph Barton's wife Sarah Catherine. Peter may have died, because on 4 Mar 1869 Sarah Catherine Barton, daughter of Levi and Catherine, was married to George Knight of Baltimore, Maryland. He was the son of Aaron and Catherine. Sarah O. Knight was buried in Union Forge Cemetery. She was born 24 Apr 1835 and died 25 Nov 1875.

Isaac O. Barton was 75 years old when he died 23 Nov 1912. He was married on 28 Dec 1865 to Mary Elizabeth Miller, the daughter of Joseph of Peter Miller and Sarah

Hausenfluke. Mary Elizabeth was the sister of Peter E.
Miller, the husband of Sarah Barton. Mary Elizabeth Miller
was born 14 Apr 1842 and died 30 Jun 1897. Isaac and Mary
Elizabeth are thought to have been buried in the Union
Forge Cemetery. Isaac was 5'5" with a sallow complexion,
dark hair and gray eyes. He was a laborer when he enlisted
on 18 Apr 1861 at Edinburg in Company C of the 10th
Virginia Infantry. He transferred to Company F on 18 Apr
1862. He was taken POW at Spotsylvania Courthouse on 12
May 1864. He was transferred to Fort Delaware in May of
1864 and was released under the Oath of Allegiance on 10
Jun 1865.

          Emma Frances Barton was married on 3 Sep 1868 to
Henry Jackson Reed of Hardy County, West Virginia. Henry
was the son of Isaac and Mary.

RELATED FAMILY:
          Joseph M. Barton, son of Levi, married Sarah
Catherine Miller on 27 Aug 1857 and resided in **dwelling
315.**
          Julia Ann Barton, daughter of Levi, married
Jonathan W. Heaton on 19 Jul 1853 and resided in **dwelling
316.**
          Mary C. Barton, daughter of Levi, married
George W. Windle on 26 Mar 1854 and resided in **dwelling
317.**

1850 CENSUS: Levi Barton was a resident of dwelling 687
          on page 49.

PAGE 47 EDINBURG DISTRICT   (Microfilm Page 571)

Dwelling 319   Family 319

Jacob Hutchinson   63 Farmer   0 56 Virginia
Margaret Hutchinson   60   "

          Jacob Hutchinson was born 15 Dec 1797 and died
24 Mar 1874. He was the son of George Hutcheson and Mary
Hottel Hutchinson. Jacob was married to **Margaret Mauck** on
10 Jun 1822. The bondsman for their marriage was Jacob Y.
Barnes. Jacob and Margaret resided on a farm on the north
branch of the Shenandoah River. Margaret Mauck Hutchinson
died at the age of 75. They were buried in Union Forge
Cemetery in Edinburg.

322

RELATED FAMILY:
        Charles Hutchinson, brother of Jacob, was married to Eliza Whissen on 15 Mar 1827 and resided in **dwelling 68.**
        Jacob Amos Hutchinson, son of Jacob, was a resident in **dwelling 81.**
        Charles W. Hutchinson, son of Jacob, married Caroline Clinedinst on 6 Apr 1850 and resided in **dwelling 78.**
        Jacob Franklin Hutchinson, son of Jacob, married Mary Ann Long on 4 Sep 1853 and resided in **dwelling 1187.**
        John Hutchinson, son of Jacob, married Mary Margaret Dirting on 20 Oct 1849 and resided in **dwelling 357.**
        William H. Hutchinson, son of Jacob, married Mary Emily Hockman on 14 Feb 1854 and resided in **dwelling 359.**

1850 CENSUS: **Jacob Hutchinson** and his family resided in dwelling 679 on page 48.

PAGE 47 EDINBURG DISTRICT (Microfilm Page 571)

Dwelling 320 Family 320

Dilmon Estep	26 Millwright	530	175	Virginia
Matilda C. Estep	32			"
Charles L. Estep	1			"

    Dilmon Estep was born 31 Mar 1834 and died 4 Jun 1918. He was the son of Reuben and Sarah. Reuben Estep married Sally Foltz on 2 Feb 1833. Dilmon married **Matilda Fry** on 12 Feb 1857. Matilda was the daughter of John and Catherine. John A. Fry married Catherine Grandstaff on 10 Jun 1815 and resided in **dwelling 353.** Matilda Estep was 86 years old when she died on 2 Jan 1915. Dilmon Estep was 5'8 1/2" with dark complexion, light hair and hazel eyes. He enlisted on 18 Apr 1861 at Edinburg in Company C of the 10th Virginia Infantry. He was a 3rd Sgt. and was promoted to 2nd Sgt on 21 Aug 1861. He later transferred to Company F of the 10th on 18 Apr 1862. He served as a private with that unit. He was taken POW at Spotsylvania Courthouse on 12 May 1864. He was assigned to Fort Delaware on 21 May 1864. He took the Oath of Allegiance on 7 Jun 1865. Dilmon was a resident of Clarke County, West Virginia after the war. He died at Millwood, West Virginia.

Charles Lee Estep was born 1 Jan 1859.

RELATED FAMILY:

Ambrose Fry, brother of Matilda, married Julia Ann Gochenour on 25 Mar 1856 and resided in dwelling 323.

Susan Fry, sister of Matilda, married Michael Patton on 12 Dec 1836 and resided in dwelling 314.

John A. Fry Jr., brother of Matilda, married Susan Beasley on 27 Oct 1857 and resided in dwelling 354.

Rebecca Fry, sister of Matilda, married Lewis Pence on 21 May 1849 and resided in dwelling 83.

William Harrison Fry, brother of Matilda, married Rosa Coffman on 6 May 1844 and resided in dwelling 355.

Leatta Fry, sister of Matilda, married David Tisinger on 27 Feb 1854 and resided in dwelling 1184.

1850 CENSUS: There is no record of this family in the 1850 census.

PAGE 47 EDINBURG DISTRICT   (Microfilm Page 571)

Dwelling 321   Family 321

Joseph B. Grandstaff	25	Millwright	300	50	Virginia
Isabella Grandstaff	23				"
John B. Grandstaff	3				"
Henrietta S. Grandstaff	1				"

Joseph Boston Grandstaff was 72 years, 11 months and 6 days old when he died 6 Feb 1897. Joseph was the son of Benjamin and Elizabeth. Benjamin Grandstaff married Elizabeth Clinedinst on 14 Oct 1820. Benjamin Grandstaff and his family resided in dwelling 324. Joseph was married on 25 Mar 1856 to Isabella Larkin, the daughter of John and Nancy. Isabella was born 26 Nov 1837 and died 22 Apr 1910. Joseph and Isabella were buried in the Old Edinburg Cemetery.

John B. Grandstaff was born 15 Apr 1857 and died 10 Oct 1944. He was buried in the Union Forge Cemetery in Edinburg.

RELATED FAMILY:

Isabella Grandstaff, sister of Joseph, wed Jacob Pence 19 Aug 1858 and resided in dwelling 337.

Arabella Grandstaff, sister of Joseph, married John Evy Jr. on 21 Apr 1857 and resided in **dwelling 1167**.

Mary J. Grandstaff, sister of Joseph, married John Chrisman on 22 Apr 1852 and resided in **dwelling 338**.

1850 CENSUS: **Benjamin Grandstaff**, father of Joseph, was located in dwelling 988 on page 69. However, Joseph was not in the household at that time.

Isabella Larkin resided with her mother in dwelling 95 on page 7.

PAGE 47 EDINBURG DISTRICT   (Microfilm Page 571)

Dwelling 322   Family 322

Lydia Clinedinst	60	2200 870	Va.	Cn'tRd
Catherine Clinedinst	29		"	
Lydia A. Clinedinst	20		"	
William R. Clinedinst	19	Farmer	"	
Isaac Clinedinst	27	Day Labor	"	
Augustus Clinedinst	23	Carpenter	"	
Alexander Clinedinst	18	Plasters Apprentice	"	
Virginia Clinedinst	13		"	School

Lydia Holler Clinedinst was born 23 Dec 1799 and died 11 Jun 1880. She was the daughter of Augustine Holler and Katherine Halderman. Augustine and Katherine had married 26 Jul 1798. Lydia was married to Isaac Clinedinst on 7 Mar 1825. Isaac was born 13 Aug 1790 and died 9 Nov 1856. Lydia and Isaac are buried in the Union Forge Cemetery in Edinburg.

Catherine Clinedinst was 53 years, 3 months and 27 days old when she died 21 Feb 1883. According to Holler family records, Catherine was initially married to a man named Getz. No record has been found of this marriage. On 12 Dec 1869 she was married to James Summers. James was the son of Jacob and Rosanna. Jacob Summers married Rosanna Coffman on 8 May 1839. Jacob and his family resided in **dwelling 356**. James Summers was a farmer. He was born 17 Oct 1842 and died 9 Jul 1914. After Catherine died in February of 1883, James was married on 12 Aug of the same year to Lydia Clinedinst, the daughter of Elizabeth. James and Catherine were buried in the Union Forge Cemetery.

Lydia A. Clinedinst was married on 27 Jan 1864 to Nimrod Milton Hoffman. Nimrod was born 14 Jul 1822 and died 19 Apr 1885. Nimrod was the son of Andrew Jackson Hoffman and Frances Stover Hoffman. Nimrod was originally married on 5 Feb 1845 to Mary C. McCord. Mary was the daughter of Catherine. Mary was born 27 Feb 1825 and died 7 Apr 1862. Nimrod Hoffman and his family resided in **dwelling 278.** Mary and Nimrod were buried in the Hoffman Cemetery. Lydia A. Clinedinst died prior to 1870 as Nimrod Hoffman married for the third time. His third wife was Mary Laura Pitman Snapp, the widow of Robert B. Snapp. She and Robert had married on 27 Dec 1855. Mary Laura was the daughter of Phillip and Mary Susan Houston Pitman.

William R. Clinedinst died 2 Aug 1915. He was buried in the Union Forge Cemetery. William had originally married Mary G. Carper. She was from Frederick County, Virginia. Mary was the daughter of William and Mary. Mary Carper Clinedinst died when she was 21 years old. She was buried in the Union Forge Cemetery. On 14 Nov 1872 William was married to Mary C. Griffey, the daughter of Mark and Elizabeth. Mark Griffey and his family resided in **dwelling 926.** Mary C. Griffey Clinedinst died on 23 Sep 1919. She was 65 years old. William Clinedinst joined his brothers as a member of Company C of the 7th Virginia Cavalry.

Isaac Clinedinst was born 12 Oct 1832 and died 5 Dec 1911. He was married to Sarah Ida V. Patton on 12 Nov 1874. Sarah was the daughter of Michael and Susan. Michael Patton married Susan Fry on 12 Dec 1836. Michael and his family resided in **dwelling 314.** Sarah Ida V. Patton Clinedinst was born 25 Dec 1857. She died 5 Mar 1938. Isaac and Sarah were buried in the Hawkinson United Methodist Church Cemetery in Mt. Jackson. Isaac was initially a member of Company C of the 10th Virginia Infantry. He enlisted on 18 Apr 1861 at Harpers Ferry as a private. He was detailed as a teamster in the regimental quartermaster department. No further record of his service with this unit is reported. At some point he joined his brothers in service with Company C of the 7th Virginia Cavalry.

Augustus Clinedinst was born in 1838. He was married on 12 May 1867 to Christena F. Coffman. Christena was the daughter of Lewis and Eveline. Lewis and his family resided in **dwelling 358.** "Tena" F. Coffman Clinedinst was born 27 Oct 1846 and died 12 Oct 1868. She was buried in the Union Forge Cemetery in Edinburg. After the death of Tena, Augustus was married to Anna Jewell on 20 Feb 1873. Anna was the daughter of Fielding and Sarah. Fielding Jewell married Sarah Silfouse on 9 May 1850. Fielding and his family were residents of **dwelling 664**. Augustus Clinedinst enlisted on 18 Apr 1861 in the 10th Virginia Infantry. He was a corporal in Company C. He rose in the ranks from 4th Cpl. to 1st Cpl on 21 Aug 1861. He transferred to Company F of the 10th on 18 Apr 1862. On 10 Oct 1862 he joined his brothers in Company C of the 7th Virginia Cavalry. After the war Augustus and his family moved to Moorefield Junction in West Virginia.

Alexander B. Clinedinst was born 21 Apr 1842 and died 6 Oct 1918. He was married on 9 Mar 1868 to his first cousin Betty Bowers. Elizabeth "Betty" Bowers was the daughter of Reuben Bowers and Mary Holler. Reuben and Mary had married on 8 Aug 1832. Mary was the sister of Lydia Holler Clinedinst. Reuben Bowers and his family resided in **dwelling 1207**. Betty was born 27 Jun 1836 and died 17 Nov 1905. Alexander and Betty were buried in the Union Forge Cemetery. Alexander enlisted in the 10th Virginia Infantry at Harpers Ferry on 18 Apr 1861. He is not found in company records after 1 Mar 1862. He apparently joined his brothers in Company C of the 7th Virginia Cavalry. A. B. Clinedinst was reported to have been wounded during the conflict.

Virginia S. Clinedinst was 21 when she married George L. Hite on 18 Oct 1866. She does not list her parents in the record of marriage. She is not in the household at the time of the 1850 census. George L. Hite was a carpenter.

RELATED FAMILY:
Leah Holler, sister of Lydia, married John Bowman on 12 Jan 1831 and resided in **dwelling 1738**.
Jonathan Holler, brother of Lydia, married Anna Bartley on 18 May 1835 and resided in **dwelling 1619**.
Alexander Holler, brother of Lydia, married Eve Price Coffman on 2 Aug 1841 and resided in **dwelling 1183**.
Isaac Holler, brother of Lydia, married Elizabeth Marshall on 24 Dec 1828 and resided in **dwelling 1591**.
Catherine Holler, sister of Lydia, married Phillip Olinger on 21 Jul 1831 and resided in **dwelling 889**.
Henry Holler, believed to have been the base-born son of Lydia, married Margaret Tasco on 9 May 1842 and resided in **dwelling 1836**.

John Clinedinst, son of Lydia, married Sarah Catherine Bowman on 30 Sep 1858 and resided in **dwelling 261.**

Michael Clinedinst, son of Lydia, married Lydia Miller on 27 Sep 1853 and resided in **dwelling 2064.**

Caroline Clinedinst, daughter of Lydia, married Charles W. Hutchinson on 6 Apr 1850 and resided in **dwelling 78.**

1850 CENSUS: Lydia Holler Clinedinst and her family resided in dwelling 678 on page 48.

PAGE 47 EDINBURG DISTRICT (Microfilm Page 571)

Dwelling 323 Family 323

Ambrose B. Fry	36	Carpenter	1000	1705	Virginia
Julia A. Fry	23				"
Samuel L. Fry	3				"
Joseph H. Fry	1				"
Rebecca Coffelt	15	Housegirl			"

Ambrose B. Fry was born 16 Feb 1825 and died 2 Dec 1889. He was the son of John A. and Catherine. John A. Fry married Catherine Grandstaff on 10 Jun 1815. John and his family resided in **dwelling 353.** Ambrose was married to **Julia Ann Gochenour** on 25 Mar 1856. She was the daughter of Joseph and Christena. Joseph Gochenour married Christena Crabill on 30 Oct 1813. Julia Ann was born 8 Jan 1836 and died 10 Sep 1883. Ambrose and Julia were buried in the Cedarwood Cemetery. Ambrose B. Fry later married Mary Ann Kibler Lineweaver on 14 Oct 1886. Mary Ann was the daughter of William and Christina. William Kibler married Christina Kibler on 13 Nov 1839. Mary Ann's first husband was John Lineweaver. She had married John on 13 Mar 1866. John was the son of John and Susan.

Samuel Luther Fry was born 20 Feb 1857 and died in 1942. He was married to Annie Virginia Bowman. Annie was the daughter of Noah and Sarah. Annie V. Bowman Fry was born 5 Nov 1853 and died 12 May 1925. Samuel and Annie were buried in the Cedarwood Cemetery.

Joseph Henry Fry was born 17 Jan 1859 and died 28 Nov 1946. He was married to Elizbeth Magruder. The date of this marriage is not known. The parents of Elizabeth are not recorded in family records. Elizabeth was born 16 Jan 1859 and died 17 Mar 1933. Joseph and Elizabeth were buried in the Cedarwood Cemetery.

RELATED FAMILY:

> **Matilda C. Fry**, sister of Ambrose, married Dilmon Estep on 12 Feb 1857 and resided in **dwelling 320**.

> **Susan Fry**, sister of Ambrose, married Michael Patton on 12 Dec 1836 and resided in **dwelling 314**.

> **John A. Fry Jr.**, brother of Ambrose, married Susan Beazley on 27 Oct 1857 and resided in **dwelling 354**.

> **Rebecca Fry**, sister of Ambrose, married Lewis Pence on 21 May 1849 and resided in **dwelling 83**.

> **William Harrison Fry**, brother of Ambrose, married Rosa Coffman on 6 May 1844 and resided in **dwelling 355**.

> **Leatta Fry**, sister of Ambrose, married David Tisinger on 27 Feb 1854 and resided in **dwelling 1184**.

1850 CENSUS: **Julia Ann Gocehenour** resided in dwelling 1299 on page 93. This was the residence of Rebecca Keller.

Ambrose Fry resided with his parents in dwelling 693 on page 49.

PAGE 47 EDINBURG DISTRICT **(Microfilm Page 571)**

Dwelling 324 Family 324

Benjamin Grandstaff	66	Shingle Maker	0	106	Virginia
Elizabeth Grandstaff	58				"
George W. Grandstaff	31	Shingle Maker			"
Jacob F. Grandstaff	28	Carpenter			"
William L. Grandstaff	18	Day Labor			"
Joseph U. Grandstaff	5				"

Benjamin Grandstaff was born in 1794 and died 22 Jan 1873. He was the son of Phillip and Elizabeth. Phillip Grandstaff married Elizabeth Haas on 21 Dec 1784. Benjamin was married to **Elizabeth Clinedinst**.

George Watson Grandstaff was married on 12 Nov 1871 to Ann Cornelia Shank. Ann was the daughter of George and Catherine. George W. Shank married Catherine Wendel on 7 Sep 1840. Ann Cornelia died 1 Mar 1914. She was 64 years old. George W. Grandstaff may have served with Confederate troops. The problem in making this determination is complicated by the presence of other men named George W. Grandstaff in Shenandoah County at the time

of this census. One of these individuals was a twenty six
year old who headed **dwelling 13**. There was a George W.
Grandstaff in Company E of the 35th Battalion. Additional
research on this matter is required.

       Jacob Franklin Grandstaff was born 2 Oct 1831
and died 27 Sep 1890. Family records indicate that his
first wife was named Isabella. However, no record of this
marriage has been established and there is reason to
question the accuracy of this report. He was married on
31 Mar 1867 to Elizabeth Bowman. Elizabeth was the
daughter of David. Elizabeth was born 22 Feb 1839 and died
2 Feb 1901. Jacob and Elizabeth were buried in the Lantz-
Bowman Cemetery. Jacob F. Grandstaff was 5'9" with dark
complexion, gray eyes and brown hair. He enlisted on 5 Apr
1862 at Hawkinstown in Myers Company C of the 7th Virginia
Cavalry. He was a private. On 1 May 1862 he enlisted at
Woodstock in Company K of the 12th Virginia Cavalry. He
was AWOL in September of 1862. He was reported as sick
during September and October of 1863. He was detailed as
a courier for court martials in March and April of 1864.
Jacob was paroled at Edinburg 4 May 1865.

       William Lemuel Grandstaff was born 18 Dec 1842
and died 7 Jul 1936. He was married on 30 Apr 1868 to
Sarah F. Burke. Sarah was the daughter of Johnson and
Catherine. Johnson Burke married Catherine Bussey on 8 Feb
1843. Johnson Burke resided in **dwelling 1737**. However,
Sarah F. Burke was a resident in **dwelling 1573** at the time
of this census. Sarah was 62 years, 4 months and 22 days
old when she died 3 Jan 1907. William and Sarah were
buried in the Bethel Lutheran Church Cemetery. William was
a member of the 7th Virginia Cavalry and appears as Lem.

       Joseph Eugene Grandstaff was listed as the son
of Jacob and Isabella. However, absent the marriage record
of Jacob to Isabella this remains open to speculation.
There is the possibility that he was accually the base born
son of Isabella Grandstaff, the daughter of Benjamin
Grandstaff. Isabella had married Jacob Pence on 19 Aug
1858 and resided in **dwelling 337**. This needs to be
investigated further. On 25 Jan 1877 he was married to
Milly Shipe. She was listed as the daughter of Ann.

RELATED FAMILY:
       Joseph Boston Grandstaff, son of Benjamin,
married Isabella Larkin on 25 Mar 1856 and resided in
dwelling 321.

Isabella Grandstaff, daughter of Benjamin, married Jacob Pence on 19 Aug 1858 and resided in **dwelling 337**.

Arabella Grandstaff, daughter of Benjamin, married John Evy Jr. on 21 Apr 1857 and resided in **dwelling 1167**.

Mary J. Grandstaff, daughter of Benjamin, married John Chrisman on 22 Arp 1852 and resided in **dwelling 338**.

Catherine Grandstaff, sister of Benjamin, married John A. Fry on 10 Jun 1815 and resided in **dwelling 353**.

Phillip Grandstaff Jr., brother of Benjamin, married Mary Cooper on 6 Aug 1816 and resided in **dwelling 267**.

George P. Grandstaff, brother of Benjamin, married Mary Reedy on 3 Oct 1810 and resided in **dwelling 63**.

Elizabeth Liggett Grandstaff, sister in law of Benjamin, had married John I. Grandstaff on 27 Feb 1826 and resided in **dwelling 46**. John I. Grandstaff had died in 1852.

Jacob Snapp, brother in law of Benjamin, had married Rebecca Grandstaff on 4 Apr 1831 and resided in **dwelling 44**. Rebecca had died in 1855.

1850 CENSUS: **Benjamin Grandstaff** and his family resided in dwelling 988 on page 69.

PAGE 47 EDINBURG DISTRICT **(Microfilm Page 571)**

Dwelling 325 Family 325

Reuben L. Allen	38 Farmer	17000 6930	Virginia	
Mary M. Allen	24		"	
Helen Q. Allen	15		"	School
Mary A. Allen	13		"	School
William A. Allen	11		"	School
Joseph H. Allen	9		"	School
Sarah E. Allen	7		"	School
John Allen	2		"	

Reuben Lee Allen was born 17 Jan 1822 and died 26 Feb 1896. Reuben was the son of Israel and Sarah. Israel Allen married Sarah Pifer on 22 Apr 1803. He was married on 24 Feb 1844 to Sarah Ann Miller. Sarah Ann Miller was born 14 Jan 1825 and died 7 Mar 1854. On her marriage record she was listed as the daughter of Reuben.

However, on her tombstone in the Old Union Church Cemetery in Mt. Jackson she was listed as the daughter of A.D. Miller. The Allen family history record that she was the daughter of Reuben and Atlantic Ocean Walton Miller. After Sarah's death Reuben Lee Allen was married in November of 1855 to **Mary Margaret Grandstaff**. Mary was the daughter of John and Isabella. John J. Grandstaff married Isabella Murray on 5 Mar 1835. John J. Grandstaff and his family resided in **dwelling 328**. Mary was born 19 Dec 1835 and died 12 Aug 1893. Reuben and Mary Margaret were buried in the Old Edinburg Cemetery. Grandstaff family records indicate that Reuben paid Alonzo "Lon" Frank Grandstaff to take his place as a substitute during the Civil War. Lon was a resident of **dwelling 328**.

Helen Q. Allen was born 23 May 1845 and died 22 May 1867. She had married on 28 May 1866 to William A. Larkin, the son of Andrew and Rebecca. Andrew Larkin married Ann Rebecca Epley on 25 Jul 1838. Andrew and his family resided in **dwelling 1206**. Helen was buried in the Cedarwood Cemetery. William married Mattie Ship on 18 Sep 1873. Mattie was the daughter of Jacob and Dorcas. She was reported to have been from Knox County, Ohio. Mattie and her parents were in Shenandoah County in 1860 and resided in **dwelling 2067**.

Mary Atlanta (Attie) Allen was born in 1847 and died in 1875. She was married to Benjamin F. Murray. Benjamin was the son of James and Margaret. Benjamin was a deputy sheriff at the time of this census. He resided in **dwelling 328**, the household of Sheriff John J. Grandstaff and his wife Isabella Murray Grandstaff. It is probable that Isabella was the sister of Benjamin. Benjamin was born in 1827 and died in 1888. Benjamin and Attie had five children. After Attie died in 1875 Benjamin is believed to have married her sister **Sarah E. Allen**. Sarah was born in 1852 and died in 1920. Benjamin, Attie and Sarah were buried in the Old Edinburg Cemetery.

Joseph Eugene Allen was a liveryman residing in Montana when he married Lurley Arlinton Ludwick on 18 Dec 1894. Lurley was the daughter of John and Sarah. John M. Ludwig married Sarah E. Grandstaff on 16 Aug 1868. Sarah E. Grandstaff Ludwig was the sister of Mary Margaret Grandstaff Allen. Joseph and Lurley were cousins. Joseph was born 21 Jul 1850 and died 11 Feb 1912 in Helena, Montana. Lurley Ludwick Allen was born 24 Nov 1871 and died 31 Jan 1912 in Helena. This marriage produced a child.

John Lee Allen was born 15 Oct 1857 and died 15 Aug 1861.

RELATED FAMILY:

Julia Ann Grandstaff, sister of Mary Margaret, married William Wightman on 20 Jul 1852 and resided in **dwelling 290.**

Joseph M. Allen, probable brother of Reuben, married Mary Catherine Walton on 10 Mar 1845 and resided in **dwelling 558.**

Israel Allen, probable brother of Reuben, and his wife Amanda West (married ca. 1842) resided in **dwelling 564.**

Catherine Kingree Allen, was the sister in law of Reuben. She had married John Jackson Allen on 23 Feb 1854. John Jackson Allen died 16 Aug 1858. Catherine resided in **dwelling 586.**

Richard Miller, brother in law of Reuben, had married Mary Allen. Mary Allen Miller died 21 Dec 1841. Richard Miller resided in **dwelling 291.**

1850 CENSUS: **Reuben Lee Allen** and his family resided in dwelling 677 on page 48.

Mary Margaret Grandstaff resided with her parents in dwelling 712 on page 50.

PAGE 48 EDINBURG DISTRICT (Microfilm Page 572)

Dwelling 326 Family 326

Henry Funk	40	Farmhand O	122	Virginia	
Sarah A. Funk	33			"	
James W. Funk	13			"	School
Charles Funk	11			"	School
Samuel Funk	9			"	School
Angeline Funk	7			"	School
John C. Hambleton Funk	4			"	
Mary E. V. Funk	1			"	

1850 CENSUS: **Henry Funk** and his family resided in dwelling 1845 on page 133. There is no other record of their presence in Shenandoah County.

333

PAGE 48 EDINBURG DISTRICT   (Microfilm Page 572)

Dwelling 327   Family 327

Abraham Stover	44 Miller	0 302	Virginia
Rachel A. Stover	37		"
Sarah A. Stover	11		"
Martin L. Stover	5		"
Benjamin F. Stover	3		"
Harvey Smootz	27 Farmer		"
Ann M. Stover	3m		"

Abraham Stover was married on 16 Dec 1848 to Rachel Ann Smootz. She was the daughter of John and Catherine. John Smootz married Catherine Kern on 29 Dec 1821.

Sarah Jane Stover, daughter of Abraham and Rachel, was born in Rockingham County, Virginia. She married Edwin G. Stover on 19 May 1870. Edwin was a carpenter from Augusta County, Virginia. He was the son of Daniel and Rachel.

Harvey Smootz was the brother of Rachel Ann Smootz Stover. He was a member of Company K of the 7th Virginia Cavalry. He worked in the company commissary. Harvey died 14 Feb 1905 at the age of 74. He was buried at the Valley Pike Brethran Church Cemetery.

RELATED FAMILY:
Catherine Kern Smootz, mother of Rachel and Harvey, resided in dwelling 920.
Henry M. Smootz, brother of Rachel and Harvey, resided in dwelling 919.

1850 CENSUS: Harvey Smootz resided with his parents in dwelling 1474 on page 105.

DRAWING

by

Michael

Varnadore

PAGE 48   EDINBURG DISTRICT   (Microfilm Page 572)

Dwelling 328   Family 328

John J. Grandstaff	49	High Sheriff	0	830	Virginia
Isabella A. Grandstaff	46				"
George J. Grandstaff	21	Deputy Sheriff			"
Sidney Grandstaff	19				"
Frank A. Grandstaff	16				" School
Sarah E. Grandstaff	13				" School
Alelia A. Grandstaff	8				" School
William L. Grandstaff	4				"
Margaret Murray	69		0	7500	Maryland
Mary A. Murray	41				Virginia
Benjamin F. Murray	31	Deputy Sheriff			"
Amos Murray	23	Farmhand			"

John Jackson Grandstaff was the son of George and Mary. George P. Grandstaff married Mary Reedy on 17 Mar 1810. According to family history he married his first wife Julia Skyrock in 1833. John was married on 5 Mar 1835 to **Isabella Murray**. Isabella was the daughter of James and Margaret. Her mother, **Margaret Murray** resided in this household. Isabella Murray Grandstaff was born in 1812 and died 25 Aug 1877. John died 9 May 1884 at the age of 71 years, 6 months and 22 days old. This couple was buried in the Old Edinburg Cemetery.

George J. Grandstaff was born 1 May 1839 and died 12 Aug 1892. He was married to Anna R. Matthews, the daughter of Thomas P. and Elizabeth Borden Matthews. Anna R. Matthews Grandstaff was born 10 May 1849 and died 14 Dec 1924. George and Anna were buried near her parents in the Cedarwood Cemetery. George J. Grandstaff had a distinguished military career. He was 5'7" with fair complexion, gray eyes and light hair. He enlisted 5 Apr 1862 as Hawkinstown in Myers Company (Company C) of the 7th Virginia Cavalry. He joined Company K of the 12th Virginia Cavalry on 1 May 1862. He rose from the rank of private and was appointed a captain in Company K on 15 Aug 1862. He was present throughout the 1862,63 and 64 years. Unofficial sources indicated that George commanded the regiment after the death of Major Knott on 6 Apr 1865. He was paroled at Edinburg on 4 May 1865. Historian John Wayland has recounted the exploits of Captain Grandstaff when he set out in pursuit, from Edinburg, of Union troops that had captured some local forces. Fighting with a make shift unit of Shenandoah County men home on leave he was

able to secure the freedom of the captured forces while
inflicting casulties on their forces.   After the war he
served for a time as a clerk in Washington, D.C.   He
returned to Shenandoah County and served as Commissioner
of Revenue and was eventually elected to the Virginia House
of Delegates in 1881 until 1883.   He is reported to have
participated in the 1884 parade of veterans at Staunton,
Virginia.

        Rebecca Sidney Grandstaff was 37 years, 6
months and 26 days old when she died on 13 Dec 1878.
Sidney married Solomon K. Moore on 6 Dec 1866. Solomon was
the son of Reuben and Sarah.   Reuben Moore married Sarah
Kingrey on 18 Dec 1815. Solomon Moore was a widower at the
time of this marriage.   He had married Wilhelmina Tate
Pennybacker on 25 Nov 1852. He and Wilhelmina resided in
dwelling 611 at the time of this census. Wilhelmina died
6 Feb 1861.   Sidney Grandstaff Moore and Wilhelmina Tate
Pennybacker Moore were both buried in the Old Union
Cemetery in Edinburg.   James and Louise Wilson have
produced a booklet on the town of Edinburg during the Civil
War.   In their work they tell an anecdote of Sidney and her
sister Sarah. One day Sidney and Sarah, or Sac as she was
known, set off from their home beyond the Massie woods to
run errands in the town of Edinburg. On the way they were
captured by Yankees. They were questioned regarding their
destination.   Sidney was constantly pleading for their
freedom with the promise they would inform no one   that
Yankee forces were in the area. Sac was angry and was not
as   willing   to   humble   herself   before   the   intruders.
Eventually Sidney was able to convince the troops that they
should be released.   However, the commanding officer
insisted that two of his men escort the girls into town.
Thus it was that the Grandstaff sisters arrived in town
with two soldiers marching at their side.   When the party
reached their destination the young men removed their hats,
bowed deeply and left Sidney and Sac standing in the street
a bit humiliated.

        Alonzo "Lon" Frank Grandstaff was born in 1843
and died 31 Mar 1916. He was married to Cora Alice Allen
on 19 Dec 1868. Cora was the daughter of Joseph and Mary.
Joseph M. Allen married Mary Catherine Walton on 10 Mar
1845.   Joseph M. Allen and his family resided in **dwelling**
588. Cora was born in 1846 and died in November of 1908.
Alonzo and Cora are buried in the New Mt. Jackson Cemetery.
Alonzo was 5'7" with fair complexion, hazel eyes and brown
hair.   He enlisted on 10 May 1862 at Woodstock in Company

K of the 12 Virginia Cavalry. Alonzo was detailed with the provost guard at Brigade Headquarter in September and October of 1863. The March 31 1864 roll indicates that he was absent with detached service. He was present for the rest of 1864 and was paroled at Edinburg on 4 May 1865. Grandstaff family history indicates that Lon originally entered the service as a paid substitute for Reuben Allen. Reuben Allen resided in **dwelling 325.**

Sarah Ellen Grandstaff died 26 Oct 1921. She was married on 16 Aug 1868 to John Morgan Ludwick. John was the son of George and Matilda. John was a miller by trade and was born in Clarke County. He was born ca. 1843. He was 6' with dark complexion, black hair and blue eyes. He enlisted on 10 Jul 1861 at Winchester as a private in Company A of the 10th Virginia Infantry. He was absent sick with typhoid fever in Apr 1862 until Jan 1863. He was absent again as a result of his illness from May 1863 until Oct 1863. John was paroled at Edinburg on 5 Apr 1865. He eventually entered the Robert E. Lee Confederate Soldiers Home in Richmond. He died there on 28 Sep 1927 and was buried in the Hollywood Cemetery in Richmond.

Lelia A. Grandstaff was married on 18 Feb 1925 to Martin A. Ashby of Jefferson County, West Virginia. Martin was the son of Martin and Elizabeth.

William Locke Grandstaff died 7 Jan 1925. He was married on 9 Nov 1881 to Martha E. Neff. Martha was the daughter of Michael and Catherine.

Mary Ann Murray, was the sister of Isabella. She married Thomas Corbin on 2 Nov 1869. Thomas was a widower from Culpepper, Virginia. He was the son of Thomas and Susan. Thomas resided in **dwelling 1585.** He had originally married Christina Coffman on 4 Mar 1823. Christina died on 8 Jul 1862.

Benjamin F. Murray was the brother of Isabella. He was married to Mary A. Allen on 26 Jan 1864. Mary Attie Allen was born in 1847 and died in 1875. She was the daughter of Reuben Lee Allen and Sarah Ann Miller. Reuben and Sarah had married on 24 Feb 1844. Mary Attie Allen and her family resided in **dwelling 325.** Upon the death of Mary, Benjamin married her sister Sarah E. Allen. Sarah was born in 1852 and died in 20 Mar 1920. Death records indicate that she died in Delaware. Benjamin was born in 1827 and died in 1888. Benjamin Murray and both of his wives were buried in the Old Edinburg Cemetery. Benjamin and Harrison Holt Riddleberger began the **10TH LEGION BANNER** in Apr of 1870. This was a weekly periodical. Harrison Holt Riddleberger eventually was elected as a United States Senator from Virginia.

RELATED FAMILY:

      Mary Frances Grandstaff, sister of John, married William J. Dinges on 25 May 1847 and resided in **dwelling 58.**

      Elizabeth Ann Grandstaff, sister of John, married William J. Koontz on 12 Aug 1837 and resided in **dwelling 60.**

      Milton M. Grandstaff, brother of John, married Emily J. A. Frye on 19 Nov 1846 and resided in **dwelling 61.**

      Phillip Marcus Grandstaff, brother of John, married Sarah Miller and resided in **dwelling 62.**

      Artemisia Grandstaff, sister of John, married Richard Miller on 18 Jan 1842 and resided in **dwelling 291.**

      Ellen M. Grandstaff, sister of John, married John R. Miller and resided in **dwelling 53.**

      Mary Margaret Grandstaff, daughter of John and Isabella, married Reuben L. Allen on 14 Nov 1855 and resided in **dwelling 325.**

      Julia Ann Grandstaff, daughter of John and Isabella, married William Wightman on 20 Jul 1852 and resided in **dwelling 290.**

1850 CENSUS: **John J. Grandstaff** and his family resided in dwelling 712 on page 50.

      Benjamin F. Murray resided with John Gatewood and his family in dwelling 249 on page 18.

PAGE 48 EDINBURG DISTRICT (Microfilm Page 572)

Dwelling 329 Family 329

George Bowman	20	Day Labor	0	400	Virginia	Cn't Rd
Martha Bowman	21				"	Can't Read
James W. Bowman	8m				"	

      No marriage record has been discovered for George and Martha. It is believed that **George E. Bowman** was the son of Samuel and Elizabeth. There was a marriage reported for Samuel Bowman and Elizabeth Colback. George was born 20 Mar 1840 and was a member of Captain George J.

Grandstaff's Company in the 12th Virginia Cavalry. He was
killed in action on May 6, 1864 at Spotsylvania Courthouse.
It is believed that he was married to **Martha Pence**. Martha
was the daughter of Joseph and Mahala. Joseph Pence
married Mahala Grim on 8 Sep 1836. Joseph and Mahala
resided in **dwelling 305**. On 23 Dec 1868, the widowed
Martha Pence Bowman married John Crawford. John had been
born in Scotland. He was a carpenter and was the son of
John and Mary.

RELATED FAMILY:

       Rebecca J. Pence, sister of Martha, married
William Ort on 6 Jan 1857 and resided in **dwelling 248**.

       Sarah Catherine Bowman, sister of George,
married John Clinedinst on 30 Sep 1858 and resided in
dwelling 261.

       Mary Frances Bowman, sister of George,
resided in the household of Phillip Grandstaff. They
resided in **dwelling 267**.

1850 CENSUS: **George E. Bowman** and his family resided in
    dwelling 1675 on page 120.
    Martha Pence and her parents resided in
    dwelling 992 on page 69.

PAGE 48 EDINBURG (Microfilm Page 572)

Dwelling 330 Family 330

Gabriel Jenkins   22 Day Labor Virginia Just Married
                                             Can't Read
Rebecca F. Jenkins 19   "   Just Married

       Gabriel Jenkins was the son of John and Nellie.
He was born in Page County, Virginia. Gabriel was married
on 21 Jun 1859 to **Rebecca Frances Drummond**. Rebecca was
the daughter of Mary Drummond. Rebecca's mother Mary
Drummond, reportedly the daughter of Thornton, had married
William Williams on 20 Aug 1857. Of interest is the fact
that Rebecca Frances Drummond was also listed in the
household of her mother and step-father. They resided in
dwelling 1172. Gabriel Jenkins enlisted on 2 Apr 1862 at
New Market in Company E of the 12th Virginia Cavalry. He
was a POW at Poolesville on 9 Sep 1862. He was exchanged
at Aikens Landing on 27 Sep 1862. He remained absent from
his unit until Sep of 1863. He was absent sick in November
and December of 1863. Unofficial sources indicate that he
was wounded at the Wilderness. He was buried at the

Reliance United Methodist Church Cemetery in Warren County, Virginia.

1850 CENSUS: There was no record of these individuals in 1850.

PAGE 49   EDINBURG DISTRICT   (Microfilm Page 573)

Dwelling 331   Family 331

Jacob Bowman	54	Farmer	10,115	2687	Virginia	
Mary Bowman	53				"	Can't Read
Robert Bowman	27	Farmhand			"	
Whiten Bowman	23	Farmhand			"	
Elizabeth Bowman	21	Housegirl			"	

Jacob Bowman was the son of John and Mary. John of David Bowman married Mary Lantz on 13 Mar 1805. Jacob was 84 years and 8 days old when he died on 28 Dec 1889. He was married to **Mary Fravel** on 19 Sep 1829. George Lantz was the bondsman for this marriage. Mary was the daughter of Jacob and Rebecca Snyder Fravel. Mary was born 16 Feb 1807 and died 28 Apr 1874. Jacob and Mary were buried in the Lantz-Bowman Cemetery.

Robert Bowman was born 19 Nov 1832. He enlisted on 10 Mar 1862 in Myers Company. This was Company C of the 7th Virginia Cavalry. He was a private and was reported as present at the 30 Apr 1862 muster. The only other official information of his service in this company reveals that he was absent with leave in Shenandoah County in November of the same year to find a new horse as his had broken down. Unofficial records indicate that he later served with the 12th Virginia Cavalry. The **Rockingham Register** for 24 Jul 1863 indicates that he was killed in action near Upperville on 21 Jun 1863 when a ball entered the left side of his heart. His tombstone in the Lantz-Bowman Cemetery confirms the date of his death and indicates that the was "killed at the battle of Goose Creek in Loudoun County, Virginia."

Whiten Bowman was born 19 Jun 1836 and died 14 Dec 1895. He was married on 7 Feb 1866 to Frances "Fanny" E. Rosenberger. Fanny was the daughter of Jacob and Anna. Jacob Rosenberger married Anna Rinker on 18 Jun 1830. Jacob and his family resided in **dwelling 1472**. Fanny was born 5 Feb 1844 and died 17 Feb 1919. Whiten Bowman was reported to have been a member of the 7th Virginia Cavalry.

He attained the rank of Corporal. He was later elevated,
according to family records to the rank of Lieutenant.
Whiten and Fanny were buried in the St. Johns United Church
of Christ Cemetery in Edinburg.

Elizabeth Bowman is not mentioned as a member
of this family in the **Hottel Family** history. However, she
does appear in the household at the time of the 1850
census.

Sarah Dodson may have been the daughter of
Moses and Diana. Moses Dodson married Diana Weatherholtz
on 23 Sep 1844. Moses and his family resided in **dwelling
1242**.

RELATED FAMILY:
William Bowman, son of Jacob and Mary,
married Sarah Rosenberger on 26 Oct 1854 and resided in
dwelling 333.
Samuel Fravel, brother of Mary, married
Polly Painter on 20 Apr 1836 and resided in **dwelling 348**.
Eli Fravel, brother of Mary, married Mary
Coffelt on 31 Aug 1835 and resided in **dwelling 1228**.
Jacob Fravel, brother of Mary, married
Mahala Cline on 14 Oct 1843 and resided in **dwelling 1227**.
William Fravel, brother of Mary, married
Leah Haun on 16 Oct 1845 and resided in **dwelling 1808**.
Rebecca Fravel, sister of Mary, married
Jacob Lantz on 18 Apr 1837 and resided in **dwelling 1173**.
Samuel, **David**, **Ann** and **Lydia Bowman**,
brothers and sister of Jacob, resided in **dwelling 350**.

1850 CENSUS: Jacob **Bowman** and his family resided in
dwelling 2127 on page 153.
Sarah Dodson is believed to have been the
daughter of Moses and Diana. She resided
with her parents in dwelling 1285 on page
91.

PAGE 49 EDINBURG DISTRICT (Microfilm Page 573)

Dwelling 332 Family 332

Peter Waserman	61 Day Labor	200	106	Germany
Christina Waserman	51			" Cn't Rd
Peter Waserman	19 Day Labor			"

This family often appears as **Waterman** in Shenandoah County records. **John Peter Waterman** was born 30 Jun 1840 and died 24 Oct 1913. He was married on 17 Dec 1872 to Susan Long. Susan was the daughter of John and Elizabeth. She was born in Rockingham County, Virginia. Her parents have not been identified. There is a marriage record in Rockingham County, Virginia which indicates that John Long married Elizabeth Swanson on 1 Feb 1838. Elizabeth Long died prior to 1860 as John Long married Rebecca Campbell. John Long, his wife Rebecca and daughter Susan resided in **dwelling 1028**. Susan Long Waterman was born 3 Mar 1845 and died 10 Jan 1911. John and Susan were buried at the St. Johns United Church of Christ Cemetery in Edinburg. Peter Waterman enlisted on 24 Mar 1862 in Company G of the 33rd Virginia Infantry. He was absent during the month of October. He was promoted to corporal on 20 Mar 1863. He was admitted to Charlottesville Hospital with a gun shot wound on 8 May 1864 and was sent to Staunton on 13 May 1864. A wartime diary in John Wayland's history indicates that on "Mar 11 1865 the Yankees at Hamburg. Cold day. Took A. Walker prisoner, J. Lutz and P. Waterman."

RELATED FAMILY:

      George P. Wasterman, a resident of **dwelling 349** may have had some relationship to this family.

1850 CENSUS: Peter Waterman resided in dwelling 1293 on page 92. This was the residence of Henry and Elizabeth Sippel. This was a couple who were also from Germany.

PAGE 49 EDINBURG DISTRICT   (Microfilm Page 573)

Dwelling 333   Family 333

William Bowman	29 Farmer	575	501	Virginia	
Sarah Bowman	26			"	
John Bowman	4			"	
Charles M. Bowman	3			"	
David A. Bowman	8m			"	
James A. P. Fravel	12			"	School
Kenchesca Garlach	12			Germany	

      William Bowman was the son of Jacob and Mary Fravel Bowman. Jacob Bowman and other family members resided in **dwelling 331**. William Bowman was born 2 Oct 1830 and died 30 Dec 1872. William is reported to have been a teamster for the Confederacy during the war. No record of his service has been located. However, there was a William M. Bowyers in the 10th Virginia Infantry. He enlisted on 10 Dec 1862 as a private in Company F at Woodstock and was detailed as a teamster with the ordnance train. In October of 1863 he was assigned as a teamster with Major Harmon's headquarters. This individual was paroled at New Market on 20 May 1865. He was described as being 5'6" with a florid complexion, light hair and brown eyes. It is important to remember that this may not have been the individual in this household. The fact that William M. Bowyers served as a teamster in the 10th Virginia Infantry with a unit from Woodstock is a source for possible speculation. William Bowman was married on 26 Oct 1854 to **Sarah Rosenberger**. Sarah was the daughter of Jacob and Anna. Anna Rinker married Jacob Rosenberger on 18 Jun 1830. Jacob Rosenberger and his family resided in **dwelling 1472**. Sarah Rosenberger was the sister of William's brother Whiten's wife Fanny. Sarah was born 14 Jul 1833 and died 1 Oct 1906. William and Sarah were buried in the Lantz-Bowman Cemetery.

John Solon Bowman was born 14 Oct 1855 and died 27 Apr 1922. He was married first to Sarah Ellen Ruby on 20 Feb 1879. Sarah was the daughter of Leah Ruby. Sarah Ellen was born 6 Jun 1855 and died 13 Mar 1884. Upon the death of Sarah, John was married to Elizabeth Hawkins on 29 Apr 1888. Elizabeth was the daughter of Rebecca. The **Hottel Family History** indicates that John married for the third time on 10 Mar 1890 to Susan V. Newham of Pendleton County, Virginia. Susan was born 18 Jun 1865 and died 20 Mar 1938. John and Susan were buried at the Pleasant View Memorial Gardens Cemetery near Edinburg.

Charles M. Bowman was born 22 May 1856 and died 5 Aug 1919. He was married on 31 Dec 1878 to Mary C. Painter. Mary was the daughter of Henry and Margaret. Henry Painter married Margaret Bowman on 8 Nov 1855. Henry and his family resided in **dwelling 346**. Mary C. Painter Bowman was born 12 Oct 1856 and died 1 Oct 1904. Charles and Mary were buried in the Cedarwood Cemetery in Edinburg. Charles M. Bowman served as the Commissioner for the Madison District of Shenandoah County.

David "Dewitt" Absalom Bowman was born 8 Mar 1860 and died 13 Jun 1937. He was married on 17 Feb 1888 to Mary Catherine Borden. Mary Catherine was the daughter of Joseph and Martha Matilda Lee Borden. Joseph Borden married Martha Matilda Lee on 14 Nov 1857. Joseph and his family were located in **dwelling 1896**. She was born 11 Mar 1862 and died in 1941. David and Mary Catherine were buried in the Massanutten Cemetery.

1850 CENSUS: **William Bowman** resided with his parents in dwelling 2127 on page 153.
Sarah Rosenberger resided with her parents in dwelling 1305 on page 93.

PAGE 49 EDINBURG DISTRICT (Microfilm Page 573)

Dwelling 334 Family 334

Rebecca Speigle   66 0 275   Virginia Can't Read

        Rebecca Spigel is thought to have been the daughter of John and Elizabeth. John Spigle married Elizabeth Sockman on 9 Mar 1791. Elizabeth was the daughter of Frederick. Elizabeth Sockman Spigel married George Root on 25 Sep 1800. In the 1850 census Rebecca was a resident in the household of her mother Elizabeth Root. It appears that Rebecca never married.

1850 CENSUS: **Rebecca Spigel** resided with Elizabeth Sockman Spigel Root in dwelling 2128 on page 153.

PAGE 49 EDINBURG DISTRICT (Microfilm Page 573)

Dwelling 335 Family 335

George Lantz	77 Farmer	10210 15575	Virginia	
Robert Lantz	22		"	
Sarah Bowman	40		"	Can't Read
Artemisia E. Bowman	8		"	School

        George Lantz was born in 1788 and died 8 Dec 1869. He was married to Christina Maphis on 27 Jan 1818. Christina died 22 Dec 1837 at the age of 42. She was the daughter of John Maphis. The 1850 census reflects that George and Christina were the parents of triplets. George was a very wealthy man and gave large sums of money to charity. One of his contributions was to the Massanutten Academy. George and Christina were buried in the Lantz-Bowman Cemetery.

        Robert M. Lantz was born 13 Nov 1836 and died 7 Sep 1915. He was a 2nd Lieut. in Company C of the 7th

Virginia Cavalry. It is reported that he received a wound
in combat. Robert was married on 11 Feb 1868 to Virginia
C. Murray Baker. Virginia was the daughter of James and
Margaret. Margaret Murray resided in **dwelling 328.**
Virginia died 3 Oct 1870 at the age of 37 years, 11 months
and 13 days old. Robert M. Lantz later married Ann Rebecca
Jackson, the daughter of Alexander and Mary Shull Jackson.
Ann Rebecca died 19 Jan 1909 at the age of 70.

RELATED FAMILY:
            Christina Lantz, the daughter of George,
married Samuel Hamman on 1 Apr 1850 and resided in **dwelling
1403.**

1850 CENSUS: **George Lantz** and his triplets resided in
            dwelling 2131 on page 152.

PAGE 49 EDINBURG DISTRICT (Microfilm Page 573)

Dwelling 336 Family 336

Jacob Estep	26 Farmhand 100	50	Virginia
Mary J. Estep	22		"
Robert J. Estep	3		"
Charles H. Estep	8m		"

            Jacob Estep Jr. was the son of Jacob and Mary.
On 12 Dec 1825 there was a marriage in Shenandoah County
for Jacob Hestep to Mary Flowers. Jacob's mother is
believed to have been present in **dwelling 1855.** These may
have been his parents. Jacob Jr. married Mary Jane Barton
on 10 Nov 1854. Mary Jane was the daughter of Nathaniel
and Elizabeth. Nathaniel Barton married Elizabeth Barton
on 16 Apr 1836. Nathaniel and Elizabeth may have been
divorced. Nataniel Barton resided in **dwelling 1751.**
Elizabeth Miller Barton had returned to the household of
her father Peter Miller. They resided in **dwelling 1615.**
Mary J. Barton Estep died 4 Jun 1906. Jacob had preceded
her in death. A Jacob Estep appears on the roll of the
12th Virginia Cavalry. Company records indicate that he
was born 5 Dec 1834. He was 5'8" with dark complesion,
black eyes and dark hair. He enlisted in Company K on 14
Aug 1862 at Woodstock. He was present in Sep/Oct 1863 and
was reported as AWOL in Nov/Dec of that year. Jacob was
paroled at Winchester on 18 Apr 1865 and died 9 Oct 1897
at Woodstock.

Robert J. Estep was married on 16 Mar 1879 to Lucretia Holler, the daughter of Henry and Margaret. Henry Holler married Margaret Tasco on 9 May 1842. Henry Holler and his family resided in **dwelling 1836**. Holler family history reports that Lucretia died in 1879 the same year as her marriage.

Charles Henry Estep was born 29 Sep 1858 and died 8 Nov 1935. He was married on 25 Dec 1879 to Phoebe E. Reynolds, the daughter of John and Lydia Wolverton Foster Reynolds. Lydia was a widow at the time of their marriage on 22 Mar 1859. John Reynolds and his family resided in **dwelling 1226**. Phoebe E. Reynolds Estep was born 12 Dec 1861 and died 12 Mar 1933. Charles and Phoebe were buried in the Fisher Hill Cemetery near Strasburg.

RELATED FAMILY:

John J. **Barton**, brother of Mary Jane, resided in **dwelling 350**.

Mary Estep, perhaps the sister of Jacob, married Lewis Burke on 19 Sep 1858 and resided in **dwelling 1580**.

1850 CENSUS: Mary Jane Barton resided in the household of her father. They were residents of dwelling 17 on page 2.

PAGE 49   EDINBURG DISTRICT   (Microfilm Page 573)

Dwelling 337   Family 337

Jacob Pence	24	Farmhand 0	170	Virginia	Can't Read
Isabella Pence	23			"	
Samuel E. Pence	1			"	

Jacob Pence was reported to have been the son of Joseph and Martha. Martha is specifically mentioned as "Martha Beach". This was rather unusual in marriage records for this period. On 5 Jan 1835 there was a marriage of Joseph Pence to Martha Beach. In 1850, 14 year old Jacob Pence resided with Joseph Pence and his wife Mahala. Joseph Pence had married Mahala Grim on 8 Sep 1836. It is probable that Martha Beach Pence had died in childbirth in early 1836. Joseph Pence and Mahala Grim Pence resided in **dwelling 305**. Jacob Pence married **Isabella Grandstaff** on 19 Aug 1858. Isabella was the daughter of Benjamin and Elizabeth Clinedinst Grandstaff. Benjamin Grandstaff and his family resided in **dwelling 324**.

Military records for Company G of the 33rd Virginia
Infantry indicate that a Jacob Pence enlisted on 10 Aug
1862. Eighteen days later, on 28 Aug 1862, he was killed
in action at Manassas. It is not known if this was the
same individual. It is known that Isabella, Belle Pence,
was a widow on 4 Jan 1877 when she married John Scroggins.
John was the son of William and Polly. John Scroggins had
married Mary Ann Piggins on 11 Feb 1836 in Frederick
County, Virginia. John Scroggins and his wife Mary Ann
resided in **dwelling 256**. Isabella Grandstaff Pence
Scroggins was born in 1842 and died in 1885. She was
buried in the Old Edinburg Cemetery.

RELATED FAMILY:
> **Joseph Boston Grandstaff**, brother of
Isabella, married Isabella Larkin on 25 Mar 1850 and
resided in **dwelling 321**.
> **Arabella Grandstaff**, sister of Isabella,
married John Evy Jr. on 21 Apr 1857 and resided in **dwelling
1167**.
> **Mary Grandstaff**, sister of Isabella, married
John Chrisman on 22 Apr 1852 and resided in **dwelling 338**.
> **Rebecca J. Pence**, sister on Jacob, married
William H. Ort on 6 Jan 1857 and resided in **dwelling 248**.
> **Martha Pence**, sister of Jacob, married
George E. Bowman and resided in **dwelling 329**.

1850 CENSUS: Jacob Pence resided with his father Joseph
and step mother Mahala Grim Pence in
dwelling 992 on page 69.
Isabella Grandstaff resided in the household
of her parents in dwelling 988 on page 69.

PAGE 49 EDINBURG DISTRICT (Microfilm Page 573)

Dwelling 338 Family 338

John Chrisman	38	Shoemaker	0	125	Germany
Mary Chrisman	26				Va. Cn't Rd
William B. Chrisman	8	.			"
Benjamin Chrisman	6				"
Emily F. Chrisman	4				"
Henry L. Chrisman	2				"
Sarah A. Chrisman	3m				"

John Chrisman married **Mary J. Grandstaff** on 22
Apr 1852. She was the daughter of Benjamin and Elizabeth

Clinedinst Grandstaff. Benjamin and his family resided in **dwelling 324.**

RELATED FAMILY:

        Joseph Boston Grandstaff, brother of Mary Jane, married Isabella Larkin on 25 Mar 1850 and resided in **dwelling 321.**

        Arabella Grandstaff, sister of Mary Jane, married John Evy Jr. on 21 Apr 1851 and resided in **dwelling 1167.**

        Isabella Grandstaff, sister of Mary Jane, married Jacob Pence on 19 Aug 1858 and resided in **dwelling 337.**

1850 CENSUS: **John Chrisman** resided in dwelling 1119 on page 79.

                  Mary J. Grandstaff resided with her parents in dwelling 988 on page 69.

PAGE 49 EDINBURG DISTRICT   **(Microfilm Page 573)**

Dwelling 339 Family 339

Absalom Painter	37	Farmer	3450	571	Virginia
Helena Painter	33				"
Ansobelia Painter	14				" School
Nathaniel Painter	12				" School
Wesley Painter	9				" School

      Absalom Painter was born 16 Jan 1822 and died 18 Aug 1868. He was married to **Helena Emswiller.** Helena was the daughter of Jacob and Elizabeth. There are two marriage listed in Shenandoah County records for a Jacob Emswiller to woman named Elizabeth. The marriage of Jacob Emswiller to Elizabeth Lutz on 26 May 1825 seems to have the highest probability of being Helena's parents. Jacob and his family resided in **dwelling 1478.** Absalom appears to have died prior to 1873 as Helena Emswiller Painter was married on 3 Feb 1873 to Herman Bearsht (Basht). Herman was the son of George and Mary. When Helena died Herman Basht married Millie E. Long. Millie was the daughter of George and Barbara. George Long married Barbara Bowman on 11 Aug 1834. The Long family resided in **dwelling 1497.** Herman Basht was born 30 Mar 1848 and died 29 Mar 1923. His wife Millie E. Long Basht was born 19 Mar 1842 and died 1 Jun 1918. Herman and Millie were buried in the Pleasant View Memorial Garden Cemetery in the Hamburg area. Absalom Painter was a private in Company B of the 11th

Virginia Cavalry. He was present from 1 Jan 1863 to 31 Aug 1863. He had his own horse since 28 February 1863. He was absent from 1 Sep 1863 until 31 Oct 1863. Absalom was a substitute for George Hawse. George Hawse was a farmer from Hardy County, West Virginia. Absalom was absent with out leave from Oct 31 1863 unti 1 Apr 1864. It was believed that he deserted. However, other events might have lead to his extended absence. Absalom was buried in the Lantz-Bowman Cemetery.

Ansolbelia Painter was born 27 Sep 1846 and died 31 Dec 1870. She was buried in the Lantz-Bowman Cemetery.

Nathaniel Painter was born 1 Jan 1848 and died 18 Dec 1862. He was buried near his sister.

Wesley Painter was born 1851 and died 1922. He was married on 8 Jun 1871 to Mary Jane Spiggle. Mary Jane was born in 1853 and died in 1927. She was the daughter of Isaac and Frances. Mary Jane and Wesley were buried in the Old Union Church Cemetery in Edinburg.

1850 CENSUS: Absalom Painter and his family resided in dwelling 1047 on page 73.

PAGE 50   EDINBURG DISTRICT   (Microfilm Page 574)

Dwelling 340   Family 340

Wilson Green	50 (Black)	Well Digger 0	50	Virginia
Amonia Green	31 (Black)			"
Godfrey Goodrich	7 (Mulatto)			"
Nelly Gaskins	66 (Black)			"

There is no record of **Wilson Green** in Shenandoah County marriage records. However, he did reside in the county in 1850.

1850 CENSUS: Wilson Green resided in dwelling 978 on page 68.

PAGE 50 EDINBURG DISTRICT   (Microfilm Page 574)

Dwelling 341   Family 341

Phillip Painter	57 Farmer	6126	556	Virginia	
Catherine Painter	39			"	Can't Read
Levi Painter	10			"	School
William Painter	9			"	School
George Painter	8			"	School
Mary A. Painter	6			"	
Susan Painter	5			"	
Christina E. Painter	3			"	
Elizabeth Painter	2m			"	
Rebecca Sine	14			"	

Phillip Painter died 30 Aug 1874.   He was 73 years, 11 months and 28 days old.   His wife **Catherine** died 4 Jan 1897 at the age of 79 years, 7 months and 8 days old. They were buried in the Painter Cemetery.   Their marriage record has not yet been discovered. On 8 Mar 1849 there is an interesting marriage record for Phillip Pamlin to Catherine Fry.   This is probably not the couple in this household.   It is of interest because of the number of Fry's in the area.

Levi Painter was born 30 Sep 1849 and died 22 Feb 1924.   He was married to Mary Magdalene Baker on 9 Feb 1871.   She was the daughter of Elizabeth Baker.   Mary and her mother were located in **dwelling 1576**.   Mary Magdalene Baker Painter was born 13 Aug 1849 and died 22 Aug 1910. They were buried in the Bethel Lutheran Church Cemetery.

William C. Painter was born 19 Jan 1851 and died 21 Feb 1931.   He was married on 13 Sep 1877 to Victoria Susan Rucker.   Victoria was born 16 Mar 1859 and died 30 Dec 1920.   She was the daughter of William and Mary.   William Rucker and his family resided in **dwelling 1742**.   William and Susan were buried in the Bethel Lutheran Church Cemetery.

George Painter was born 10 Nov 1852 and died 29 Jan 1931.   He was married to Elizabeth Rucker. Elizabeth may have been the sister of Victoria Susan Rucker.   She was born 4 Jan 1846 and died 13 Jul 1895. George was remarried on 5 May 1901 to Mary E. Draper.   Mary had been born in Washington County, Maryland.   She was the daughter of John and Cordelia.   George and his wives were buried in the Bethel Lutheran Church Cemetery near Hamburg.

Mary Anna Painter was married on 18 Nov 1875
to Joseph L. Estep. Joseph was the son of Thomas and Mary
Ann. Thomas Estep was married to Mary Ann Betz on 17 Nov
1836. Thomas Estep and his family resided in **dwelling
1575.** Joseph Estep was born 18 May 1852 and died 28 Oct
1915. He was buried in the Ruby Cemetery in Edinburg.

Elizabeth Painter was born 10 Apr 1860 and died
10 May 1910. She was married on 9 Apr 1876 to John Wesley
Bowers. John was the son of William and Lydia. William
Bowers married Lydia Fryman on 6 May 1848. William Bowers
and his family resided in **dwelling 385.** John W. Bowers was
born 13 May 1854 and died 2 Jul 1913. They were buried in
the Zion Lutheran Church Cemetery in Hamburg. John Wesley
Bowers was married for the second time to Rebecca Painter
on 23 Feb 1911. Rebecca was the sister of Elizabeth. She
was born 28 Mar 1862 and died in February of 1935. She is
also buried at the Zion Lutheran Church Cemetery in
Hamburg. Hamburg is located near Edinburg.

Rebecca Sine may have been the daughter of
George and Anna. She was born in 1845 and died in 1913.
Rebecca married John Adam Sine on 20 Jan 1867. John was
the son of George and Mary. John Sine was born 28 Jun 1830
and died 23 Mar 1894. Rebecca and John were buried in the
Zion Lutheran Church Cemetery.

1850 CENSUS: Phillip Painter and his family were located
in dwelling 1046 on page 73.

PAGE 50 EDINBURG DISTRICT (Microfilm Page 574)

Dwelling 342 Family 342

Moses Painter	40 Farmer			Virginia	
Catherine Painter	68	4000	1447	"	Can't Read
Rebecca Wetzel	50			"	Can't Read
Phillip Painter	73 Farmer			"	

Moses Painter was the son of Phillip and
Rachel. Phillip Painter had married Rachel Lindamood on
9 Nov 1815. Phillip Painter appear in this household. It
is possible he was deceased at the time of this census as
his name appears at the end of the household. Moses
Painter was married on 27 Sep 1868 to 20 year old Laura
Louise Emswiller. Laura was the daughter of Henry and Ann.
Henry Emswiller and his family resided in **dwelling 1438.**
Moses Painter was 5'8 1/2" with ruddy complexion, blue eyes

and dark hair. He enlisted on 7 Apr 1862 at Hawkinstown in Company K of the 12th Virginia Cavalry. He was discharged on 14 Jul 1862 at Harrisonburg, Virginia for being over 35 years of age. However, he reenlisted at Front Royal on 7 Apr 1863 in the same unit. He was present from September 1863 until February 1864. The roll of his unit shows him AWOL on 1 Mar 1864. He was absent as a result of illness in July and August of 1864.

Phillip Painter had originally married Rachel Lindamood on 9 Nov 1815. Rachel was listed as the daughter of Christopher. On 11 Aug 1826 Phillip married **Catherine Lindamood**. Catherine was the daughter of Jacob Lindamood.

Rebecca Wetzel may have been the sister of Jackson Wetzel. She appears in his household in 1850. Jackson Wetzel had married Dorothy Helsley on 28 Aug 1849.

RELATED FAMILY:
Henry Painter, brother of Moses, married Margaret Bowman on 8 Nov 1855 and resided in **dwelling 346**.

1850 CENSUS: **Phillip Painter** and his family resided in dwelling 1044 on page 73.
Rebecca Wetzel appears in dwelling 671 on page 47. This was the household of Jackson Wetzel.

PAGE 50 EDINBURG DISTRICT (Microfilm Page 574)

Dwelling 343 Family 343

Solomon Sigler	44	Farmhand	400	431	Virginia	
Mary Jane Sigler	33				"	Can't Read
Amanda Sigler	9				"	School
John Sigler	8				"	School
Joseph Sigler	4				"	
Sarah C. Sigler	1				"	

Solomon Sigler was the son of Jacob and Catherine. Jacob Sigler married Catherine Lickliter on 11 Mar 1807. Catherine Lickliter Sigler resided in **dwelling 2075**. Solomon Sigler originally married Leah Speigle on 29 Nov 1848. She was the daughter of Samuel. On 10 Sep 1857 Solomon Sigler was married to **Mary Jane "Polly" Conner**. Polly was the daughter of James and Margaret. James Conner married Peggy Huddle on 21 Apr 1817 in Frederick County, Virginia. Polly Sigler was born in 1826

352

and died in 1919. She was buried in the Bethel Lutheran Church Cemetery in Woodstock.

Amanda Sigler was born 22 Sep 1850 and died 16 Nov 1922. She was married on 23 Dec 1869 to Harvey Holler. Harvey was the son of Alexander and Evey. Alexander Holler married Evey Price Coffman. Evey was a widow. Alexander and his family resided in **dwelling 1183**. Harvey Holler was born 6 Jul 1847 and died 3 Jan 1903. They were buried in the Union Forge Cemetery in Edinburg.

Sarah Catherine Sigler died in Maryland on 7 Mar 1942. She was married on 4 Nov 1880 to George W. Day, the son of William and Sarah. William Day married Sarah Ellen Ship on 26 Apr 1847. William and his family resided in **dwelling 1288**. George was a widower at the time of their marriage. He had originally married Phoebe Alice Huddle on 9 May 1872. Phoebe was born in 1853 and died 16 Jun 1879. She was the daughter of William and Jane Irwin Huddle. Phoebe was buried in the Old Columbia Furnace Cemetery. George W. Day died 7 Feb 1930.

RELATED FAMILY:
      Mary Sigler, sister of Solomon, married William Lewis on 2 May 1858 and resided in **dwelling 1499**.
      Susannah Sigler, sister of Solomon, married Joseph Crabill on 7 May 1849 and resided in **dwelling 2075**.
1850 CENSUS: **Solomon Sigler** resided with his wife Leah in dwelling 2101 on page 151.
      Mary Jane Connor Sigler resided with her parents in dwelling 1999 on page 143.

PAGE 50 EDINBURG DISTRICT (Microfilm Page 574)

Dwelling 344 Family 344

Phillip Trook	57	Farmer	2700	571	Virginia	
Rebecca Trook	57				"	
Rosetta V. Trook	17				"	
Amanda S. Trook	15				"	School
Lemuel Trook	13				"	School
Charles Trook	7				"	School
Ann R. Trook	21				"	

      Phillip Trook was born 1 Jan 1800 and died 18 Mar 1871. He was the son of John and Susan. He was originally married to **Rebecca Painter** on 30 May 1826. She was the daughter of Adam and Elizabeth. Adam Painter married Betsy Bowman on 3 Jul 1802. Rebecca was born 9 Jun 1803 and died 18 Mary 1865. Rebecca died of smallpox. Upon the death of Rebecca, Phillip was married on 17 Apr 1869 to Mary Miller Barton. Mary Miller had married William Barton on 6 Nov 1839. She and William were present in this census in **dwelling 1203**. Mary was the daughter of Peter and Christina. Peter Miller Jr. had married Christina Hisey on 1 Aug 1805. Peter and Christina resided in **dwelling 1615**. Phillip and Rebecca were buried in the Painter Cemetery near Edinburg.

NOTE: Trook was often written as "Druck" or "Drick" in early county records. The name Painter sometimes appears as "Bender".

      Amanda Trook was born 1 Jan 1848 and died 24 Mar 1872. She was married to Samuel Evans on 15 Mar 1870. Samuel was a member of the 7th Virginia Cavalry. He was listed as the son of C. Artz Evans and Susan. However, when Samuel married for the second time after the death of Amanda, he was listed as the son of William. Samuel Evans married Mary C. Cook of Rockingham County on 30 Dec 1873. Mary was the daughter of John and Mary. Rockingham County records indicated that John Cook married Mary Ward on 23 Nov 1848. Samuel resided in **dwelling 21** at the time of this census.

      Lemuel P. Trook was living in Grant County, Indiana when he married Susan Peters on 12 Mar 1872. Susan was the daughter of John and Sarah. John Peters married Sarah Mowery on 23 Dec 1856. John Peters and his family resided in **dwelling 1078**.

      Phillip and Rebecca had a daughter named **Ann R. Trook** at the time of the 1850 census. She may have been deceased at this time. On 16 Nov 1865 Artemisia Trook, daughter of Phillip and Rebecca married John W. Pence. John was the son of David and Missouri. David Pence married Missouri Barnes on 13 Mar 1832. Missouri Pence and her son David resided in **dwelling 571**. Artemisia Trook was 11 at the time of the 1850 census.

RELATED FAMILY:
      Mary Painter, sister of Rebecca, married Samuel Fravel on 20 Apr 1836 and resided in **dwelling 348**.
      Jacob Painter, brother of Rebecca, married Elizabeth Bowers on 1 Nov 1847 and resided in **dwelling 1404**.

Joseph Painter, brother of Rebecca, married Ellen Shank on 22 May 1849 and resided in **dwelling 1437**.

1850 CENSUS: **Phillip Trook** and his family resided in dwelling 1043 on page 73.

PAGE 50 EDINBURG DISTRICT (Microfilm Page 574)

Dwelling 345   Family 345

William Estep	30 Master	675	151	Virginia	
Mary C. Estep	32			"	
Eli H. Noel	12			"	School
Emma J. Noel	10			"	School
Jacob A. Noel	9			"	School
Luther M. Estep	5			"	
John A. Estep	3			"	
Charles L. Estep	5m			"	

William Estep was the son of Samuel and Sarah. Samuel Estep married Sally Silfuss on 2 Feb 1828. Samuel Estep resided with his family in **dwelling 1391**. William was married on 13 Sep 1853 to **Mary Catherine Frinkl Noel**. Mary Catherine was a widow. She had married Jacob Noel on 12 Jan 1847. The bondsman for that marriage was Phillip Druick. Druick was another way that the name Trook was written. Phillip Trook resided in **dwelling 344**. There is a chance that Mary Catherine was the daughter of Phillip. The surname Frinkl is not common in Shenandoah County and may have been an abberation of the surname Druick. Mary Catherine was 37 years, 7 months and 7 days old when she died on 1 Aug 1866. She was buried in the Painter Cemetery next to Phillip and Rebecca Trook. Upon the death of Mary Catherine, William Estep married Elizabeth Baker on 26 Jan 1867. Elizabeth was the daughter of Elizabeth. According to marriage records William Estep was a stone mason. It is possible that William served with Confederate forces. However, his unit is not known. There was a William Estep who enlisted on 1 Jan 1863 in Company G of the 18th Virginia Cavalry. There was also a William Estep on the roll of Company K of the 7th Virginia Cavalry. Further investigation will be necessary to determine if William Estep served during the war.

Emma J. Noel was listed as Emma C. in marriage records. She married George L. Grim on 16 May 1871. George was a carpenter. He was the son of Hiram and Leah.

Hiram Grim married Leah Sheetz on 1 Feb 1847. Hiram and his family resided in **dwelling 1398.**

       Luther Monroe Estep appears to have spelled his name **Eastep.** He was born 24 Dec 1854 and died 16 Dec 1938. He was married on 8 Feb 1880 to Sarah Catherine Hamman. Sarah was the daughter of Lewis and Barbara. Lewis Hamman married Barbara Rosenberger on 7 Apr 1856. Sarah Catherine Hamman Eastep was born 15 Mar 1860 and died 25 Mar 1937. Luther and Sarah were buried at the St. Stephens Church Cemetery near Lebanon Church.

       Charles L. Estep was born 23 Dec 1859.

RELATED FAMILY:
       Julia Ann Estep, sister of William, married John Moore on 8 Jan 1857 and resided in **dwelling 1518.**
       Benjamin Estep, brother of William, resided in **dwelling 961.** This was the household of Harrison Pence.

1850 CENSUS: **William Estep** resided with his father in dwelling 1384 on page 100.
       Mary Catherine Frinkl Noel resided with her husband Jacob in dwelling 1409 on page 101.

PAGE 51 EDINBURG DISTRICT (Microfilm Page 575)

Dwelling 346 Family 346

Henry Painter	25	Farmer	Virginia
Margaret Painter	25		"
Mary C. Painter	3		"
Rebecca J. Painter	2		"
Cora A. Painter	5m		"
Christina Miller	25		"

       Henry E. Painter was born 10 Feb 1834 and died 9 Jul 1900. He was the son of Phillip and Catherine. Phillip Painter married Catherine Emswiller on 11 Aug 1826. Phillip and his family were located in **dwelling 342.** Henry was married to **Margaret Bowman** on 8 Nov 1855. Margaret was the daughter of David and Rebecca. David Bowman married Rebecca Cline on 4 Nov 1833. David Bowman resided in **dwelling 350.** Margaret Bowman Painter was born 22 Feb 1835 and died 7 Sep 1892. Henry E. Painter was 5'11" with dark complexion, blue eyes and dark hair. He enlisted on 21 Aug 1862 at Culpepper in Company K of the 12 Virginia Cavalry. He was a private and was absent sick from September until

December of 1863. He was present beginning in January of
1864 and was AWOL in March of that year. He was paroled
at New Market on 20 Apr 1865.

Mary C. Painter died 1 Oct 1904. She was 47
years, 11 months and 19 days old when she died. She was
married on 31 Dec 1878 to Charles M. Bowman, the son of
William and Sarah. William Bowman married Sarah
Rosenberger on 26 Oct 1854. William and his family resided
in **dwelling 333**. Charles M. Bowman was born 22 May 1856
and died 5 Aug 1919. They were buried in the Cedarwood
Cemetery.

Rebecca J. Painter was born 6 Mar 1858 and died
30 Jun 1892. She was married on 12 Dec 1878 to John J.
Barton. John was a teacher. He was the son of Nathaniel
and Elizabeth. Nathaniel Barton married Elizabeth Miller
on 16 Apr 1836. John J. Barton was a resident of **dwelling
350**. He was born 11 Sep 1848 and died 17 Dec 1916.
Rebecca and John were buried in the Lantz-Bowman Cemetery.

Cora A. Painter was born 19 Jan 1860 and died
19 Jun 1944. She was married on 5 Aug 1880 to Reverend
Milton M. Long. Milton was born in Rockingham County,
Virginia. He was the son of John and Rebecca. John Long
married Rebecca Campbell of Page County, Virginia on 2 Apr
1858. John Long and his family resided in **dwelling 1028**.
Reverend Milton M. Long was born 27 Nov 1858 and died 30
Dec 1894. Cora and Milton were buried in the Lantz-Bowman
Cemetery.

1850 CENSUS: **Henry E. Painter** resided with his father in
dwelling 671 on page 47.
Margaret Bowman resided with her father in
dwelling 1039 on page 72.

PAGE 51 EDINBURG DISTRICT (Microfilm Page 575)

Dwelling 347 Family 347

Ephramin Bowman	42	Farmer	5070	1020	Virginia
Josephine Bowman	29				"
Sarah M. Bowman	9				"
Mary E. Bowman	7				"
Elizabeth F. Bowman	5				"
Rebecca D. Bowman	2				"
Elizabeth Fry	30				"

Ephramin Bowman married **Josephine M. Dyer.** The date of this marriage is not known.

Sarah Mary Bowman was married on 4 Nov 1869 to Jacob Hyre of Grant County, West Virginia. He was the son of Solomon and Mary. He was born in Hardy County, West Virginia. Sarah Mary Bowman died soon after this marriage. She was 19 years, 5 months and 19 days old. She was buried in the Zion Lutheran Church Cemetery in Edinburg. Jacob Hyre remarried on 4 Nov 1873. He married Lydia A. Stoner Rosenberger. Lydia had married Erasmus Rosenberger on 21 Oct 1860. Her husband Erasmus was a Lt. in Company K of the 7th Virginia Cavalry and had been killed at Gettysburg. At the time of this census Lydia resided with her mother Catherine in **dwelling 1476.** Catherine was the widow of David Stoner. Jacob Hyre also appears to have been a member of the Confederate forces. There was a Jacob J. and a Jacob S Hyre listed on the roll of Company E of the 18th Virginia Cavalry. Both of these men were from Hardy County, West Virginia. Jacob S. Hyre also appears on the roll of Company H of the 18th Virginia Cavalry.

Elizabeth Frances Bowman was born 16 Mar 1856 and died 27 Mar 1885. She was married on 26 Oct 1874 to George Wilkins. George was the son of Isaac and Catherine. Isaac Wilkins married Catherine Hockman on 6 Dec 1839. Isaac and his family resided in **dwelling 1592.** George L. Wilkins was born 9 Sep 1845 and died 24 Jan 1919. He was married to Mary E. Sheetz on 21 Feb 1888. Mary was listed as the daughter of Henry and Susan. Henry Sheetz had married Caroline Phillips on 1 Dec 1853. Caroline actually appears to have been her mother. Henry and his family resided in **dwelling 1794.** George and both of his wives were buried in the Zion Lutheran Church Cemetery. Ephramin and Josephine had a daughter **Josephine D. Bowman** who had been born on 30 Nov 1860. She married Gideon Wilkins, the brother of George on 16 Aug 1881.

Mary Virginia Bowman was 89 years old when she died on 26 Apr 1943 at Woodstock. She was married to John Samuel Cline. John had died 19 Oct 1929.

Elizabeth Fry may have been listed twice in this census. She was probably the daughter of Samuel and Catherine. Samuel Fry married Catherine Irwin on 24 Jan 1828. Elizabeth appears with her parents in **dwelling 1358.** There were no other members of the Fry family in this age bracket listed in this census.

1850 CENSUS: Elizabeth Fry resided with her parents in
dwelling 1706 on page 123.

PAGE 51 EDINBURG DISTRICT   (Microfilm Page 575)

Dwelling 348   Family 348

Sarah Fravel	51	Farmer	4720	0	Virginia
Mary Fravel	45				" Can't Read
Martha E. Fravel	19				"
Sarah C. Fravel	17				"
Ann E. Fravel	12				"
Emma P. Fravel	11				" School
Lydia A. Fravel	8				" School
Virginia A. Fravel	2				"
William F. Ludwick	17				" School

Samuel Fravel was born on Stony Creek near
Edinburg on 25 Apr 1809.   He was the son of Jacob and
Rebecca Snyder Fravel.   Samuel died 30 Dec 1887.   He was
married to **Mary "Polly" Painter (Bender)** on 20 Apr 1836.
She was the daughter of Adam and Elizabeth.   Adam Painter
married Elizabeth "Betsy" Bowman on 3 Jul 1802.   Polly was
born 27 Aug 1814 and died 30 Mar 1888. Samuel and Polly
were buried in the Painter Cemetery in Hamburg, Virginia.

Martha Ellen Fravel was born 8 Dec 1840 and
died 24 Jan 1907.   She was not married.   Martha was buried
in the Painter Cemetery.

Sarah Catherine "Kate" Fravel was born 6 May
1843 and died 15 Feb 1911.   She was married on 22 Dec 1870
to William Bowman.   William was the son of Isaac and
Elizbeth.   Isaac Bowman married Elizabeth Ann Bender on 18
May 1840.   Isaac and his family resided in **dwelling 1477.**
William Bowman was born 29 Dec 1842 and died 19 Jul 1923.
Kate and William were buried in the New Mount Jackson
Cemetery.

Annie E. Fravel was born 6 Jun 1845 and died
15 Mar 1903.   She was married on 15 Nov 1866 to Isaiah
Bowman, the brother of William Bowman.   William Bowman was
the husband of Annie's sister Kate.   Isaiah was born 13 Aug
1845 and died 23 May 1918.   Isaiah served in the Civil War.
Upon the death of Ann, Isaiah was married on 9 May 1906 to
Emma Frances Fravel, the daughter of Aaron.   **Emma Frances
Fravel Bowman** was born 15 Jan 1857 and died 29 Dec 1919.

Annie, Emma and Isaiah were buried in the Bethel Lutheran Church Cemetery near Hamburg, Virginia.

Emma Jane Fravel was born in 1849 and died in 1916. She was married on 14 Feb 1893 to Perry S. Coffelt. Perry was born in 1848 and died in 1930. He was the son of William and Catherine. William Coffelt married Mary Ann Corbin on 24 Feb 1859. Perry and his parents resided in **dwelling 1217.** Perry S. Coffelt was born in 1848 and died in 1930. Perry was a widower at the time he married Emma. He had originally married Arbelin R. Seiver, the daughter of William and Sarah. His first marriage took place on 19 Dec 1876. Arbelin died 17 Dec 1889. This family was buried in the Cedarwood Cemetery.

Lydia A. Fravel was born 7 Jun 1851 and died 21 Sep 1863. She was buried in the Painter Cemetery.

Virginia Alice Fravel was born 4 Oct 1857 and died 1 May 1861. She was also buried in the Painter Cemetery.

William F. Ludwick may have been the son of John and Sophia. John A. Ludwick married Sophia Flowers on 26 Jun 1838. He appears with this family in 1850. William was of age to serve at the outbreak of the Civil War. No record of his service has been found. However, there was a William Luquirck in Company B of the 18th Virginia Cavalry. He was described as 5'8" with light complexion, light hair and gray eyes. He was paroled on 4 May 1865 at Winchester. This should be checked by scholars interested in the investigation of the Ludwick family.

RELATED FAMILY:

Rebecca Painter, sister of Mary, married Phillip Trook on 30 May 1826 and resided in **dwelling 344.**

Mary Fravel, sister of Samuel, married Jacob Bowman on 19 Sep 1829 and resided in **dwelling 331.**

Eli Fravel, brother of Samuel, resided in **dwelling 1228.**

Jacob Fravel, brother of Samuel, resided in **dwelling 1227.**

William Fravel, brother of Samuel, married Leah Haun and resided in **dwelling 1808.**

Rebecca Fravel, sister of Samuel, married Jacob Lantz on 18 Apr 1837 and resided in **dwelling 1173.**

Joseph Painter, brother of Mary, married Ellen Shank on 22 May 1849 and resided in **dwelling 1473**.

Jacob Painter, brother of Mary, married Elizabeth Bowers on 1 Nov 1847 and resided in **dwelling 1404**.

1850 CENSUS: Samuel Fravel and his family resided in dwelling 1038 on page 72.

William F. Ludwick appears in the household of John A. Ludwick. John is believed to have been his father. They resided in dwelling 52 on page 4.

PAGE 51 EDINBURG DISTRICT (Microfilm Page 575)

Dwelling 349 Family 349

George P. Waserman	46	Farmhand	Germany
Catherine Waserman	52		"
Ferdinand Waserman	9		Virginia School
Franklin P. Waserman	4		"

Franklin P. Waterman was born 19 Mar 1857 and died 27 Jun 1941. He was married on 24 Jun 1883 to Martha Jane Sine. Martha Jane was the daughter of George and Cornelia. George Sine and his family resided in **dwelling 391**. Martha Jane was born 13 Jul 1856 and died 3 Jan 1921. Franklin and Martha were buried in the Bethel Lutheran Church Cemtery near Woodstock.

NOTE: The name **Waserman** appears as **Waterman** in later Shenandoah County records. It is probable that this family has some relationship to **dwelling 332**.

1850 CENSUS: George P. Waserman and his family resided in dwelling 1048 on page 73.

PAGE 51 EDINBURG DISTRICT (Microfilm Page 575)

Dwelling 350 Family 350

Samuel Bowman	40	Farmer	6190	1114	Virginia	
Lydia Bowman	53				"	Can't Read
Ann Bowman	43				"	Can't Read
Amanda Bowman	23		3480	537	"	
Louisa Bowman	16				"	
John J. Barton	11				"	
David Bowman	51				"	

Samuel Bowman died 7 Mar 1888 at the age of 68. He is believed to have been the son of John of David Bowman and his wife Mary. John Bowman married Mary Lantz on 13 Mar 1805. In the 9 Nov 1847 will of John Bowman (Will Book Y-Page 411), John mentions his unmarried son Samuel and unmarried daughters Lydia and Ann. **Lydia Bowman** was born 1 Jan 1807 and died 7 Jul 1880. **Ann Bowman** died 26 Feb 1866 at the age of 50 years and 10 months. Members of this family were buried in the Lantz-Bowman Cemetery.

David Bowman was the brother of Samuel. He was born 19 May 1808 and died 25 Feb 1860. He had married Rebecca Cline, the daughter of Henry on 4 Nov 1833. According to census regulations he was listed despite the fact that he was deceased at the time of this census. The names of deceased individuals were listed at the bottom of the household. His wife Rebecca preceded him in death.

Amanda J. Bowman was the daughter of David and Rebecca. It was her task to manage David Bowman's estate for other members of his family. Amanda probably never married. She was born 6 Nov 1836 and died 2 Jan 1915. Amanda was buried in the Lantz-Bowman Cemetery.

Louisa E. Bowman, daughter of David and Rebecca, married Dr. Nathaniel Q. Humston on 12 Nov 1872. He was the son of Nathaniel and Margaret. Nathaniel Q. Humston Sr. married Margaret Stephenson on 5 Dec 1826. Nathaniel and Margaret resided in **dwelling 246**. Nathaniel Jr. was not in the household in 1860. It is probable that he was away at medical school. Dr. N. Q. Humston was born in 1832 and died in 1906. He was buried in the Cedarwood Cemetery.

John Josiah Barton was born 11 Sep 1848 and died 17 Dec 1916. He was the son of Nathaniel and Elizabeth. Nathaniel Barton married Elizabeth Miller on 16 Apr 1836. Nathaniel and Elizabeth appear to have separated as their children were dispersed throughout the area. Nathaniel Barton resided in **dwelling 1751**. Elizabeth Miller Barton resided in **dwelling 1615**. John Josiah Barton married Rebecca J. Painter on 12 Dec 1878. Rebecca was the daughter of Henry and Margaret. Henry Painter married Margaret Bowman on 8 Nov 1855. Henry and his family resided in **dwelling 346**. Rebecca was born 6 Mar 1858 and died 30 Jun 1892. John and Rebecca were buried in the Lantz-Bowman Cemetery.

RELATED FAMILY:

Mary Jane Barton, sister of John, married Jacob Estep on 10 Nov 1854 and resided in **dwelling 336.**

Margaret Bowman, sister of David, married Henry Painter on 8 Nov 1855 and resided in **dwelling 346.**

Jacob Bowman, brother of David, married Mary Fravel on 19 Sep 1829 and resided in **dwellinig 331.**

1850 CENSUS: **Samuel Bowman** and his sisters resided in dwelling 1040 on page 72.

David Bowman and his children resided in dwelling 1039 on page 72.

John Josiah Barton resided with his parents in dwelling 17 on page 2.

PAGE 51   EDINBURG DISTRICT   (Microfilm Page 575)

Dwelling 351   Family 351

Garret Dore 25 Day Labor on R.R. 0 20 Ireland Can't Read
Ellen Dore   25   "
Kate Dore   1   "

1850 CENSUS: There is no record of this family in 1850.

PAGE 51   EDINBURG DISTRICT   (Microfilm Page 575)

Dwelling 352   Family 352

Isaac R. Hite   47 _____in Chancery 1400 400   Virginia
Rhoda F. Hite   23   "
Virginia Hite   15   "
Milton L. Hite   2   "

Isaac R. Hite was the son of Michael and Mary. He was born 28 Jun 1809 and died 16 Aug 1891. Isaac was married on 19 Jun 1834 to Lucinda Humston, the daughter of John. When Lucinda died, Isaac was married on 26 Aug 1857 to **Rhoda Frances Miley**. Rhoda was the daughter of Martin and Catherine. Martin F. Miley married Catherine Rhodes on 7 May 1836. Martin and his family resided in **dwelling 2307.** Rhoda Frances Miley Hite was born 10 Jul 1837 and died 16 Aug 1887. She was buried in the Massanutten Cemetery. A tombstone for Isaac R. Hite was located nearby indicating that he was a veteran of the Civil War. No record of his service has been located. There is a 5 foot tall tombstone located in the Hite Cemetery indicating that

Isaac, Lucinda and some of the Hite children were buried
in this cemetery.

Virginia K. Hite is one of the children listed
on the tombstone in the Hite Cemetery. She was 20 years
old when she died in 1866.

Milton Lloyd Hite was born 12 Apr 1858 and died
9 Apr 1930. He was married to Emma J. Sheetz on 3 Jul
1881. Emma was the daughter of Daniel and Harriet. Daniel
W. Sheetz married Harriet J. Siebert on 13 Feb 1863. Emma
J. Sheetz Hite was born 12 Feb 1866 and died 15 Nov 1935.
Milton and Emma were buried in the Massanutten Cemetery in
Woodstock.

1850 CENSUS: **Issac R. Hite** and his family resided in
dwelling 675 on page 48.
Rhoda Frances Miley resided with her parents
in dwelling 809 on page 57.

PAGE 52 EDINBURG DISTRICT (Microfilm Page 567)

Dwelling 353 Family 353

John A. Fry	67	Farmer	11,300	4454	Virginia	
Catherine Fry	63				"	
Artemissia Fry	21				"	
George Patton	22	Farmhand			"	Can't Read

John Anthony Fry was the son of John Fry. He
was born 14 Jan 1791 and died 31 Mar 1873. In the 1870
census John A. Fry is reported to have come from Loudoun
County, Virginia. John was married on 10 Jun 1815 to
Catherine Grandstaff. Catherine was the daughter of
Phillip and Elizabeth. Phillip Grandstaff married
Elizabeth Haas on 21 Dec 1784. Catherine was 80 years old
when she died 31 Mar 1878. John A. and Catherine were
buried in the Cedarwood Cemetery in Edinburg. According
to the 1840 census, this couple may have had as many as
nine children.

Artemissia Fry died at the age of 74 on 4 Dec
1912. She was married on 26 Nov 1862 to Elias W. Sheetz.
Elias was the son of George and Elizabeth. George of Jacob
Sheetz married Elizabeth Bowman on 14 Feb 1826. Elias was
a resident of **dwelling 64** at the time of this census.
Elias is listed in the Cedarwood Cemetery as having served

as a member of Company C of the 7th Virginia Cavalry. He also saw service in the 10th Virginia Infantry.

George Washington Patton, grandson of John and Catherine, was the son of Michael and Susan. Michael Patton married Susan Fry on 12 Dec 1836. Susan was the daughter of John and Catherine. Michael Patton resided in dwelling 314. George would marry Mary C. Myers on 1 Nov 1860. Mary was listed as Leah on their marriage certificate. She was the daughter of Abraham and Susan. Abraham Myers married Susan Pence on 8 Jan 1827. Susan Pence Myers and her family resided in dwelling 307. George died 30 Nov 1920. Information available regarding his death indicates that he had married Mary Shank after Mary Myers Patton had died. George Patton was probably a member of the Confederate Army. It is not known which unit he joined. There was a George Patton in Company C of the 7th Virginia Cavalry. Individuals named George Patton also appear in Company G of the 18th Virginia Cavalry and in Company G of the 33rd Virginia Infantry.

RELATED FAMILY:

Ambrose B. Fry, son of John, married Julia Ann Gochenour on 10 Mar 1856 and resided in dwelling 323.

Matilda C. Fry, daughter of John, married Dilmon Estep on 12 Feb 1857 and resided in dwelling 320.

John A. Fry Jr., son of John, married Sarah Beazley on 27 Oct 1857 and resided in dwelling 354.

Rebecca Fry, daughter of John, married Lewis Pence on 21 May 1849 and resided in dwelling 83.

William Harrison Fry, son of John, married Rosa Coffman on 6 May 1844 and resided in dwelling 355.

Letta Fry, daughter of John, married David Tisinger on 22 Feb 1854 and resided in dwelling 1184.

Elizabeth Liggett, sister in law of Catherine, had married John I. Grandstaff on 27 Feb 1826. John I. Grandstaff, the brother of Catherine had died in 1852. Elizabeth resided in dwelling 46.

George P. Grandstaff, brother of Catherine, married Mary Reedy on 3 Oct 1810 and resided in dwelling 63.

Phillip Grandstaff Jr., brother of Catherine, married Mary Cooper on 6 Aug 1816 and resided in dwelling 267.

Benjamin Grandstaff, brother of Catherine, married Elizabeth "Betsy" Clinedinst on 14 Oct 1820 and resided in dwelling 324.

Jacob Snapp, brother in law of Catherine, married Rebecca Grandstaff on 4 Apr 1831 and resided in **dwelling 44**.

1850 CENSUS: **John A. Fry** resided with his family in dwelling 693 on page 49.

PAGE 52   EDINBURG DISTRICT   (Microfilm Page 576)

Dwelling 354   Family 354

John Fry	26	Carpenter	0	100	Virginia
Sarah Fry	22				"
Franklin M. Fry	1				"
John E. Fry	2m				"
Seatie Beazley	24				"

John A. Fry was the son of John A. and Catherine. John A. Fry married Catherine Grandstaff on 10 Jun 1815. John and Catherine resided in **dwelling 353**. John A. Fry Jr. married **Sarah Beazley** on 27 Oct 1857. This marriage took place in Page County, Virignia. She may have been the daughter of Isaac and Ann R. It is likely that **Seatta Beazley** was the sister of Sarah. John A. Fry probably served in the Civil War. However, his unit is not known. In records for Company B of the 33rd Virginia Infantry there was a John Andrew Fry on the roster. He is suppose to have died in January 1902 at Mt. Jackson. There was a John Fry in the 2nd Virginia Infantry who was born in 1834. He was wounded in combat and was paroled at Mt. Jackson. It is not clear that either of these individuals was the head of this household. However, circumstances surrounding their military record produces interesting parallels.

Franklin M. Fry was listed as Franklin L. Fry in marriage records. He was married to Sallie G. Landis on 17 Apr 1884. Sallie was the daughter of Daniel and Margaret. Daniel Landis married Margaret Whitzel on 4 Jan 1844. Daniel Landis and his family appear in **dwelling 1867**. Sallie was born in Rockingham County, Virginia. In the Borden Cemetery book there was a Frank Fry in the Old Union Church Cemetery near Mt. Jackson. No record of the grave site is preserved as many of the tombstones in the cemetery were wooden. Cemetery records indicate that Frank Fry was born 5 Sep 1858 and died 10 Dec 1895.

John E. Fry was born 25 Dec 1859 and died 3 Mar 1924. He does not appear to have married. He is buried in the New Mount Jackson Cemetery. Buried near him was Sarah E. Fry. It is likely this was his mother. She was born 22 Oct 1837 and died 23 May 1923.

RELATED FAMILY:

Ambrose B. Fry, brother of John A., married Julia Ann Gochenour on 10 Mar 1856 and resided in **dwelling 323.**

Matilda C. Fry, sister of John A., married Dilmon Estep on 12 Feb 1857 and resided in **dwelling 320.**

Susan Fry, sister of John A., married Michael Patton on 12 Dec 1836 and resided in **dwelling 314.**

Rebecca Fry, sister of John A., married Lewis Pence on 21 May 1849 and resided in **dwelling 83.**

William Harrison Fry, brother of John A., married Rosa Coffman on 6 May 1844 and resided in **dwelling 355.**

Letta Fry, sister of John A., married David Tisinger on 22 Feb 1854 and resided in **dwelling 1184.**

1850 CENSUS: John A. Fry Jr. was present in the household of his parents. They resided in dwelling 693 on page 49.

PAGE 52   EDINBURG DISTRICT   (Microfilm Page 576)

Dwelling 355   Family 355

Harrison Fry	39 Carpenter	0	250	Virginia	
Rosanna Fry	35			"	
William H. Fry	15			"	School

William Harrison Fry was the son of John and Catherine. John Fry married Catherine Grandstaff on 10 Jun 1815. John and Catherine resided in **dwelling 353.** William Harrison Fry married **Rosa Coffman** on 6 May 1844. Rosa was the daughter of George Coffman. When William died, Rosa Coffman Fry married David Bowers on 16 Oct 1879. David was a widower from Hardy County, West Virginia. He was the son of John and Mary.

William H. Fry was listed as William A. on his marriage record. He was married on 14 May 1868 to Sarah E. Shipe. Sarah was the daughter of Levi and Susan. Levi Shipe married Susan Wendle on 2 Mar 1854. Sarah Shipe and her parents resided in **dwelling 1832.** William may have

served in the Confederate Army. There was a William Fry
on the roll of the 11th Virginia Cavalry and the 12th
Virginia Cavalry. This needs to be confirmed by
individuals interested in the Fry family.

RELATED FAMILY:
> **Ambrose B. Fry,** brother of William, married
Julia Ann Gochenour on 10 Mar 1856 and resided in **dwelling
323.**
> **Matilda C. Fry,** sister of William, married
Dilmon Estep on 12 Feb 1857 and resided in **dwelling 320.**
> **Susan Fry,** sister of William, married
Michael Patton on 12 Dec 1836 and resided in **dwelling 314.**
> **John A. Fry Jr.,** brother of William, married
Sarah Beazley on 27 Oct 1857 and resided in **dwelling 354.**
> **Rebecca Fry,** sister of William, married
Lewis Pence on 21 May 1849 and resided in **dwelling 83.**
> **Leatta Fry,** sister of William, married David
Tisinger on 22 Feb 1854 and resided in **dwelling 1184.**

1850 CENSUS: There is no record of William and his family
in 1850.

PAGE 52   EDINBURG DISTRICT   (Microfilm Page 576)

Dwelling 356   Family 356

Jacob Summers	51 Day Labor	250	75 Va.	Can't Read
Rosanna Summers	45		"	Can't Read
Mary J. Summers	20 Housegirl		"	
James H. Summers	17 Day Labor		"	
Samuel Summers	13		"	

Jacob Summers was married to **Rosanna Coffman**
on 8 May 1839. John Coffman was the bondsman for this
marriage.

Mary Jane Summers was married to Marion Cave
on 2 Aug 1871. Marion was the son of Noah and Sarah. Noah
Cave married Sarah Jenkins on 16 Jul 1819 in Page County,
Virginia. Marion was born in Page County, Virginia.
Marion Cave died 27 May 1901 and was buried in the Union
Forge Cemetery. Marion Cave was located in **dwelling 452.**
He was a widower.

James H. Summers enlisted on 4 Mar 1862 in the
Eighth Star New Market Artillery. He was present on all
rolls but was reassigned to the Danville Artillery in

September of 1862. He was paroled at Appomattox on 9 Apr 1865. James was married to Catherine Clinedinst on 12 Dec 1869. Catherine was the daughter of Isaac and Lydia. Isaac Clinedinst married Lydia Holler on 7 Mar 1825. Catherine Clinedinst and her parents resided in **dwelling 322**. Catherine Clinedinst Summers was older. She died 21 Feb 1883 at the age of 53 years, 3 months and 27 days old. She was buried in the Union Forge Cemetery. James married Lydia Clinedinst on 12 Aug 1883. Lydia was the daughter of Elizabeth. Lydia and her mother are found in **dwelling 1736**. After the death of Lydia, James married Annie Holler on 28 Jan 1885. Annie was about 58 years old when she died in October of 1900. She was the daughter of Isaac and Millie. Isaac Holler married Millie Clem on 29 Jan 1851.

       Samuel Summers (Sommers) is reported to have been born in Rockingham County, Virginia. He married Sarah Frances Smith on 29 Apr 1868. Sarah was the daughter of Ellen.

1850 CENSUS: Jacob **Summers** and his family resided in dwelling 682 on page 48.

PAGE 52   EDINBURG DISTRICT   (Microfilm Page 576)

Dwelling 357   Family 357

John Hutcheson	37	Farmer	600	207	Virginia
Mary M. Hutcheson	37				"
Elizabeth M. Hutcheson	7				"
Daniel W. P. Hutcheson	6				"
John A. Hutcheson	3				"
Marcus L. Hutcheson	1				"

       John T. Hutcheson was born 14 Mar 1824 and died 15 Oct 1878. He was the son of Jacob and Margaret. Jacob Hutcheson married Margaret Mauck on 10 Jun 1822. Jacob Hutcheson and his wife resided in **dwelling 319**. John was reported in the Hottel Family history to have served in the Confederate Army. No record of his service has been located. John was married on 20 Oct 1849 to **Mary Margaret Dirting**. The bondsman for that marriage was Adam Dirting. It is believed that she was the daughter of Adam and Elizabeth. Adam Dirting married Elizabeth Hisey on 30 Dec 1829. Adam and his family resided in **dwelling 1744**. Mary Margaret Dirting Hutcheson was born in 1832 and died in 1909. John and Mary Margaret were buried in the Union Forge Cemetery.

Elizabeth Margaret Hutcheson was born 8 Sep 1851 and died 28 Nov 1923. She was married to Emanuel G. Shipe on 29 May 1879. Emanuel was the son of Jacob and Catherine. Jacob Shipe married Catherine Fogle on 26 Jan 1848. Jacob Shipe and his family resided in **dwelling 1871**. Emanuel G. Shipe was born 5 Apr 1856 and died 23 Apr 1938. Elizabeth and Emanuel were buried in the Union Forge Cemetery.

Daniel Wilmore (Wilbur) Prescott Hutcheson was born 21 Nov 1853 and died 5 May 1911. He was married to Delilah Hettie McInturff on 11 Oct 1888. Hettie was the daughter of Delilah and Branson. Branson McInturff married Delila Ridenour on 15 Sep 1853. Branson McInturff and his family resided in **dwelling 472**. Hettie was born 31 Jul 1866 and died 13 Nov 1938. Daniel and Hettie were buried in the Dry Run Cemetery No. 2 at Seven Fountains. Several of their children were buried in the Hutcheson Cemetery at Carmel in the Fort Valley.

John Amos Aiken Hutcheson was born 22 Feb 1857 and died 9 Jul 1907. He never married and resided in West Virginia at the time of his death. His sister Nellie V. Hutcheson was buried near him. She was born 19 Feb 1872 and died 22 Nov 1906. They were buried in the Cedarwood Cemetery.

Marcus Delaffette Hutcheson was born 9 Feb 1859 and died 18 Dec 1921. He was married on 18 Oct 1892 to Alice Frances Heisey of Union, in Montgomery County, Ohio. She was born 28 Jul 1867.

RELATED FAMILY:

Charles Hutcheson, brother of John, married Caroline Clinedinst on 6 Apr 1850 and resided in **dwelling 78**.

Jacob Amos Hutcheson, brother of John, was a resident in **dwelling 81**.

Joseph Franklin Hutcheson, brother of John, married Mary Ann Long on 4 Sep 1853 and resided in **dwelling 1187**.

William Hutcheson, brother of John, marrried Mary Emily Hockman on 19 Feb 1854 and resided in **dwelling 359**.

1850 CENSUS: There is no record of this family in 1850.

370

PAGE 52   EDINBURG DISTRICT   (Microfilm Page 576)

Dwelling 358   Family 358

Lewis Coffman	41	Day Labor	700	60	Va.	Can't Read
Eveline Coffman	33				"	Can't Read
Christena Coffman	14				"	School
Elizabeth Coffman	69				"	Can't Read

Lewis Coffman was believed to have been the son of John and Elizabeth. His mother **Elizabeth** appears in this residence. Lewis was born 27 Oct 1814 and died 26 Dec 1891. His wife **Eveline** was 56 when she died on 26 May 1885. Lewis and Eveline were buried in the Union Forge Cemetery in Edinburg.

Christena "Tena" F. Coffman was born 27 Oct 1846 and died 12 Oct 1868. She was buried in the Union Forge Cemetery in Edinburg. Christena was married on 12 May 1867 to Augustine Clinedinst. Augustine was the son of Isaac and Lydia. Isaac Clinedinst married Lydia Holler on 7 May 1825. Lydia Holler Clinedinst and her family resided in **dwelling 322**. Augustine was born inn 1838. After Tena died, he was married on 20 Feb 1873 to Anna Jewell, the daughter of Fielding and Sarah Silfouse Jewell. Augustine was a veteran of the Civil War. He served in Company F of the 10th Virginia Infantry and in the 7th Virginia Cavalry. After the war Augustine moved to Moorefield Junction, West Virginia.

1850 CENSUS: **Lewis Coffman** resided in dwelling 680 on page 48.

Elizabeth Coffman, mother of Lewis, resided in dwelling 681 on page 48. She lived with her husband John.

PAGE 52   EDINBURG DISTRICT   (Microfilm Page 576)

Dwelling 359   Family 359

William H. Hutcheson	26	Farmer	1120	950	Virginia
Mary E. Hutcheson	23				"
Amanda J. Smith	17	Housegirl			"
John S. Marston	11				"

William Henry Hutcheson was born 10 may 1834 and died 22 Jun 1905. He was the son of Jacob and Margaret. Jacob F. Hutcheson married Margaret Mauck on 10

Jun 1822. Jacob and Margaret resided in **dwelling 319**. William H. Hutcheson was married on 14 Feb 1854 to **Mary Emily Hockman**. Mary was the daughter of Jacob and Elizabeth. A marriage for Jacob Hockman to Elizabeth Munch was reported on 24 May 1817. These may have been her parents. Mary Emily was born 4 Sep 1837 and died 26 Jul 1912. William and Mary Emily were buried in the Old Edinburg Cemetery. Unofficial sources report that W. H. Hutcheson was a member of Company K of the 12th Virginia Cavalry.

Amanda J. Smith was born in 1842 in Page County, Virginia. She was the daughter of Samuel and Nancy. Samuel Smith married Nancy Fleming on 3 Jan 1839 in Page County. Amanda was married on 8 Sep 1867 to Mahlon Holler. Mahlon was the son of Jonathan and Anna. Jonathan Holler married Nancy Bartley on 18 May 1835. Mahlon was born 19 Sep 1844 and died 26 Sep 1919. Amanda and Mahlon were buried in the Bethel Lutheran Church Cemetery at Bowman's Crossing. Mahlon Holler was a member of Company C of the 7th Virginia Cavalry.

John S. Marston is believed to have been the son of Fountain and Mary. He appears as a one year old in their household in 1850. There is no record of the marriage for this couple. However, Shenandoah County records reveal Fountain <u>Martin</u> married Polly Ann Beener on 27 May 1830. This needs to be checked by Marston family researchers.

RELATED FAMILY:

Charles Hutcheson, brother of William, married Caroline Clinedinst on 6 Apr 1850 and resided in **dwelling 78**.

Jacob Amos Hutcheson, brother of William, resided in **dwelling 81**.

John Hutcheson, brother of William, married Mary Margaret Dirting on 20 Oct 1849 and resided in **dwelling 357**.

Joseph Franklin Hutcheson, brother of William, married Mary Ann Long on 4 Sep 1853 and resided in **dwelling 1187**.

1850 CENSUS: **Mary Emily Hockman** resided with her parents in dwelling 193 on page 14.
John S. Marston appears with his parents in dwelling 1107 on page 78.

PAGE 52 EDINBURG DISTRICT (Microfilm Page 576)

Dwelling 360   Family 360

John J. Kibler	38 Farmer	2370	351	Virginia	
Mary Kibler	37			"	Can't Read
Andrew J. Kibler	17			"	School
Rebecca Kibler	16			"	
James Kibler	14			"	School
Virginia Kibler	12			"	
Perry Kibler	10			"	School
Mary Kibler	8			"	
Ellen Kibler	6			"	
Dallas Kibler	2			"	
Alice Kibler	2			"	
Ida B. Kibler	7m			"	

John J. Kibler was born 5 Jul 1820 and died 5 Jul 1860.   John was married on 1 Jun 1840 to **Mary Wolverton**, the daughter of John and Polly.   John W. Wolverton married Polly Hottel on 3 Nov 1821.   John W. Wolverton and his family resided in dwelling 1749.   Mary Wolverton Kibler was born 3 Aug 1821 and died 16 Jun 1901. John and Mary were buried in the Massanutten Cemetery.

Andrew Jackson Kibler was born at Columbia Furnace on 19 Oct 1842.   He died at Waxahachie, Texas.   He was married on 4 Apr 1867 at Easton, Texas to Martha King. Martha was a native of Lincoln County, Tennessee.   She died 1 Apr 1900.   Andrew is thought to have been a member of the 12th Virginia Cavalry.   He enlisted at Winchester on 15 Aug 1861 in Myers Company.   Myers Company was Company C of the 7th Virginia Cavalry.   On 1 May 1862 he enlisted in Company K of the 12 Virginia Cavalry.   He was absent at the 30 Nov 1862 muster and had not been seen since the 29 Nov 1862 fight at Berryville.   He was reported as a POW at Millwood on 4 Apr 1863.   He was sent to Fort McHenry on 11 Apr 1863 and sent to Fort Monroe for exchange on 19 Apr 1863. Confederate rolls show him absent from September 1863 until August 1864 as a result of having been captured when he served as a scout for General Lomax.

Rebecca Kibler was born 31 May 1844 and died 12 Jan 1925.   She was married on 8 Jun 1871 to John O. Bauserman.   John was the son of Reuben and Mary.   Reuben Bauserman had married Mary Smith on 20 Jun 1831.   Reuben and his family resided in **dwelling 1480**.   When John died Rebecca married John David Coffman on 17 Aug 1884.   John was the son of Joseph and Elizabeth. Joseph R. Coffman married Elizabeth Coffelt on 20 Aug. 1828. Joseph and his wife resided in **dwelling 1282**. John David Coffman was a widower at the time of his marriage to Rebecca. He had originally been married to Caroline Kessler. Caroline was born 6 Jun 1837 and died 21 Feb 1884. John David was born 4 Jun 1832 and died 10 Feb 1905. John David and Caroline were buried in the Coffman Cemetery at Columbia Furnace. Rebecca Kibler Bauserman Coffman was buried with her first husband John O. Bauserman in the Union Forge Cemetery.

James Kibler was born 8 Dec 1845. He was married three times. His first marriage was to Josephine Tibbitts of New York on 3 Jun 1873. Josephine died 30 Sep 1879. His second wife was Elizabeth Gates of Isle Anglesey, Wales. They were married on 8 Dec 1880. Elizabeth died 7 Sep 1894. On 5 Nov 1918 James married Annie Frost. James eventually moved to Jacksonville, Florida and earned his living as a carpenter. James was reported to have been a veteran of the Civil War. No record was discovered on his service.

Virginia Kibler was born 3 Apr 1848 and died 20 Nov 1931. She was married on 18 Dec 1870 to Nicholas W. Baker. Nicholas was a carpenter. He was the son of Thomas and Elizabeth. Nicholas was born 3 Apr 1845 and died 8 Aug 1927. Virginia and Nicholas were buried in the Mt. Jackson Cemetery.

Perry Kibler was born in 1850 and died in 1930. He was a teacher and a farmer. He was married on 25 Mar 1903 to Malinda J. Fravel. Malinda was the daughter of Jacob and Mahala. Jacob Fravel married Mahala Cline on 19 Oct 1843. Jacob and his family were located in **dwelling 1227**. Malinda was born 18 Sep 1854 and died in 1932. Perry and Malinda were buried in the Union Forge Cemetery.

Mary Kibler was born 31 May 1852 and died 18 Jun 1918. She was married to Robert S. Holler on 21 Feb 1872. Robert was the son of Isaac and Elizabeth. Isaac Holler married Elizabeth Marshall on 24 Dec 1828. Isaac Holler resided in **dwelling 1591**. Robert S. Holler is found in **dwelling 991**. Robert was born 23 Feb 1839 and died 20 Jun 1909. Mary and Robert were buried in the Massanutten Cemetery.

Ellen Kibler was married to Joseph L. Mauck on 26 May 1879. Ellen was born in 1853 and died in 1930.

Joseph L. Mauck was the son of James and Mary. James Harvey Mauck married Mary Catherine Marston on 17 Jun 1852. The Mauck family resided in **dwelling 377**. Joseph L. Mauck was born in 1856 and died in 1931. Ellen and Joseph were buried in the Massanutten Cemetery.

Alice Kibler was born 5 Aug 1857. She died 8 Mar 1944. Alice was married on 25 Dec 1877 to John L. Shaeffer. John was a school teacher. He was the son of Levi and Annie. Levi Shaeffer married Anna Crabill on 9 Mar 1841. Levi Schaeffer and his family resided in **dwelling 918**. John was born on 8 Mar 1843 and died 3 Mar 1919. Alice and John were buried in the St. Marys Pine Church Cemetery.

Ida Bell Kibler was married to Ira L. Olmstead on 1 Oct 1902. Ira was the son of Israel and Sarah. He was born in Greene County, New York. He was 62 years old at the time of this marriage and operated a hotel in Highmont, New York. Ida Bell Kibler Olmstead died 3 Sep 1941. Ida was buried in the Union Forge Cemetery.

RELATED FAMILY:

Martha Kibler, daughter of John, resided in **dwelling 50**.

Rosa Ann Wolverton, sister of Mary, married Jonathan Chilcott and resided in **dwelling 1214**.

David Wolverton, brother of Mary, married Mary Catherine Heltzell on 7 Feb 1848 and resided in **dwelling 1369**.

Lydia Wolverton, sister of Mary, married John Reynolds on 22 Mar 1859 and resided in **dwelling 1226**.

John Wolverton, brother of Mary, married Sarah Ann Riffey on 26 Jan 1854 and resided in **dwelling 1756**.

George Wolverton, brother of Mary, married Leanna Foltz on 14 Oct 1850 and resided in **dwelling 1733**.

Nathaniel Wolverton, brother of Mary, married Rebecca Lambert on 11 Sep 1851 and resided in **dwelling 1748**.

Wesley Wolverton, brother of Mary, married Catherine Shadwell on 17 Dec 1857 and resided in **dwelling 1244**.

1850 CENSUS: **John J. Kibler** and his family resided in dwelling 684 on page 48.

PAGE 53 EDINBURG DISTRICT   (Microfilm Page 577)

Dwelling 361 Family 361   .

Eli Coffelt	38	Farmer	3600	720	Virginia	
Sophia Coffelt	35				"	
Mary V. Coffelt	12				"	School
Ellen F. Coffelt	11				"	School
Elizabeth H. Coffelt	8				"	
Benjamin F. Coffelt	6				"	

Eli Coffelt was born 6 Oct 1821 and died 24 Aug 1898. He was married on 13 Apr 1846 to **Sophia Saum**. Sophia was the daughter of Daniel and Mary. Daniel Saum married Mary Brubaker on 28 May 1813. Sophia was born 7 Feb 1825 and died 16 Jan 1909. Eli and Sophia were buried in the Mt. Zion Lutheran Church Cemetery in Woodstock.

Mary Virgina Coffelt was born 10 Sep 1847 and died 5 Jul 1877. She was married to James Knox Polk Hoover on 13 Sep 1866. James was the son of Abraham and Rebecca. Abraham Hoover married Rebecca Marshall on 16 Nov 1840. Abraham and his family resided in **dwelling 1874**.   James Knox Polk Hoover was born 8 Mar 1845 and died 12 May 1907. When Mary Virginia died, James married Catherine Miller on 24 Mar 1878.   Catherine was born .in Rockingham County, Virginia. She was the daughter of George and Elizabeth. She was born 27 Jan 1858 and died 1 Sep 1915. James and both of his wives were buried in the Hoover Cemetery in Woodstock.

Ellen Frances Coffelt was born 24 Mar 1849 and died in 1921. She was married on 26 Mar 1868 to John Tyler Sager. John was the son of John and Christena. John Sager married Christena Wiseman on 10 Oct 1838. John was born 29 Nov 1841 and died 1914.   He was 5'6" with light complexion, light hair and blue eyes. He enlisted as a private at Woodstock in Company F of the 10th Virginia Infantry. He was detailed as a nurse in May 1863. He was taken POW at Spotsylvania Courthouse on 20 May 1864 and was released under oath on 7 Jun 1865. Ellen and John were buried in the Jonas Gochenour Cemetery near Woodstock.

Elizabeth Helen Coffelt was born 22 Feb 1852. She married Jacob Harvey Gochenour on 31 Dec 1874. Jacob was the son of Jonas and Mary Ann. Jonas Gochenour married Mary Ann Coffman on 17 Mar 1843. Jonas and his family are found in **dwelling 1835**. Jacob Harvey Gochenour was born

6 Nov 1848 and died 30 Dec 1914. Elizabeth and Jacob were buried in the Jonas Gochenour Cemetery in Woodstock.

Benjamin Franklin Coffelt was born 18 Nov 1853 and died 25 Nov 1941. He was married on 24 Dec 1878 to Ida Virginia Smootz. Ida was the daughter of P.W. and Hannah. She was born in 1857 and died in 1936. Ben and Ida were buried in the Mt. Zion Lutheran Church Cemetery in Woodstock.

RELATED FAMILY:

Maria Saum, sister of Sophia, married Isaac Hockman on 3 Nov 1834 and resided in **dwelling 1930**.

Samuel Saum, brother of Sophia, married Catherine Olivia Hisey on 10 Aug 1844 and resided in **dwelling 1888**.

1850 CENSUS: **Eli Coffelt** and his family resided in dwelling 1 on page 1.

PAGE 53 EDINBURG DISTRICT (Microfilm Page 577)

Dwelling 362 Family 362

Raphael M. Conn	54	Farmer	12,750	20,700	Va.	Just Mar
Mary E. Conn	37				"	Just Mar
Thomas E. Conn	18	Law Student			"	
William Conn	16				"	School
Sarah B. Conn	9				"	School
Richard Argenbright	18				"	School
John Williams	30	Carpenter			"	Just Mar
Margaret Williams	35				"	Just Mar
William Shown	28	Farmhand			"	
Julia Hall	21	(Mulatto) Houseservant			"	
Peter Hall	20	(Mulatto)			"	
Scot Hall	2m	(Mulatto)			"	
Martha Baker	17				"	

Raphael Morgan Conn was born 13 Nov 1805 and died 1 Mar 1887. He was one of a group of men who received approval to begin the Mt. Jackson Mfg. Company on 1 Apr 1848. Their task was to produce woolen goods. Raphael was also the individual who joined with D. H. Walton to organize the **Tenth Legion**. This was a group of Shenandoah County men who enlisted to support the southern cause at the outbreak of conflict. He is remembered in John Wayland's book for a stirring speech that he gave in Columbia Furnace to enlist men to the cause. He was given the rank of Colonel at the start of the conflict. He was orginally married on 23 Feb 1835 to Ann Eliza Almond of Page County, Virginia. His first wife was born 5 Mar 1815 and died 30 Oct 1836. In the 1850 census his wife was listed as Sililia A Conn. In 1859 he married **Mary E. Bussell**. Mary was born 20 Jul 1820 and died 6 Jun 1871. Rapahel Morgan Conn was buried in the Green Hill Cemetery in Luray, Virginia. Two of his wives are buried with him.

Thomas Erwin Conn enlisted on 15 Jul 1861 in Company K of the 33rd Virginia Infantry. He was made Color Sergeant of the unit in October 1861. He was absent sick in late October of that year. He was transferred to Company E and made a Lt. on 22 Apr 1862. He was taken prisoner on 27 Aug 1862. He was exchanged on 13 Dec 1862 and resigned soon thereafter.

William Conn appears as W. Conn on the roll of Company C of the 7th Virginia Cavalry.

Sarah Bell Conn was born in 1851 and died 23 Mar 1927. She was listed as the daughter of Raphael and Sililia. Sarah was married to Akin Robinson on 13 Aug 1884. Akin was the son of John and Mahala. John Robinson married Mahala J. Burke on 21 Feb 1848. John Robinson and his family resided in **dwelling 299**. Sarah Bell Conn Robinson was buried in the Lebanon Church Cemetery.

John Williams was from Stafford County, Virginia. He was the son of Tama and Scarlett. He was married on 31 May 1860 to **Mary Margaret Allison**. She was born 23 Oct 1820 and died 5 Oct 1897. She was buried in the Union Forge Cemetery.

William Shown was the son of Sarah. Sarah Shown resided in **dwelling 365**.

RELATED FAMILY:

Susan Margaret Conn, daughter of Raphael, married Samuel A. Danner on 12 May 1859 and resided in **dwelling 528**.

1850 CENSUS: **Raphael M. Conn** and his family resided in dwelling 1097 on page 77.

PAGE 53 EDINBURG DISTRICT (Microfilm Page 577)

Dwelling 363 Family 363

James McCoy	27	Farmhand 0	120	Ireland	Can't Read
Elizabeth McCoy	24			Virignia	
Thomas McCoy	2			"	
Sarah McCoy	1			"	
Nancy Rosenberger	59			"	

James McCoy was born in 1835 and died 18 Apr 1910. He was married on 4 Mar 1856 to Margaret Elizabeth Rosenberger. Margaret was the daughter of Nancy Rosenberger. James was born in Northern Ireland. He was the son of George and Margaret. James Mccoy was buried in the Mt. Zion Lutheran Church Cemetery near Woodstock. He is believed to have enlisted on 23 Mar 1862 at Rude's Hill as a Private in the 5th Virginia Infantry. He was in Company K and was captured on 17 Sep 1862 at Sharpsburg. He was paroled on 20 Sep 1862. James returned to the Company in December of 1862. He was on detached service to the Shenandoah Valley in 1863. He was captured again on 12 May 1864 and was sent to Fort Delaware. He was released on 10 Jun 1865 and is said to have died at his home in Mt. Airy on 18 Apr 1910.

Sarah "Sallie" McCoy was married on 2 Mar 1882 to William Perry Stultz. William was the son of Jacob and Lydia. Jacob W. Stultz married Lydia Naugle on 20 Nov 1849. William Stultz was a widower at the time of this marriage. He had married Roberta S. Smootz on 20 Sep 1877. Roberta was the daughter of William and Barbara. William H. Smootz and Barbara Gochenour were married on 15 Nov 1849. William Perry Stultz resided with his parents in dwelling 1841. William Perry Stultz married for the third time after Sallie's death. His third wife was Luella Shank. Luella Shank Stultz was born in 1859 and died in 1923. William and Luella were buried in the St. Luke Cemetery at St. Luke, Virginia. Roberta Smootz Stultz and Sallie McCoy Stultz are both believed to have been buried in the Stultz Cemetery in Alonzoville, Virginia.

1850 CENSUS: No record of this family has been located in 1850.

PAGE 53 EDINBURG DISTRICT   (Microfilm Page 577)

Dwelling 364   Family 364

Luke Racey	52 Day Labor	0	75 Virignia
Lydia Racey	52		"
William H. Racey	19 Day Labor		"
Eliza J. Racey	17		" School
Christopher C. Racey	13		" School
Luke Racey	11		" School
Linden Racey	9		" School

Luke Racey was married on 10 Aug 1835 to **Lydia Tidewich.** The bondsman for the marriage was John Lindenburg. Many of the children in this family were born in Hardy County, West Virginia.

William H. Racey was born 10 Sep 1842 and died 16 Dec 1908. He was married on 9 Mar 1862 to Eliza Jane Fry, the daughter of Phillip and Leah. Phillip Fry was married to Leah Ann Dysert on 19 Feb 1845. Phillip Fry and his family resided in **dwelling 1741**. She was born in 1845 and died in 1872. William H. Racey would remarry after the death of Leah. He married Isabella Irwin on 23 Jul 1876. Isabella was the daughter of Benjamin and Lucy. Benjamin Irwin married Lucy Coffelt on 7 May 1838. Benjamin and his family resided in **dwelling 1231**. Isabella Irwin Racey was born 2 Mar 1844 and died 16 Aug 1906. William and Isabella were buried in the St. Luke Lutheran Church Cemetery in St. Luke, Virginia. William was married for a third time to Luella V. Weast of Augusta County, Virginia on 12 Jun 1909. Luella died 31 Aug 1910 at the age of 43. She was buried in the Sherman Cemetery in Columbia Furnace. William H. Racey enlisted in Company C of the 33rd Virginia Infantry on 3 Jun 1861. He was absent sick in August 1861 and was home on furlough in February of 1862. He was reported to have deserted in December of 1862.

Eliza J. Racey was listed as Louisa Jane in marriage records. She married Joseph Hines on 23 Jul 1868. Joseph was the son of William and Sophia. William Hines married Sophia Wolverton on 18 Dec 1837. Joseph Hines died 25 Oct 1929 at the age of 81. Eliza was reported to have been born in Hardy County, West Virginia.

Christopher C. Racey was born in Hardy County on 21 Jul 1848. He died 26 Dec 1916. Christopher was married to Sarah Ellen Holler, the daughter of Henry and

Margaret on 17 Sep 1868. Henry Holler married Margaret Tascoe on 9 May 1842. Henry Holler and his family resided in **dwelling 1836**. Sarah Ellen was born 6 May 1847 and died 27 Mar 1935. Christopher and Sarah Ellen were buried in the Gravel Springs Cemetery in southwest Frederick County, Virginia. Christopher C. Racey was 5'7" with dark complexion, dark eyes and hair. He enlisted in Company C of the 12th Virginia Cavalry at Waynesboro on 19 Apr 1864. He was present in April through July of that year. He was paroled at Winchester on 9 May 1865.

Luke St. Racey was married on 31 Aug 1869 to Lydia Ann Shireman (aka Sherman). She was the daughter of Levi and Elizabeth. Levi Shireman was married to Elizabeth Holler on 4 Aug 1836. Levi and his family resided in **dwelling 1268**. Lydia Ann Shireman Racey was born in February of 1848 and died 6 Apr 1908.

Linden Racey was married on 20 Feb 1876 to Hannah Groves, the daughter of John and Sarah. John Groves married Sarah Hausenfluke on 11 May 1850. John and his family resided in **dwelling 1270**.

RELATED FAMILY:
James Madison Racey, son of Luke and Lydia, married Mary Ann Fadely on 12 Oct 1858 and resided in **dwelling 1229**.

1850 CENSUS: There is no mention of this family in Shenandoah County in 1850. It is likely they were residents of Hardy County.

PAGE 53 EDINBURG DISTRICT (Microfilm Page 577)

Dwelling 365 Family 365

Sarah Shaun	48	0	80	Virginia	Can't Read
Sarah Jane Shaun	22			"	Can't Read

Sarah Shaun and her family were present in Shenandoah County in 1850. The family name is listed as **Shown**. In the household two additional children, Elizabeth and William, were listed.

RELATED FAMILY:
William Shown, son of Sarah, resided in **dwelling 362**.

1850 CENSUS: **Sarah Shown** and her family resided in dwelling 1018 on page 71.

PAGE 53   EDINBURG DISTRICT   (Microfilm Page 577)

Dwelling 366   Family 366

Elias Hottel	57 Lawyer 0 244		Virginia	
Margaret Hottel	57		"	
David H. Hottel	22 Engineer		"	Just Mar
Mary E. Hottel	17		"	
Nathan Hottel	16 Shoemakers Apprentice		"	School
Margaret Hottel	12		"	School
Ann R. Hottel	8		"	School
Sophia Hottel	23		"	Just Mar

   Elias Hottel was born 24 Sep 1808 and died 11 Jun 1882. He was the son of John and Elizabeth. John W. Hottel married Elizabeth Swartz on 12 May 1803. Elias was married on 25 Jul 1833 to **Margaret Walter**. The bondsman for the marriage was Henry Gochenour. Margaret was born 5 Sep 1809 and moved with her daughter Ann R. Hottel Barr to Fletcher, Ohio after the death of Elias. Margaret died in Ohio on 8 Jul 1884. Elias Hottel served as Superintendent of the Shenandoah County Infirmary.

   David H. Hottel was born 5 Aug 1837 and died 16 Nov 1910. He is listed twice in this census. He also appears in the household of his wife's parents. David was married on 19 May 1860 to **Sophia Sheetz**. Sophia was the daughter of George and Elizabeth. There are several marriages for individuals named George Sheetz to women named Elizabeth. The most likely parents of Sophia were the George Sheetz and Elizabeth Bowman who were married on 14 Feb 1826. Sophia, David and her parents are reported to have resided in **dwelling 1796**. Sophia must have died shortly after the census was published. David enlisted in Company K of the 7th Virginia Cavalry. He married Sarah Catherine Barton on 21 May 1863. Sarah was located in **dwelling 1797** at the time of this census. She was the daughter of Nathaniel and Elizabeth. Nathaniel Barton married Elizabeth Miller. It is possible her parents were divorced as both reside independently in this census. Sarah Catherine Barton Hottel was born 28 Nov 1840 and died 3 Jul 1931. David and Sarah were buried in the Mt. Zion Lutheran Church Cemetery near Woodstock.

Mary Elizabeth Hottel was born 6 Mar 1842 and died 14 Jul 1902. She was married to T.P. Duncan of Troy, Ohio in 1876.

Nathan Hottel was born 12 Sep 1844 and died 13 Jul 1924. He was one member of this family who chose to go by the name Huddle. He was a member of Company K of the 7th Virginia Cavalry. He was called "Dock" by other members of his unit. Nathan married Mary E. Dewer of Augusta County, Virginia. She was born 7 Jan 1833 and died ca. 1903. Upon her death, Nathan married Lydia Shafer of Shadyside, Ohio. Nathan died in Armstrong Mills, Ohio. He may also be found in dwelling 208 of this census. He was an apprentice shoemaker in the residence of Josiah Heller. Josiah was a master shoemaker.

Margaret Hottel was born 12 Oct 1846 and died 22 Aug 1863.

Annie R. Hottel was born 21 Mar 1852 and died 21 Aug 1922. She was married on 23 Dec 1875 to Jacob D. Barr, the son of George and Maria. Annie and her family moved to Ohio in 1883. Jacob died 17 Apr 1912. They lived in originally in Piqua, Ohio, but later moved to Columbus, Ohio where Jacob was employed as a mechanic for the Columbus Buggy Company. He later worked for the Ralston Steel Car Company.

RELATED FAMILY:
        Jacob Hottel, brother of Elias, married Julia Ann Ramey on 19 May 1834 and resided in dwelling 1863.
        Mary Catherine Hottel, sister of Elias, married William Fravel on 12 Mar 1838 and resided in dwelling 1933.

NOTE: This was one family where brother literally fought brother during the Civil War. Amos Hottel, son of Elias and Margaret had removed to the west prior to this census. At the outbreak of armed conflict he enlisted in the Union army and was killed in combat on 17 Oct 1863 at Memphis, Tennessee.

1850 CENSUS: Elias Hottel and his family resided in dwelling 966 on page 67.

383

PAGE 54   EDINBURG DISTRICT   (Microfilm Page 578)

Dwelling 367   Family 367

```
Joseph S. Sheetz      42 Millwright  1520  695   Virginia
Ann R. Sheetz         36                          "
Calvin J. Sheetz      12                          "   School
James W. Sheetz        8                          "   School
Virginia C. Sheetz     6                          "
Albert Sheetz          4                          "
Catherine Sheetz      27                          "
```

      Joseph Sheetz was married on 21 Sep 1846 to **Ann Rebecca Utz.** The bondsman for the marriage was Abe Beidler. Rebecca was 86 years old when she died 6 Aug 1912.

      Calvin J. Sheetz, a carpenter, was married on 11 Mar 1868 to Sarah C. Litton. Sarah was the daughter of Abraham and Lucinda. Abraham Litton Jr. married Lucinda Miller on 3 Aug 1843. Sarah and her family resided in **dwelling 1851.**

      James W. Sheetz, died on 4 May 1923 at Narrow Passage Creek. He was 72 years old. Obituary records indicate that he had a wife who had died prior to this date. Her name is not known.

      Virginia C. Sheetz was married on 7 Mar 1876 Isaiah Kibler. Isaiah was the son of Samuel and Lydia. Samuel Kibler married Lydia Wiseman on 18 Sep 1849. Samuel Kibler and his family resided in **dwelling 1811.** Virginia Sheetz Kibler was born 30 Jan 1853 and died 22 Jan 1903. She was buried in the Sheetz Cemetery near Woodstock. Isaiah Kibler married Mary Elizabeth Shipe Lichliter on 8 Jan 1905. Mary Elizabeth was the daughter of Lorenzo and Catherine. Lorenzo Shipe had married Mary C. Rinker on 30 Oct 1870. Mary Elizabeth was born in 1873 and died in 1958. Her first husband was William B. Lichliter. Mary Elizabeth married William on 25 Dec 1892. William Lichliter and Mary Elizabeth Shipe Lichliter Kibler were buried in the Dedrick Cemetery in the Fort Valley. Isaiah Kibler was born 23 Nov 1849 and died 1 Mar 1931. He was buried in the Patmos Lutheran Church Cemetery in Woodstock.

      Catherine Sheetz may have been the daughter of Mathias and Catherine. Twenty year old Catherine appears in that household in 1850. Mathias Sheetz had married

Catherine Phillips on 2 Nov 1816. If this were the same
young lady, she would marry James W. Cooley on 3 May 1864.
James was the son of John and Elizabeth John Cooley
married Elizabeth Rebecca Hottel on 3 Aug 1836. James was
a veteran of the Civil War. He was a member of Company K
of the 33rd Virginia Infantry. He died 14 Mar 1922.
Catherine Sheetz Cooley was born 2 Feb 1830 and died 12 Mar
1895. She was buried in the Saint Pauls Lutheran Church
Cemetery.

1850 CENSUS: Joseph S. Sheetz and his family resided in
dwelling 142 on page 11.

PAGE 54   EDINBURG DISTRICT   (Microfilm Page 578)

Dwelling 368   Family 368

Phillip Sheetz	62	Farmer	8000	7311	Virginia
Sarah Sheetz	58				"
Abraham Sheetz	29	Farmer			"
Elizabeth A. Sheetz	30				"
Henrietta Sheetz	6				"
Joseph F. Sheetz	4				"
Sarah C. Sheetz	2				"
Francis Marion Sheetz	9m				"

       Phillip Sheetz was born 24 Feb 1798 and died
24 Jan 1875. He may have been the son of Jacob and Eva.
Jacob Sheetz married Eva Walker on 3 Jan 1788. Phillip was
married to **Sarah Kibler** on 27 Feb 1830.   Sarah Kibler
Sheetz died 7 Jun 1879 at the age of 78. Phillip and Sarah
are buried in the Mt. Cavalry Cemetery in Woodstock.

       Abraham Sheetz was born 16 Nov 1830 and died
3 Dec 1904. He was married on 13 Jan 1853 to **Elizabeth Ann
Layman**.   Elizabeth was the daughter of William and
Christena Hamman Layman. Elizabeth Ann Layman Sheetz was
born 12 Oct 1829 and died 8 Jul 1919.   Abraham and
Elizabeth were buried in the Mt. Calvary Cemetery.

       Henrietta Sheetz was born 20 Oct 1853 and died
16 Feb 1930. She was married on 10 Aug 1879 to William H.
Sheetz, the son of Samuel and Lydia. Samuel Sheetz married
Lydia Coffman on 5 Dec 1850. Samuel and Lydia and their
family resided in **dwelling 1792**. William H. Sheetz was
born 9 Jun 1852 and died 27 Jun 1935.   Henrietta and
William were buried in the Massanutten Cemetery.

Joseph Frank Sheetz was married on 29 Jul 1880 to Ella V. Miller, the daughter of Christley and Catherine. Christian Miller married Catherine Saum on 1 Apr 1844. Christian Miller and his family were located in **dwelling 1615**. Joseph was born 3 Jul 1855 and was a carpenter in Portsmouth, Virginia.

Sarah Catherine Sheetz was born 23 Aug 1857 and died 26 Dec 1862.

Francis Marion Sheetz was married on 25 Dec 1884 to Virginia Alice Litten. Virginia was the daughter of Abraham and Lucinda. Abraham Litten married Lucinda Miller on 3 Aug 1843. Abraham Litten and his family resided in **dwelling 1851**. Francis was born 29 Aug 1859 and died 9 Aug 1939. Virginia was born 10 Aug 1865 and died 30 Jan 1895. Virginia and Francis were buried in the Mt. Calvary Cemetery.

RELATED FAMILY:

William H. Sheetz, son of Phillip, married Lucy Hisey on 30 Dec 1855 and resided in **dwelling 369**.
Elizabeth Sheetz, daughter of Phillip, married Joseph Rosenberger on 30 May 1846 and resided in **dwelling 372**.

1850 CENSUS: Phillip Sheetz and his family resided in dwelling 147 on page 11.
Elizabeth Ann Layman resided with her parents in dwelling 794 on page 56.

PAGE 54 EDINBURG DISTRICT (Microfilm Page 578)

Dwelling 369 Family 369

William H. Sheetz	21 Farmer	0	100	Virginia
Lucy E. Sheetz	17			"
Charles M. Sheetz	10m			"
Amanda Rucker	13			" School

William H. Sheetz was the son of Phillip and Sarah. His mother was listed as Clara in marriage record. Phillip Sheetz had married Sarah Kibler on 27 Feb 1830. They resided in **dwelling 368**. William H. Sheetz was born 25 Mar 1838 and died 11 May 1920. He was married on 30 Dec 1855 to **Lucy Hisey**. Lucy was the daughter of David and Lucy. David Hisey married Lucy Boyer on 4 May 1820. Lucy Hisey Sheetz was born 29 Mar 1841 and died 25 Mar 1909.

William and Lucy were buried in the Mt. Calvary Cemetery in Woodstock. William H. Sheetz probably served in the Confederate Army. However, specific information regarding his service is not known. It should be noted there was a William H. Sheetz who enlisted on 27 Aug 1862 at New Market in Company K of the 12th Virginia Cavalry. He was absent sick in November of 1862. The last entry in December of 1863 indicated that he had been sick since 5 December 1862. There is no further record.

       Charles M. Sheetz was born 24 Jul 1859 and died 8 Oct 1935. He was married on 20 Oct 1880 to Mary E. Sheetz. Mary was the daughter of William and Christena. William W. Sheetz married Christena Frances Hottel on 28 Mar 1861. Mary E. Sheetz was born 18 Jan 1862 and died 27 Jan 1934. Charles and Mary were buried in the Mt. Calvary Cemetery.

       Amanda E. Rucker was the daughter of William and Mary. She was listed with her parents in **dwelling 1742**. Amanda was married on 8 Dec 1872 to Walton H. Farra. Walton was the son of Whiting and Harriet. Whiting D. Farra married Harriet Gray on 25 Feb 1833. The Farra family resided in **dwelling 598**. Walton was a widower at the time of the marriage. He was first married to Adaline Rosenberger on 31 May 1870. Adaline was the daughter of John and Sally. John Rosenberger married Sarah Shaffer on 24 Nov 1837. Adaline and her parents were residents of **dwelling 592**. There is a tombstone for Walton H. Farra in the New Mount Jackson Cemetery. It reports that he was a member of Company B of the 17th Virginia Infantry.

RELATED FAMILY:

       Elizabeth Sheetz, sister of William, married Joseph Rosenberger on 30 May 1846 and resided in **dwelling 372**.

1850 CENSUS: **William H. Sheetz** resided with his parents in dwelling 147 on page 11.
                   Amanda Rucker resided with her parents in dwelling 129 on page 10.

PAGE 54 EDINBURG DISTRICT   **(Microfilm Page 578)**

Dwelling 370 Family 370

William Thompson	22	Day Labor	0	40	Va.	Just Mar
Elizabeth S. Thompson	20			"		Just Mar

387

There are few records related to this family.
The couple appears to have been buried in the Massanutten
Cemetery. **William Thompson** was born 31 Dec 1835 and died
30 May 1911. His wife **Elizabeth S. Thompson** was born 25
Dec 1842 and died 22 Apr 1903.

1850 CENSUS: There is no record of this family in the
census.

PAGE 54   EDINBURG DISTRICT   (Microfilm Page 578)

Dwelling 371   Family 371

Elias Hottel of Joseph	27 Miller	2520	2135	Virginia
Julia Ann Hottel	29			"
Eliza J. Hottel	5			"
William H. Hottel	3			"
Lucy E. Hottel	2			"
Mary A. Hottel	3m			"
Isaac Hottel	20 Millers Apprentice			"
Susan McInturff	21 Housegirl			"

Elias Hottel was born 13 Jul 1833 and died 9
Apr 1906. He was the son of Joseph and Catherine. Joseph
Hottel married Catherine Snarr on 18 Jun 1815. Joseph
Hottel resided in **dwelling 1854.** Elias was married on 2
Feb 1854 to **Julia Ann McInturff.** She was the daughter of
Henry and Elizabeth. Henry F. McInturff "Mountain Henry"
married Elizabeth Ridenour on 28 Feb 1821. Elizabeth
Ridenour McInturff and her family are found in **dwelling
455.** Julia Ann McInturff Hottel was born 3 Jan 1831 and
died 27 Dec 1898. Elias and Julia were buried in the
Hottel Cemetery at Pughs Run. Elias Hottel was exempt from
military service during the Civil War as he was making
flour for the government. He had mills at Narrow Passage,
Valley and White Sulfur. Upon the death of Julia, Elias
married Annie R. Miller on 13 Sep 1900. Annie was the
daughter of Christian and Catherine. Christian Miller
married Catherine Saum on 1 Apr 1844. Christian Miller and
his family resided in **dwelling 1615.**

Elizabeth Jane Hottel was born 10 Nov 1854 and
died 2 Jan 1909. She was married to Samuel Krebs Hottel
on 24 Dec 1878. Samuel was born 27 Feb 1854 and died 3 Jul
1917. Elizabeth and Samuel were buried in the Massanutten
Cemetery. Samuel was the son of Jacob and Ann. Jacob
Andrew Hottel and Ann Maria Mort were married on 14 Mar
1850 and resided in **dwelling 2000.**

William Henry Hottel was born 5 Oct 1856 and died 29 Feb 1920. He was married on 26 Oct 1880 to Lydia V. Funkhouser. Lydia was the daughter of Phillip and Elizabeth. Phillip A. Funkhouser married Elizabeth Hottel on 11 Mar 1841. Phillip and his family resided in **dwelling 1935**. Lydia V. Funkhouser was born 9 Mar 1858 and died 8 Dec 1920. William and his family resided in Luray, Virginia and were buried in the Green Hill Cemetery in that city.

Lucy E. Hottel was born 5 Oct 1856 and died as a young child.

Mary Alice Hottel was born 25 Feb 1860 and died 26 Mar 1928. She was married to Daniel Hottel on 13 Feb 1879. Daniel was the brother of Samuel Krebs Hottel, the husband of Mary Alice's sister Elizabeth Jane. Daniel was born 11 Mar 1852 and died 28 Jun 1919. Mary Alice and Daniel were buried in the Toms Brook Cemetery.

Isaac T. Hottel was listed twice in this census. He appears in **dwelling 1745** with his parents. He was the son of George and Cassandra. George Hottel married Cassandra Fleming on 25 Dec 1837 in Rockingham County, Virginia. Isaac was born 25 Jan 1840 and died 14 Sep 1902. He was born in Page County, Virginia. He was married to Frances Jane Victoria Wetzel on 22 Feb 1866. Frances was the daughter of Henry and Mary Catherine. Her father was a minister. Hottel family history indicates that the Reverend Henry Wetzel had married Mary Catherine Hilker of Augusta County, Virginia. Augusta County marriage records indicate on 5 Dec 1839 Henry Wetzel married Mary Catherine Staubus. This should be checked by individuals interested in this family. France Jane Victoria Wetzel Hottel died 22 Mar 1871 at the age of 28 years, 3 months and 2 days old. She is buried at the Zion Lutheran Church Cemetery in Edinburg. Upon the death of Frances, Isaac was married to Catherine Fansler on 11 Oct 1872. Catherine was the daughter of William and Nelly. William Fansler married Nelly Walters on 28 Jan 1833. The Fansler family resided in **dwelling 2003**. Catherine Fansler Hottel was born 23 Oct 1836 and died 25 May 1883. When Catherine died Isaac T. Hottel married her sister Barbara. Isaac and Barbara were married on 5 Mar 1885. Barbara was born 14 Feb 1840 and died 24 Feb 1906. Isaac T. Hottel was born 25 Jan 1840 and died 14 Sep 1902. Isaac, Catherine and Barbara were buried in the Massanutten Cemetery. Isaac T. Hottel enlisted in Company C of the 33rd Virginia Infantry on 29 Apr 1861.

He was wounded on 5 Sep 1861 near Woodstock. He was absent through February 1862. He returned to his unit in April and was reported as AWOL on the 29 May 1862. There was an Isaac Hottel listed on the roll of Company C of the 7th Virginia Cavalry.

Susan McInturff was the sister of Julia Ann McInturff. She was married on 9 Jun 1867 to Joseph Smoke. Joseph was the son of Jacob and Christena. Jacob Smoke married Christena Lineweaver on 8 Dec 1840.

RELATED FAMILY:

Marcus M. McInturff, brother of Julia, married Mary E. Long on 16 Dec 1858 and resided in **dwelling 456.**

Henry F. McInturff, brother of Julia, resided with his mother in **dwelling 455.**

Elizabeth Miller McInturff, sister of Julia, married Jacob M. Lichliter on 3 Mar 1841 and resided in **dwelling 542.**

Lewis McInturff, brother of Julia, married Margaret Ann Edwards on 16 Nov 1854 and resided in **dwelling 1944.**

Nancy Ann McInturff, sister of Julia, married Elanson Reynard on 5 Dec 1848 and resided in **dwelling 250.**

Alfred McInturff, brother of Julia, married Mary Teeter on 24 May 1855 and resided in **dwelling 232.**

1850 CENSUS: **Elias Hottel** resided with his father in dwelling 2060 on page 148.

Julia Ann McInturff resided with her parents in dwelling 1923 on page 138.

Susan McInturff resided with her sister Elizabeth Lichliter in dwelling 1897 on page 137.

Isaac Hottel resided with his parents in dwelling 683 on page 48.

PAGE 54   EDINBURG DISTRICT   (Microfilm Page 578)

Dwelling 372   Family 372

Joseph Rosenberger	41	Shoemaker	4000	586	Virginia
Elizabeth Rosenberger	35				"
Sarah C. Rosenberger	14				"

Joseph Rosenberger was born 28 Oct 1816 and died 6 Feb 1908. He was married to **Elizabeth Sheetz** on 30 May 1846. Elizabeth was the daughter of Phillip. Elizabeth was born 21 Jan 1822 and died 27 Aug 1863. It is believed that she was the daughter of the Phillip Sheetz who appears in **dwelling 368**. However, marriage records indicate that he was married to Sarah Kibler on 27 Feb 1830. The discrepancy regarding the birth of Elizabeth and his marriage date creates a problem. Phillip may have been married prior to his 1830 marriage to Sarah Kibler. However, at this time no other marriage record has been located. Joseph and Elizabeth were buried in the Mt. Calvary Cemetery near Woodstock. After Elizabeth died Joseph was married on 29 Aug 1865 to Margaret Ann Kibler. Margaret Ann Kibler was the daughter of Catherine and William. William Kibler married Catherine Lineweaver on 26 Dec 1820. William Kibler and his family resided in dwelling 1802. In that marriage Joseph was listed as the son of Abraham and Ann.

Sarah C. Rosenberger died 8 Nov 1922 at the age of 75 years, 9 months and 28 days old. She was married on 7 Mar 1867 to George Washington Sheetz. George was the son of George and Elizabeth. George Sheetz married Elizabeth Kibler on 22 Mar 1836. George and his family resided in **dwelling 2161**. George Washington Sheetz was born 25 Jul 1843 and died 24 May 1919. They were buried in the Sheetz Cemetery near Woodstock.

RELATED FAMILY:

William H. Sheetz, probable half brother of Elizabeth, married Lucy Hisey on 30 Dec 1855 and resided in **dwelling 369**.

1850 CENSUS: Joseph Rosenberger and his family resided in dwelling 151 on page 11.

PAGE 55 POWELLS FORT (Microfilm Page 735)

Dwelling 373 Family 373

Name	Age	Occupation	Value	Birthplace	Notes
Lewis Marston	57	Wagon Maker	300	60 Virginia	
Margaret Marston	49			"	Can't Read
George Marston	18	Farmhand		"	
Thornton Marston	12			"	School
Edward Marston	6			"	
Andrew Marston	3			"	

Lewis Marston was one of three Marston brothers who are found in Shenandoah County during this period. According to Marston family records he was the son of Thomas Marston. The Marston family were originally located in Spotsylvania, Rappahannock and Culpepper Counties. No marriage record for Lewis has been discovered. However, Marston records indicate that he was married to Fannie Scothern. Fannie was the sister of Phoebe Scothern, the wife of Joseph Homer Hisey. Lewis was also a minister.

George T. Marston was married to Mary C. Evans on 19 Sep 1867. She was the daughter of David and Mary. David Evans married Mary Walters on 4 Jul 1843. David and his family resided in **dwelling 1873**. Mary C. Evans Marston died shortly after their marriage and George was married to Caroline J. Coffman Bell on 14 Mar 1875. Caroline was a widow. She was the daughter of Henry and Catherine. Henry Coffman married Catherine Ann Hupp on 10 Oct 1831. Caroline died 1 Dec 1919. George T. Marston died 19 Apr 1915. It is reported that they were buried in the Ketochin Cemetery in Purcellville, Virginia. George Thomas Marston enlisted in Company C of the 33rd Virginia Infantry on 3 Jun 1861. He was wounded at Chancellorsville on 3 May 1863. He was absent with his wound through June of 1863. On 28 Sep 1863 he was admitted to Chimborazo Hospital with diarrhea. He returned to duty on 28 Nov 1863. He was admitted again to Chimborazo with an eye injury on 29 Nov 1863. He returned to duty on 19 Dec 1863. He was paroled on 4 May 1865. George Thomas Marston was 5'6" with fair complexion, brown hair and hazel eyes. There is a tombstone in the Old Edinburg Cemetery which commemorates his service in the Confederate Army. His obituary reports that he was married three time. Only two of these marriages are known to this researcher.

Thornton Jefferson Marston died 17 Apr 1926 at the age of 78. He was married to Rebecca F. Scothern on 5 Aug 1869. Rebecca was the daughter of David and Sarah. David Scothern was married to Sarah Walker on 13 Mar 1845. David and his family were located in **dwelling 660**. Rebecca F. Scothern Marston died 16 Sep 1918 at the age of 69.

Andrew Jackson Marston was married on 26 Jul 1887 to Mollie B. Jordan. Mollie was the daughter of Lydia. Andrew Jackson Marston died 29 Feb 1920. He was 68.

392

RELATED FAMILY:
   Joseph H. Marston, son of Lewis, married Eva Rebecca Grove on 19 Dec 1858 and resided in **dwelling 74**.
   Joseph G. Marston, brother of Lewis, married Hannah Eppley on 14 Nov 1832 and resided in **dwelling 374**.
   Powell Marston, brother of Lewis, was located in **dwelling 391**.

1850 CENSUS: **Lewis Marston** and his family resided in dwelling 740 on page 52. Lewis was reported to have been deaf in that census.

PAGE 55 POWELLS FORT (**Microfilm Page 735**)

Dwelling 374 Family 374

Joseph Marston	45	Marston, Buck and Co. Pig Iron Mf.
	38,731 13,675	Virginia
	2,730	
Hannah L. Marston	44	"
Joseph Marston	17 Hotter	"
John R. Marston	15	" School
Caroline Marston	9	" School
Charles B. Marston	2	"
Green B. L. Marston	3m	"
Francis P. Marston	6m	"
Jane E. Barton	22 Housegirl	"

   Joseph G. Marston is believed to have been the son of Thomas Marston. The family was scattered throughout Spotsylvania, Rappahannock and Culpepper counties. Joseph operated the Caroline Furnace for the Lobdell Car Wheel Company of Wilmington, Delaware. The furnace produced about 3 tons of pig iron each day. The operation consumed about 200 bushels of charcoal for each ton of pig iron produced. Furnaces had existed for many years in the Fort Valley area. They were originated by an individual named Blackford from Page County. He operated three furnaces which were named after his daughters. Caroline Furnace was the one operated by Joseph Marston. It was in the southern end of the Fort and was located near the Luray road. Elizabeth Furnace was at the other end of the Fort near the Strasburg and Front Royal areas. The final of Mr. Blackford's furnace was the Isabella Furnace in Page County. The furnaces in the Fort Valley were burned and destroyed by Federal forces during the Civil War. Joseph G. Marston was 64 years old when he died 20 Nov 1873. He was married in Page County, Virginia to **Hannah Eppley** on

14 Nov 1832. Hannah was born about 1806 and died ca. 1880 at the home of her son Charles Bush Marston in Lost River, West Virginia. Joseph and Hannah were buried in the Isaiah Clem Cemetery in the vicinity of Edith in the Fort Valley.

Joseph G. Marston Jr. was born 8 Nov 1841. He was a carpenter at the time he joined the 10th Virginia Infantry on 18 Apr 1861. He was a private in Company C. He appears as a 4th Corporal on 2 Aug 1861. He later served with Company F of the 10th Virginia Infantry. Eventually he enlisted in the 35th Virginia Cavalry. On 9 Sep 1862 he was appointed a 2nd Lt. with Company E of the 35th. Joseph was married on 17 Aug 1863 to Martha J. Barton. Martha was the daughter of Mathew and Mary. Mathew Barton married Mary Boyd on 14 Mar 1832. Martha and her parents resided in **dwelling 396**. Martha J. Barton Marston was born 10 Oct 1843 and died 22 Apr 1902. She was buried in the Isaiah Clem Cemetery in Edith.

NOTE: Joseph Marston, son of Joseph and Hannah, married Catherine Good on 13 May 1869. This is a bit of a problem. According to records Martha J. Barton Marston did not die until 22 Apr 1902. Joseph G. Marston Jr. and Martha J. Barton Marston had a daughter Frances Blanche Marston who was born 25 Mar 1871. This needs to be clarified. Catherine Good Marston was the daughter of Abraham and Elizabeth.

John Robert Marston was born 22 Dec 1844. He joined the 10th Virginia Infantry on 1 May 1861 at Harpers Ferry. He served as a private in Company C. He died on 26 Mar 1862 in the Chimborazo Hospital of Typhoid Fever. He was buried in the Isaiah Clem Cemetery on Rt. 675 in the vicinity of Edith in the Fort Valley.

Caroline "Carrie" Marston was born in 1846 and was married on 23 Jun 1872 to Henry W. Shipp. Henry was from Knox County, Ohio. He was the son of Jacob and Dorcas.

Charles Bush Marston was born 4 Jun 1854 and died 11 Jul 1915. He was married to Phoebe Josephine Glenn. She was the daughter of John Clark and Harriet Catherine Wilson Glenn. Josephine was born 24 Nov 1855 and died 16 Jul 1939. He resided in Lost River, West Virginia.

Greenberry L. Marston was born 22 Mar 1858 and died 11 Jul 1858. He was deceased at the time of this

census. Greenberry was buried in the Isaiah Clem
Cemetery.

Francis Perry Marston was born 18 Dec 1859 and
died 1 Aug 1860. Francis was a male. He is listed as
Frances on his tombstone in the Isaiah Clem Cemetery in the
Fort Valley.

RELATED FAMILY:
    Andrew J. Marston, son of Joseph, married
Sarah Isabella Miller on 29 Jul 1858 and resided in
dwelliing 375.
    Mary Catherine Marston, daughter of Joseph,
married James Harvey Mauck on 12 Jun 1852 and resided in
dwelling 377.
    Ann Elizabeth Marston, daughter of Joseph,
married Lewis Clem on 12 Feb 1857 and resided in **dwelling
397**.
    Thomas Marston, son of Joseph, married Susan
A. Mauck on 5 Aug 1857 and resided in **dwelling 378**.
    Lewis Marston, brother of Joseph, resided
in **dwelling 373**.
    Powell Marston, brother of Joseph, resided
in **dwelling 391**.

1850 CENSUS: **Joseph Marston** and his family resided in
        dwelling 1823 on page 131.

PAGE 55 POWELLS FORT **(Microfilm Page 735)**

Dwelling 375 **Family 375**

Andrew J. Marston	22 Wagoner	0	50	Virginia
Sarah I. Marston	23			"
George F. Marston	1			"

    Andrew Jackson Marston was the son of Joseph
and Hannah. Joseph Marston married Hannah Eppley on 14 Nov
1832 in Page County, Virginia. Andrew's father was the
wealthy manager of the Caroline Furnace. They resided in
dwelling 374. Andrew was married to **Sarah Isabelle Miller**
on 29 Jul 1858. Sarah was the daughter of Timothy and
Julia Ann. Timothy Miller married Julia Ann Glenn on 17
Jun 1823. Julia Ann Miller resided in **dwelling 501**. Julia
Ann was reported to have been born in Pennsylvania. Andrew
Jackson Marston was born in Page County, Virginia. He was
5'9" with fair complexion, dark hair and grey eyes. Andrew
enlisted as a private in Company E of the 35th Virginia

Cavalry. He enlisted on 30 Jul 1862. He was AWOL on 31 Aug 1864 and was paroled at on 20 Apr 1865.

George F. Marston was a miner at the time of his marriage. He was married to Martha Ellen Good on 19 Feb 1885 in Page County. Martha was the daughter of Henry and Frances. Henry Good married Frances Aleshire on 13 Jan 1852 in Page County, Virginia.

RELATED FAMILY:
Mary Catherine Marston, sister of Andrew, married James Harvey Mauck on 17 Jun 1852 and resided in **dwelling 377**.
Ann Elizabeth Marston, sister of Andrew, married Lewis Clem on 12 Feb 1857 and resided in **dwelling 397**.
Thomas Marston, brother of Andrew, married Susan A. Mauck on 5 Aug 1857 and resided in **dwelling 378**.
Thomas Miller, brother of Sarah, married Margaret Barton on 21 Nov 1854 and resided in **dwelling 1263**.
John Miller, brother of Sarah, resided in **dwelling 497**.

1850 CENSUS: **Andrew Jackson Marston** resided with his parents in dwelling 1823 on page 131.

PAGE 55 POWELLS FORT (Microfilm Page 735)

Dwelling 376   Family 376

Jacob Sine	58	Furnace Filler 0	60 Virignia	Can't Read
Mary Sine	57		"	
Sarah Sine	23	Housekeeper	"	Can't Read
Elizabeth Sine	21		"	Can't Read

Jacob Sine was born 24 Oct 1800 and died 11 Sep 1874. He was married to **Mary Beeler** on 13 Jan 1823. The bondsman for the marriage was Nicholas Druck. Mary Beeler Sine was born 3 Nov 1793 and died 20 Jun 1859. Jacob and Mary were buried in the Sine Cemetery near Edith in the Fort Valley.

RELATED FAMILY:
Susan Sine, daughter of Jacob, married Hezikah Mysinger (aka Mozengo) on 26 Jan 1854 and resided in **dwelling 388**.

John P. Sine, son of Jacob, resided in dwelling 501.

Christina Sine, daughter of Jacob, married George Allen on 7 Dec 1846 and resided in dwelling 591.

Margaret Sine, daughter of Jacob, married Enoch Duncan on 6 Jan 1857 and resided in dwelling 386.

1850 CENSUS: Jacob Sine and his family resided in dwelling 1510 on page 108.

PAGE 55 POWELLS FORT   (Microfilm Page 735)

Dwelling 377   Family 377

Harvey Mauck	30	Farmhand 0	136	Virginia
Mary C. Mauck	26			"
Joseph Mauck	3			"
Lucy A. Mauck	1			"

James Harvey Mauck was the son of Henry and Margaret. Henry Mauck married Margaret Eleshite on 28 Jul 1828. They were married in Page County, the site of James Harvey Mauck's birth. He died 24 Jan 1865 at the age of 35 years, 1 month and 3 days old. The cause of death was listed as spasms. He was married to Mary Catherine Marston on 17 Jun 1852. Mary Catherine was the daughter of Joseph and Hannah. Joseph Marston married Hannah Eppley on 14 Nov 1832. Joseph and Hannah resided in dwelling 374. On 22 Mar 1866 the widow Mary Catherine Marston Mauck was married to John P. Sine. John was the son of Jacob and Mary. Jacob Sine married Mary Beeler on 13 Jan 1823. Jacob and his family resided in dwelling 376. John P. Sine was located in dwelling 501. John P. Sine died 19 Feb 1883. Mary Catherine died 4 Jan 1888. They were buried in the Pughs Run Cemetery.

Joseph L. Mauck was born in 1856 and died in 1931. He was married on 26 May 1879 to Ellen Kibler. Ellen was the daughter of John and Mary. John Kibler married Mary Wolverton on 1 Jun 1840. John Kibler and his family resided in dwelling 360. Ellen Kibler Mauck was born in 1853 and died on 30 May 1930. They were buried in the Massanutten Cemetery.

Lucy H. Mauck listed her age as 28 when she married 29 year old James M. Strickler on 5 Aug 1893. James was born and resided in Rockingham County, Virginia. He was the son of Phillip and Mary. He was a miller.

RELATED FAMILY:
              William Thomas Marston, brother of Mary
Catherine, married **Susan A. Mauck** (sister of James) on 5
Aug 1857 and resided in **dwelling 378.**
              Ann Elizabeth Marston, sister of Mary
Catherine, married Lewis Clem on 12 Feb 1857 and resided
in **dwelling 397.**
              Andrew Jackson Marston, brother of Mary
Catherine, married Sarah Isabelle Miller on 29 Jul 1858 and
resided in **dwelling 375.**

1850 CENSUS: **James Harvey Mauck** resided in dwelling 1826
                    on page 131. He was a joiner and resided
                    in the home of William Litten.
              Mary Catherine Marston resided with her
                    parents in dwelling 1823 on page 131.

PAGE 55 POWELLS FORT (Microfilm Page 735)

Dwelling 378 Family 378

Thomas Marston	24 Wagoner	0	52 Virginia
Susan Marston	25		"
Emma J. Marston	3		"
Hannah Marston	3m		"

      William Thomas Marston was born 24 Aug 1835 and
died 21 Nov 1899. He was the son of Joseph and Hannah.
Joseph Marston married Hannah Eppley on 14 Nov 1832. They
were married in Page County, Virginia. William Thomas
Marston married **Susan A. Mauck** on 5 Aug 1857. They were
married in Page County, Virginia. Susan was the daughter
of Henry and Margaret. Henry Mauck married Margaret
Eleshire on 28 Jul 1828. Susan was born 10 Feb 1835 and
died 29 Jun 1910. William and Susan were buried in the
Henry McInturff Cemetery in the Fort Valley.

      Emma J. Marston is believed to have been Emma
Susan Marston. She married John W. Abell. She was born
21 May 1858 and died 15 Aug 1920. John W. Abell was born
22 Jul 1854 and died 15 May 1916. Emma and John were
buried at the Zion Cemetery near Woodstock.

      Hannah Marston was born in 1860 and died in
1942. She was married originally to John F. Grim on 22 Jan
1888. John was the son of Phillip and Elizabeth. Phillip
Grim married Elizabeth McCullough on 12 Oct 1835. Phillip
Grim and his family resided in **dwelling 587.** John Grim was

born 6 Aug 1840 and died 8 Apr 1893. After John died, Hannah was married to Samuel Keller on 28 Jun 1900. Samuel Keller was the divorced son of John and Mahala. John Keller married Mahala Lichliter on 2 Jan 1845. Samuel Keller died in 1927. Hannah and Samuel were buried in the McInturff Cemetery Number 2 in the Fort Valley. John Grim appears to have been buried in the Hawkinson United Methodist Church Cemetery.

RELATED FAMILY:

Mary Catherine Marston, sister of Thomas, married **James Harvey Mauck** on 17 Jun 1852. James Harvey Mauck was the brother of Susan. Mary Catherine and James resided in **dwelling 377**.

Ann Elizabeth Marston, sister of Thomas, married Lewis Clem on 12 Feb 1857 and resided in **dwelling 397**.

Andrew Jackson Marston, brother of Thomas, married Sarah Isabelle Miller on 29 Jul 1858 and resided in **dwelling 375**.

1850 CENSUS: William **Thomas Marston** resided with his parents in dwelling 1823 on page 131.

PAGE 55 POWELLS FORT (Microfilm Page 735)

Dwelling 379 Family 379

William Moreland	55	Farmer	700	287	Virginia
Mary M. Moreland	45				" Can't Read
Joel Moreland	25	Collier			"
Levi Moreland	23	Farmhand			"
William J. Moreland	18	Farmhand			"
Mary C. Moreland	14				" School
Henry C. Moreland	12				" School
Isaac T. Moreland	9				" School
George W. Moreland	6				"
John G. B. Moreland	3				"

William M. Moreland died 15 Oct 1881 at the age of 77 years and 2 months old. He was married on 24 Jul 1833 to **Mary Magdalene Ross**. Mary was the daughter of Adam Ross. Adam Ross married Mary Magdalene Walters on 29 Oct 1796. Mary was 65 years, 5 months and 14 days old when she died in November of 1881. William and Mary were buried in the Isaiah Clem Cemetery.

Joel Moreland was married on 22 Nov 1866 to Ellen Simpson. Ellen was the daughter of David and Ann. Two sisters of Ellen resided in **dwelling 389**. Joel Moreland was 5'9" with dark complexion, light hair and blue eyes. He enlisted in Company E of the 35th Battalion Virginia Cavalry. He enlisted as a private on 30 Jul 1863. He was present on April 1864 and AWOL on 31 Aug 1864. Joel was paroled at New Market on 20 Apr 1865.

Levi Moreland enlisted in the 33rd Virginia Infantry in Company C on 29 Apr 1861. He was present through April of 1862. He was absent sick in September of 1862 and returned to his unit in October of the same year. On 3 July 1863, Levi Moreland was killed in action at Gettysburg.

William J. Moreland followed his brother Levi into action on 29 May 1861. He joined Levi in Company C of the 33rd Virginia Infantry. He was present at every muster until April of 1862. He became the first of the Moreland brothers to fall in action. He was killed on 27 Jun 1862 at Gaines Mill outside of Richmond.

Mary C. Moreland was born 24 Jun 1845 and died 10 Jan 1909. She was married in December of 1881 to Manoah Harmon. Manoah was the son of Benjamin and Peggy. Benjamin Harman married Margaret "Peggy" McInturff on 25 Aug 1815. Manoah Harmon was born 25 Feb 1822 and died 22 Nov 1903. He was a widower at the time of his marriage. Manoah had married Elizabeth Ann McInturff on 22 Nov 1856. Elizabeth was the daughter of David and Mary Polly Coverstone McInturff. Manoah and Elizabeth resided in **dwelling 414**. Elizabeth McInturff Harmon was born 16 May 1826 and died 24 Feb 1867. Manoah, Elizabeth and Mary C. Moreland Harmon were buried in the Sponaugle Cemetery in the Fort Valley.

Henry Clay Moreland was born 21 May 1847 and died 7 Oct 1921. He was married on 23 Apr 1874 to Minerva Munch. Minerva was the daughter of Silas and Rebecca. Silas Munch married Rebecca Jane Barr on 18 Sep 1843. Silas and his family resided in **dwelling 525**. Minerva Munch Moreland was born 20 May 1855 and died 4 Jan 1918. Henry and Minerva were buried in the Munch Cemetery.

Isaac Thomas Moreland was born 1851 and died 1925. He was married on 13 May 1880 to Emma Sophia Shuff. Sophia was the daughter of William and Margaret. William

Shuff married Margaret Glenn on 20 Jul 1833. William Shuff and his family were located in **dwelling 393**. Sophia was born 5 Aug 1857 and died 18 Dec 1906. She died in Mills County, Texas and was buried in the Pleasant Grove Cemetery in that county.

George Moreland died 26 Sep 1906 at the age of 52 years, 5 months and 3 days old. He was buried in the Sponaugle Cemetery in the Fort.

RELATED FAMILY:

Rebecca Moreland, daughter of William, married Jackson Lehew on 2 Mar 1857 and resided in **dwelling 382**.

Abraham Ross married **Lydia Ross** on 24 Jan 1831. One of these two was the sibling of Mary Magdalene. They resided in **dwelling 406**.

1850 CENSUS: **William Moreland** and his family resided in dwelling 1828 on page 131.

PAGE 56 POWELLS FORT (Microfilm Page 736)

Dwelling 380 Family 380

Adam Proctor	37	Miner 0	25	Virginia
Abelia Proctor	29		"	Can't Read
Nancy C. Proctor	7		"	
James M. Proctor	6		"	
Rebecca J. Proctor	3		"	
Nancy Ward	70		"	Can't Read

The surname **Ward** was difficult to read. It may be that this is not correct. It is possible that **Nancy** was related in some manner to the family in this household. The fact that the eldest daughter was named Nancy leads one to speculate that she was the parent of Adam or Abelia.

1850 CENSUS: **Nancy Ward** and her daughter **Arbelia** resided in dwelling 933 on page 335 in Page County, Virginia. **Adam Proctor** was a resident of their household.

401

Dwelling 381   Family 381

Daniel Bynaker	57	Miner 0	56	Hanover, Germany	Can't Rd
Mary Bynaker	37			Virginia	
Elizabeth Bynaker	14			"	
John W. Bynaker	11			"	School
Regina Bynaker	9			"	School
Samuel Bynaker	7			"	
Alexander Bynaker	5			"	
Mary C. Bynaker	2			"	

Alexander Bynaker, a laborer, was married to Mary Catherine Pence on 8 Aug 1878. Mary was the daughter of John and Lydia.

1850 CENSUS: There is no record of this family in Shenandoah County.

PAGE 56 POWELLS FORT   (Microfilm Page 736)

Dwelling 382   Family 382

Jackson Lehew	28	Miner 0	75	Virginia
Rebecca Lehew	21			"
William H. Lehew	2			"

Jackson Lehew died 19 Apr 1898 at the age of 66 years and 8 months old. He was the son of Abner and Sarah. Abner Lehew married Sarah Forsythe on 16 May 1824. In marriage records it was reported that Jackson Lehew was born in Warren County, Virginia. The Lehew family was very prominent in Page County, Virginia. The Lehew family was granted a 1,000 acre tract by Lord Fairfax in the early 1700's. The family home, Black Oaks is listed as one of the distinguished old homes of the county. Jackson was married to **Rebecca Moreland** on 2 Mar 1857. Rebecca was the daughter of William and Mary. William M. Moreland married Mary Magdalene Ross on 24 Jul 1833. William and his family resided in **dwelling 379**. Rebecca Moreland Lehew died 14 Sep 1885 at the age of 46 years, 8 months and 3 days old. Jackson married after Rebecca's death. On 11 Nov 1886 in Page County, 50 year old Jackson Lehew married Susan R. Bixler. Susan R. Lehew, listed as the wife of Jackson buried in the Moreland Cemetery. She died 3 Feb 1898 at the age of 44 years, 8 months and 15 days old. She was the daughter of Morgan and Ellen. Jackson resided in his later life in Page County. After his death an infamous activity occurred at his former residence. The **Page Courier** relates that on Saturday night 2 Jan 1915 Bessie Booth Burner and three of her children were hacked to death by an axe wielded by William Nichols. This activity took place 7 miles northwest of Luray. Two miles north of the Bixler's Ferry the tragedy occurred at the old Jackson Lehew place. William Nichols romantic advances had been spurned by Bessie Booth Burner.

RELATED FAMILY:

        William Lehew, brother of Jackson, married Emily Frances Balthis on 30 Nov 1854 and resided in **dwelling 1629.**

        Richard Lehew, brother of Jackson, married Rebecca Duncomb (Duncan) on 31 Dec 1857 and resided in **dwelling 383.**

1850 CENSUS: Rebecca Moreland resided with her parents in dwelling 1828 on page 131.

PAGE 56 POWELLS FORT (Microfilm Page 736)

Dwelling 383 Family 383

Richard Lehew	35 Miner 0	50	Virginia
Rebecca Lehew	21		"
Laura Lehew	1		"
Mary V. Lehew	1m		"

        Richard Lehew was the son of Abner and Sarah. Abner Lehew married Sarah Forsythe on 16 May 1824. Richard was born 19 Oct 1833 and died 30 Jan 1902. He was born in Warren County, Virginia. He married **Rebecca Duncomb (Duncan)** on 31 Dec 1857 in Page County, Virginia. Rebecca was the daughter of Charles and Anna. Charles Duncomb married Anna Roadcap on 3 Jun 1816. Richard was a widower when he married Sarah C. Riley on 11 Jan 1863. Sarah was the daughter of Nancy. She was born 26 Apr 1841 and died 10 Aug 1908. They were buried at the Rileyville Cemetery in Page County, Virginia.

RELATED FAMILY:

        William Lehew, brother of Richard, married Emily Frances Balthis on 30 Nov 1854 and resided in **dwelling 1629.**

        Jackson Lehew, brother of Richard, married Rebecca Moreland on 2 Mar 1857 and resided in **dwelling 382.**

George Duncan, brother of Rebecca, married Sarah Ellen McDaniel on 26 Jan 1860 and resided in **dwelling 506.**

Enoch Duncan, believed to have been the brother of Rebecca, married Margaret Sine on 6 Jan 1857 and resided in **dwelling 386.**

1850 CENSUS: There is no record of this family in Shenandoah County.

PAGE 56 POWELLS FORT (Microfilm Page 736)

Dwelling 384   Family 384

Henry Bowers	36	Miller	0	700	Virginia
Caroline Bowers	37				"
Prince Albert Bowers	15				"
Ann E. Bowers	14				" School
Joseph J. Bowers	10				" School
Mary C. Bowers	7				" School
James H. Bowers	6				"
Uriah L. D. Bowers	1				"
Sarah Green	39				"

Henry T. Bowers was born 6 Oct 1823 and died 7 Jan 1897. He was married to **Caroline Green** on 28 Jan 1843. The bondsman for the marriage was Harrison Green. Henry was the son of Ann. Caroline was born in March of 1822 and died 3 Jan 1891. They were buried in the St. Paul's Lutheran Church Cemetery in Jerome.

Prince Albert Bowers was born 12 Nov 1845. He was married on 31 Mar 1867 to Susan McInturff. Susan was the daughter of David and Mary. David McInturff married Mary "Polly" Coverstone in 1816. Susan was a resident of **dwelling 399.** She resided with her sister Mary McInturff Harman and her husband Hiram. Mary was born 17 Feb 1842 and was buried in the Sponaugle Cemetery at St. David's Church. Albert Bowers was a private in Company E of the 35th Battalion Virginia Cavalry. He enlisted on 30 Jul 1862 for the duration of the war. He was present until 1864 when he was AWOL during the month of August. He was paroled at New Market on 20 Apr 1865. Albert was 5'8" with dark complexion, dark hair and hazel eyes.

Ann Elizabeth Bowers was born in April of 1845 and died 6 May 1911. She was married to Franklin Clem on 4 Apr 1867. Franklin was the son of Abraham and Elizabeth.

Abraham Clem married Elizabeth Ross on 9 Sep 1834. Abraham and his family resided in **dwelling 398**. Franklin resided in **dwelling 417**. This was the household of his grandmother Barbara Murdock Clem. He was born 24 Aug 1835 and died 14 Apr 1909. Ann and Frank were buried in the Franklin Clem Cemetery at Edith in Fort Valley. Franklin Clem was a private in Company E of the 35th Battalion Virginia Cavalry.

Uriah David Bowers was born in 1858 and died in 1935. He was a miner at the time he married Etta M. Day on 5 Feb 1880. Etta was born in 1861 and died in 1950. She was listed in marriage records as the daughter of Jacob and Mary. Her obituary states that her fathers name was Henry. Jacob Day married Mary Ann Lindamood on 10 Sep 1860. David was supposedly born in Hardy County, West Virginia. Etta and David were buried in the Massanutten Cemetery.

RELATED FAMILY:
John W. Bowers was the son of Henry and Caroline. He has not been located in this census. He was born in 1847 and died in 1906. He was married on 1 Sep 1870 to Bettie Ferrel. Bettie was from Page County, Virginia. She was the daughter of William and Polly. William Ferrel married Mary Dalton on 26 May 1834. John was a widower when he married Levinia Miller on 5 Dec 1878. She was the daughter of Aquilla and Elizabeth. John later married Mary C. Miller Funkhouser. Mary was the daughter of George W and Nellie Dellinger Miller. She was the widow of Thomas F. Funkhouser. Mary C. Miller Funkhouser Bowers was born in 1862 and died in 1936. They were buried in the St. Paul's Lutheran Church Cemetery at Jerome.

Sarah Green is believed to have been the sister of Caroline Green Bowers.

1850 CENSUS: **Henry Bowers** and his family resided in dwelling 1967 on page 142.

405

PAGE 56 POWELLS FORT   (Microfilm Page 736)

Dwelling 385   Family 385

William Bowers	36	Collier	0	70	Virginia
Lydia Bowers	35			"	Insane
Lucinda Bowers	13			"	
Cornelia F. Bowers	11			"	School
Henrietta C. Bowers	9			"	School
John W. Bowers	6			"	
Phillip W. Bowers	3			"	
George W. Bowers	6m			"	
James M. Bowers	6m			"	
Caroline Bowers	15			"	

William H. Bowers was married on 6 May 1846 to **Lydia Fryman**. The bondsman for the marriage was Phillip W. Bowers. William H. Bowers is believed to have been the son of Phillip and Lydia. Phillip W. Bowers married Lydia Ryan on 11 Aug 1823. Lydia Ryan Bowers was a resident of **dwellinig 1304**.

Lucinda Bowers was born 8 Feb 1847 and died 19 Jun 1925. She was married to William H. Craig on 5 Apr 1868. William was the son of Peter and Ann. William was born 18 May 1846 and died on 6 Jan 1921. He was 74 years, 7 months and 18 days old. Lucinda and William were buried in the Old Columbia Furnace Cemetery.

Cornelia F. Bowers was born in 1849 and died in 1908. She was married to Joshua Miller on 4 Jul 1878. Joshua was the son of Jacob and Leah. Jacob of Jacob Miller married Leah Barb on 1 Feb 1842. Joshua was a farmer and resided with his family in **dwelling 1286**. Joshua was named after his maternal grandfather Joshua Barb. Cornelia was buried in the Zion Lutheran Church Cemetery in Hamburg, Virginia. Joshua Miller was the brother of Simon Miller, the great great grandfather of Marvin J. Vann, the compiler of this book.

John Wesley Bowers was born 13 Mar 1854 and died 2 Jul 1913. He was married on 9 Apr 1876 to Elizabeth Painter. Elizabeth was the daughter of Phillip and Catherine. Phillip Painter and his family resided in **dwelling 341**. Elizabeth was born 10 Apr 1860 and died 10 May 1910. Upon the death of Elizabeth, John Wesley was married to Rebecca Painter on 23 Feb 1911. Rebecca was the sister of Elizabeth. Rebecca was born 28 Mar 1862 and died

21 Feb 1935. John Wesley, Elizabeth and Rebecca were all buried in the Zion Lutheran Church Cemetery.

Phillip W. Bowers was married on 17 Nov 1878 to Mary E. Helsley. Mary was the daughter of Aaron and Martha. Aaron Helsley married Martha Warner on 15 Jun 1854.

Caroline Bowers was the daughter of George and Polly. George Bowers married Polly Miller on 19 Dec 1826. She was married on 5 Sep 1867 to Robert Fry. Robert was the son of George and Magdalene. Robert Fry and his family were located in **dwelling 1562**. Caroline resided with this family at the time of the 1850 census. Other members of the family of George and Polly were also in residence in the household. Apparently one or both of their parents were deceased prior to 1850.

RELATED FAMILY:

James Bowers, brother of William, married Susan Sheetz on 11 mar 1851 and resided in **dwelling 1098**.
Elijah Bowers, brother of Caroline Bowers, married Elizabeth Barb on 3 Jul 1851 and resided in **dwelling 1254**.

1850 CENSUS: **William H. Bowers** and his wife **Lydia Fryman Bowers** resided in dwelling 6 on page 1. This was the home of Lydia Ryan Bowers, mother of William.

DRAWING BY Michael Varnadore

BIBLIOGRAPHY

INDEX

BIBLIOGRAPHY

Armstrong, Richard L.; **11th Virginia Cavalry**, H. E. Howard, Inc., Lynchburg, Virginia, 1989.

Artz, Sydney M.; **Priest-Hamrick and Other Kin: A Genealogy,** 1985.

Baker, Robert H.; **Genealogy of the Baker Family,** 1955.

Bertrand, Phillip J. and Turpin, Joan; **Page County, Virginia: Marriages 1831-1864,** Heritage Books, Inc. 1986.

Bly, Daniel W.; **The Hockman Family,** 1970.

Brown, Doris Reeves and Stainbrook, May Collins; **Grandstaff-Grindstaff Family,** D'Amato Printing Specialities, Inc., Brockway, Pennsylvania, 1991.

Borden, Duane; **Tombstone Inscriptions: Toms Brook and Vicinity, Shenandoah County, Virginia,** Yates Publishing Co., Ozark, Missouri, 1981.

_____; **Tombstone Inscriptions; Strasburg and Vicinity, Shenandoah County, Virginia,** Yates Publishing Co., Ozark, Missouri, 1982.

_____; **Tombstone Inscriptions; Woodstock and Fort Valley Vicinities, Shenandoah County, Virginia,** Yates Publishing Co., Ozark Missouri, 1983.

_____; **Tombstone Inscriptions; New Market, Mt. Jackson & Edinburg Vicinities, Shenandoah County, Virginia,** Yates Publishing Co., Ozark Missouri, 1984.

_____; **Tombstone Inscriptions; Page County, Virginia,** Yates Publishing Co., Ozark, Missouri, 1986.

_____; **Tombstone Inscriptions; Shenandoah and Page Counties, Virginia.** Yates Publishing Co., Ozark, Missouri, 1984.

_____; Tombstone Inscriptions; Prospect Hill Cemetery, Front Royal and other Warren County Vicinities, Yates Publishing Co., Ozark, Missouri, 1985.

_____; Tombstone Inscriptions; Shenandoah County, Virginia and Bordering Counties: Frederick, Rockingham, Warren, Fauquier, Rappahannock and Hardy Counties. Yates Publishing Co., Ozark Missouri, 1986.

Borden, Duane L. and Ritenour, Jeanette C.; Marriages: Shenandoah County, Virginia, 1850-1882, Yates Publishing Co., Ozark, Missouri, 1987.

_____; Marriages: Shenandoah County, Virginia, 1882-1915, Dogwood Printing, Ozark, Missouri, 1990.

_____; Tombstone Inscriptions; Page County, Virginia, Volume II. Dogwood Printing, Ozark, Missouri, 1991.

Clower, James I.; The Clower Family, 1974.

Delauter, Roger U.; 18th Virginia Cavalry, H.E. Howard, Inc., Lynchburg, Virginia, 1985.

_____; 62 Virginia Infantry, H. E. Howard, Inc., Lynchburg, Virginia, 1988.

Denniston, Elmer L.; Genealogy of the Stukey, Ream, Grove, Clem and Denniston Families, 1930.

Divine, John E.; 35th Battalion Virginia Cavalry, H.E. Howard, Inc., Lynchburg, Virginia, 1985.

Frye, Dennis E.; 12th Virginia Cavalry, H. E. Howard, Inc. Lynchburg, Virginia 1988.

_____; 2nd Virginia Infantry, H.E. Howard, Inc. Lynchburg, Virginia, 1984.

Gilreath, Amelia C.; Haller-Hollar-Holler Genealogy, 1981.

_____; Shenandoah County, Virginia: Abstract of Wills, 1772-1850, 1980.

Golladay, Ralph J.; **Golladays in America**, The Shenandoah Press, Dayton, Virginia, 2nd Edition, 1983.

Hale, Laura Virginia; **Four Valiant Years: In the Lower Shenandoah Valley 1861-1865**, Shenandoah Publishing House, Inc. Strasburg, Virginia, 1968.

Huddle, Rev W.D. and Huddle, Lula Mae; **History of the Descendants of John Hottel**, Shenandoah Publishiing House, Inc., Strasburg, Virginia, 1930.

Kleese Richard B.; **Shenandoah County in the Civil War: The Turbulent Years**, H. E. Howard, Lynchburg, Virginia, 1992.

Kringer, Raymond L.; **The McInturffs (McInturf/McEnturff/McEntarfer) Volume I**, Brady-Drake Company, St. Louis, Missouri.

McDonald, William N.; **A History of the Laurel Brigade**, Reprint edition, R.W. Beatty, Ltd., Arlington, Virginia, 1969.

Moore, Robert H., II; **The Danville, Eighth Star New Market and Dixie Artillery**, H. E. Howard, Inc. Lynchburg, Virginia, 1989.

Murphy, Terrence V.; **10th Virginia Infantry**, H.E. Howard Inc., Lynchburg, Virginia, 1989.

Pitman, Levi; (Bly, Daniel W., editor and compiler); **Extracts from the Diaries of Levi Pitman of Mt. Olive, Shenandoah Co., Virginia, 1845-1892**, by the compiler.

Reidenbaugh, Lowell; **33rd Virginia Infantry**, H. E. Howard Inc., Lynchburg, Virginia, 1987.

Stickley, Judy C.; **Someone You Knew: A Necrology**, 1987.

Vogt, John and Kethley, T. William; **Virginia Historic Marriage Register: Frederick County Marriages, 1738-1850**, Iberian Press, Athens, Georgia, 1984.

_____; **Virginia Historic Marriage Register: Warren County Marriages, 1836-1850**, Iberian Press, Athens, Georgia, 1983.

_____; Virginia Historic
Marriage Register: Page County Marriage Bonds, 1831-
1850, Iberian Press, Athens, Georgia, 1983.

_____; Virginia Historic
Marriage Register: Rockingham County Marriages, 1778-
1850, Iberian Press, Athens, Georgia, 1984.

_____; Virginia Historic
Marriage Register: Shenandoah County Marriage Bonds,
1772-1850, Iberian Press, Athens, Georgia, 1984.

Wallace, Lee A., A Guide to Virginia Military
Organizations, 1861-1865, H.E. Howard, Inc.
Lynchburg, Virginia, 1986.

_____, 5th Virginia Infantry, H. E. Howard, Inc.
Lynchburg, Virginia, 1988.

_____, 17th Virginia Infantry, H. E. Howard,
Inc. Lynchburg, Virginia, 1990.

Wayland, John W.; A History of Shenandoah County, Virginia,
Shenandoah Publishing House, Inc., Strasburg,
Virginia, 1927, 2nd Edition, 1969.

Wilson, James D. and Wilson, Louise E.; Edinburg 1861 to
1865-Civil War Incidents & Anecdotes, American Speedy
Printing Centers of Shenandoah County, Woodstock,
Virginia, 1982.

Yarlick, Iva C.; Adam and Magdalene (Munch) Ridenour and
Some Related Families, Cooper-Trent, Arlington,
Virginia, 1973.

INDEX

Last Name	First Name	Dwelling
Bird	Mark	164
Black	Elizabeth	139
Blair	Serena	147
Blanhour	Rebecca	286
Boehm	Samuel	33
Bolen	Charles H.	50
Borsh	Addison	121
Borum	George M.	97
Bovey	Jacob	23
Bowers	Henry	384
Bowers	Joseph	142
Bowers	William	385
Bowman	Alexander	227
Bowman	Catherine	304
Bowman	Daniel S.	254
Bowman	Ephramin	347
Bowman	George	329
Bowman	Isaac	280
Bowman	Isaac N.	204
Bowman	Isaac R.	11
Bowman	Jacob	331
Bowman	Joseph	124
Bowman	Joseph	258
Bowman	Mary F.	267
Bowman	Samuel	350
Bowman	Sarah	335
Bowman	Stephen	28
Bowman	William	333
Branin	John W.	70
Broadus	Clarence L	82
Burke	John	309
Burner	Daniel	133
Burner	Jane	132
Bynaker	Robert	381
Cahoun	Robert	104
Campbell	Josiah L.	226
CAN'T READ	....	274
Carder	Stephen H.	175
Carper	Henry	259
Caruthers	Ebenezer	292
Carver	Hiram	35
Cavanaugh	Cornelius	92
Chrisman	John	338
Clanahan	Samuel	238
Clinedinst	Barnet	168
Clinedinst	John	167

Last Name	First Name	Dwelling
Clinedinst	John	261
Clinedinst	Lydia	322
Clower	Henry	93
Clower	Jacob B.	176
Clower	Joseph H.	107
Clower	Samuel V.R	109
Clower	Virginia C	171
Coburn	James M.	169
Coffelt	Eli	361
Coffelt	Rebecca	323
Coffer	Timothy	66
Coffman	Ezra	273
Coffman	John P.	194
Coffman	Lewis	358
Coffman	Obed	102
Collins	John	285
Collins	Martin	128
Comer	Christian	73
Cone	William H.	2
Conn	Raphael M.	362
Conner	Atwell	237
Cooper	Jacob	77
Cooper	Joseph P.	17
Cullen	Michael	127
Cullers	Andrew J.	230
Davis	John J.	212
Day	Caroline	96
Day	Louisa	121
Dean	Sarah C.	134
Dean	Zedekiah	170
Dellinger	Elenora	51
Dellinger	Israel	83
Dinges	Maria	143
Dinges	William J.	58
Donaldson	William	175
Donovan	Lawrence	245
Dore	Garret	351
Dosh	William	112
Downey	Amelia A.	76
Downey	Eleazer	274
Downey	Frances	275
Drummond	Samuel	308
Eakin	Mary C.	166
Elick	Barbara	217
Estep	Dilmon	320
Estep	Elizabeth	254

Last Name	First Name	Dwelling
Estep	Jacob	336
Estep	Sarah	308
Estep	William	345
Evans	Aaron B.	71
Evans	Henry H.	6
Evans	Jerimiah S	57
Evans	John	277
Evans	Joseph W.	38
Evans	Samuel	21
Evans	Sarah	247
Fadely	Harrison	182
Farra	Mary	98
Feete	Daniel	193
Fetzer	Ann	195
Fetzer	Isaiah	105
Fetzer	Mary E.	127
Fetzer	Nancy	94
Few	William H.	100
Firrel	Athferrath	215
Fitzpatrick	Andrew	187
Flernice	James	92
Fogle	Frank	192
Fogle	Jacob	152
Fogle	Samuel	266
Fox	John	254
Fox	Joseph	259
Fox	Samuel	255
Fravel	David	200
Fravel	Ellen C.	201
Fravel	George	177
Fravel	Henry C.	199
Fravel	James A.P.	333
Fravel	James G.	114
Fravel	John H. J.	145
Fravel	Joseph	189
Fravel	Joseph	283
Fravel	Mary	207
Fravel	Phillip J.	111
Fravel	Sarah	348
Freet	Elizabeth	221
Fry	Ambrose B.	323
Fry	Elizabeth	347
Fry	Harrison	355
Fry	John	354
Fry	John A.	353
Fry	John H.	146

Last Name	First Name	Dwelling
Fultz	Jacob	306
Funk	George	37
Funk	Henry	326
Garlach	Kenchesca	333
Gaskins	Nelly	340
Gatewood	John	169
Gaw	Sarah C.	161
Gill	Susan	151
Gillock	David	126
Gillock	Harrison	197
Gillock	Mary	117
Goladay	William	108
Goodrich	Godfrey	340
Grabill	Ephramin	96
Grainton	Mary	131
Grandstaff	Benjamin	324
Grandstaff	Branson	313
Grandstaff	Elizabeth	46
Grandstaff	George	63
Grandstaff	George W.	13
Grandstaff	John J.	328
Grandstaff	Joseph B.	321
Grandstaff	Joseph F.	54
Grandstaff	Marcus	62
Grandstaff	Mary S.	264
Grandstaff	Milton M.	61
Grandstaff	Phillip	267
Grandstaff	Robert H.	45
Grant	Malinda	241
Grantham	Mary	222
Grayson	Granville	73
Grayson	Walter	49
Grayson	Washington	286
Green	Sarah	384
Green	Wilson	340
Grey	Susan	233
Grove	Catherine	74
Grove	Lewis W.	52
Grove	Robert P.	103
Gumby	James	312
Haas	Isaac	137
Haas	John	95
Haas	Sarah A.	176
Hall	Julia	362
Hamaker	Margaret A	140
Hammack	Cornelius	243

Last Name	First Name	Dwelling
Hamman	George C.	174
Hamman	John	47
Hamrick	Martha	220
Hamrick	Nimrod F.	239
Hanson	Thomas J.	73
Hardy	Henry	121
Harris	Mary	150
Haun	Ellen	90
Hays	John	92
Heartshorn	William	142
Heaton	John W.	316
Heller	Adolph	117
Heller	Elizabeth	118
Heller	Josiah	208
Helsley	George W.	175
Hess	Mary C.	206
Hickman	Benjamin D	205
Hickman	John T.	150
Hill	Mary	233
Hines	Jacob	171
Hisey	Emily F.	91
Hisey	Frederick	18
Hisey	James M.	31
Hisey	Robert	21
Hisey	Samuel	15
Hisey	William H.	69
Hite	Isaac R.	352
Hockman	Henry M.	10
Hockman	Jacob F.	293
Hockman	Phillip J.	107
Hockman	Samuel	121
Hockman	William	12
Hockman	William M.	295
Hoffman	Joseph W.	34
Hoffman	Julia A.	266
Hoffman	Nimrod M.	278
Hoffman	Rebecca	272
Holden	Benjamin D	42
Hollar	Mary L.	43
Holler	Caroline	53
Holtzman	Benjamin B	56
Hoover	James	283
Hoover	Silas	282
Hottel	Elias	366
Hottel	Elias	371
Hounshour	David D.	224

Last Name	First Name	Dwelling
Hounshour	Margaret	104
Hounshour	Peter	116
Hounshour	Peter	130
Howe	Edward	225
Huddle	Madelene	271
Huddle	Nathan	208
Humston	Nathaniel	246
Hunt	Glover	178
Hunton	John H.	154
Hutcheson	Amos	81
Hutcheson	Charles W.	78
Hutcheson	John	357
Hutcheson	William H.	359
Hutchinson	Charles	68
Hutchinson	Jacob	319
Iden	George	142
Ireland	John	307
Irwin	James	157
Irwin	Joseph S.	141
Jack	Samuel	25
Jackson	Caroline	208
Jacobs	Adda C.	292
Jenkins	Gabriel	330
Jenkins	Zachariah	298
Jennings	Henry	1
Johnson	Hattie	288
Johnson	Henry T.	186
Johnson	James N.	142
Jones	Ann	209
Jones	Samuel	190
Keffer	John	101
Keiffer	Charles W.	277
Keiran	Sarah	44
Keller	Daniel	270
Keller	Ellenora	179
Kelly	Patrick	296
Kern	Barbara	283
Kibler	James	121
Kibler	John J.	360
Kibler	Martha	50
Kidwalder	Catherine	6
Kneisley	Harvey C.	189
Kneisly	Lewis	136
Kneisly	Luther B.	169
Kniesley	Timothy	92
Knight	Lovett	297

Last Name	First Name	Dwelling
Koontz	Elizabeth	60
Koontz	Harrison	91
Koontz	William	253
Krause	John A.	113
Krebs	William F.	153
Lantz	George	335
Laughland	Michael	92
Leacount	Thomas	262
Lee	Caroline V	209
Lee	Richard	121
Lehew	Jackson	382
Lehew	Richard	383
Lersner	Gustavus	84
Lewis	Mary J.	52
Lewis	Nancy	214
Lichliter	Conrad	122
Lichliter	Jacob	123
Lichliter	Sarah	135
Liggett	William	26
Lillie	George	121
Lindamood	Jackson	300
Linder	Catherine	86
Linn	Sarah A.	124
Litten	Mary	185
Loder	Rebecca H.	164
Lowenback	Josepha	117
Luckins	Neetow	235
Ludwick	William F.	348
Ludy	William	142
Lutz	Flora	163
Magruder	William W.	209
Maphis	George	304
Maphis	Jacob	244
Maphis	Joseph	302
Maphis	William	303
Mars	Eliza	289
Marshall	William H.	72
Marston	Andrew J.	375
Marston	John S.	359
Marston	Joseph	374
Marston	Joseph H.	74
Marston	Lewis	373
Marston	Thomas	378
Martin	Rebecca	229
Martz	Dorilas J.	257
Mauck	Harvey	377

Last Name	First Name	Dwelling
McCoy	James	363
McDonald	William	167
McFee	Catherine	168
McInturff	Alfred	232
McInturff	Susan	371
McMahon	Nancy	228
McMan	John	140
McNance	James	92
McPherson	Lydia	134
Melhorn	Michael	181
Miley	Abraham	30
Miley	Isaac W.	75
Miley	John W.	20
Miley	Joseph R.	35
Miller	Christina	346
Miller	Ellenora	29
Miller	John R.	53
Miller	Mary E.	315
Miller	Nancy W.	188
Miller	Phillip	3
Miller	Phillip	225
Miller	Reuben	168
Miller	Richard	291
Miller	Sarah	257
Miller	Sarah	318
Miller	Susan	80
Milligan	John D.	51
Moler	John	156
Moore	Isaac	242
Moore	Rachel A.	240
More	Mark	165
Moreland	William	119
Moreland	William	379
Morris	Harvey	126
Morrison	Edward	84
Morton	Peggy	164
Mountz	Jacob	167
Mowery	Salus	167
Murray	Margaret	328
Myers	Julia A.	62
Myers	Margaret	173
Myers	Margaret	184
Myers	Nancy	271
Myers	Susan	307
Neeb	Curtis	162
Newman	Artemisia	21

Last Name	First Name	Dwelling
Newman	Robert	5
Newman	Rosanna	310
Noel	Eli H.	345
Nugent	Patrick	92
Offner	Sarah C.	93
Orndorff	Catherine	133
Orndorff	Israel	7
Orndorff	Jesse	180
Orndorff	Sarah J.	118
Ort	William H.	248
Ott	George H.	125
Ott	Jacob	179
Ott	John W.	159
Ott	William	203
Painter	Abraham	339
Painter	Henry	346
Painter	Moses	342
Painter	Phillip	341
Painter	Samuel	269
Palmer	Cornelius	132
Patton	George	353
Patton	Michael	314
Pence	Beale S.	308
Pence	Jacob	337
Pence	Joseph	305
Pence	Lewis	83
Pence	Perry	260
Pence	Susan	309
Pitman	Phillip	247
Prescott	Daniel W.	49
Preston	Sarah	115
Pritchard	Thomas	103
Proctor	Adam	380
Purvis	Hugh	148
Racey	Luke	364
Ralls	Andrew	183
Ramey	Peter P.	89
Rau	Barbara J.	36
Rau	David S.	65
Rau	John H.	64
Reed	Henry L.	158
Reedy	Anne M.	67
Reeser	John	279
Reifsnider	Elizabeth	100
Reynard	Abraham	252
Reynard	Elanson	250

Last Name	First Name	Dwelling
Reynard	Elizabeth	251
Reynolds	Lucretia	150
Rhorback	Mary H.	49
Richards	Lucy A.	286
Rickerson	Joseph	242
Riddleberger	Madison	40
Riddleberger	Robert	24
Riley	Patrick	284
Rinker	Elizabeth	37
Rinker	Samuel	2
Rinker	Thomas J.	219
Rinker	William	255
Ripley	Valentine	301
Ripley	William	300
Ritter	Isaac	14
Robinson	Ann	19
Robinson	Caloub	227
Robinson	Eliza	210
Robinson	John	299
Rodeffer	David	139
Rodeffer	George B.	106
Rodeffer	Jacob	131
Rodeffer	Phillip	134
Rosenbaum	Lewis	202
Rosenberger	Joseph	372
Rosenberger	Nancy	363
Ruby	Catherine	10
Ruby	Isaac	55
Ruby	Ann S.	12
Rucker	Amanda	369
Rudy	Ann	33
Rudy	Elizabeth	236
Rudy	Rachel	170
Rye	George	156
Samuels	Green B.	199
Samuels	Joseph G.	218
Samuels	Samuel C.	174
Saum	Abraham	19
Schmitt	Bernadotte	110
Schmitt	Talisandra	236
Scroggins	John	256
Shaffer	Frederick	121
Shaffer	Henry	185
Shank	Andrew	16
Shaun	Sarah	365
Shea	William	8

Last Name	First Name	Dwelling
Sheetz	Elias	64
Sheetz	Joseph S.	367
Sheetz	Phillip	368
Sheetz	William H.	369
Shifflet	Moses	113
Shirk	David B.	213
Shown	William	362
Sibert	Daniel	249
Sibert	Emily	280
Sibert	George W.	80
Sigler	Solomon	343
Sine	Jacob	376
Sine	Rebecca	341
Smith	Amanda J.	359
Smith	Catherine	203
Smith	Owen	92
Smith	William	288
Smoot	John W.	29
Smootz	Daniel	138
Smootz	Harvey	327
Smootz	Roberta	141
Snapp	Jacob B.	44
Snyder	Christophe	137
Sonnestine	Catherine	19
Sourbaugh	Michael	94
South	Jane	168
South	John M.	167
Southard	Payton	9
Speigle	Rebecca	334
Spengler	Fanny	121
Spengler	Joseph H.	39
Spengler	Mary C.	115
Spengler	Mary J.	269
Sprigs	John	44
Steel	Charles	191
Stephens	Jonas	165
Stewart	William T.	140
Stidley	Robert	223
Stoneburner	Charles	121
Stoneburner	John J.	50
Stover	Abraham	327
Sullivan	Edward	285
Sullivan	Willis	160
Summers	Jacob	356
Supinger	Sarah	88
Supinger	William J.	87

Last Name	First Name	Dwelling
Swann	James N.	51
Swartz	James H.	302
Teeter	Jacob	231
Tharp	George	265
Thompson	Frances A.	160
Thompson	William	370
Triplett	William H.	141
Trook	Phillip	344
Trout	Isaac	196
Turner	John	311
Turner	Milton	241
Tusing	Elizabeth	281
Valentine	Jacob	84
Valentine	Rachel	27
Vansickle	Gilbert	121
Vena	John	276
Viands	Nancy	43
Visery	Mary L.	51
Walker	Rebecca	156
Walsh	Thomas	285
Walton	Moses	120
Walton	Reuben	165
Wanzer	Ann	164
Wanzer	Elanson	287
Wanzer	Levi D.	34
Ward	Nancy	380
Warfield	Laura	176
Waserman	George P.	349
Waserman	Peter	332
Webster	George	300
Welch	Charles A.	103
Welden	Rebecca	183
Weldon	Ann	287
Wetzel	Catherine	166
Wetzel	Elizabeth	73
Wetzel	Jacob	268
Wetzel	Martin M.	43
Wetzel	Rebecca	342
Whane	James	92
Whissen	Edward B.	80
Whissen	Francis M.	68
Whissen	Jane	22
Whissen	Salome	79
White	Sarah	174
Wierman	John R.	41
Wierman	William	174

Last Name	First Name	Dwelling
Wightman	William A.	290
Wilcher	Calvin	59
Wilkins	John	121
Williams	Henry	263
Williams	John	362
Williams	Samuel C.	174
Wilson	James	172
Windle	Andrew J.	4
Windle	George	32
Windle	George	317
Windle	William	28
Winter	Albert	80
Wiseman	Charles H.	117
Wolff	John W.	166
Zimmer	Peter	216
Zimmerman	John G.	48

Made in the USA
Middletown, DE
08 June 2023

32270855R00245